Under the Linden Trees

Love and Loss Behind the Iron Curtain

Under the Linden Trees
©2014 by Thomas P.W. Schardt

This is a work of creative nonfiction. The people, places and events depicted within are depicted as true events to the best of the author's knowledge and memory. Any inaccuracies are the error of the author alone, and he requests the readers understanding in advance.

Published by the Piscataqua Press
An imprint of RiverRun Bookstore
142 Fleet St., Portsmouth, NH 03801

www.riverrunbookstore.com
www.piscataquapress.com

ISBN: 978-1939739-32-2

Printed in the United States of America

Under the Linden Trees

Love and Loss Behind the Iron Curtain

Thomas P.W. Schardt

My Grandmother and I

My Aunt and Cousin

My Parents Wedding Photo

My Stepfather, My Mother, and I

My Mother, My Brother, Klaus, My Stepfather

Klaus And I

My Uncle Ernst

Prologue

It's a warm and sunny spring day. The enormous Rhododendrons leading to the funeral hall are in full bloom. Mourners come to pay their last respects; they file in calmly through the tall and wide open doors. On a small table is a black-and-white photograph of the deceased. Next to the silver picture frame are three candles, flames flickering, in a simple wrought-iron candelabra, approximately twenty centimeters long with ornamental openings in the footings. It is easily recognizable as Klaus' work, the man I came to say a final goodbye to. He was my lover and partner until he became my nightmare. Today I sit together with his friends, some whom I know, many I don't, to seek closure for a part of my past that began when I was twenty-one years old and ended, painfully, ten years later.

After a somber hour of remembrances we all follow Klaus' urn to be placed in the "Ground of the Anonymous." I begin to wonder if I should write our story— his and mine — now that Klaus has passed. I have thought about it more than once but until today I never knew where to begin, where to end. I always felt that if I would put on paper one day it shouldn't be just a simple report about our tumultuous and abusive life together. Our own upbringing with its roots and tragedies have to be part of the story as well as the life-stifling environment we had been a part of. Maybe somewhere in all that lies the answer — why were we unable to make our relationship work? One day I will write it all down, I promise myself. Then I watch the urn with Klaus' ashes disappear. All that's left now of Klaus is what I remember.

Time passed. Excuses always prevented me from sitting down at my laptop to fulfill the promise I made at Klaus' graveside so many years ago. I still remember Klaus. Every year when I go skiing I think of him. He taught me how to ski. I think of him every year on his birthday, August 10th. I even think about Klaus on February 13th. On that day in 1945 the Allies bombed Klaus' hometown of Dresden to rubble. He was seven months old at the time. The apartment building where he and his grandparents lived was hit. Everybody who had sought shelter in the basement survived including baby Klaus. His grandmother asked a neighbor to take him downstairs after the bomb alarm went off while she and her husband went to get their belongings out of the apartment, then they would follow in a couple of minutes. Seeking shelter was mandatory but his grandparents didn't make it in time, so that day Klaus lost half of his family. His mother was working outside of the city and his father was a soldier fighting in the East.

Still nothing was motivating enough for me to finally sit down and start writing, other things got in the way including my move to New York in 1989. After almost fifteen years I had left my partner Bruce and I was single again. My doctor diagnosed me with a pre-cancerous growth in my colon. For the next two years I had to come to grips with my new life. My doctor's diagnosis was wrong. I settled into my new place in a new city. I had a future. Then on a visit to Germany my friend Franz told me that his brother Ferdinand was dying of AIDS and I was totally caught off guard. Hearing that Ferdinand had AIDS was like somebody telling me that I had AIDS.

"Only very few know that he is sick," Franz told me. "He has been fighting death for the last five years, but now he is losing that fight." Ferdinand got infected in 1984, the year he met Stefan. At that time Stefan was an aspiring musician who played the flute and wanted to attend the Conservatory. I remember how surprised I was when Stefan switched careers and went to nursing school instead. In hindsight, it was all part of Ferdinand's plan. He promised Stefan a financially stable life upon his death. I didn't know it at the time, but the arrangement was that Stefan will take care of Ferdinand and his needs.

Ferdinand died three months after his brother told me about his illness. Ferdinand was one of Klaus's lovers. Stefan, his partner, helped Klaus to settle his estate and lead his funeral. I felt like life had come full circle, it was time to write. I didn't know how long and where this would take me, I only knew that I was ready.

2

The Beginning

The bar is loud, packed and smoky as it always is on a Friday night. I have a hard time getting through the door. No one notices me. I squeeze between the coat rack, bar counter and wall. I am hidden because there is a huge glass jar on top of the counter filled with pickled cucumbers and eggs. The wall of chatting men closes me in, and I feel isolated and alone. I usually never have the guts to push further into the bar, but now I have to because I need to pee. The chairs are so close together that I get up onto my toes to make it through the crowd. I do so, pressing against tabletops, shoulders and chairs. I try to be polite assuming patrons would make room for me, but no one does. Reaching the bathroom is one thing, coming back is another. I try to get back where I was, hoping the bartender will see me raising my hand this time. Maybe tonight someone will talk to me, maybe even buy me a drink? I was looking forward to being here at Burgfrieden, one of three gay bars in East Berlin that existed in the Seventies. I couldn't wait to get out of the house. It took me half an hour to walk here.

Every time I plan to go out I feel excited about it. I try so hard to look my best, choosing the right outfit, hoping to catch someone's attention. I don't have a round ass to show off, and when I look in the mirror it looks flat. My face is not right. My lips are too fat. I have pimples. I am only twenty-one and I already have gray hair that is thin and straight. But somehow I always manage to dress decent. Tonight I choose tight white pants and a white cotton top with a zipper and dark blue collar, a gift from a friend who lives West Germany. I am sure everybody will notice that. I add sandals and just three rings. I love jewelry. I can only afford fake gold, but after a few hours my fingers get stained so I have to keep rubbing it off.

I am on my second beer and feel the effect, having not eaten today. It's one week away from payday and I had to choose between buying food or beer, which I don't even like, but it is the cheapest alcohol you can buy — a glass of it only costs 51 Pfenning.

"Hey boy, what's up? How come you are not smiling?" hollers a guy next to me. Other men turn around, causing me to blush. I look down at my glass. I hate that. People always say that I look so serious. Why don't I smile? I don't know. I can't help it. I practice smiling in the mirror, squeezing my face muscles, opening my lips to show my teeth. I try to remember this when I walk down the street so I will look friendly and happy, but it feels silly and it hurts. So, here I am again. The stranger is scolding me in front of everybody in the bar. I down my beer and leave. I feel awful. Lost. Totally alone and ugly. My chest is tense, my breathing labored. I am a mess. Another unsuccessful night out. But what's new? I reach the street corner and turn right.

"Good evening." I almost jump because I hadn't noticed someone coming up right next to me. I look at him and whisper back "Hi." He has blond hair. He is slim. Good looking.

"Where you going?" he asks.

"Home." I suddenly become shy.

"Can I come with you?" our eyes meet.

"Ah, sure. My apartment is kind of a mess. Not much furniture. I just moved in. Not sure, if you would like it."

We keep walking, slowly.

"Oh that's okay. I don't mind. But we can go to my place!" I feel relieved because my place is rather depressing. It's dark. It needs paint and wallpaper. There is just a toilet. I have to wash up in the kitchen sink. I have a pullout couch as a bed, a matching chair and coffee table, some self-made shelves and a huge wardrobe. I don't have enough money to buy things to match. I am happy to have my own place but I am also too embarrassed to invite people in. I always tell friends that I just moved in even if that's not true. I have lived in the apartment for the past three years.

"That's fine. Where do you live?" I asked him. Without answering he is waving for a cab.

"I live fifteen minutes from here. Come, it's getting late." He opens the car door and slides in. I follow. He gives the driver the address. Christburger Strasse 3. I never heard of that street before. I wonder if I should get worried. We don't speak. I look out the window. Sure enough, fifteen minutes later the cab stops at a dark street lined with big old apartment buildings. There are no trees and few streetlights, some lit, some not. I feel nervous as we approach the door to his apartment building. The hallway is dark. I follow close behind him. We cross the courtyard and turn left. It's pitch black. I am getting scared. Maybe I shouldn't have come here. My inner alarm goes off. He must sense my hesitation.

"Are you scared?" He turns around, "Don't be. The lights never work here. There is no money to fix them, but what can you do? He takes my hand. I like the feel of it, his fingers clasping mine.

"I don't even know your name," I say as he pulls me towards another door, turning on the lights. This light works. We start climbing the stairs. He still holds my hand, reassuring me.

"I am Klaus. I am thirty-four and I live on the fourth floor. What else do you want to know?" I can't believe what I am hearing. He is thirty-four. He looks younger than me. He must be lying.

"My name is Thomas. I am twenty-one," I reply. I am behind him. He doesn't look back, he is still holding my hand. We reach the top floor and he reaches for his key with his free hand. He doesn't let go of me and I don't mind.

He pulls me into a small hallway, turns and puts his arms around me. He pushes the apartment door shut with his foot and I start to shake and feel warm inside. I am getting hard and he notices, sliding one hand down my pants. His lips close around mine. I can't believe this is happening. A guy is kissing and feeling me up at the same time and I like it. I push my tongue through his teeth and I am running my hands down his back. I touch his ass. Everything is happening so fast. He gets down on his knees, pulling down my pants and underwear. He takes my dick in his mouth. My legs are shaking. I bend over and kiss his head and reach for his cheeks. He holds my ass tightly and goes back and forth on my cock. I feel like I am getting close.

He stops, gets up and pulls me into the living room. My pants are still around my ankles so I almost trip. He pulls down the zipper on my sweater and then helps me out of my pants and underwear. I am naked. He is not. Then Klaus steps back and looks at me.

"Very nice," he says. No one has ever said something like this to me. *What's so nice about me*, I wonder. He must be joking. He takes my head in his hands and kisses me again. Eyes. Lips. Nose. Forehead. Neck. *Maybe this is for real*, I think before I fall back, moaning. I grab his belt and start to undo it, unzipping his jeans. He is not wearing any underwear. I touch his hard dick and he smiles at me. I pull his t-shirt up. We are both naked, except for our socks. I must be dreaming. I look at Klaus. He has the most beautiful body; no chest hair, a flat stomach, a nicely shaped dick. Not too big. Just right. He has big low hanging balls. His legs are muscular. I can't see his ass but I bet it's nice too. We pull each other close. We are getting intense, our hands touching each other everywhere. We sink to our knees. I fall on my back. He is on top of me, going down, taking me in, lifting my ass, licking my balls. He pushes my legs back and spreads my cheeks with his mouth. I feel his tongue going inside of me and I arch my back, holding his head. It feels like the first time to me. Then he pauses, spits in his hands, wets his dick and my ass. He pushes inside of me and it hurts like hell.

He keeps in and out of me. I grab Klaus' ass to slow him down. He puts the pile of our clothing under my ass and starts to push harder, while stroking my dick. The pain eases and pleasure takes over. I am getting wet. I want him inside me to stay. We haven't spoken one word but our breathing says it all.

"Are you coming?" I ask.

"Oh, I like your ass. You feel so tight. I don't want this to end, but I am close. How is it for you?" Klaus asks, "I hope we come together. I can't hold off much longer."

I push myself against him. "I am ready, too. I am coming. Are you?"

Klaus shouts, "Yes! Please come! I am there! Yes! " As the sperm runs out of me, Klaus tenses up and I feel the warmth inside of me. Klaus pulls out, resting his head on my chest. I am not sure how much time has passed, by but slowly we come back to reality again. He looks at me. "That was great." I pull his head up and kiss him. "Why don't you take a shower and I make the bed?"

I get up and go into the kitchen where the shower is, realizing Klaus' apartment has no bathroom. The toilet must be out in the hallway down the stairs, typical for an old building like this. I notice that he has a washing machine, a refrigerator and a nice new kitchen stove all lined up on next to the shower. On the other side of the kitchen is a row of newer kitchen cabinets. Opposite from the kitchen door is the window with a built-in cabinet underneath. Klaus sure has good taste.

I step into the shower, turn on the water, slide down and put my arms around my knees. I am hurting. There was not enough spit to open me. I start to pee. My urine mixes in with the water running down my shoulders and think about Klaus, the first man to be nice to me in a long time. He didn't take me into bushes or alleyways. Most men I have met before him didn't bother to bring me to their places. Anywhere was good enough for a quickie, and I always let it happen, never turning them down, being horny never made me proud. Tonight, this man took me home and said nice things to me before fucking me. I feel so good, so happy. I finally met someone who at least cared where we had sex, even if I may not see him again. A good-looking man like him doesn't need me. He probably has a boyfriend, but at least I have a good memory to dwell on. I shut the water off, step out off the shower and dry off. Klaus comes in and turns the water back on.

"The bed is ready. Go ahead. I will be right there," Klaus says, closing the shower curtain.

I go back into the living room and look around. The huge couch is pulled out to a queen-size bed. Two matching chairs are pushed to the side. Above the couch are two shelves with candlesticks and glass vases. Between the two windows is a bookshelf. Across from the couch is a wall of shelves, bureau, a wardrobe and a desk. Next to the tiled coal oven is a folding table with two chairs. Very cozy and tasteful as well.

I slide under the covers. I am tired. I stare at the ceiling. That's a first, too. None of the men who had taken me home in the past had ever asked me to stay over, but he has.

Klaus comes in, walks over to the floor lamp and turns it off. I see his ass for the first time. It is perfect like everything else. I am getting hard again. Klaus comes under the covers and kisses me lightly. "Good night, handsome. See you in the morning," he says and turns around. I say nothing, putting my hand on his back. It is way past midnight on June 6th, a day I will never forget.

"Hey, sorry to wake you up. I have to get going. Take your time. Just pull the door shut when you leave." At first I didn't know who was talking to me. I open my eyes and feel a kiss on my forehead. I try to look awake and push the covers off me. "No, no. Sleep as long as you want to. But I have to be out the door — actually a while ago. So long." I hear the door shut. I sit up. I am not sure what to think, what to do? I must have slept like a baby, I didn't even notice him get up. What a night. It is all coming back to me. I look at my clothes, still piled on the floor where he took me. I smile. No one would know by looking at my white jeans, underwear and sweater that that was the place where raw sex had happened, meaningful only to me. My ass hurts. I have to go the bathroom. I open the apartment door and listen. No one is using the toilet so I run down the stairs to it, still naked, and I lock the door. I hear another door open.

"Klaus, Klaus," a woman's voice calls out. Oh shit. "Klaus are you in the bathroom?" I don't know what to do. Someone is coming down the stairs. The door handle moves.

"It's occupied."

"Goddamn it," she says, "I guess I have to use the other toilet down below." The door handle snaps back into place.

"Sorry," I whisper. I hear footsteps on the stairs. I am really hurting, it is so painful. I feel something warm and I know it's blood. I always bleed after sex. It takes days before it stops. I wonder if everybody bleeds after having anal sex. Maybe one day I won't bleed anymore and it won't hurt as much. I clean myself carefully and I feel a burning sensation. I press my ear against the door and I hear a toilet flush. It must be her again. I push the door open and run up the stairs, quickly closing the apartment door behind me. I realize that I don't have a key. Just imagine, the door could have closed shut leaving me outside naked. Next time I will be more cautious, maybe there won't be another time? Klaus didn't say anything about calling. I get in the shower.

I hope I can visit Klaus again. I shake my head, turn off the water, dry myself and I grab my clothes, get dressed and then put the couch back together, bruising my finger. I rearrange the coffee table and chairs the way I remember them from last night. I wish I could stay. It's so nice here, so cozy, so together. Klaus even has a telephone, so he must be important or have connections since the average waiting period for a phone is fifteen years. He never told me what he does for a living, but I didn't tell him what I did either. I look for piece of paper to leave him a note.

"Dear Klaus," I write, "thanks for last night. It would be great to see you again. Call me. Here is my work number. I don't have a home phone. Goodbye, Thomas ." I take one more look around the apartment before I shut the door.

I shriek. An old woman in a worn-out bathrobe is standing right in front of me, her greasy and thinning hair hanging down on her shoulders. "Where is Klaus?" she barks at me.

"He already left." Feeling like an intruder, I try to compose myself but she doesn't move an inch.

"You are his new friend?"

I look at her, my face turning red.

"Don't play shy. I know all Klaus' friends. You seem a little younger than all of the others. What's your name?"

"Thomas," I reply, offering my hand which she ignores.

"He has lots of friends. Some seem nice but I wish he could find a good one for a change. Don't get me wrong. I have had my share of men. Every one of them liked to fuck me. I was good, but none of them stayed around for long. Now I am old and only that old geezer of a super wants me to blow him."

I wish she would stop talking. I can't believe what she is telling me. I visualize her with the super, her greasy hair spread over his lap. "I really have to go," I say, trying to get by her.

9

"When did you meet?" she probes.

"A while ago," I lie.

"You are lying. I have never seen you before. So, you met last night, right?" She is right, but I don't tell her. "You have nice honest eyes. He is a good man. He helps me bring buckets of coal up from the basement. Sometimes he even buys me groceries. He knows I don't have any money. My state pension does not buy much. He is a good man." She turns around, "I hope to see you again. I can't say that for most of the guys Klaus brings home," she snarls, slamming the door behind her.

I am bewildered. What was she trying to tell me? Maybe she has it all wrong. Maybe the guys she is talking about are just friends of Klaus' and nothing more. Does she really know? On the other hand, Klaus is attractive; he must attract a lot of guys but it doesn't mean he sleeps with them. Last night was so nice. Sure it was casual but our encounter was a meeting by chance. Wasn't it? Did Klaus see me inside the bar, or just run into me outside of the bar? Who knows? Does it matter? What we had counts. I just want to get home and keep the memory of last night. What his neighbor was saying shouldn't matter. Maybe I won't hear from him. Maybe it was a one-night stand, who knows? I pull the Klaus' door shut and walk down to the street.

I am not sure where to turn. Nothing looks familiar. This is a part of Berlin I have never been in. It's kind of seedy. The homes are in disrepair. For the most part people who are live here are not well off. There are pubs on every corner. "A sure sign of difference," as my mother would say. My family is snobbish, educated and proud of where they came from, even if that is part of our history and has nothing to do with the present. "We were well known and respected," my grandmother never forgets to mention. I always feel embarrassed whenever I hear that, but I have to admit I also have some of that arrogance in me.

It is eleven o'clock in the morning and a drunk guy stumbles out of a corner pub. I avoid him by crossing the street. I finally know where I am and how to get home. I am looking at one of the major roads that cuts through the city.

This one is special; it starts on the outskirts of Berlin, in the Wannsee area, and ends in the city's political center, the entire road is nicely paved with no potholes. Officials from the Party and government use this road. When the fleet of black limousines — they recently changed from the Soviet-made Tschaikas to Sweden-made Volvos — speed through the city all of the traffic lights turn red so that the city's traffic comes to a halt and the officials have their uninterrupted passage . All of the building façades along the smooth roadway are nicely painted so as to be more pleasing to the Party bosses' eyes.

I have to switch streetcars to get home but I don't really want to be alone. Maybe I will go for a walk. The weather is beautiful. Long walks always cheer me up.

Even though it's already warmer than usual for this time of the year my large one-room flat is still cold and dark. It's on the first floor and all of my windows face a small courtyard surrounded by buildings. The sun never makes it down to my floor. If I want to see the sky I have to lean out the window.

Nylons, Coffee, and Chocolate for an Apartment

As a kid I was always fascinated with this apartment. Old Sister Gertrude lived here. She was a nurse in a Catholic home for the elderly. My grandmother lived on the top floor of the building and became friends with her at church. They visited, had coffee and shared memories of better days. Sister Gertrude was very sweet and always friendly. I liked her, too. She always invited me in to have cookies that she got from the nursing home. "The old ladies can't chew them. They are too hard," she would say.

I never stayed long because she didn't talk much. We just sat in her room. One day she would not get out of bed anymore, so my grandmother looked after her but there was not much she could do. "She wants to die," my grandmother said. One day she did. Sister Gertrude had a nephew who didn't know what to do with all of the stuff his aunt had left him so he asked my grandmother to give it away. She contacted the priest to see if he knew if any of his parishioners could use it, and he did. After the apartment was empty it looked much bigger.

"Do you think I should try to get the apartment, Tata?" I asked my grandmother.

"How? They never will give you the permit," she responded.

"I will try anyway. Give me the key."

She looked at me. "That's illegal. You know that. I have to return the key to the Housing Authorities."

"I know it's illegal to keep access to the apartment, but what can happen? They could evict me, but at least I want to try." Who would want to live in this dark apartment anyway? It's too small for a family, not nice enough for an important person. I convinced myself that I had a good chance of getting a permit to occupy the apartment.

"Well, I suppose you are right," Tata said, "Why not? Maybe Ms. Barry would help?" Ms. Barry who worked for the Housing Authority rented a room just below my grandmother's. Ms. Barry is very plain looking and quiet, but always friendly. I think she is a lesbian. Her landlady once told my grandmother that she has seen her with a woman dressed in men's trousers and shoes.

My grandmother and I are of the same mindset. We always see the light at the end of the tunnel, we never give up. She is a fighter and a very feisty one at that. She is always diplomatic, but not afraid to challenge authority. At five foot five inches you would not expect the energy and anger that was packed into such a small frame. She is smart, and I always wanted to be like her. Grandmother and grandson made a plan. She would fetch Ms. Barry at the earliest time possible with nylons and coffee in hand which Ms. Barry likes, as nylons and coffee are from the West. Tata has had success with this method before. For example, when she needed the permit for a new kitchen stove she was told by Housing Authority that there was a waiting list and she was number twenty·three which meant a two·year waiting period.

The Western products for Ms. Barry put my grandmother immediately at number four. Two months later the kitchen stove was delivered. Hopefully the nylons/coffee bribe would work miracles for me as well. In East Germany apartments are rare — more than bananas, lean tenderloins or cars; my grandmother' products from the West would get her the fresh fruit from the greengrocer across the street from our apartment building and the filet from the butcher shop next door. She never tried to force a car application because no one in our family had the money to buy a car, so there was no need to bribe us into a good position on the car waiting list.

To obtain a favored status within the Housing Authority is a whole different story. Families with kids and at least one parent with working·class credentials are allowed to submit an application for an apartment. There is no space in the entire application form to put down the desired number of rooms or even location. That was in the power of the Housing Authority alone. Policemen and military personnel are also considered working class, as are shop clerks and persons who worked in Party bureaus. Part of the working-class classification were also people who had survived the Nazi camps or had to immigrate to the Soviet Union in the Thirties and were lucky enough to have survived the first Paradise of the Proletariat to return to Germany after the war. I am an aspiring librarian, so I'm not in a good category.

My mother is an economist with a law degree working at an international trade company, my stepfather is a teacher, my aunt is teaching at the University in Leipzig and her husband is a scientist working at a museum in Leipzig. My mother's brother is a teacher as well. My grandmother's homeland is now part of Poland. And my biological father lives in West Germany. It can't get really any worse. I am basically just "one gene" away from officially branded as a bourgeois. If I am lucky I might be eligible to submit an application for an apartment in about five years from now with an additional waiting period of about ten years to get an apartment assigned. God knows were? So, here I am, eighteen years old with a very sketchy social background wanting an apartment of my own. A hope made in an asylum, really. But it is a challenge I feel I can take. And with the help of nylons, coffee and some Sarotti milk chocolate that my grandmother can add, I might be able to work the system.

The presents for Ms. Barry produced a "I am not sure if that will work, but Thomas should come to my office to fill out the paperwork." So I did. A subordinate clerk to Ms. Barry looked at the filled-out form again and again.

"You're kidding young man, aren't you?" She glares at me. "You are single, right."

I nod my head.

"You don't have a wife or children do you?"

I nod.

"You are not serving in the National People's Army, are you?"

I nod.

"What are you?" She gives me a glaring look again.

"I am an A-student at a library school. I got the permission to graduate six months earlier because of my

14

good grades."

She looks at me in total disbelief.

"And because of that you think our State of the Workers and Farmers should assign you an apartment? Young man, the State of the Workers and Farmers provided you with an education without charge. Now it's your turn to earn the trust of the proletariat before even thinking about getting an apartment." She closes my file. But I was not dismissed that easily.

"I am very thankful for the opportunity that I was given by the proletariat. Because of my grades the proletariat will pay six months less for my education and I will be part of the work force six months earlier. In order to be a productive member of the socialist society I think I should have my own place. And I will be forever thankful for the understanding and generosity of the proletariat."

She looks at me. I could tell by her wordless expression that she knew that I being cynical but she wouldn't dare to question my thanks to the proletariat.

"You will hear from us." Now was time for me to leave.

Somehow I knew I would get the apartment. About two weeks after my visit to the office of the Housing Authority I got a note that a committee of the Housing Authority would inspect the apartment to evaluate the situation. The weather Gods were with me. It was freezing cold, meaning my apartment would be freezing cold, too. The water was frozen and a thick icicle was hanging out off the faucet. I don't have any decent lighting fixtures yet. In the kitchen a single bulb hung from the ceiling. In my living room I have only a table lamp. The place was gloomy. The scene was set when the committee marched into my apartment. They were very hostile. The woman I had the exchange with hardly acknowledged me. Everybody had a notebook. As they spoke to each other their breath turned to white fog. It was easy to see that they couldn't wait to get out of this place. They stopped speaking to each other, just scribbling in their note books. "I think we are done," said the woman I met before. The committee exited the apartment.

"Are you sure you want this place? This is almost uninhabitable. But if you want it you must sign off on any

15

future wishes to apply for an apartment. That's it."

Yes, I think and look at her. "Thank you very much. When should I be at your office to sign whatever is necessary and to get the written assignment for the apartment?"

"Tomorrow afternoon at 4:15 sharp. Don't be late. We are closing at 4:30." And out the door she went. I ran up the stairs. "Tata we did it! We did it! I got the apartment. Tomorrow I will sign the papers." She looks at me. "You are my grandson. I don't know where you got from but you did it." I look at her. "Yes." I put my arms around her. She pushes me away. She doesn't like warm and fuzzy emotions. "Let's eat."

I enter my apartment. What a contrast to Klaus'. I almost feel depressed. I never will be able to afford any changes that would make it look like his. I open the windows to let some warm spring air in. And I think about last night. No one but me knows how much I want a real a home for me and my heart. I feel so aimless, without answers. Yesterday I felt a little bit of the comfort that I so long for. I wish Klaus would appear out of nowhere. But how could he? He does not have my address, only my work phone number, and in all likelihood he never will call.

I am hungry. I decide to go to my grandmother's. She always has something on the stove or already prepared in the pantry. After that I will take a long walk. Probably lost in the Klaus-and-me-and-our-future dream world. Some self talk. Escaping from reality. I like these moments. Sometimes it feels really real. Being alone is not that bad, but loneliness hurts me. Creating an imaginary world makes me happy. I wonder if others do the same when they feel lonely. There are times I am convinced that I am the only one with no real friends, that I am ugly and have no exciting future. I imagine a world where I am attractive with a nice ass, a bigger cock, less lips, thick hair and no pimples. A future where a beautiful man takes care of me and reads my mind, ready to fulfill any wish I have. A future where I am the center of attention, with a good job that makes me feel adequate. I want to be admired, but most of all I want to be wanted. This is the future I can daydream myself into for hours at a time, and how I like that. Back to reality. My nose tip starts to tickle, tears on my face. Back to self pity.

Nazi Past, Pizza, Poisonous Bookcase, and Paragraph 175

It's Monday morning and I am working the service desk in the catalog department of the library. I have few visitors, but none of them need my help right now. I have some books to file away. I like working at the service desk, because that means working with the public. It's the mix of people I deal with that I like. There are the ones who never need any help; they can do the research for certain book titles and magazines on their own. But the majority — faculty members and students —don't have the time to go through the index catalog and search for the right literature, and this is where I come in. I love the challenge of finding the specific index card with the information about where in our vast collection this particular book is to be found. We have three different catalog systems: There is the alphabetical index catalog where books are sorted according to the author or title, there is the alphabetical subject index catalog and there is the so-called "old catalog" that are big leather-bound ledgers, where book titles are recorded by hand. Sometimes you get requests via phone or pneumatic tube from other libraries inquiring for a book on behalf of one of their readers.

My service desk shift is scheduled for four hours at a time. Then I am replaced by another colleague and I have to go back to the less exciting work of cataloging books, a task that happens in a stuffy and dusty room I share with three other workers and an endless amount of new books to be worked on. Day in and day out. Therefore the time the service desk is a welcome interruption of my boring routine.

My eyes scan the room to make sure none of the visitors removes index cards out of the catalog drawers. Everything seems in order. As a matter of fact, I have never experienced an unruly visitor on my watch...but it happens. The head of the service desk department for the last forty-five years tells us on every possible occasion that readers steal. She has basically spent her entire life in the library. No wonder. She lives with her mother, a retired teacher. Miss Arnold is in her early sixties and never, ever socializes without her mother, Mrs. Arnold. At library functions you would think they were sisters. They dress alike, head to toe. It's a riot. Miss Arnold never speaks in the presence of Mrs. Arnold. Because the mother, always and without pause, talks in an almost lecturing manner. I like Miss Arnold. She is kind and gentle. Her mousy looks fit her demeanor. She was one of my teachers at Library School. Her trademark is a short and always sharpened pencil behind her left ear.

The phone rings. "Service desk. How can I help you," I answer.

"Good morning. I would like to speak to Thomas Schardt."

"Speaking," I answer, as I wonder who it could be.

"Hi, I didn't recognize your voice. How are you?" I take the phone from my ear to look at it. I can't believe what I am hearing. It's Klaus.

"Hi. What a surprise! I thought I would never hear from you." I whisper into the phone. I am in a public area and private phone calls are not encouraged.

"Well, here I am. Just wondering if and when I can see you again. I thought maybe we could have a beer tonight."

"Yes, I can do that," I try to be as official as possible.

"Let's say at six. Meet you at Burgfrieden."

"All right. That's fine." I don't know what else to say.

"O.K., see you tonight." He hangs up.

I have to get up from my seat. I almost can't contain myself. *He called. He called!* I walk around the desk to open the window. I see my reflection. I have to change, I think. I look so librarian. Buttoned- up shirt, sweater with a v-neck, pleated pants. How boring. And of course a big pimple is growing under my nose. It's still red. But just in time for tonight it will be white. Great. I try to concentrate and go back to my seat. I pretend to catalog a book.

All I do is stare into space and think about how I can get out of work to go home in order to change and be on time for the date with Klaus. It's impossible, unless I leave work earlier. Maybe I should take the whole afternoon off? That

19

gives me plenty of time to work on my pimple and figure out what to wear. Somehow I manage to make it through the rest of my desk shift. I also have come up with an excuse that will get me out of work earlier.

"The meter man is coming today between noon and four to read my electric usage. I totally forgot about it," I tell my supervisor knowing she cannot deny me leaving early.

"Of course. But next time maybe your grandmother can be home for you since you live in the same building." I almost got caught in a lie.

Of course I am ready to meet Klaus much earlier than the agreed time, but I don't want to be the first one to arrive. I take a long detour, the whole time playing in my mind over and over what to say when we meet. Do we kiss or just shake hands? I try my face-smiling exercises. I am totally aware of my pimple. I really tried hard to make it disappear, but it just gets bigger and redder. Walking down the street I try to catch myself in the reflection of shop windows. You really can't see it, can you, I convince myself for one minute. Passing another window reflection the pimple is so obvious. It's not fun to be so unattractive. Finally, it's five minutes after six. I open the door to the bar. I have never seen it so empty. Of course it's kind of early to be packed. I let my eyes circle the place as I am still standing in the doorway. No Klaus. Maybe he is in one of the other rooms. I have to make myself move further inwards. I am so tempted to turn around and run outside.

I pretend to go to the bathroom and walk quickly in that direction with my head down. The few men sitting at the tables don't take notice. I rush in the bathroom nodding to the woman attendant in front of it. She is older and always next to a small round table with a white tablecloth. In the center and very visible is a small porcelain decorated with a flower garland around the edge. It's for the twenty Pfennig that's expected for using the urinal plus hand washing. Thirty Pfennig for the use of the john, plus hand washing. Toilet attendants make a lot of money, so everybody says. I wouldn't know. How much money can you really make collecting twenty or thirty Pfenning a pop? Somebody told me that it's not easy to lease public bathrooms in restaurants, bars and hotels. There is always a waiting list. Especially for those in places with a lot of Western tourists because they mostly pay in hard currency as opposed Easterners who only have the other less desired kind of money. If someone pays with Western Pfennig that puts him or her right in the high position of toilet users. The attendant usually will check the john to make sure it's really clean. And for Westerners the air gets sprayed with a room freshener before he does his business. Easterners can expect a clean toilet but no nice scent. Anyway the attendant at Burgfrieden bar likes her men, since the more alcohol consumption there is the more the men need to use her facilities. The clinging noise of falling Pfennig into the flowered plate becomes at some point an uninterrupted sound of "music" as the evening goes on. Rumor also has it that the bathroom attendant looks the other way when two guys disappear in the stall at the same time. That means more Pfennig on her plate.

Anyway I pay my twenty Pfennig and unzip at the urinal. I don't have to pee but I pretend. I return back to the bar room. No Klaus. Oh well, maybe he forgot or he will just be a no-show. I get a beer, pay and disappear into the corner right next to the entrance.

The door opens and three men walk in, among them Klaus. At first I think they are not together. But they talk to each other as they pass by me. He is with some friends. I am disappointed. I had not expected that. I could leave right now because Klaus has not seen me. The three sit down in the other room, their backs to me. What should I do? This is exactly the situation I want to avoid. I wanted to be the one coming in after Klaus, expecting him right at the bar counter, waiting for me. I had it all planned. Now what? I could leave altogether and come in again, maybe then I would be noticed by Klaus right away. I could leave and not come back. Or, I could just start moving towards the table undoubtedly blushing all over. I push myself away from the wall. I feel my face getting hot. The table is only a couple of meters away but it feels like forever to reach the group. I go around the table and face them.

"Here you are. I just said to my friends, I wonder if he

21

will show up. Hi. How are you?" He gets up from his chair and gives me a hug. I still have the beer glass in my hand. Klaus' hug shakes it and beer drips on the table barely missing one of his friends. Now I am dark red. I wish I could disappear. I feel so clumsy.

"Hi," I say.

"Sit down. These are my friends Ferdinand and Matthias," Klaus introduces me. Ferdinand is a little bit pouchy, but has beautiful curly black hair. He gets up and gives me an unexpected hug. Matthias stays seated. He is very slim and dark haired as well. He looks familiar to me. He shakes my hand. His grip is very soft, almost nonexistent. He doesn't look me in the eyes. I sit down. There is an awkward moment of silence.

"What do you do for work?" Ferdinand breaks the silence.

"I am a librarian at University Library of Humboldt University," When I say that I feel like I am bragging.

"Oh, I thought only women would be librarians," Ferdinand responds, "but I guess being gay is almost the same...I am joking." I feel embarrassed and offended.

"Sure, I was the only male in my class. But there are male librarians where I work," I try to overcome being red-faced again.

"Oh, I am a waiter. Most of my colleagues are women and the male ones are all faggots." Ferdinand laughs. Klaus and Matthias don't say a thing. That would be the moment to ask Klaus what he does for work but I don't want to let his friends know that I don't know.

"What do you do? I think I have seen you before." I look at Matthias.

"You probably have. I am a ballet dancer at the Deutsche Staatsoper." Another typical gay profession, I think.

"That's right. Now I remember. You were in Swan Lake, weren't you?" I say. "I loved the production. Odette was super. I think Preuss danced that evening. I don't remember who did the Prince?"

"Yes, it must have been the night I almost danced the lead. But I had a gig the night before in Leipzig, so they couldn't reach me to ask me if I could dance the Prince the next day. But I did the next three performances. Too bad you haven't seen me. It was fabulous. I got great reviews."

I don't know what to say. That sounded a little bit too much like bragging. I look at Klaus. He rolls his eyes. "Do you want another beer or do you want to go someplace else to have something eat?" he asks. I am glad he asks.

"Oh, that would be great. I haven't eaten yet."

"Well, then let's go. Ferdinand, I'll see you tomorrow at the rehearsal. Matthias, I will call you later." Klaus gets up from his chair. I get up as well, and I wonder what kind of rehearsal Ferdinand and he are having. "Bye," I say. "No, no. I want a hug." Ferdinand pulls me down and gives me a kiss. I like him. Matthias nods. His demeanor is clear: No hug from me, and no handshake. I lift my hand, give a quick wave and then I follow Klaus.

"Matthias can be a little obnoxious at times. He really thinks that he is better than any of the soloists at the ballet. But I like him anyway. He is funny. Hope, you will see that side of Matthias at some point, too." I don't say anything, just look at Klaus.

"Thanks for asking me to tonight. I am glad you called."

"I would have done it earlier. But I was busy at work. And then I wanted to call you last week but I couldn't find your number. I looked everywhere. I even asked Matthias if he had seen it. By mistake I had thrown it into the trash can." He puts his arm around me. *He asked Matthias*, I think, *what is the story here?* Klaus must have read my thoughts. "Matthias and I were lovers. We broke up a while ago. But he still has the key to my apartment. He saw your note. Even before me. He came to my apartment when I was still at work that day. He called me right away. He was furious. I think he finally realized that it was over between us. He is a drama queen." I feel relieved.

"What rehearsal are you going to have tomorrow?" I ask.

"I belong to this dance group. We are all non-professional dancers. It's mostly folk dance we do. Our boss tries sometimes to do classical stuff. We train once a week. I like it. We are always looking for more men. You should come. We can talk about it over dinner." He takes my hand and pulls me across the street. "There is a pizza place just a couple streets down, I thought we should go. Do you like pizza?" I have to admit I never had pizza. I have heard about this new place. It's the first pizza restaurant in Berlin.

"Sure," I say. I like being with Klaus. He is so easy to be with. I don't feel intimidated. I also totally forgot about my pimple. (For a while at least.) And he apparently has no problems being physical with me in public. "Ferdinand dances too?" I ask.

"Yes, he is a little bit clumsy and overweight as well. But he is strong. He can lift the girls very easily. Most of our dances we do involve a lots of lifting. Kurt, our boss, loves that. He always says the main purpose of male dancers is to carry women across the stage and make it look very easy at the same time. Most of our men are a little bit on the heavy side. Folk dance is not about slim, beautiful, artificial-looking dancers. It's more about the reflection of everyday people having fun dancing and moving in a realistic way."

We are at the pizza place. Of course there is a long line outside. "Just a moment," Klaus says and makes his way to the door. A couple minutes later he waves at me to come up front. "We can sit at the counter. I know one of the waiters. You don't mind, do you?" I don't. We squeeze through the door. Some of the people in line start to complain. "We were here first. That's not right that these guys get seats..." A waiter pulls us in and shuts the door. I feel special.

Klaus's waiter friend comes up. "And who is this new beauty?" He slaps Klaus on the shoulder. "That's Thomas. Thomas, that's Henry. He dances with me."

"We don't just dance together. Let me tell you that much. Hope to see you soon at one of Klaus' parties." Henry is one of those loud gays who doesn't give a damn if anybody listens, but I do and my red face shows it.

"Look at him. Isn't that sweet. He blushes. You must have him over pretty soon. I like the innocent ones. So hard to find them anymore." I wish Henry would go away.

"Stop it, Henry. You are impossible today. Bring us something to eat." I am glad Klaus puts an end to this.

Our order arrives. It's my first pizza. I have heard about pizza. But my family is pretty conservative where food is concerned, including my grandmother. Any food that is to be eaten with your hands would not come on the table.

That's not how we eat. So, I kind of enjoy using my hands to grab my first slice. "You know this is my first pizza?" I say.

Klaus looks at me. "You never had pizza before? I can't believe that. It's the easiest meal to prepare. You are not a cook?" I am sure not. I take another slice. If my mother could see me eating with my hands she would die. I love it and take another bite. The tomato sauce drips down my fingers. I look around. Everybody in the place eats without forks and knives. A restaurant where there is no silverware, I have to tell Tata about it. She probably won't believe it. Maybe I can take her here someday.

"So tell me a little about you," Klaus says.

I am not sure where to start. I have a pretty boring life. I don't have many friends. I have a dysfunctional family that projects perfection to everybody on the outside. I don't want to tell him that I will be leaving Berlin in a couple of months for Leipzig to work there. That's a long and complicated story, and who knows when the time comes to move I might already be history for Klaus. I want to enjoy us as long as possible.

"Well you know what I do for work. My family made the decision that I should become a librarian since I couldn't make it to the university on the direct path. I am still kind of embarrassed to say what I do. It's a women's job. The few men are very stuffy. But I have to say I like where I work because I can pretty much read what would normally be impossible." The University Library has a big and broad collection. Part of it is marked restricted and only available for researchers with a special clearance. For instance works by Nietzsche and Schoppenhauer fall into the restricted category as well as Rosa Luxemburg, Stalin, Trotsky and Ulbricht, the previous Party chairman, dismissed in disgrace.

And then there is the so called "Poison Bookcase." It's located in the office of the special assistant to the Library Director. In order to get books from there you have to put a special request in, usually issued by the head of whatever school the student or faculty member is from. The special assistant reviews the request. If he grants the permission he signs it. Some of the books from the "Poison Bookcase" are so "poisonous" that they can only be read in the library reading room. Very few can be taken home, and only for a maximum of five days. As a librarian, one has some privileges and can get restricted books as well, and it surely helps when you are friendly with the special assistant. Since the time I went with him on a drinking binge he kind of likes me, but he has no clue I am gay. That would probably end our friendship. He is a man's man and he likes his women. Rumor has it he gets blow jobs from pretty and young students. Anyway, my special connection to the special assistant allowed me so far to read all the Solzhenitsyn books, Boris Pasternak's *Doctor Zhivago*, Camus' *Pest* and Günter Grass' *The Tin Drum*.

I can tell by his face that Klaus has no clue what I am talking about. "That's great. I don't read much. I have to confess. I work with my hands. I never was a good student. I hated school and I made it with the worst possible grades." At least he is honest. "I am a blacksmith and work at the Deutsche Staatsoper. Everything metal on the stage we build. Sometimes it's very challenging because the producers have very little technical understanding. They just want their artistic views made into stage reality. And that changes with each new production. We don't recycle anything from previous ones."

He talks about how he spends a lot of time directly on stage. Close cooperation and understanding with all the other tradesmen like the carpenters, painters, electricians, stagehands, costume makers and make-up people is key. His blacksmith shop then creates the foundation for the illusion called opera or ballet. Fascinating. I had never been behind the scenes of any theater. I never really think about what is needed to make the performance come together. Any possible occasion I have, I try to go to the opera and the ballet. It's the non-reality I love. It takes me away from my life. I enjoy the music, the theatrical aspect, the story, the voices, the bodies and the effects. Whoever came up originally to create this world of dreams, love stories and fantasy in a totally controlled setting did mankind a great service. I can't imagine not having that escape to slip away from what surrounds me daily. And the way Klaus talks about his work and how much he loves the theater makes me feel very connected to him. We both must have a desire to submerge into a bubble that is outside of reality, I think. I want to know everything about him, about his past, about his family and his life that is already thirteen years longer than mine. Despite the age difference I sense many parallels between our lives.

I have the urge to touch him, to at least hold his hand. I press my knee against his. I feel his knee pressing against mine. A wave is going down my body. I sense a gentle flow to my stomach, my heart and my face. As I search for his eyes I see his eyes searching for mine. I realize I have a hard on. "Thanks," is all that I can say. Klaus puts his left hand over my right arm. "What are you thanking me for?"

"Thank you for spending time with me," I answer. Klaus smiles. We are one for a moment.

"Hi, guys how are we doing?" Henry is back. He looks at us both. One hand on my shoulders the other hand on Klaus' back. I don't say a word. I fear another embarrassing moment.

"Well, well, well. Aren't we the little lovebirds? Hey, boy be careful," he turns to me. "This man is dangerous. I don't know what it is about him but he breaks everybody's heart including mine." Henry lowers his head. I feel his breath close to my ear. "He is not worth crying over. He is not even that good in bed. Have fun with him. But if you need somebody good let me know. I can show you a better time. You are cute."

I am not sure how much of that Klaus actually could hear. Of course I am red-faced again. Henry makes me uncomfortable. Why is he telling me all this? Henry straightens up. "Do you want anything else? How about another beer?" Klaus tips his head. Henry is off. He is tall, slim, and his pants fit snugly around his nice ass.

"Listen, whatever Henry told you is probably true. I am not good with just one man. I have to be honest with you." I am not sure what to say. I look at Klaus. I remember what his neighbor had told me at that first morning after. Now this waiter friend of his warned me. Klaus confesses a multitude of men. Being frank and straightforward can be unwanted at times; for instance right at this moment. He is just too honest and it hurts. I am nervous. My little dream that this gorgeous man could be all mine seems short lived. The center of my attention implodes into reality. Why am I so ahead of everything? This is only our second encounter. I certainly enjoy it...minus his friend Matthias' attitude, Henry's directness and Klaus's honesty. Maybe I can be different for him? If he lets me, I will try. I don't want to let go.

"I see this big cloud on your forehead. What are you thinking?"

"This is all new to me. The first night you took me home, you let me stay in the morning. You called me to ask me out again. I meet friends of yours. We are having dinner together. I mean, I have seen other men, but none of them ever treated me with respect. We always did it in the dark, someplace hidden. If I went home with somebody I was asked to leave quietly afterwards. One guy even didn't want me to use the bathroom. The noise could have woken up his neighbors. It made the just spent time and enjoyed pleasure feel so dirty. With you it's so normal. So easy. You are not ashamed of being with me. You already introduced me to some of your friends."

"What's wrong with that?" Klaus asks "And what do you mean by not being ashamed? Why would I be ashamed? I know a lot of people. Some of them are very different. Like Henry. I am not ashamed of being his friend. Yes he is a faggot. He likes to dress up in women's clothing. Would I do that? No. Yes, he sometimes totally misses boundaries. He can be offensive. Some are turned off by that. I really don't believe that I am defined by who I know. My friends mirror me. No, no, no. Absolutely not. I am my own man. I have friends, lots of them. Some are closer to my heart than others. I want to have fun. That's what I want. When you know me better and longer — and I hope you do —you will see I am not a serious person, going through the world analyzing things, reflecting on everything and everyone. I know it sounds superficial. Bu I live in the moment and not what comes after that. So, now I don't want to talk about serious stuff anymore. Let's have another drink, shall we?"

Klaus seeks Henry's attention and puts two fingers up. Moments later two vodka colas are in front of us. I feel already a little bit lightheaded, but I take a big gulp. It's the moment that counts. Isn't that what Klaus just said? Maybe I can be a little bit like Klaus and less uptight about everything? I want to be like Klaus. I take a couple of fast sips. I feel the impact almost immediately. I am more than tipsy. A new round of drinks arrives. I am in la-la land. I feel happy. I even start to like Henry. More drinks arrive in a fast line-up. I stop counting how many I've had. However, I decide I have enough. "Klaus, I can't drink anymore."

"Oh, bullshit. Don't be a wuss." I look at him. I realize that he is pretty gone, too.

"Maybe we should pay and leave?" I suggest.

"You can leave if you want. I am staying." He gives me a push at my shoulder. Klaus is really drunk. I don't know what to do. But I also feel very uncomfortable. I hadn't seen this coming. I try again.

"Maybe I can show you my place?"

"I don't want to see your place. I want to stay here. You can leave." It's like somebody hit a switch. Klaus is suddenly a different person. I don't know what happened to him? What did I do that he is so unpleasant?

"Do you want me to stay?"

"Didn't you just say you want to leave? Then just leave and don't bother me anymore." He turns his back. I look at his neck.

My, God, what just happened? I notice the couple next to me is looking at me. They must have listened to our little exchange. I want to sink into the ground. But at the same time I want to talk to Klaus and make the whole incident disappear. I push my chair back and tap Klaus on the shoulder. He totally ignores me. He has another drink in his hand. I look for Henry.

"I want to pay."

"Is that together?" Henry asked.

"Yes, he can pay for us. He is a librarian at the Humboldt University," Klaus mocks me.

This is awful. Henry gives me the bill. Thirty-two Marks. I have only twenty on me. Everything around me disappears. I feel like I am in a hole. I try to think clearly. What can I do? Panic. Embarrassment. But I have to do something. I will ask Henry if I can pay him the rest later. But I am also afraid he would make a scene. I can't ask Klaus to help me out. I am lost. I don't want to be here. I touch Klaus' arm.

"Can you lend me some money? I will pay you back, I only have twenty Marks. It's not enough."

"Then you have a problem, I guess." Klaus stares at his glass. His words are slurred. He can't be that drunk, I think. He only had two or three more drinks than I had, if even. I feel totally sober now after the shock. What is happening now is quickly sobering me up.

Henry must have realized what is going on. "Give me what you have. And don't worry about the rest." I am tearing up. I feel so embarrassed and humiliated. I give him the money.

"Thanks. I will bring the rest tomorrow."

"I said don't worry about it." He shakes my hand. "Don't get involved with him or you will regret it. Mark my words." I just look at Henry. I feel terrible. I turn towards Klaus. "Good night." He does not answer. Maybe he didn't hear me. But I feel the best thing to do right now is just to leave. I feel invisible.

Unable to walk, I lean against a lamppost outside of the restaurant. All the energy is sucked out of me. I catch the eyes of pedestrians passing by me. I wish somebody would just hold me. My knees feel like rubber and I want to sit down, but I keep holding on to the lamppost. A couple more minutes, I say to myself, and then I will start walking home. After a while my surroundings come alive again. I can hear the traffic noise. I hear people talking and the clicking of their shoes on the cobblestones. I am back. I start to walk. My legs are wobbly. My feet feel like they are made of iron. I am overcome by pity. I don't care about the tears running down my face. I just want to be home. Lie down, sleep and forget what just happened.

A little while after I go to bed I wake up. It's still dark. I have to pee. As I stumble to the bathroom I notice that I have a headache from too much drinking. I sit down, and everything comes back: Klaus, the pizza place, the drinks, everything. Why did the evening turn out the way it did? I still can't figure it out. It went from sweet to bitter in a second. I flush the toilet and go to bed, but I can't go back to sleep. My brain is in overdrive, thinking I must have done something last evening that triggered Klaus's reaction. Didn't he want to be with me anymore? Maybe I shouldn't have told him how good it felt to be with him. Maybe he felt that I was getting too close. Maybe he doesn't want it to be too serious between us. Like he said he wants his life to be fun and nothing else. I certainly am not very loose. I am not all giggly and happy. He must felt that. Klaus was the one, who made the first move, spoke the first word. I don't understand it but I want to. I don't have anybody to talk to about it.

The people that I hang out with are mostly co-workers at the library and some fellow students from the library school: All girls. We are a core group of five. I feel very comfortable with them —around them. It is Claudia, Sonia , Maria, Marlene and me! All four still live at home with their parents. We go to movies together and away on weekend trips. Claudia and Marlene have their own cars, bought by their relatives in the West through Genex, a front company where Westerners can buy East German products for their East German relatives. My friends' relatives also paid for the driving school. West Marks make it possible. There is no waiting list for a car or a place in driving school for them.

Anyway, Claudia's and Marlene's cars mean that the five of us very mobile. We always get attention wherever we go. For one thing, twenty-one-year-old girls usually don't have and drive their own cars in East Germany, except when these girls have West German relatives. So the looks we get are mostly out of curiosity, jealousy or both. And then when we pile into a restaurant or hotel, four girls and one boy, that certainly makes heads turn. Needless to say, we all enjoy the attention and let the spectators speculate. Once we went to Wittenberg to stay at a youth hostel that was part of the Wittenberg Castle. The manager asked us point blank what this was: "Four for one?" He made it very clear that there wouldn't be any nightly interactions.

I told him that we were a youth group of librarians doing some research on Martin Luther and it just happened that I was the leader of this group. I am not sure if he brought that explanation. In any event, he let us stay under one condition: I had to have my own room on the ground floor and my friends had to sleep hostel-style in a room full of bunk beds on the top floor. We still had a blast. And in the end, the manager told us that he never had such a fun and well-behaved group and that we would be welcomed back any time.

We really enjoy each other and my friends' parents like that we hang out together, the only exception being my own parents. I don't live at home anymore and I am not on good terms with them, or rather, with my stepfather. Anyway Claudia's father is a chef. So any party at her house is a great feast: lots of cakes, cold cuts, and salads. When it's over everyone gets a bag full of food to take home. Marlene's parents have a small farm with mostly chickens and a pig or two so good and heavy food is guaranteed there as well. Marlene is a pretty good cook and baker herself.

Sonia's parents are simpler, her mother has some mental problems which sometimes send her to a hospital and her father is an insurance agent. They live on the top floor of a two-family home with use of a nice garden. We never go to Maria's house and I'm not sure why. We can talk about God and the world, politics, church, books we read, but we never mention boyfriends or girlfriends. Maria disappears from time to time when she sees someone. Claudia, Marlene and Sonia don't have boyfriends and I am alone too. I don't know if they know that I am gay. They must, maybe. We talk a lot about Dr. Klotz, who works at the library and supposedly lives with a younger man. No one has ever seen him, except that Dr. Klotz mentions a roommate who studies philosophy at Humboldt University. When we talk about "questionable" men we don't call them gay. The term is "175er" because the paragraph 175 in the Civil Code or "Buergerliche Gesetzbuch" addresses the gay issue. (Some gay men in East Germany celebrate May 17th as their holiday.)

Sometimes I wish I would have the courage to talk to

them about being different. I am not fearful that they would quit our friendship, I am sure they wouldn't. It's me who would be uncomfortable to start this conversation. Every time I come close to telling them, I have a vision that they would imagine what two men do to each other in bed. I know it's me and not everybody would make this immediate mental transition, but I can't help it. This means that I can't even vent about my crazy experience with Klaus. I am a true product of my family, whether I want to be or not. We don't talk about feelings, distress. It's strength that ultimately leads us through all the pain. Defeat is not part of my family's way of life because that means weakness and giving into failure. Self-pity and crying out for help is considered an inconvenience to others. Even my family has to admit that living life means dealing with problems once in a while. But when you talk about problems out loud it means you have to confront these problems; therefore, we don't talk about problems. And when you don't talk about them then they don't exist. My family's mantra!

Hat Maker, Business Woman, and Cleaning Lady

My grandmother had lost her own mother early on, then her father remarried and the classic stepmother story unfolded. The stepmother had children of her own and only had their best interest in mind so my grandmother and her brother were pushed aside. Their father was not strong enough to equalize the situation. When my great-grandfather died my grandmother and her brother were left without any money and were sent off to live with an aunt. My grandmother was the stronger one of the siblings. When she was eighteen years old she opened her own business — a shop for hats in Wartenberg a tiny town in Silesia what would become Poland after the Germany lost the war. Anyway, my grandmother had a good business sense and sailed through the turmoil of the twenties when a lot of people lost a lot of money due to high inflation, the Great Depression and the stock Market crash.

At the wedding of a relative she met her future husband; a master carpenter. More rational than emotional, she saw her future as a wife and owner of a furniture factory. After a short courtship they got married. My grandmother sold her shop, and then went to the bank to get a loan to purchase a big corner building in nearby Namslau with enough room for a future machine shop, a couple of apartments and the possibility for expansion. "For a business it's important to be visible. That's why you should always be on a corner. You will be seen from two sides," was one of her many self-taught business rules.

That my grandmother was the driving force in her marriage right from the beginning is evident through the fact that she had picked the property without consulting her husband. After she had secured the loan and the real estate she called her husband, who up to this point had rented a machine shop to start the business, to ask him to come to the bank to sign the papers.

"Shouldn't I see the house before I commit to it?" he asked.

"We can look at it afterwards. Trust me it's the right thing." He did. It's one of my grandmothers' favorite stories to this day. "He was a good man and a very good carpenter. But he had no business sense. He always needed to think things over and over. I was the opposite," remembers my Grandmother. The couple prospered into money, social status and three children. As shrewd as my grandmother was in business dealing she was a good Catholic.

As someone amongst the "who's who" in town she was responsible for the decoration of the Joseph's altar in her church. My grandparents had reserved seats in the church with their nameplate attached to the pew. But she was her own woman. The priest was not "God" to her and, she disagreed with the church's closeness to the politics and the Nazi regime. "They tried very hard to get us in the Party. But I made it very clear that I don't belong to anyone." An attitude she kept all her life. "We didn't know how far the Nazis would go. But I was not blind." She remembers Jewish business owners in town who would leave. One of them, a good friend of my grandparents wanted to sell them his villa for next to nothing.

"It was a good deal. But I knew it would have been close to robbery if I bought the house and I told him so. He just wanted us to have it. He told me that he wanted the assurance that someone would take good care of it. But we didn't need another house. I offered to drive him to Breslau to the train station. At first he didn't want me to do that, more out of concern for me. But I didn't care. The next day we went to Breslau." The man and his family were lucky enough to buy themselves out of Germany just in time. My grandparents were visited by the town's Nazi Party-boss to be questioned about their "help for a Jew." "I told him that is not his business and please don't ever came to my house again. If he has to talk to me then I would come to his office. I would not have it any other way."

However, the furniture making flourished as well as their reputation to put out a quality product. Through the local Chamber of Commerce my grandfather was offered the opportunity to take over a factory in Lodz. My grandparents saw that as a fantastic moment to expand — until their visit to Lodz and the factory. The foreman at the factory greeted my grandparents with "Heil Hitler" "That turned me off right then and there. I told your grandfather that I am not interested in a tour. Your grandfather was too polite to just leave. So he asked who the owner was. 'Oh, he was a Jew. He left the country.' The man told us. I had had enough, so we left. As we walked down the street back to the train station I saw a couple approaching us. As they came closer I noticed the Yellow Star on the coats. When they saw us they stepped down onto the street. Later I learned it was the law that Jews should not use the sidewalk. I never could have lived there."

Later, during the war my grandparents' company was ordered to build special boxes for ammunition. On January 19th, 1945, the citizens of Namslau were told to leave. The Russians were quickly approaching. "It was total chaos. I went to the bank to get some money. No money was left. I had some jewelry to be repaired. The store owner had already left taking everything with him. I went home and packed some suitcases absolutely sure we will back in a couple of weeks." My grandmother remembers how she covered up the furniture to protect it from dust. The family took the train to seek refuge at my grandfather's in-laws in the countryside. When they arrived there most of the people had already left. Her mother-in-law had refused to leave the farm against the wishes of her husband. The Russians came and ransacked everything. My grandfather went in hiding just in time. His brother did not. He was put on a transport toward the East. No one ever heard from him again. (Later they learned that a sister of my grandfather, who was a nun and lived in a cloister in Breslau, was killed.)

My grandmother felt it was time to head toward the West. They somehow managed to secure space on a Russian army truck. Before my family headed West my grandmother decided to try to get back to Namslau one more time to fetch some clothes for her three children. She and her husband made it. As they tried to get into their house they were greeted by a Polish family, who apparently had moved in. My grandmother didn't grasp the situation at first and went straight into the building. "These people I have never seen before were screaming at us not to enter their home. 'This is all mine,' this Polish woman screamed at me in broken German. I couldn't believe what I was hearing. Their house. This was *my* house. Thank God your grandfather kept his cool. He grabbed me by my collar and said come, come. We should leave. I was beside myself. I was walking in a trance. How can this have happen to me?"

After they reunited with their children, my grandparents joined all of the other expelled Germans. That was the beginning of the real nightmare: Weeks of freezing temperatures, hunger and death. If people died their bodies would be left at the side of the road. There was no time to bury them, it was all about survival. Two hundred and twenty five miles on foot. Eventually the family made to the small town of Pratau in the Russian-occupied East. The occupiers assigned my family an apartment. My mother and her sister started school again. My uncle was just five years old at the time. My grandmother found a carpenter workshop that was for rent.

My mother and her sister were sent at night to the railroad tracks to wait for trains loaded with coal. When a train stopped they had to climb into the cars to grab as much coal as they could and then jump off before the train would start moving again. My grandfather didn't have enough orders to make a living. My grandmother came up with another plan: Make it to Düsseldorf. She had relatives there. They would help. She was convinced of that. The family packed and went off without their eldest daughter, my aunt. She believed in Communism and wanted to stay in East Germany.

When the family arrived in Düsseldorf the relatives were not happy, nor eager to help. They offered my grandparents a room in the basement. But my grandmother was not to be discouraged. She looked for a better living situation. She found a bunker she could rent, it was dark, wet and moldy. The future never looked so uncertain. My grandfather has reached his end. The life was draining out of his body, leaving his wife and two small children in a desperate situation. "For the first time in my life I didn't know where to go. I was 50 years old and I had lost everything."

But my grandmother, being my grandmother, marched on. She realized she had to find work. She had no skills to show except that she was a successful wife, mother and business owner in the past, now living in a bunker. She was a refugee in her own country. And her countrymen, including her family, stayed away as far as they could. She made a plan. She needed a suitable apartment for her two children and herself. She needed to find work and she needed to start the process getting restitution for her lost property now in Poland. By law she was entitled to compensation. She found a one-bedroom flat. With the help of social services and some distant relatives she furnished it —— sparsely but with a sense of welcomed normalcy. She made window valances out of newspaper, it was a start. And she got a job cleaning at the post office. One of the perks was the free food in the cafeteria.

"When I got the job, I felt like the happiest person in the world. After the first week I asked if I could get a cash advance thinking maybe ten Marks. I got fifty Marks. For the first time since we had left Namslau almost eight years ago I cried. I was Frau Wilk from Namslau way back. People respected my family and me. We had it all. And here I am washing floors and have a breakdown over fifty Marks I had earned." She ran home to share the joy with her two kids. The three of them went to a coffee shop for hot chocolate. "We sat in the window, watched the street scene and felt a little bit at home. I wished Paul, your grandfather, could have been with us."

My mother became an apprentice in a large department store, my uncle went to school and my grandmother cleaned the post office. Life was tough and did not resemble the life a decade ago. But they were together, alive and healthy. "I learned that regrets and dwelling on the past is a waste." My mother met my father, thirteen years her junior. He was tall and showed confidence. I think she saw in him in a way her father whom she had adored and vice versa. My father's family was on the very left side of the political spectrum and members of the West German Communist party, which was eventually outlawed in the '50s. Anyway the socialist East Germany was the desire of many including my father. After my parents got engaged against the will of my grandmother they moved to the outskirts of East Berlin. My father, a trained locksmith, got a job in the "Herman Rau" factory. So did my mother, as office help. They were a novelty and part of the propaganda machinery of the East Germans. Two young people left the evil empire of the capitalist West to come to the future, the eventual victors of history. They got a nice one-bedroom apartment for the conviction. My parents married in 1954. The only wedding guests were my aunt and her husband. I was born one year later.

My mother's older sister had progressed from a refugee from the East to a student at Humboldt University in Berlin, where she had met a future husband. In the mid-'50s she became a high school teacher, her husband worked at the ministry of education. Both were members of the Socialist Unity Party. Things looked very bright for them. Except that my grandmother and her son lived still in enemy land. When trying to make it up the East German stepladder a mother and a brother in the West did not look good. This black spot was prohibitive for any future *Nomenklatura* "membership." My aunt and uncle went to work on my grandmother to convince her to move to East Germany. This was when two Germanys existed and their territories were cut up in allied sectors. The borders were still crossable. The Iron Curtain not yet as iron.

After several visits back and forth, fueling the guilt my family is so good at, and an endless exchange of letters, my grandmother gave in and moved from Düsseldorf to East Berlin, the capital of the "First Dictatorship of the Proletariat on German Soil." My uncle started the extended high school at the Carl von Ossietzky Schule in Pankow, where I would be sent twenty years later. The irony is it that my parents got divorced in 1959, and my father went back to his hometown, Düsseldorf. He had enough of the proletarian paradise. I was four years old. I would never see my father again. My memories of him are almost nonexistent. He never paid a dime for my support and never wrote or initiated any contact. He died in the late '80s in Spain, mourned by his fourth wife.

Linden Trees, Intershops, and Vacation Plans

I have the late shift at the book return counter. The last visitors are leaving the large reading room. I like the late shift. It is quiet and I have time to read. Sometimes I fantasize about certain regulars that they are gay and, that they will ask me out to have a drink with me. Of course it never happens. I turn off the lights and sign myself out. I have no plans for tonight. I step through the enormous library door. A nice breeze meets me. A streetcar squeaks by. I noticed that the tracks are sinking below the street surface. It's time to lift the tracks again. I never understand why there is not a permanent solution to make the tracks stable enough so they do not shift. Repairing them means many, many months of disrupted service, and as soon everything is back to normal the tracks start to sink again. Like with so many other things there is a constant presence of misery. Some say we have it so much better here in East Berlin. Things get done because it's the capital, but go outside of the city they conditions in the rest of the country are much worse. Well, that might be true but that makes our inconveniences no less inconvenient.

I decide to walk to Unter den Linden boulevard towards Alexanderplatz to catch the subway home from there. I like the boulevard lined with Linden trees and benches. Passing by the impressive building of the Staatsbibliothek and the Humboldt University on the one side and the Deutsche Staatsoper and the Cathedral on the other gives it a sense of worldly flair I always imagine I would find in Paris, London or Vienna...places in all likelihood I will never see. The traffic is still buzzing. I am lost in enjoying the vastness of the only world city I know, next to Prague and Budapest that is. The daylight slowly switches to night. I love the twilight on a summer evening.

"Hey." Someone stops me. I look up. It's Klaus.

"What are you doing here?" Thinking that it's a

coincidence to run into him.

"I had called earlier to see if you are working today. They told me you would be finished by seven." As much as I have missed him, I am not sure if I want this. I have a flashback to our last evening together that ended so abruptly. I look at him overcome by my ridiculous shyness, totally speechless. He is what I am not, but I what would like to be. His shirt is unbuttoned and is only held together because its tucked into his jeans. His jeans are tight. He wears wooden clogs. I would dress exactly the same. His face is narrow. I hadn't noticed his slight overbite. Sexy. His blond hair is curled, parts hanging over his forehead. I slept with this guy, I think. My dick gets hard. Hoping he wouldn't notice I clear my voice. "What a surprise," I manage to say.

"I thought we could have a beer." So, he is assuming that I don't have any plans. For a split second I want to say no. But I don't.

"Sure. Where do you want to go?" I ask.

"How about the Espresso Bar across the street?" I tilt my head. I like the place. You can sit outside and watch the traffic and the people . We cross Unter den Linden boulevard and walk to the corner of Friedrichstrasse. Klaus puts his arm around my shoulder with confidence. I wonder where he gets that self-assurance, but I know the answer. Beautiful people have no reason to hide. I notice pedestrians staring at us, their eyes wandering from Klaus to me. I like the attention.

We find two empty seats on the patio. Klaus orders two beers. Life is good again. "I missed you," he says. I look up from my beer, blushing.

"It's nice to run into you," is the only thing I can think of to say.

Klaus says, "I loved our evening at the pizza place, but to this day I can't figure out why you left so suddenly." For a moment I am not sure that I hear him right. I am kind of shocked. I left all the sudden and he doesn't know why? *Is he teasing me*, I wonder. I try to read his face. "No good reason. I had to leave," I said.

"Oh, I thought you were mad at me or something. I wasn't sure if I should try to see you again. Glad that I did.

But you could have visited me too, couldn't you?"

"I was kind of busy," That's a total lie. "But let's forget this. It's super that we are having a beer here and now," I am determined to save the situation. "What have you been up to since I saw you last?" I ask.

"I am really busy at work. We are working on the production of Salome. The set designer has great ideas but it's a challenge to make it work and budget at the same time." Klaus takes a big gulp of his beer. I notice his glass is almost empty. "And we are getting very close to our next performance with the dance group. I have a solo. Therefore I have a lot additional training hours. By the way, you should come and join us. We are always short on men." I have to laugh.

"I never have danced. In school I did ballroom dancing, but that was the extent of it. I am not in good enough shape for it."

"I don't think that's true. Remember I have seen you. You have great legs and a nice ass."

I am blushing again but at the same time I like his complements. I also like the thought of trying. When I was about twelve years old I saw a billboard promoting the State Ballet School. There was a picture of a couple in a classical dance pose, one man lifting a woman way above his head. It looked so beautiful. The man had a great body. I was standing in front of him, imagining being that man. The same evening I told my mother that. She looked at me. "Absolutely not. Don't ask me again." I remember feeling very hurt, but being a good kid I did not challenge her. Yet, almost ten years later I was asked to join a dance group.

Klaus is on his second glass of beer. "I'll tell you what. Tomorrow is our regular training in the evening. Why don't you come and just watch us? I will introduce you to the choreographer and his assistant. What do you think?" I feel tickled, attending a rehearsal won't hurt.

"Sure," I say, relieved to be doing more than watching Klaus get drunk.

"Do you want to walk a little bit? The evening is gorgeous."

"That's a great idea. I love to. Why don't we walk to my

place? Can you stay for the night?" Klaus looks me straight in the eyes. He has a beautiful smile. I feel another sensation in my groins.

"I suppose I can stay, but I don't have a change of clothes with me." I don't like to wear the same things twice.

"Don't worry. I have enough stuff," Klaus offers. "You can just pick something out."

Klaus was always full of surprises. I had never been offered to wear another man's clothes before. I get up from the chair, covering the front of me with my bag. I have a boner and it shows. Klaus pays the waiter. It's almost dark. Only the street lights illuminate the walkways. We join the many who enjoying an evening stroll.

We pass the Staatsoper and the Opern Café, just over the bridge the Marx-Engels-Platz big looks like a vast dark blob. People and cars seem to shrink. After a while we see the Marien Kirche, the hundreds of fountains at the base of the TV Tower with the rows of benches that are so pleasing to the eye. Coffee shops and restaurants under the wing-shaped cement roofs at the base of the tower have the aura of modernity. Often I go to the Espresso Bar if I am lucky enough to find a seat; it's always so crowded. The packs of cigarettes betray most of the patrons being from West Berlin, coming here for the day, living it up with the 25 GDR Marks they have to exchange at the checkpoint, the compulsory for every Westerner in order to get into the Paradise of the Proletariat. The West Mark is very much desired by the Party bosses. Sometimes the Western visitors are pay in hard currency, the desired Marks. It's illegal for the wait staff to accept the money without reporting it to the manager, but they are all in it together. Being in the restaurant business in East Berlin means you have it made. With the West Marks you can get almost anything. A couple of Marks open doors for daily goods such as lean meat or quick access to handymen from plumbers to carpenters to car repair men. The West Marks allows you also to buy West goods in the Intershops that are filled with chocolate, perfumes and clothes such as the so sought after Levi jeans. Officially, these Intershops are meant for people from the West visiting the East, but you go in any of those shops and you see some Westerners, but a lot more East Germans. I am not one of the lucky ones who have access to West Marks as I am a librarian.

Klaus and I cross the Alexanderplatz, the pinnacle of socialist architecture framed with the box-shaped department store. We pass the Hotel Berlin —another hangout for Westerners —and the complex of the House of the Teachers, adjacent to the Kongress Halle where I had my Youth Inauguration, the mandatory socialistic rite of passage which takes place when one is fourteen years old. In the middle of Alexanderplatz is an enormous round fountain with a spiral shaped insert for the water display. Near it stands the giant round World Clock which has the exact time of all the major cities in the world suggesting unity; ironic, since citizens of East Germany are not allowed to travel to most places on this planet. (Yet we can see what time it is in New York or Paris.)

Alexanderplatz is always busy until the wee hours. There you can meet friends, strangers or just socialize. The underground public bathroom is cruised by gays. I never dare to go there even though I want to. I am always afraid people I know, but shouldn't know, cruising toilets would see me. Klaus must have read my mind.

"You ever been down there? Lots of action." His head points in the direction of the stairs.

"No, but I have heard about it."

"Oh come on. Don't play innocent! You would be the first gay man I've met who hasn't had his fun there." *Well, then I am the first*, I think.

"Honestly, I have never been down there."

"You are a strange guy." Klaus puts his right arm around me, his hand squeezing my shoulder. As soon as he touches me I get hard. "Let's take the streetcar. I want to get home. Can't wait to get you naked." He pulls me in the direction of Prenzlauer Allee. I feel like everybody sees my dick pushing against the inside of my zipper. I giggle. We both start running. We are lucky. The right streetcar pulls up. We get off at the fourth stop. It's not long until we reach Christburger Strasse.

We start running again. The street slopes downwards to

number 10. I reach for his hand before we walk through the spooky hallway, crossing the courtyard. Dark, yet familiar. I take two steps at a time, faster than Klaus until he catches me by my waistband and I turn around. I am higher up than he is. I put my arms around his neck, pressing his head against my chest. His hands are at my back sliding down into my pants. His fingers touch the top of my underwear. I feel one hand going inside, smoothing over my buttocks from one cheek to the other. I start breathing harder. It feels so good. His one hand goes further down; the other is pressing me closer towards him. I feel his finger circle around my anus. I push my hips a little bit away from him. I want his finger. I kiss the top of his head. My tongue finds his ear, just as his finger is inside of me. Our moaning is intense. I want him right here and now, but I remind myself that we are still in the hallway. My lust is strong and so is his. I open my pants. Klaus pulls them down, then my underwear. His head goes down on my chest and my stomach as he steps down. He slightly pushes me to sit down. I spread my legs, lean back. He has my dick in his mouth. One hand straddles my balls while two fingers from the other hand enter deep inside of me, beginning a slow rhythm.

I have never felt such a sensation through my whole body. No one has ever satisfied me like this. My hands guide his head. I want to touch him but I can't. I am lost in the moment. I start to shake. I am close to an orgasm. Klaus knows and he is goes faster. He now has three fingers inside of me. He takes my balls and my cock in his mouth at the same time. The warmth and the moisture of his spit are putting me over the edge. I lift my hips and I push deep inside of his mouth, then I am coming. Klaus takes it, swallowing every drip. He releases me. What a wonderful feeling. He looks at me and smiles. I slide down to kiss him, tasting myself.

"Thank you, "I say.

"Thank you. You taste sweet," he says. "It was great."

All of a sudden we realize that we are still in a public place. I pull my pants up, but Klaus slides his hand in my pants and grabs my ass again. We take the last steps up to his apartment. As soon as the door closes behind us I finger

46

at his zipper to get his cock out.

"Wait," he says as we undress and look at each other. Now he is hard and I am soft.

"Think you can get it up again?" Klaus laughs. I wonder if I can. Klaus kisses me. I put my hands on his ass, massaging it, pulling his cheeks apart as he rotates his hips. I can tell he likes it. His moaning makes me hard again. I spit into my hand and wet his hole. "Yes, yes. Fuck me with your fingers. Go deep." I follow his lead. His inside is so soft and moist. We are gliding to the floor. He is on his back, his head resting on my left arm. My right hand caresses his thighs. I slide my fingers in and out. I kiss the tip of his penis as he lifts his hip, wanting more. I free my left arm, lift his legs and tease his ass with my tongue. A drip of his pre-cum touches my lips. I wet him and myself, guiding my cock into his hole as he grabs his ass and pulls it apart. I slide in. Klaus and I are one, savoring the moment. I look at his ass. I am all the way inside. Just looking at this excites me even more. I pull Klaus on top of me. I bend over and take his cock in my mouth until we are at the same tempo.

"Oh, Thomas. I like having you in me. It's the perfect size. Oh, God." Our moaning mixes with the sound of his ass slapping on my hips. I am close. So is he. "Are you ready?" I want that we come together; it feels so good. I have his penis in my hand. I feel pressure against my palm.

"Yes, I am close. Are you? I am coming."

"Yes, yes." We come at the same time. I push against him, my hips lifting both of us. His semen lands on my chest as he collapses on me. I pull out. His cum glues us together like the first time. Feeling and hearing each other's orgasm. My hands move up and down on his back. Klaus kisses me softly. "What a perfect match," he says, rolling off me. I now feel the harshness of the carpet. I put my hands under my head. I am lucky. We are one, equal.

All the guys I have been before always made sure they would come, but didn't care if I did. Klaus is first guy who would allow me to enter him. I never felt adequate until now. Until now sex was just a fast release. Nothing more. Hardly with any foreplay. For me sex with men was something I wanted yet felt ashamed and dirty. This was

Klaus kisses me on the shoulder. We are both naked.

"I think dinner is ready," I say.

"Not quite. Ketchup is missing." Klaus grabs the bottle and shakes it over the pan. "That's the icing. Hope you like it?" I smile and kiss him. He divides the food onto two plates and brings them to the living room. Our clothes are strewn all over the floor. Klaus sets the table as I separate socks, t-

48

shirts, pants. I hear the sizzling noise of matches. Klaus lights a candle. We sit down. I look at him. If he only could imagine how much this evening, this moment means to me, thinking how this evening began and would end with Klaus and I together and calm with dinner and candlelight. I slide my arm over the table, our hands meet in the middle. "Thank you," I say and start eating. "I am glad we ran into each other."

His fork scratches over the plate, then he says "Next week I'll take a couple of days off. I have no plans. Want to do something together?"

"Sure, what do you have in mind? I figured you would be busy with work and the dance group."

"I know. I wouldn't leave town for more than two or three days, but I need to get away."

"I certainly have vacation time. I am sure I can get some days off. Where would you like to go?" I ask

"Friends of mine went to Jelenia Góra in Poland. They said it's nice there and cheap too."

Jelenia Góra was called before the war Greenberg and was then part of Germany. My grandparents used to take my mother and aunt in summer to a nearby town on vacation. One of her relatives owned an inn there.

"Sounds like fun. How do we get there?" I ask.

"By train. And there are always vacancies in the university dorms," Klaus responds.

"Then let's do it. I have never went on vacation with a man, I mean a lover. I mean another gay man. This is so exciting!" I get up from my chair and kiss Klaus, feeling as if I was on cloud nine.

"You've never had a lover before?" he asks. *So, he considers me his lover and not a fling?* I wonder.

"No," I said, "I am not so lucky in this department. I never had a boyfriend. The longest I saw somebody was for two months, but we never did anything together except have sex. It's a long story."

.

"Were you thinking of going to Jelenia Góra during the week or over the weekend? I have to clear this with my boss at the library." I asked Klaus.

"I was thinking of leaving this Saturday and coming back on Tuesday. That way I wouldn't miss dance rehearsal on Wednesday."

"Let's plan on that. I will find out tomorrow if I can take next Monday and Tuesday off." We finish dinner. I clear the table. Klaus pulls out the couch bed. I have to pee. That means putting some clothes on and hopefully not meeting his neighbor on the way to the bathroom. When I come back he is already in bed. I slip under the covers and put my head on his chest. His right arm pulls me close.

"I enjoy being with you. I really look forward to our little trip to Poland," Klaus says. It's nice that he says that. My hand goes over his chest. "Yes," is all I can say, feeling very sleepy. "See you tomorrow."

"Good morning. When do you have to be at work?" I open my eyes and look at Klaus. He smells fresh. Showered, dressed and ready to leave the house. I didn't even hear him get up.

"Good morning. Yes, I have to be at work today." I push the blankets off me. Klaus looks at my hard-on. "You better cover that up otherwise I will be late." He kisses the tip of my dick, embarrassing me. "I left you a key. It's here on the table. Keep it. I'll call you at work to see if you can get the days off for Poland. Thanks. Talk to you later," Klaus says. He closes the apartment door.

I am late for work, but no one really cares as long I'm there. I ask my supervisor if I can get next week off. She gives me the okay. My first vacation with a man is going to happen. I daydream throughout the morning. Everything is happening so fast. Yesterday morning everything was as dull, boring, routine, but now forty-eight hours later I have a boyfriend with whom I enjoy good sex, giving me the keys to his apartment and we are planning a trip! Tonight I am invited to be a part his of hobby and meet some of his friends.

"You never know. We meet angels when we don't expect to. All bad things will eventually lead to something good," my grandmother often says. How often she has told me that I can't count, and her unbroken optimism often seems so ridiculous that I am always quick to dismiss it: "Oh, Tata, how can you says that? Every life is so different." And yet she remains steadfast, and her life has proved it true. The events of the past validate her philosophy even more.

I would like to tell everybody about Klaus. I am about to burst. My brain, my heart, my blood pressure, my body soars. I am not even hungry or thirsty at lunch. My surroundings fade into bliss. How can it be that things turn so quickly as if you flip a switch, and all hurt and pain is in the distant past.

Stepfather, Step-Aunt, and Westcar

No one knows how much I have longed for a shoulder and two arms to lean on since my stepfather stepped between my mother and I. This separation led me into loneliness and losing my childhood, both at the age of 13, becoming an instant adult. On the outside we were the perfect family, and I played my part because I wanted that perfection I had seen in my classmates' families so much. But reality couldn't be more different. I walked on eggshells in my parents' home because of my stepfather.

Our living room door was locked when they left for the evening so I couldn't watch television. My room was only heated on weekends. He reminded me not to use too much hot water, wash my hair only once a week, to eat my boiled eggs only in conjunction with a piece of bread, not to touch any of his stuff, never mix my bedsheets at the laundry with his and never even think about bringing friends home. My parents and brother went on vacation but I was left at home, either spending time with my grandmother or my aunt and uncle in Leipzig.

Once my stepfather's sister from West Berlin came to visit us. I had met her before and she liked me. She was an opera singer who had a car. The plan was that we all would drive into the countryside for the day. I was so excited because I would see her. But most of all we would drive in a Western car. All morning I was looking out of the window to see her to drive around the corner. When I saw her I ran down to the street. She asked me if I wanted to sit up front. Of course I wanted to. She opened the door and I got in. We were talking and waiting for my parents and brother to come out. After a while my aunt pushed the horn to get my parents to hurry up.

All of the sudden I see my stepfather open the window and yell down to us: "We are not coming. I wanted to spend a day with my family. But there is not enough room in your car for us!"

I was mortified and ashamed, because everybody could hear him yelling. It was clear that he didn't want me in the car. I was not part of his family.

"What is he talking about? We all fit into my car." I looked at her, choking up.

"He doesn't want me in the car. That's all right. I will stay here," I said, opening the door.

"What? What did you just say?" grabbing my arm and turned me towards her. She saw me crying.

"Oh my God. He is mean to you, isn't he? Why didn't you tell me before? I will talk to my brother. You are coming with us today."

"Please don't talk to him," I pleaded, "it only makes it worth."

"Does he hit you?"

"No, he never gets physical with me, he just hates me. He hated me from the first day we." My aunt hugged me.

"What about your mother?" I shrugged my shoulders.

"I don't want to talk about it." She looked at me. "My brother is not a good person. He is selfish. As kids he was always a tattletale and our mother would always take his side, but I would never cave in, telling her that he was lying. I never took shit from him. Do you smoke? Here take one." So we both sat in her car and smoked a cigarette. We didn't speak a word, just puffed and it felt good. At least I felt protected by her. "I will go up and get your parents. I promise you we will have a fun day." And we did. But this was one of the very few times my stepfather could be appeased.

My stepfather was a teacher, so we both were home every day in the early afternoon. Between that time and my mother's coming home from work, or me picking up my brother from kindergarten, he would let me have it. One day after he told me that my room smelled like a pig sty he yelled: "I wish you were never born!" That was the only time I rebelled and told my mother after she came home. She looked at my stepfather and me. "I am working so hard. I am trying to make this a family. Why does no one see that? Sometimes I want to leave just everything behind. So, here

I am. Coming home and have to listen to this. I had a stomachache all day long. I couldn't eat. Now it's getting worse. I won't have any supper tonight. I will go to bed."

I didn't know what to say. Of course I didn't want my mother to leave us or have chronic stomachaches. I learned a lesson: Keep my mouth shut. I went to my room. I didn't have supper either. For the next three years I never said a word to my mother about her husband. He had won. He continued to abuse me.

I didn't make it into college and I was devastated. No one in my family came to me to say anything encouraging. Except for my grandmother, but I wanted to hear it from my mother. My stepfather said: "You are a loser. I want you out of the house as soon as possible."

So I had failed. My stepfather had been right all along. "You are worthless." During my final high school exams I collapsed and had to be admitted to the hospital. My whole digestive system had shut down. The doctor told my mother that I almost died. She came to visit me in the hospital every day. My stepfather only visited once. When my mother left the room my stepfather being my stepfather told me that I better get better very soon, that I had become an inconvenience and a burden for his family.

"I know and you know this is a big game here. You want your mother to cater to you all the time, but let me tell you, I know you are a phony." I looked at him; my arm was attached to an IV. I was in the hospital during which time I had lost twenty pounds.

I was released from the hospital, took my final high school exam and started the following September at the librarian school. After one year in librarian school I couldn't take my stepfather's nagging anymore, I left my parents house for good, moving in with my grandmother.

Besides my clothes I wanted to take with me two old chairs I had found on the sidewalk and had painted white. I loved the chairs. But my stepfather would not give them to me. I was very sad about that, but I felt it was worth fighting for. I just wanted to get away from him and this unhappy home. My mother cried when I left.

Because of my excellent grades I was offered the

opportunity to finish library school six months earlier. I took
the chance. After graduating with library diploma I started
evening classes right away to get my college degree. I got
my own apartment and things started looking good for me.
I was determined to prove to myself I was not a loser, but
this was only one part of my life. Since my early teens I
realized that I was attracted to men rather than to women.
I had slept with two girls, but it didn't excite me, so I cruised
parks and restrooms at night. All encounters were
"quickies" or one-night stands.

At the library I fell for co-workers wishing they would be
gay, the same way I once fell for a classmate in our final
years of high school.

Michael was hot and a hunk, but I was not. I could not
stop watching him at gym class. He had strong hairy legs. I
always fantasized that his balls and cock were covered with
the same thick blond hair. I bought him cigarettes and
alcohol. I think he liked me for that, just for that. On our
last summer vacation in high school he invited me on a
camping trip with four other guys. I would ride with Michael
on his motorbike to the Baltic Sea. I was so excited, but I
ended up in the hospital and couldn't go on the camping trip.
Neither Michael nor any of my other classmates visited me
at the hospital. Months later I ran into Michael and asked
him how the camping trip was. He had a blast, but didn't
mention my absence, so I left it at that. From time to time I
still think about him; my first love.

Dance Pose, Frankfurter, and an Untouched Beer

We meet a little bit before six in the evening at the S-Bahn station Marx-Engels-Platz. Klaus kisses me then we walk to the rehearsal hall, which is tucked away in the second courtyard of this rambling building complex, so typical for Berlin. At one time it housed factories, small businesses, and way in the back, apartments—all under one roof. However, the small rectangular courtyards would only allow very little sun in. These complexes were not built in order to comfort their inhabitants and workers, and to this day nothing has changed. It is a home to the disenfranchised, the undesired fringe of the socialistic society. The rulers of the Worker's Paradise couldn't be bothered with theses hidden slums. This section remains the city's underbelly. Before the war it was known as the "Scheunen Viertel" or shed quarters. A lot of poor Jews lived here as well. They were there to produce all kinds of goods, house the producers and make sure they were sealed off and away from a brighter and flourishing outside. Nothing has been done to repair and improve these places since before the war.

Most of the factories are gone now, closed because they either didn't survive the war, or the owners had left for the West after East Germany became the afterbirth of the Soviet Union in 1949. Very few small business owners stayed, hoping stubbornly to outlive the German Democratic Republic; however the big Nationalizing Campaign in the 1960s put an end that dream. The last existing small and middle-sized businesses became the property of the proletariat. It was believed that private ownership of producing and creating goods is imperialistic and therefore inhuman, not tolerated in a world where everybody owns everything. Only some small enterprises were spared the nationalizing nightmare, among them were shop owners like bakers, cobblers or butchers. Shutting

56

down small manufacturing businesses like machine shops added to the notorious shortage of consumer products that is so common in nationalized economies. The Party explained these shortfalls as "little bumps on the road to a bright future" or the "birth pains of a new society. " Of course the spin comes from those who live behind walls of Wandlitz with their own shops fully stocked and readily available for the "avant garde of the proletariat."

Empty factories were left to rot and fall into total disrepair, but some were put to use as "ateliers" or rehearsal lofts by theater and ballet companies, including the dance troupe that Klaus belongs to. Some of them had classical training but chose not to become professionals. I had heard about the group before, because it is generously sponsored by FDGB, the government-run union and the FDJ, the state-mandated youth organization. The dance group is part of the huge cultural propaganda machine. The arts have become tools and weapons to persuade citizens to accept the Party and its teaching becomes a tool and a weapon! Theater, literature, dance, singing, painting and architecture are all used to manipulate the masses. Art is less obvious than dull manifestos and a comatose constituency is a willing constituency. I am skeptical how I will feel to be made part of the message through happy feet. I am also not in physical shape to dance. But we will see won't we?

Klaus introduces me to choreographer Kurt Klein, who looks disheveled and a little bit unkempt. His clothes don't fit. He needs a haircut. I always look at people's fingernails, if they are clean that's a sign that everything else is well taken care of too. But Klein's nails are long and dirty.

"How old are you?" Kurt asks, shaking my hand.

"Twenty-one."

"Good. We need young guys. Everything else you will be taught." Kurt checks me out, top to bottom, turns me around. I feel uneasy. I am blushing. Dancers trickle in look curious about me.

"Hey guys look at him. He is blushing. He must be a virgin. Not like you sluts." Kurt howls. I hear giggles. I want to run, but then I see a familiar face. It's Henry, the waiter from the Pizza restaurant. I must look miserable because he comes over.

"Welcome handsome. Did Klaus talk you into joining us? Well, you are not his first lover to end up with us." Henry slaps me on my ass and leaves to change into his rehearsal gear. Klaus is talking to a girl. She is blond and has a pretty face and wide hips. She is shorter than Klaus. I am not sure what do to? Everybody knows his place. The accompanist sorts through his music notes. Kurt tends to Cocco, his poodle, dirty and unkempt like his master. Cocco. What a ridiculous name. Then an older woman comes in. She is short, overweight and waddles.

"Marianne, come here," Kurt calls her not in a very nice tone. I sense a tension and an almost disdain between the two of them. "This is Thomas. Check him out. He is our new one." Marianne extends her hand. Nice and soft, very long and manicured fingers with that never worked.

"I am Kurt's assistant. Have you danced before?"

"Never. I am not sure if I can or even should try."

"Don't worry. Most of our dancers never did before they joined us. If you have natural posture and a sense for rhythm then you are in. The rest you can learn, but you won't become a professional dancer."

With that she takes me by the arm and leads me away towards a smaller training room. One wall is totally mirrored. All four walls have ballet railings. I am told to face the mirror.

"Let's try a couple of poses. Put your legs together, feed turned outwards as far as you can. Shoulders down and back. Arms in front of you, forming a slight oval, stomach in, butt tight."

I am trying to follow her instructions, but my own image in the mirror looks miserable. I stumble and fall out of the pose.

"Don't worry. You are doing fine," Marianne lies. I like her. She is very kind and gentle. She instructs me to get back in position, this time my legs a little apart.

"Go up on your toes. Don't move the rest of your body. Keep everything tight." Again, I fall out before I can keep balance.

"We have work to do, but I like your posture and slim proportions. We will take it from there. I have to go back to the group to start training."

I follow Marianne into the larger ballet hall. There are about thirty women and men, mostly women, all in place at the ballet railing.

Marianne starts the warm up. I retreat into a corner and watch. Of course I look more towards the men. They are all in tight leggings. Fitted shirts. Ballet shoes. Most of the men have great asses and big bulges in the crotch. Klaus has the nicest ass, round, well-formed legs. So has Henry. He is much taller than Klaus. I recognize another guy. He was at the bar when I met Klaus for the second time. Now I remember. Ferdinand. He does not look like a dancer. He is very stocky, no neck. His large torso looks very loose to me. If he can be part of the dance group, I can too.

After the classical training the group works on a couple of folklore dances, all in preparation for the upcoming performances. The more I watch the more excited I get. I really should try this out. I once had the wish to become a dancer. Why not do it as a hobby? I drift into a dream, seeing myself dancing, forming circles with the others, moving into straight lines, and lifting my partner onto my shoulder. My friends and family in the audience. Amazed by my talent. Hugging me after the performance. "We didn't know you can dance."

"Hey." I am back in realty. "After the training we always go out for a beer. Want to come?" It's the first time that Klaus has talked to me since we arrived here three hours ago.

"Sure." I am a little bit disappointed. I thought he and I would just go home and be alone. The pub is around the corner; dingy, smoky and noisy. The bartender greets our group. "Must be Wednesday." He throws the coasters on the table. "Beer for all. Anybody want to eat? I have potato salad and frankfurter."

"What's new?" Henry grabs this man's waist. "How about your frankfurter for me?" The guy just laughs. "I could do him anytime." Henry doesn't even lower his voice. This is not a gay bar. The other patrons look rough.

59

"Henry, stop it. You don't have any shame," says one of the guys from the dance group. Klaus drinks his beer with one big gulp.

"I'll have another one," he calls out.

"Yeah, Henry and I could do you whenever you want to. Or you can do me." Everybody laughs except for me. I am blushing with embarrassment.

"You always get red. Why do you play the innocent? I know you are not." Klaus says, finishing his second beer. I look down. Why is he humiliating me in front of the whole group?

A girl next to me introduces herself. "What's your name? My name is Sophie." She is the blonde that Klaus had talked to before the rehearsal had started. She is Klaus' dance partner.

"Thomas," I reply, holding onto my beer glass.

"Have you danced before? How did you learn about us?" Strange that Klaus hasn't mentioned me. How odd, I think. "Klaus suggested that I should come and watch you guys. I am not sure if I can join. I have never danced before."

"Oh don't worry. You will learn. None of our men had any training before they came to us. Look at Klaus and Henry; they are now soloists. Maybe someday you will be too? Give it try. It's a lot of fun." I nod my head.

"Oh I don't think he will be a soloist. He is not very flexible. I know that for a fact. He is group material at best." Klaus laughs, but no one else does. I can't believe what he just said. Why does he do that to me? I flash back to when he was embarrassing me at the pizza place. This looks like a repeat, but I won't allow it this time. I try to keep my composure.

"I think I will go home. It was nice meeting you all and watching your rehearsal." I get up from the table. I look at Klaus. He is ignoring me, emptying another glass of beer. I pay for my untouched beer at the bar.

"Don't take it to heart." I feel a hand on my shoulder. It's Ferdinand. "Klaus is a good guy and lot of fun, but he has a dark streak. He does this to me all the time." I catch a glimpse of myself in the mirror behind the bar. I try to smile but it looks like an accident. So, Ferdinand is one Klaus' ex-lovers too. It's the fourth time seeing Klaus and I have already met two of his former boyfriends.

"I know," I say. "Nice seeing you again. But I really have to go."

"O.K. You should seriously think about joining us. Looks like you could use a little fun. Hope to see you." Ferdinand gives me a hug.

The breezy air outside feels good. What is going on? I can't understand the two sides of Klaus. They seem so contrary. Maybe I am too uptight: I know I am. But he just humiliated me in front of his friends and made remarks to the bartender. I never experienced that before. Boyfriends should not do this to each other. Shouldn't we be gentle and nice with each other? Looking at the stars, walking in the park, sleeping together, holding hands when and wherever we can. That is what I want and had always wished for. I hoped Klaus and I will become something special, something that would be so different from blowjobs behind bushes and quickies in front of stinky urinals. I long so much for tenderness and kindness. When will I ever have that? It can't be that this is only dreamed up in movies and books. Aren't hands and arms there to touch and hold? Isn't happiness of the heart what life is all about?

It's a long walk home, but I need the distance to settle my anger and anguish. I will not go on a trip with him. I wipe the tears off my face. I maybe will not see him again. Why is my happiness always short lived and then caves in on me? What is the reason that I always pay so dearly for just a moment of happiness? Why can't my life be balanced like everyone else's?

"You are taking a couple of days off next week. After you come back I want you to work in the shipping department." I am sitting in the office of the Deputy Director of the library. Her decision hits me like a hammer on the head. Working in shipping is a total demotion and has nothing to do with my qualifications. Employees in the shipping department are unskilled; most of them barely finished middle school. Packing books to send off to other libraries doesn't take a whole lot of brains.

I look at the director. "It's a punishment, isn't it?" I can't believe that I am that frank and direct with her.

"I don't know what you mean. I need somebody responsible and knowledgeable there. And you will be supervising four employees."

"This is a first, I believe, that someone with a library degree is needed to watch over packers." I respond, while anger grows in me.

"Well if you see it like that then you should decide if you still want to work here. Nothing prohibits me from filling the position with someone who has a degree. I want to elevate our shipping department to a qualified place. The book exchange with other libraries in the country is growing. You let me know here and now if you want to continue your employment with one of the most prestigious scientific institutions not only in our country but in all of the socialist countries in the world."

"Bullshit," I say. "You're barking up the wrong tree. You've wanted me out for a long time, and here is an opportunity to do so. Now you are trying to manipulate me into making a decision. Your real intent is for me to quit, isn't it?"

I still don't know where I take the courage from to talk back to her. But it feels good. She is startled. I can see by the way she acts. She fumbles as she takes a cigarette out of an open package. I could give her a light because the lighter is right in front of me, but I don't. I hate that woman's guts, and feeling is mutual. "I am not willing to discuss this any further. What is your decision?" She sits erect. She is Director Kiefer again.

"I guess I have no other choice. I will take the job." I stand up and leave the room. Total silence follows me. I can feel her eyes on my back. I think she is surprised, that her coup has not worked. I close the door behind me and my knees almost buckle. Thank God it's lunchtime. I need to walk.

It is beautiful outside. The streets are filled with people strolling along Unter den Linden Boulevard toward Brandenburg Gate. Its lunchtime not only for me; but employees from the university, Deutsche Staatsbibliothek, the Ministry for Education, banks and the headquarters of the state youth organization.

I look for a bench to sit in the shade of the Linden trees. Friends had warned me. "You don't swim against the tide without repercussions." I always thought it would be different for me. I was a good employee; the first one to sign up for Subtonics, the extra and unpaid work on Saturdays.

"They value my work," I thought, "Their outrage and anger with me will soften with time." How wrong I was. It took them almost a year to prove me that I am nothing without their blessing. The haunting began, slick like snakes. It was calculated; then time passed until I became a nullified Party member. The elite of the working class acted, but not on behalf of their peers whom they didn't give a damn about either; their action is an excuse to further strengthen their own power in the name of the people and their own future.

The Party cannot kill their enemies anymore. But they can end their career, blacklist them, threaten them and make their life miserable until they cave in and denounce their stray from the socialist ideology. Others will just be reduced to nothingness. The Party's ultimate goal is to brainwash individuals, for them to swear and follow like sheep. The very few who can resist their pressure are traitors. Unable to change them, the elite sells them to the West German government for 20,000 West Marks per head. I fear that will happen to me.

Vicious Dogs, Estate Jewelry, and a Peek Over the Wall

One afternoon my friend Sonia and I are summoned to the director's office. "What a great day," she commented, "I think you are the first ones to graduate six months ahead of your class because of your persistent achievements. The working class has given you the opportunity to study for free and you in return have given your best. You have shown that you are productive members of our society. Congratulations." The director shakes our hands and presents us with our diploma. I feel very proud and happy. For the first time in my life I have proven to my family that I am not a failure. I may have disappointed them when I was not allowed to go on to University, but it appears I just have taken a detour. I am now on my way to get my extended high school diploma and with that I can apply to the University.

The director tries a little small talk. I can tell she feels very awkward. She wants this little ceremony over as quickly as possible.

"You have worked so hard these last couple of weeks to get prepared for the finals. Therefore, I give you the permission to take this afternoon and the whole day tomorrow off. Please report back in two days."

She shakes our hands again, and we are dismissed. Relieved. Grateful for the free time ahead. Ecstatic about the future. I will have lunch with my mother. Afterwards, I will sign up for the evening class to get my extended high school degree. The course starts next month, four times a week for the next two and half years. Then I can go to the University assuming that the library will sponsor me, but that's down the road. First steps first.

After the little ceromonie, I meet my mother. Our lunches become routine and it's the only time we see each other. She works as an economist for an international trading company. Her office is near the Berlin Wall, overlooking the Brandenburg Gate, the border guards and the vicious German shepherds who ensure that no one escapes. Their chains are attached to an overhead rail. These dogs are trained to run constantly back and forth. No one has to be told what would happen if you approach them. You would either die from the sharpshooters or you would be ripped to pieces by the dogs.

If someone against the odds actually made it to the fence he would either be blown up by mines, activate the self-shooting rifles aimed inwards or be electrocuted by the live high-voltage fence. At the same time, bombastic sirens would start to blast. If you had a miracle on your side and the cement wall was your last obstacle you could only pray that you will be shot at this point, because your attempt to jump on top of the wall will be certainly stopped by the rolling tubes. You would have no chance of getting a firm grip to pull yourself over the Wall and fall into the West. The minds that engineered the devilish fence considered every possibility. Some of them must have studied the walls at the Soviet gulags and the Nazi death camps. All of this is designed to protect the proletariat, their comrade leaders, the people's paradise and the future. According to the Party, communism symbolizes the end, history definition is the end of history. From here on everything else will be discharged onto the dump of human past.

Ironically the East German "anti-fascist protection wall" is primarily built to keep its constituency in. If the enemies of the working class want to visit the paradise they are allowed to come in through checkpoints after paying the compulsory 25 West Marks. The imperialistic money keeps on coming and supports the lifestyle of comrade leaders and their patrons: Volvo limousines, groceries for their stores, appliances for their *datschas* and so on. Of course they have an excuse for that: The current system is not perfect. These are but the birth pains of the Communist society. After all the *Nomenklatura* is living the future with all its amenities as a taste of what is to come for all the people at some undetermined time ahead. Soviet leader Krushev and East German leader Ulbricht had predicted the paradise meaning the Communist society would be reality by the end of the twentieth century. By then capitalism will be just crumbs on a dustbin.

But enjoying Unter den Linden boulevard on a sunny day lets one forget that Brandenburg Gate is the end of life as we know it. Meeting my mother here on the buzzing street is always a highlight. I love my mother despite her failure to stand up for her oldest son. I hate her husband, but she deserves a life as well. I am not sure how happy she is in her second marriage, as her first with my father was ill-fated. The little I know about my father makes me wonder if my mother saw in him a ticket out of the misery and hardship she had endured since fleeing with her parents from what's now Poland. Politically they were close, left on the political spectrum. The new East Germany looked more promising than West Germany.

My grandmother could not fathom the decision by her youngest daughter and her fiancé to move eastwards where her oldest daughter and her husband already lived. Grandmother didn't like Communists like my father. She kind of liked the Russians, because they had protected her against the Poles. A Russian officer had told her that it would be better if she and her family leave their home in September of 1945. But that was the end of my grandmother's sympathy for all "Made in the East."

I was born in 1955, less than a year after my parents got married. Two young and good-looking people had their firstborn, a son. They had a nice apartment and secure jobs at the Herman-Rau plant, but their perfect life was short lived as my father was a womanizer, drifting from job to job, and my mother had a miscarriage. She divorced my father in 1959. He had had enough of the East and went back to the West, never to be seen again. Here was my mother with a small child, looking for a new life. For the next ten years she was a single mother, working, going to school at night and struggling. In school I was one of three pupils without a father, in the category of "raised by a single mother." I think some parents looked down on me and the other two pupils in our category.

I had a close friendship with a guy named Michael, whose

parents ran a state-owned appliance store. His mother was once a model. Their apartment was spotless and even as a kid I could see that a lot of their stuff was not produced in East Germany. There was an uncle in West Germany. Michaels parents were the first I knew of who had a Polski Fiat car paid by that uncle through the East-West Trade company Genex. One day I was at Michael's house to do some homework and his mother made some sandwiches for us. As she was putting them in front of us she said: "Poor thing. Your mother probably has no time to make you sandwiches, doesn't she? It must be so hard not to have a father. Does your mother have a boyfriend? Does she go out dancing a lot?" I was so embarrassed. My face turned deep red. I didn't answer her. From then on I made sure I would not run into Michael's mother again.

I do have good memories of the time my mother and I lived alone, but there were boyfriends. One was serious. He was from Sweden and he worked in East Germany. Plans were made to marry, but things didn't work out. The hurdles to get permits for a life together in Sweden were too high. East Germany was part of the Eastern Bloc countries and countries behind the Iron Curtain refused to let go of their people. Freedom and human rights were not objective conditions, but defined by the authorities. I think that the rest of my family had something to do with it as well. My mother's sister and brother were teachers as well as members of the Party. That alone made them pillars of the system. My mother, willingly or not, must have stepped back into the "herd" while Jack went back to Sweden, so their life together went up the chimney of the house of socialism.

At some point my mother's friend Lilo and her husband Guenther convinced my mother to place an ad in the newspaper, which eventually produced Heinz, an army veteran who lost his left arm at the East Front during World War II. Unable to be in an active fighting unit he went to Officer School in Potsdam. After that he became the personal adjutant to General Heydrich, stationed in France. Heydrich belonged to an intimate group of officers that wanted to topple Hitler. Secret messages between the fed-up high-ranking military were sent through military postal service.

As the personal adjutant to General Heydrich, Heinz was the first to open the daily mail and learn about the conspiracy. However, neither man ever talked about the imminent assassination attempt on Hitler; the less words the better, but their silence made them co-conspirators.

The bomb went off on July 20th, 1944 at the military outpost Wolfschantze, but Hitler survived the explosion. The General and his adjutant were lucky not to be shot on the spot. But they were ordered to report to Copenhagen to face the Military Tribunal. Heinz didn't want to face a military court. He volunteered to be sent back to the Eastern Front.

At that time in the war there was a ninety percent chance of being killed in action. His assignment: Defending Pressburg, known as Bratislava today. A head shot ripped part of his skull off, but that severe injury saved his life. He stayed hospitalized until the end of the war. A short incarceration in an American prison camp followed. Due to his partial involvement in the assassination attempt of Hitler my stepfather sailed through the de-Nazification by the Allies, becoming one of the first so called New-teachers, a fast track program in East Germany designed to have as many educators in the school system as possibly, who did not have a questionable past rooted in the Third Reich. When Heinz met my mother he had three failed marriages and four children. He probably never intended to marry again.

At the time he met my mother, my future stepfather Heinz lived in a restricted area. The Berlin Wall was about fifty meters away from his apartment building. From his window he could see not only the Wall, but also watch the people on the other side of it in West Berlin, walking their dogs and enjoying the outdoors. Not only did he need a permit to live where he lived, anybody who was going to visit him needed a permit as well, which was obtained at a designated police station. This permit was good for about six months, but after that it had to be renewed. For many years only my mother could visit him. I think he tried as long as he could not to have a permit issued for me, as he was not interested in his girlfriend's son. Years into their dating I finally was added to my mother's permit. I felt so special, because I was now allowed into a restricted area. I could watch the people on the other side of the Iron Curtain and I bragged about it in school.

Their years of courtship eventually lead to a breakup. Soon after that my mother realized that she was pregnant. I remember the many family gatherings that followed. At twelve years old I knew something was up, I pieced things together. There were hushed talks about an abortion, which was illegal at that time in East Germany. The idea of a back-alley abortion was discussed, because there were apparently women in Communist East Germany who would do these procedures on their kitchen tables. Another option was going to Poland where you also could find someone, but time was running out for all these options. My mother was far too long into her pregnancy. As so many times before and after, the family made the decision for her. My mother had to marry Heinz. Both gave in under the pressure.

When my mother was seven months pregnant a small wedding ceremony was held at the town hall in Pankow. My mother cried through the whole ceremony. Afterwards we had lunch at Café Moskau, one of the top restaurants in East Berlin. The three of us were joined by my grandmother and Gretel, a friend of my mother, whom I think was in love with my mother.

After my mother got married, I felt a sense of normalcy. I had a father, a real family, even if we were still living apart. My stepfather was still in his flat in Treptow district, my mother, my baby brother and I stayed in the Pankow district. The search for an apartment where we all could live together would take a long time and ended almost a year after my brother was born. Until then my stepfather was not really part of my parenting. My mother, a full time student at the time, and I took care of the infant: Bringing him in the morning to day care, picking him up in the afternoon, changing diapers and feeding him. My brother was a very sick baby who couldn't keep food down. He always had a cold and was very thin. He would always cry.

He was stillborn and the doctor had a hard time helping him breathe. I think that was the reason for his frail condition later on.

I still remember the morning that my mother said I should call an ambulance because the contractions had started. Since we didn't have a phone I had to run to next public phone booth praying that no one was using the public phone and most of all that the phone would work. I was lucky. When I talked to hospital to order the transport I was asked if I was the father.

I chuckled. "No, I am the son."

"Where is your the father?"

"He is not living with us. He is at school."

"Oh boy, one of those mothers." I was so embarrassed. I never told my mother about the conversation. The ambulance arrived and my mother and I got in. I was so scared because I didn't know better. The hospital in Buch district was about a thirty-minute drive away.

When we arrived I grabbed the suitcase and lead my mother to the door. A nurse took the suitcase and my mother inside, shutting the door. I was not allowed further. My mother and I had it all planned out before and now I had to call my stepfather and then her friend Gretel, whom I would stay with for a day or two. After that I would take the train to my aunt and uncle in Leipzig and spend a month with them. The good kid that I was, I did everything according to our plan. Of course I was eager to see my new brother as soon as possible, but I also felt like my life had changed forever.

Quotas, Nomenklatura, and First Encounter

This paralleled the heat waves of puberty and the first signs of me being more attracted to boys than girls, as well as the pressure to get a spot in the twelve-grade school. My inner world was a total battleground with me as the only fighter. Neither victory nor defeat seemed the outcome. Just war. Personal matters were kept private, within the boundaries of my own family. Major changes came into play as well. My parents finally found an apartment. I cleared the first hurdle and was accepted after finishing the eighth grade to change over to an extended high school. The next two years would be crucial as well. At the beginning of the tenth grade students would be told who has made the final cut to continue onto the eleventh and twelve grades. Five or six of us wouldn't make it just because of a set quota.

Our new apartment was in a not-so-nice part of Mitte district in the center of Berlin. It had four rooms, with one for me. Since I wanted to stay in the school system of Pankow district my daily ride from now on took almost an hour via streetcar. My new school, the Carl-von-Ossietzky-Schule, was the same one that my uncle Paul had graduated from. I felt I had accomplished something and met the expectations of my family, but the joy was short lived. Living with my stepfather turned into a nightmare.

The East German leader Walter Ulbricht was ousted by his protégé Erich Honecker. That should have a decisive impact also on my future. Access to higher education was from now on not a right and privilege for everyone. Ulbricht's vision of an "Educated Society" was done in by his successor. From now on only a selected group would give the chance to a higher education. Ten-year school attendance was still mandatory. The wish to go university was from now on scrutinized by a new selection process. Academic achievements were not the decisive factor anymore.

A student's social background became equally important.

71

Children whose parents were either working class or farmers had priority. Of course, "working class" was defined by the authorities. The same way as Hitler once famously said "I determine who is Jewish," the GDR authorities copied that as well. Members of the working class were not only manual laborers but also members of the People's Police as well as members of the National People's Army, the State Security Service and Party bosses. The next group was the intelligentsia like teachers and faculty members at universities. Another group was the artists like actors, painters, writers. Then there was the employee group and all the rest of society. My mother is classified as an employee. My biological father was a laborer but went "MIA" in West Germany. All the rest of my family are teachers or scientists and therefore part of the intelligentsia.

My grandmother was a senior citizen. That didn't amount to anything. She had worked as a cleaning lady in a post office. That almost could have been in my favor except that the post office was in Düsseldorf, West Germany. When we had to fill out the social status form we had left out that my grandmother once owned a furniture factory in Silesia. My mother put down as Tata's profession: hatmaker. That was not a lie, but my grandmother was a hatmaker in the Twenties. To top off my weird and fucked-up social heritage is my mother's birth place. Born in Namslau. A name that does not longer exist. It's now Namyslov as part of the socialist brother country Poland. I remember my mother's outrage when she needed a new ID card and the clerk at the police station wanted to change my mother birthplace to Polish Namyslov. After much screaming and arguing a higher-up People's Police man settled the dispute and my mother was allowed to continue to call her town of birth Namslau. I on the other hand could not count on any leniency from the school authorities. My social status was like mud. My educational career was finished, at least for now.

It was my last summer before I would start library school. My parents and brother, like every year before, went on vacation without me. I was kind in a limbo what to do. I could have visited my aunt and uncle in Leipzig. I was always welcomed there, but I wanted to do something different. So, I was happy when my uncle's ex-wife Renee invited me to visit her at her parents' *datscha* in Bansin at the Baltic Sea.

I took the train to Bansin, and I was looking forward to some relaxing days at the ocean. Renee's parents' *datscha* was a very nice old style wooden structure tucked away in the woods and about 10 minutes from the beach. All of the neighbors were part of the conformed intelligentsia with perks; mostly painters and writers with obscure fame and bundles of money. Because of their names and fortunes they would always find a nice table at the very few nice restaurants in town, have access to tons of fresh lobster and take over the typical beach chairs that a normal person would have a hard time to rent. I certainly enjoyed all of these privileges and dreamed at the same time that one day I will get that as well.

The day after I arrived in Bansin Renee had to leave for Berlin because of work. Unexpectedly I had the house to myself. In a way I liked that, but on the other hand I would be alone — again. I spent my days on the beach and my evenings strolling along the promenade in hopes of finding somebody to talk to. It didn't happen. One day I decided to take the bus to Swinoujscie, a seaside resort in Poland. The visa law between the countries had just changed and as an East German you could travel to Poland without obtaining a visa, your ID card was enough.

Poland, because of the strength on the Catholic Church, had a relative freedom of small enterprise that was a kind of heaven for us East Germans. You could buy all of the knickknacks that you wouldn't find in East German shops; perhaps they were unimportant but they brightened our otherwise gray East German daily life with items such as crystal, fine glassware, costume jewelry, and interesting clothes including Levi's jeans. Outdoor Markets were everywhere and there were restaurants, ice cream shops and street cafés. From Bansin it was about a two-hour bus ride to the border, from there you just could walk into town.

As I was strolling along I noticed a man watching me. I

don't know what it was, but I felt some kind of an unexplainable sensation rushing through my body, heat waves going from my toes up to my head and back down. I met his eyes. Confused, I looked down. But I didn't move. I pretended to be interested in some antiques displayed on the sidewalk. Out of the corner of my eye I saw him approaching me. I couldn't move.

"Hi. How are you?" His German had an unmistakably Polish accent. I tilted my head. "Do you want to go for a walk?" he asked.

"Sure. Where to?" I replied.

"We could go to my hotel," he said. I can't describe what was going on inside of me. I felt very nervous. I even started to shiver a little bit, but at the same time I got a hard on. Again, I tilted my head. He walked in front of me. I followed without looking up. His hotel was only a few steps away. We took an outdoors staircase upwards. I noticed the shabbiness of the place. The paint was peeling off the siding. The glass in the door was missing and replaced with a piece of plywood. He unlocked the door. The carpet was dirty. The bed unmade. Next to a two-door-ward rope with mirrors was a sink. A pile of socks, underwear and a towel on the floor. All the sudden he pulled me inside and locked the door behind us. He started to kiss me. His hands pushed my shorts down. My dick jumped out. I looked at my reflection in the mirror. He went down on his knees and took me inside his mouth. It did hurt. I saw his shoulder and his hairy ass. His cheeks spread, his asshole visible. My dick went in and out of his mouth. One of his hands grabbed my ass; the other one stroked his dick. I felt a sensation. Soon after, I came in his mouth.

He was not ready yet. He kept me inside and at the same time he jerked his dick very fast. I watched everything in the mirror and at the same time I wanted to leave. I felt so disgusted and ashamed. I tried to get away. But his grip was strong. I went limp. He looked at me. "You little slut. You are not going anywhere before I am finished. Go down and suck me."

He pulled my head into his crotch. I smelt urine. His pubic hair was scratching my eyes. His dick smelt so unclean. He pushed himself in my mouth and guided me back and forth. I started to gag. I could taste something salty. He came. I didn't want to swallow it, but he would not let me go. I knew I wouldn't like the taste. I tried to collect my own spit as fast and as much as I could. His slimy stuff was now watered down enough that I was able to swallow. His body jerked back. He pressed his breath through his tired lips. His ass cheeks were still tense but wrinkly, kind of saggy and shapeless, nevertheless. He did let go of me. All I wanted was to clean myself. But there was only this small sink. I turned on the faucet.

The water was running over my hands. I wanted to spit, but I didn't dare doing it in front of him. "You never did this before?" he asked.

"No, you are the first." I looked in the mirror. My face was red, my neck all blotchy. *How can I get out of here?* was all I could think. The mixture of being ashamed, having this really bad taste in my mouth, being watched by this man, I don't even know his name, these cheap surroundings. I just felt awful.

"So, you never had anybody up your ass? Do you want to? I know you want it." He moved closer to me again. We both looked into the mirror. I felt his hands pulling my ass apart. I started to panic. What should I do? I don't even know what he is talking about. He can't be serious to fuck my ass? Of course I heard that some guys do that. It's seemed disgusting. I can't imagine I would do such a thing. I turned around.

"Maybe later. I would like to have something to drink". We faced each other.

"Sure. But I really would like be the real first man for you. You are so sweet and innocent." He touched my dick. Shit. I was hard again. Why? I pulled away. "Let's get something to drink." I said again.

"You are horny. I can't wait to open you slowly. First with my fingers. What do you think?" His voice became smooth and whispery. He sounded so slimy. I pulled up my underwear and shorts. I could see he was hard too. Curved upwards. How ugly. I opened the door. He was right behind me. With one hand closing his zipper, the other on my

75

shoulder. "You are not running away, aren't you? Don't be afraid. I will be careful. You are not the first virgin I've had."

I scouted out the area from the top of the stairs. Where can I run to? His hotel had a restaurant on the first floor. We sat down. He ordered coffee and lemonade. I looked around. I felt like everybody in the place was looking at us, knowing what we just did. My hands smelt like him. I had to pee. "I have to go to the bathroom." I had noticed a toilet when we came in. It was around the corner from the main dining room and on the way to the exit. I made myself go slowly, but as soon as I turned the corner I started to run. It was fifteen minutes to the border, straight down the main road. I didn't look back. I had to make it to the checkpoint before he would come after me, I thought. I was afraid. Then I could see the border police. Thank God. No waiting line. I was still running, pulling my ID card out of the pocket. I realized that I shouldn't run anymore. I didn't want to give anyone cause for suspicion. I slowed down and started walking. Breathless. One more time I turned around. He was not following me. Relieved, I handed my ID to the guard.

I am back in East Germany. I never felt so relieved. My legs start to shake. I have to sit down on the side of the road. My head sinks into my hands. I am not gay. I never will touch another man. Why did I let this happen to me? Maybe my stepfather is right? Maybe I am a loser? I still can't believe that my first sexual encounter was with a man. I willingly went to his hotel room. Excited, curious. Ashamed, disgusted, frightened afterwards.

It seems like that nothing, absolutely nothing, is normal in my life. I am probably the only sixteen-year-old kid who goes alone on vacation. In a couple of weeks I will enter a library school I don't even want to be in. I hate living with my parents. I have no friends. The guy I had a crush on and who invited me to go camping didn't even care that I spent two weeks in the hospital. What it is wrong with me? I am totally lost in my tumbling thoughts on the side of this faceless road, just yards away from a strip of no-man's land. What could be more fitting to describe my state of mind?

The rest of my vacation I spent mostly at the beach,

either sunbathing or walking for miles. The wind, the sand and the gentle pounding of the waves makes me feel better no matter what time of the day it is. Even the occasional rain does not bother me. It all helps me sort through the recent events, failures and disappointments and where I want to go from here on.

My life as a high school student is definitely over. A new phase is going to start. I am a grown up. I want to show everybody that I will make something out of my life. I will be strong enough. I feel like I weathered my first big test and survived. Lying in that hospital bed for two weeks and going through pain and agony not knowing if I can finish my graduation ever? Even the doctors said I almost wouldn't have made it. But I did. I survived and I graduated. Now on through the next door! I leave Bansin with a lot of resolutions. As the beautiful scenery passes by my window I make another promise to myself. Someday I will have also a vacation home at the sea.

My days of cataloguing and filing books are coming to an end. Starting next Monday I will have the time off that Klaus and I had planned to spend together. But it seems so distant, that Klaus had asked me to go on a trip with him. The thought pains me. It could have been so nice but regrets are just a waste of time. I make the best out of it, without Klaus. If the weather is nice I could go to the Pankow district public pool or spend a day at Lake Mueggelsee. After my mini-vacation I go back to work, demoted to the shipping department. I have no choice. But that will be short lived. After the summer is over I will move to Leipzig. My uncle Ernst is probably right in suggesting that I should get out of Berlin for while. Start a new chapter in my biography. Let the grass grow over the whole Party membership mess. In a couple of years I might be off of the blacklist. Being out of the "spotlight" could be very well in my favor. This is what my uncle Ernst thinks. I trust him. It also seems like the only option I have right now. I am done at the library. Packing books is really just one step away from a cleaning person. I am neither that nor packer material.

Uncle Ernst is my surrogate father, friend, confidant

and the "head" of our family. He is always calm in the midst of stress, excitement and the onslaught of problems. Everybody in our family turns to him to get advice. I love him. When he offered that he could find me a job at the archive of the Museum for Ethnology where he is the head of the educational outreach department, it appealed to me. There he can protect me against the odds and the fist of the Party he is a member of. He has status and is almost part of the *Nomenklatura*. Things can turn around for me. With his support I will have a career again — maybe not soon but later. I have not given notice yet at the library that I will be leaving. I will wait until the last minute. I feel so upbeat that *I* can determine when to quit my job, *not* them. I think they will be surprised. I am sure they think that they have me in the palm of their hand and can do with me whatever they want. Placing me in the shipping department is only the beginning. The next thing would probably be a job as an assistant to the library janitor.

The Party Knows Best!

Of course I feel defeated by the apparatus. I was naïve to believe honesty ultimately will convince them that I am not a bad person. Telling them that I don't want to continue on the path to a full Party membership was the truth. It did not feel right to me to be a member of the Party. The first excitement to be part of the elite wore off pretty fast. It felt like I had sold myself. The price being closely watched, controlled and guided in order to be promoted at the pleasure of the Party is too high a price to pay. Not worth it. But despite the three-month turmoil following my announcement to leave the Party, the seemingly endless meetings including the interrogation for twenty-four hours at the Stasi secret service gave me an incredible glimpse into the functioning of the East German machinery. It was totalitarianism on display. I have to give them that. In principle they always speak of the dictatorship of the proletariat as their governing structure. And a dictatorship it is. The society as a pyramid.

The use and privilege of power goes only in one direction: from top to bottom. You will be made to be less than nothing if and when you step out or question their rules. Worse even, when you call on their rules to be applied to your case. And nothing else was what I did. I just wanted to discontinue my Party affiliation as written in the statutes. There is the written word of rules, worthless the moment one holds the mirror in their faces and reads to them what they themselves put to paper. The operating reality of constitutions and laws in countries with the power structure of a dictatorship of the Proletariat is such as of any dictatorship in past, present and future: just a bunch of papers neatly made into books and folders and ignored from here on. It's the fig leaf, an alibi, a cover up, the Janus head of the perverted heirs of Marx and Engels. The book of rules is the mortar to hold the pyramid together, the stick that can be also a carrot as well. Free health care and education, subsidized apartment rents and basic food items, the promise of a bright and paradise like future should make the mass adore and follow the righteous leaders. In the end the Socialist Society is nothing more than a Fata Morgana. Distant. Blurry. An illusion masterfully cooked up in the propagandists' minds, where only one has it all. The *Nomenklatura*. The rest is held in suspense. Sometimes the gate to the herd is opened to let few sheep's cross over. After all the *Nomenklatura* needs to procreate to survive.

I have to admit I liked belonging to the few privileged ones. Of course I enjoyed being special and different from the rest of my colleagues. The Party button was the visible sign for the distance between us and them. Paraphrasing Lenin, you can't be part of a society and at the same time free of it. How true. How easy to adopt its structure. On the other hand I was taught by my family to be always critical and ask questions. But by the same token, being guarded doesn't mean necessarily to be against something. I grew up with the notion that things are not perfect but you can change things from within. You are not born with an inherited gene that makes you fight your surroundings right from the beginning. You learn by living. When I was asked to become a candidate of the Party I felt proud and honored. I envisioned myself as someone big someday, someone critical but also productive. Someone who would be a mover and a shaker. I also felt validated by being invited into the "inner circle." Validated because I could show my family, my former high school friends, my colleagues and my whole small world I am worth something. Because the Party, the elite, the advancement of the people had invited me to be part of them.

To top off my validation was the fact that my two sponsors for Party candidacy were prominent leaders within the party hierarchy of Humboldt-University: Dr. Gross, the head of the party group of the library, and Mrs. Kleinhart, the deputy director of the library. Being their protégé meant I was on my way. I was golden from here on. Life appeared good.

One Monday evening a month is Party meeting time. Not just at the library, but all over East Germany members of the Socialist Unity Party come together pledge their alliance to the Secretary General, to the Soviet Union, to the Proletariat and to the World Communism. Before adopting the newest marching orders as well as the talking points handed down from the Politburo of the Party all of the attendees have to express their utter disgust with the enemy, the capitalistic West. Attending the monthly meeting is mandatory. Nothing but your own death will be accepted as an excuse. Monday night belongs to the Party. No matter what!

It's always the same procedure. We all dutifully take our seats at the u-shaped conference table. As the forefront of the working class people, Party members might be the narrowing section of the pyramid, closer to the peak. But we are still a herd. The herd above the crowd, an elite herd so to speak. However, getting to the *Nomenklatura* level commands you to show discipline, nod your head and absorb the teachings of Marx, Engels and Lenin without any questions. The Party constitution is written in stone, not to question *ever*. Every Party member has to carry his or her Party-ID card and the red leather booklet of the Party rules at all time. The Party button with the two folding hands becomes a daily accessory. As routine as the monthly Monday meeting is the agenda. Dr. Gross will lecture about the daily struggle we face because the enemy never sleeps. Being in Berlin means also that the enemy is just on the other side of the Berlin Wall, watching and infiltrating us through airwaves, television and the daily visitors. As Party members we have to watch our fellow citizens constantly, listen into their conversations and know what channel they are watching, which radio station they are listening to? How often they have what is called "Western contact"? In other words, how often they are visited by their relatives from the behind the Wall? Because the enemy is not only dangerous but also very sneaky.

Therefore, only the steadfast and principled vanguard of the people is able to detect their underhanded methods to undermine the achievements of the working class. Only the Party is able to see clearly and explain convincingly the superficiality of the enemy. An enemy that tries constantly to bait with bananas, oranges and Levi's jeans. Not every citizen can see that and understand the intent of the West Germans whose only goal is to discredit the socialist system. Therefore, it is each Party member's role to help his fellow citizen to resist temptation and not to stray away from the march into a bright future. The enemy will never give up. He is finicky and has an arsenal of disguises. A wolf in a sheep's clothing. Aunts, uncles, cousins, grandmother's — you name it — if he or she lives in the West they are the willing tools of the revanchists. Delicious smelling soaps and perfumes, nylon stockings, smooth tasting chocolate bars or rich smelling coffee are nothing less than teasers, cheap lures to entrap the weak and the lost. But the Party is wise and all knowing. The Party knows best and is always ready to step in to pull the fallen and the doubter back onto the path to real satisfaction, life's purpose and socialist ideals.

At eighteen years old I am the youngest Party member in our organization. When they inducted me I swore with my hand on the red Party book to be a fearless fighter against the West for the common good of the proletariat. I am reminded whenever possible that the Party made an exception when they made me a "novice."

"Your biological father turned his back on the GDR when he moved back to the revanchist BRD. The Party and the proletariat are really putting a lot of trust in you. Don't become a disappointment," said Dr.Gross, "The Party hopes that you will never forget the great opportunity you are be given to be part of the forefront." Every time I am told that I feel a mixture of pressure and thankfulness. Of course, I don't want to let them down the same way I don't want to be loser in the eyes of my stepfather and the rest of the family. I even will try to be better than all my Party comrades. I really think I have it in me to step up the ladder. One day I want become a leader. I already lead the "FDJ" youth group within the library. That makes me a valuable liaison between the party group and my fellow young librarians. I am going in the right direction.

Dr. Gross made very clear during our the first Party meeting I attended that from now on he expects a report about the present state of the thinking of the young employees in the library.

"Comrade Thomas, don't get me wrong. I don't want you to spy on your young colleagues, but the Party has to know what they are thinking. How they are spending their free time? What are they complaining about? How many of them have regular contact with their relatives in the West? Comrade Thomas, you get the picture, don't you? With the answer to those questions we can prepare ourselves much better in our ideological fight. It will help us to have the right arguments and tools handy to talk to our citizens. Of course we know that they have doubts and questions about current shortcomings. Why can't we provide everybody with an apartment to their liking at this point? Why don't we have enough meat in our butcher shops sometimes? We have to explain to them over and over again that these are only temporary situations and not signs of weakness in our system. These are reflections of the birth pains of our socialistic society."

Sounds somehow reasonable and convincing to me, but what I will not do is spill the beans about who is and who is not watching Western TV or listening to radio stations such as RIAS or SFB amongst my fellow young co-workers. Turning the television or radio dial to Western programming is not allowed. If it is known that someone does it he or she will have a notation in his or her personal file. Therefore, I certainly will not be an accessory to blacklisting people. Of course, I don't tell Dr. Gross about the promise I made to myself not to rat out any of my co-workers who watch Western TV or listen to Western radio stations. It's nobody's business how one spends his free time.

In any event, I am part of Dr. Gross and his world. Now mine too. I will not disappoint him or my fellow comrades. I know that I will have to double my effort to become a reliable foot soldier for the party. I am someone they can count on. I will show them that I am valuable to them. I will erase their sentiments towards me. That my biological father lives in the West does not make me thin-skinned and open for infiltration from behind the Wall. The man who fathered me, has already caused a black mark on my biography. It's time to banish this guy, who never cared about me, from my life.

My friends and my co-workers question my motivation to become a Party apprentice. Don't I see the lies they are telling us every day? What do I make out of the fact that they restrict us to travel? Why are they so afraid that we want to read Western newspapers, listen to their news, and watch their movies? Why are they working with the secret service scouting out roofs to see which antennas are directed toward the western sky to receive TV from the other side? Of course they have a point. I try to have an intellectual conversation with them. I believe strongly one has to be at the inside to actively change things. Just complaining does not do anything. I can tell I don't convince them. But I will show them that over time I can be a positive force. I know some of my Party comrades are similarly critical in a positive sense. I will seek them out. Together we should have an impact. Dr. Gross encourages constructive criticism.

"We need people with suggestions based on conviction and Party principles. Comrade Thomas, I know you have it in you." He looks me straight in the eyes and grabs my shoulders. I feel his energy. I admire his steadfast believes. In these one-on-one moments I want to be like him. He tells things how they are. I trust him. "It's only a detour from our principles when, for instance, we get rid of criminals and offer them to the BRD, who is willing 20,000 Deutsch Marks per head. Do I like it that we have to deal with the other side in such manner? No. But look at the flip side. Let them deal with these unworthy elements. And we sure can use the money to buy fruits and vegetables on the international market." I like his frankness. The Dr.Grosses in the Party will change things. I want to be right beside them.

I also can't help but think that Dr.Gross likes me on a more personal level. He is good looking. Dressing very smart and almost looks like someone from the West. Excellent fitting suits, crisp shirts, unbuttoned at the collar. No tie. Pocket square. Maybe he is gay.

Party Apprentice, Martin Luther, and Repentance

This year's May 1st, the International Workers Day, falls on a Monday. That means we have a three-day weekend. Claudia, Sonia, Marlene and I decide to drive to Wittenberg. We have been there before and liked the town. Wittenberg's one fame to claim in the history books is that Martin Luther nailed his Ninety-Five Theses to the church door here. It was the start of the Reformation movement, and the beginning of the split from the Catholic Church. Our decision to spend our mini-vacation in city of Luther coincided also with the International Church Day, a yearly event organized by the Lutheran Church of East Germany with the support from their religious brothers and sisters from West Germany. That the event is held around May 1st is certainly no accident.

May 1st is a big show-off day for the leading Communist Parties in all of the Eastern Bloc countries. Citizens are made to march in columns to the cities' main squares to salute the Party elders waving from huge stages. Military units display heavy weaponry to intimidate the enemy of the workings class but also to convince their own fellow citizens how strong, undefeatable and superior the Socialist society is.

Taking part in these marches is mandatory. Excuses have to be given ahead of time and they have to be approved. If one does not show up for the march without prior approval he will get a notation in his personal file. That certainly will be put into account when it comes to a promotion in the workplace, applications for apartments or a vacation spot in one of the state-run hotels in desirable locations like the Baltic Sea or the mountains. Big Brother at work. How true that is, I got a firsthand taste of it. I had asked to be excused for my participation in the May Parade for personal reasons. I didn't tell my supervisor that I was going to Wittenberg. I didn't see a reason to do so. Claudia, Marlene and had Sonia also asked their department heads for time off. We all got the permission, reluctantly, but with the promise that we definitely would be part of the march next year.

"I hear you were in Wittenberg," Dr.Gross stops me in the hallway, "What was that about?"

I look at him not sure what his question means. "Yes. It was great. We had beautiful weather," I said.

"And how was the International Church Day?" His voice sounds very loud all of the sudden. "Come with me. We have to talk." His eyes turned into a frosty stare. I feel a tingling in my fingertips. I feel a little bit uneasy. Dr. Gross smashes the door into the lock. "What were thinking, Comrade Thomas? You were attending the International Church Day, a clear provocation to all honest and good citizen of our Republic. You, as a Party member, amongst our enemies disguising as Christians? I am disgusted and disappointed. Did you pose with any of those people for photos? Tell me the truth. I have to know if we can expect a picture on the front page of the *Bild-Zeitung* showing you in tête-à-tête with these religious fanatics."

I can't believe what I am hearing. I feel unjustly accused. *What is wrong with him?* I think. It's like I am seeing the other face of a Janus head I did not know was there. I address the Party secretary very formally.

"Comrade Dr. Gross, I did not attend the International Church Day. I visited Wittenberg. My being there at the time as the International Church Day was held is a total coincidence." I take a deep breath. "I did not pose for any pictures with any enemies of our German Democratic Republic. Quite frankly I don't understand your anger."

"I knew it. I should have never sponsored you for candidacy to become a full member of the Party. But what's done is done. I want a full written report about your trip to Wittenberg. I want to know with whom you were there and what you did there! Who did you talk to? I expect a minute-by-minute account from you. That's the only way the Party, who welcomed you with open arms, can forgive you. It won't happen right away. It will take time. From now on I want that you tell me about any trip you are planning outside of

Berlin." His every sentence is accompanied by his flat hand hitting the desk. "You have to contact me immediately if and when any person you don't know tries to contact you. You understand? For your own good and the safety of our country you have to work to regain our trust. You can leave now."

I am totally incensed by what Dr. Gross is trying to imply. Why in the world would I pose for pictures taken by a photographer from the West? And why would a stranger try to contact me? Why is he so suspicious about my weekend trip? Why does he assume that I would do anything that could endanger anything or anyone? What is going on here? My confusion turns into anger. Of course I will not do what he is asking me to do. I will not give over my life to Dr. Gross. I will not write that stupid report. I did nothing wrong. I look him straight in the eyes.

"I will not write a report you just asked me for. I am willing to answer any questions at the next Party meeting. Comrade Dr. Gross, you are turning my weekend trip to Wittenberg into something it was not."

"Pah, here we go. Comrade Thomas, you do not understand the severity of your actions at all. On May 1st all working men and women are proud to celebrate with marches to show support for the heavy and extraordinary obligation our First Secretary of the Party faces every day, and you opted out in order to spend time in a town with a questionable history. I am afraid you need to re-focus your time and energy onto what is really important. What you are calling a weekend trip can very easily be misinterpreted by our enemies. I can see their headline: *Young Party member in the grip of the church.*"

This is ridiculous. But I also realize I have no chance in hell to defuse this man's paranoia. "Again, I will answer any questions you may have at next Monday's meeting." I leave the room.

My face is hot. I am walking towards my office. Marlene stops me in the hallway. "So, you were questioned too? I could hear Dr. Gross screaming. My supervisor wanted to know if we met up with people from the West, and if someone paid for our trip. It is absolute crazy. I feel sorry for you, because you are in real trouble now, aren't you? Remember I told you not to get into their net."

"I know. But I am not sure if Dr. Gross really meant his accusations. Maybe he had a bad night or two? This was a short vacation for God's sake," I said.

"Well that's exactly what they are thinking," said Marlene. I smile realizing the double meaning of my last remarks. "Let's go out for drinks after work, shall we? I will call Claudia and Sonia."

"That's a good idea. We are probably now under observation. Let them second guess what we are about." Marlene really doesn't give a shit. She always has a healthy distance from politics. It just does not interest her. She does her work and enjoys her free time. Party, Socialism and all the other propaganda nonsense does not concern her at all. She knows that her family is watched. Her parents own a big parcel of land close to the airport in Schoenefeld district, plus an old farmhouse. An aunt and uncle live in the West. They have lots of money, which some of it benefits her and her family through Genex.

The Western money of her relatives makes Marlene immune to any repercussions. Because the East German authorities won't do anything to jeopardize the cash flow of Western money and goods. Every transaction her relatives make means hard currency in the pockets of the *Nomenklatura*. It is a fruitful cooperation between self-anointed victors of history and rich capitalist losers from behind the Iron Curtain. They all need each other to keep the world in balance. It's just interesting how each side rationalizes its actions. The socialistic East demonizes everything from the West but likes Western currency. The West thinks about the East as total idiots but behaves as a total opportunist. As my grandmother always says: "Money does not stink."

Of course the next Party meeting is all about me and my trip to Wittenberg over May 1. My comrades display total disbelief. They question my judgment by choosing the International Workers Day holiday to spend in the City of Martin Luther. Over and over again I tell them there was no hidden agenda or conspiracy behind my trip to

Wittenberg. Nor was I guided by revanchist-imperialistic motives.

"If that is all true what you tell us here, then we have misjudged your readiness to be a Party apprentice. But I suspect you're hiding something from us. And that something tells us, dear comrades, that the enemy of the Germany Democratic Republic never sleeps. The enemy is clever, vicious and relentless. The action of Comrade Thomas is an example that the enemies infiltration and manipulation still works." I watch Comrade Martina as she continues her tirade. "Our citizens are getting bombarded on a daily base with the filth and lies from the West. And there are some in our society that think the capitalist garbage propaganda has no impact. They believe everybody's mind is mature enough to withstand the enemy's propaganda. They think everybody in his right mind will see through the falsehood and mean spirit of our enemy. No, no, no. As they advance on our society we, as the Party, must one hundred percent conclude that our citizens are mentally ready and ripe to withstand the ideological onslaught of the capitalists, until then we are the keeper, the provider and the controller of our people for their own good. What happened with Comrade Thomas cannot happen again. If the enemy of the working class ever learns about this inexcusable behavior we are toast. I suggest that one of us should mentor our Comrade Thomas until we can trust him again. I am very disappointed in you, Comrade Thomas." The air in the room is full of tension. The silence is deafening.

"Well, that was quite a speech Comrade Martina." Comrade Dr. Krause breaks the utterly uncomfortable silence. It seems like everybody comes out of a coma. Some lean back into their chairs to a more relaxed position. I am so thankful that Dr. Krause is the one to take it from here.

"Some can argue that Comrade Thomas' weekend trip appears to be a bad decision. But to accuse him of being a willing victim of our enemy or even deliberately provoking our GDR goes a little bit too far. I believe Thomas that it was just what it was. A weekend in Wittenberg. Why don't we leave it at that? I would be more than happy to become kind of a mentor to Thomas so he has somebody to talk to if he has any kinds of questions. Of course, that is only a suggestion. Our Party group should vote on that. But I also think we have talked about this long enough. Let's go on with our agenda, shall we?" Some in the room nod their heads.

"Comrade Thomas, we as a Party group strongly criticize your action on the International Worker Day. We hope that in the future you won't be so careless with your choice of weekend destinations. It is our recommendation that you will meet with your mentor, Dr. Krause once a week to work on your ideological steadfastness. Comrade Dr. Krause will give us a weekly report on your progression. We also will inform the Central Party office of the Humboldt University about our decision. Comrades, are you in support of this?" Dr. Gross looks around the room. "I need your vote." Everybody's hand goes up including mine. "Thomas, I am glad that you voted for this resolution. This is the first step to your betterment. Thank you Comrades. The Party acknowledges your repentance."

I keep my head down. If a weekend trip can cause this kind of reaction, what are these people able to do to you if you really fall out of favors? My inner voice does not stop talking. Maybe I am not ready for this kind of discipline. I understand that in a time of systems struggle the defense of principle and ideology is asked for. The Party constantly tells us it's a fight for survival and that the Party is only as strong as its weakest member. On the other hand I don't have the stamina and the sense of collectivisms to give up my individualisms nor do I want to. Maybe they make such a big deal out of this because I am the most recent member. As the youngest maybe they feel obligated to show me the ropes? Maybe this is all in good fun? Maybe I should not have gone to Wittenberg when the church has a sizable event? My grandmother would probably say: "Nothing will be eaten as hot as it was cooked." Tomorrow is another day. Who knows what the purpose of all that nonsense will be? Wouldn't Tata also say: "All bad will lead to something good"?

After the meeting Dr. Gross catches up with me.

"Thomas, I want you to understand that the Party has only your best interests in mind. We are looking out for you. You know that, don't you?" He puts his arm around me. It feels good. It's a man's touch. I feel the squeeze of his hand. It's longer than it should be, I think. Or do I wish it to be? I look at him. At this moment I am so appreciative and thankful. He really likes me. He has forgiven me. I tear up. He notices it. "Relax. You should come out this weekend to visit me and my family at our *datscha*. What do you think?"

"I would love that. Thanks." His arm is still around me. His face is just a breath's distance from mine. I feel a light sensation in my groin. Is he playing me? Is there really some physical stuff going on? He lets go of me. "Have a good night." He puts his key in the car door. A white Wartburg deluxe with black leather seats, a symbol of privilege. For a split second I thought he would offer me a ride. He shuts the door and starts the car. I look at his red lights.

What happened at the meeting does not make sense to me, his invitation for this coming weekend either. Not one of my comrades has spoken to me after the meeting, not even a good night. I am poison right now. No one wants to risk doing the wrong thing and being seen with me. I want to know what they really think. Some are dickheads but others are not. They must agree that this is a total non-issue, don't they? It's a charade isn't it? Except it isn't. Not only have I had to sit through the Party meeting. In addition I also have to weekly meet with Dr. Krause to be mentored and guided. Oh, boy.

Orphanage, Vegetable Patch, and Suicide

I hear a knock at my apartment door. Who can that be? My grandmother has a key. She never knocks. She just comes in. I don't expect anybody. I press my ear against the door. I can't hear anything. Slowly I turn the key and open the door. Klaus! I look at his smiling face.

"How are you? I called the library and they told you were gone for the day. You told me once the street you live on. So I went from door to door to check name plates. Thank God you live at number 4." I am startled. I haven't really thought about Klaus much. He humiliates and embarrasses me almost every time we meet. I have no desire to see him. But here he is. Acting like nothing bad happened. Something is wrong with this guy. He puts his arms around me. I am motionless. "I don't get a hug?"

I move my right arm around his back. He kisses me. At the same time he walks me into my apartment, closes the door. His hand fingers my belt open. He pushes my pants down, takes me in. I let it happen. It feels good. I am growing hard. He works slowly. I want to pull him up. "No, I want you to come. I like to watch you when you come. Relax." He is on his knees. He slides his thumb around my balls. He knows my G-spot. It feels so good. My heads falls back. I let him do it. He fingers me deep. He does not let go of my dick. I grab his shoulder. I am ready to explode. Klaus tilts his head up. We are looking in each other eyes. I am all the way in when I come. He swallows every drop. I fall forward, bending over his head. We untangle our positions. Klaus comes up. Kisses me.

"I like you a lot. I missed seeing you." I smile at him. I pull my pants up. We are still in my hallway. Klaus looks around. I am not sure what's next. He on the other hand seems totally relaxed. "This is an interesting looking place. You can do a lot with it." He inspects my kitchen, walks into my living room.

92

"I guess you are right. I always liked the place. But I don't have the money to fix it up. All I did is wallpaper my living room. I am not very handy," I say.

"Oh, I will help you. We should renovate your apartment." *We*, I think. This guy has no clue what he did to me. That he put me down the first time in the restaurant and again in front of his friends from dance group. This guy must have multiple personalities.

Klaus says, "I was wondering if we are still on for our trip this week. I hope so."

"Well, I have it off, but this is all a little bit confusing. The last time I saw you, you were not really nice to me. I considered us done."

Klaus takes me in his arms. "You are too sensitive, aren't you? I joke a lot. I don't remember what I said to you that pissed you off. So let's forget it. I am here. I like you. I want to go on this mini vacation with you. What do you think?"

Maybe he is right. He is right, that I take things sometimes too serious. I really should loosen up. But he also did hurt my feelings more than once. Should I just forget all that? It would be nice to get away for a couple of days. Maybe it is time for me to try just live for the moment. That would make life much easier, wouldn't it? I should go for it. What is the worst that can happen? He will embarrass me and, my ego gets bent.

"Okay, let's do it. We will have a chance to know each other better. "

Klaus takes my hand. We sit down on the couch. "Want to still go to Poland? It's cheap." That sounds still good to me. I am getting excited. I can't wait to tell Tata about that.

I turn to Klaus and kiss him. He does not let me go. He slides on his back and pulls me on top of him. Our hands are all over the place. With our legs we push down each other's pants. I go down on him. Klaus lifts himself up. His legs are on my shoulders. His hands are going up and down on my back. His tongue goes into my ear. It feels unbelievable.

"I want you to fuck me," he whispers. "Yes, yes." I grab his legs and push him up. His cheeks are spread. I tongue him. I hear him scream. I found his G-spot. It is so exciting. My hand is stroking his dick. "Come inside of me, come.

Don't wait any longer."

Klaus grabs my dick and spits on it. He is guiding it. I feel a slight squeeze from his hole. "Push, harder. Don't be afraid. It won't hurt me." I am going inside. I feel the soft flesh around me. I stop and look at him. Our eyes lock. He lifts himself up. I put my legs under him. His legs go around my hips. He is sitting on me, my cock still inside. He does not let go of my eyes. He moves up and down. I hold his cock. He does all the motion. One hand is around my neck. The other one is on my leg. He moves faster and faster. Our breathing becomes louder and heavier. We are crying out to each other. He puts his other hand around my neck pulls me closer. "I am coming. You too?"

"Yes. I have never been with somebody I can come at the same time ever. I like you so much." I feel his cock tightening in my hands. I am ready as well. As his cum hits my chest I am coming inside of him. We both scream at the same time. I see heaven. Nothing else exists but us at this moment. "Oh, Klaus you are wonderful. That was good." I squeeze him tight.

He kisses my shoulder. "I am glad that I met you. I hope we can make it work."

"Yes, I hope so too. Thanks for coming today."

Our days together in Jelenia Góra are like a dream. I notice things and at the same time they are a blur. The train ride, our walks through town with its cobblestone streets, the window shopping. The sun shines at us. We enjoy each other. And we tell our stories to each other.

Klaus has almost no family left, just one distant cousin in Munich. There is also a great aunt, living in Czechoslovakia, the part that was once Sudeten Germany. After World War II all of the Germans had to leave because it was not longer Germany anymore. (A similar story to my mother family's, except she is from Silesia.) Anyway, his aunt Anna and her husband refused to leave. Their house was taken away. The both had to work in a glass blowing factory for almost no money. The officials tried to make them learn Czechoslovakian. Anna refused, her husband tried. In the sixties they got their house back. Her husband died shortly after that. Anna never was eligible for any state pension or social services. Klaus' Cousin in Munich wires money every month via a state agency. They keep the West Marks and Anna gets the local currency. Klaus speaks very nicely about his great aunt. "I want you to meet her some day. She is like a mother to me." I would love to. What happened to the rest of Klaus family is the micro history of the big events of the past, only that it will never be in any history books.

His mother was a war bride. She had met Klaus' future father at a dance. He already had the papers to go to the Eastern Front. After a night together they got married. A day later her husband went. She was pregnant. Klaus was born on August 10, 1943. His mother was sent to work in an ammunition factory outside of Dresden. Her parents took care of the infant. Then came the fateful night of February 13, 1945. The Allied forces had chosen the historic city of Dresden to bomb to the ground in order to demoralize the German population. Baby Klaus survived the horror. His grandparents did not. Klaus was brought to an orphanage. Months later his mother found him there but couldn't take him. She had no place to live and only enough food for herself. The war ended. There was no word from Klaus' father, and his mother was on the lookout for work and a flat. She found work and a new man who would take care of her and her son. The Red Cross had told her that her husband is missing in action in Russia. Her marriage was annulled.

She re-married. Klaus left the orphanage after six years. Normalcy eventually set in, but things were turned upside down. In the fifties the Russians agreed to let go of German prisoners of war and Klaus' father was amongst those who came home. The family he thought of during all of those years in the Soviet Union working in the gulags was no more. He was an ex-husband to an ex-wife now. The son he had never seen before was a stranger. There was no other choice for everybody involved to accept the new status quo. Life went on.

Klaus' mother and stepfather worked for the postal service. They didn't care much about politics and the new rulers of what was now the German Democratic Republic. His stepfather was an avid gardener and got lucky when the authorities assigned him a tiny piece of land at the outskirts of Dresden, were he could grow flowers and vegetable. Over the years he built a small cabin there as well. He spent every free minute at his oasis. Klaus' mother liked to stay home at the apartment. On weekends either she or Klaus would bring lunch to him. One day Klaus' mother was a little late with the lunch. She rushed to get it to her husband. Probably wondering why she was late he left his garden and walked towards their home. Halfway husband and wife saw each other, just separated by a busy street. Klaus' stepfather didn't see the car coming as he tried to cross the street to greet his wife.

It was not so much the lost love but the comforting routine and companionship his mother mourned as well as the sudden loneliness. Klaus was twenty-two at the time and attending vocational school to get his blacksmith's certificate. He knew he liked men; not openly but living it out when and wherever he could. One day his mother found a love letter. She screamed, cursed and ordered him to make a choice: be a fag and move out or become "normal." Klaus didn't want to make this choice. The next evening Klaus was stopped by a neighbor on his way home to tell him the devastating news. That morning, just as Klaus had left for school his mother committed suicide. In the kitchen, on her knees, her head stuck in the oven, breathing in gas.

I am looking at Klaus, tears running down my face. I am overwhelmed with emotions. His face is calm. I grab his hand. He squeezes it. "Let's do better than our parents. Lets hold on to what we have," is all what I can say.

Klaus hugs me. "You look like a lost soul, too. That makes two. Yes, let's try to make it together."

"I want to." I wish I could crawl under his skin to be just one. I have found my mate, I think. "If you give us a chance, I will do whatever it takes. Being alone hurts so much."

"I know," Klaus says and let go of my shoulders. For a split second I feel guilty that I have not told him yet that in two months I will start working in Leipzig. I quickly let the thought go. There will be the right time. It's the last evening of our trip, and I want to hold on to the moment. I look at Klaus. "I want to have sex with you right now."

"Me too." We run back to the hotel.

Not Mature Enough to be a Party Soldier

The harsh consequences of being part of the Party slowly sinks in. My thought to become part of the elite and the "in the know" has its price. I start to realize that being a Party member adds an additional level of being controlled and watched. For some reason I thought, it would be just all about privilege. No question that being a Party apprentice gives me access to the inner workings of the library management. But it really doesn't mean a thing except as a member we address each other informal and on the first name basis. So what? I feel uneasy and out of place. The more I think about my short time in the Party the more I begin to question if it was the right decision to join. My nights become increasingly sleepless. I can't stop reflecting over and over again why my weekend trip to Wittenberg has become such a big deal? I really feel that I don't deserve that fury and criticism of my fellow comrades. In my wee hours of tossing around I begin to think the unthinkable: What if I tell them I want to end my apprenticeship?

Why did I think this was such a good idea to become an official Communist? My life is complicated enough. I still have to figure out what I want to do with my professional life. And here I am adding the responsibility of a Party member to my life. Do I really need that at this point? Why did I forget that one step at time is a more reasonable approach to master life? Why did I think that I can handle everything at once? It is my own doing that I am in such a mess, isn't it? I have to free myself from something, shouldn't I?

The more I step back and look at what has happened to me during the past couple of weeks the clearer it becomes to me. The Party I wanted to be part of is the elephant in the room. It's that weight that puts so much pressure on me. There is no reason to show gratitude to those who are trying to control me. There is no reason to repent. If I now let them

98

to have their way with me how could I avoid any future patronizing and controlling? I can't. I am not cut out to do the goose step for the rest of my life. I don't want to be "Party-rized." Not now. Not later. I have to get out. Right away!

My appointed ideological mentor is very gentle and nice. He doesn't make me read the Party paper The New Germany to memorize the daily wisdom of the Party elite. We just talk how I am doing. Dr. Krause encourages me to come to him at any time I want to. He acts more like a friend than some Party ideologue I am thankful for that.

Most of the Party members of my group stay away from me in a very settled manner. When I pass them in the corridors of the library we greet each other and talk small talk. But the air of uneasiness surrounds us each and every time we meet. Even my other colleagues at the library feel that there is something up. No one asks. I don't tell. But the word must be out that I am on probation by the Party.

Again, I have no one to talk to about my true thoughts and feelings. The few friends I have I don't want to be involved. My family. That would be my uncle Ernst. But I know what he will tell me: "Do as they say. Time will be on your side. If all goes well this whole thing will be just an episode fading soon." He probably is right. But what about honesty and integrity? Aren't we supposedly better people with the future on our side? Disagreements and open discussions are part of the process and progression aren't they? How else can we represent tomorrow when we are not being honest and valuing opinions of others? To create a society of equal standing shouldn't mean that individualism has to be eradicated, does it? If a weekend trip can be as easily misconstrued as a threat to the Party and the country, how weak then is the scaffolding of what is considered mankind's ultimate destiny?

But wasn't at any given time any current establishment the antidote to the previous establishment? A utopia only the masses shall believe in and work for. Nothing else than a distraction for the common man, created by the powerful with the only purpose to stay in power.

Anything that would even in the minutest way endanger the status quo will be suppressed. What else would explain the fury of the Party, when I travel to Wittenberg, a town were Martin Luther openly challenged the Catholic Church? Why else is the Party so eager to know who watches Western TV and enjoys a visit from relatives from behind the Wall? I don't want to become a puppet on strings dancing to the tune of a Party that is only interested in holding on to the power to enjoy the perks that comes with it.

The Party statue says that one must start as a candidate of the Party before gaining full membership status. The apprenticeship lasts for one year. During that time the candidate will be prepared for his or her entrance into the inner sanctum of the Party. The full membership is not only an honor and privilege it's also a lifetime commitment. Only the Party can end one's membership. Depending on the severity of the offence a Party member can be expelled or just deleted. Being expelled is the worst that can happen to someone because it often goes hand-in-hand with losing a job. His or her name will be blacklisted forever. Requests of any kinds for such things as a new apartment, a visa to travel or a job application will be next to impossible to get.

In many cases also the ex-member's relatives will be subjected to a "guilty by association" verdict. Children can be denied access to higher education. Siblings will have a harder time advancing in their jobs. The list of possible repercussions by the authorities is as endless as their sick minds are as inventive. Incarceration as political prisoner can be a punishment. Often, an expelled Party member will receive what's called a Berlin-Ban, which prevents anyone from leaving or visiting the capital of the GDR. Only the Party and his underlings have the power to lift that ban, if ever. The less severe procedure with less follow-up punishments is the simple deletion of a member. A deleted Party member usually does not lose a job. He or she will be downgraded to non-essential work. As times passes the blacklisting will fade assuming that the ex-Party member behaves, repents and does not draw any negative attention.

Very recently the Party adopted a new statute. Part of

the re-write is to include a third way to end a membership. Any Party member can now leave by his own free will and at any time. Why the *Nomenklatura* added that one can only speculate. One explanation could be that the Party wants appear more democratic and worldly, less dictatorial. Whatever the leader's true intent is, it gives me a sudden and unexpected opening to end my membership. It makes my decision so much easier to revoke my Party apprenticeship. That way I don't have that "expelled party member" mark hanging over my head for the rest of my life. My professional future wouldn't look as dire anymore. Yes, I will invoke that new rule for me. I will tell my soon-to-be-former Party compatriots I am not mature and qualified enough at this point in my life to carry the enormous responsibility that comes with a full Party membership. Therefore I am ending my apprenticeship. They must understand that.

I will tell them that my trip to Wittenberg — even done without any hidden agenda — is a glaring example how distant I am from seeing the whole picture. Yes, I will throw their ridiculousness right back at them, making it work in my favor. The more I mentally script my resignation the better and confident I start to feel that all will go well. Sorting out my thoughts seems to slowly bring back my self-confidence and focus. Now that I know how I can present my case I sense the lift of a heavy burden off of my shoulders. Yes, I am ready to face the members of my Party group one more time for the last time. I have a plan. I know how to execute it.

Tomorrow I will ask for an appointment with Dr. Gross. After that I will explain my decision to my other Party sponsor. With the whole Party mess soon behind me I can solely concentrate on my career. How stupid of me to think I could handle so much pressure at the same time. I will have time to concentrate on my next step: getting a university degree. There is no reason to be a Party member to get ahead. Sure it would have made it a lot easier. But there are enough people who are not in the Party and have a professional career. I will be one of them. I will have my Monday nights back. I will boost my self-esteem by

101

continuing my education. Just having a high school diploma and a low-level library degree will soon be the past. Today is my first day of the future.

Until now I didn't realize how the Party apprenticeship has weighed me down. I wanted something I was not ready for. I wanted to expedite my career by becoming a Party member for all the wrong reasons. I am not a believer in socialism and communism, and never will be. I was going to fake it as many do. But I am not faker material. I wanted so much to validate myself for my family, my former classmates and everybody who knows me. I felt I had to show all of them that despite the fact I am gay, I am an achiever and purpose driven. On top of that I wanted to do that in a sprint. Why did I think it was a good idea to be on a fast track? Time is not of essence, isn't it? I have to learn to be true to myself, not to others. I am not a loser. I am a learner. I am obviously not one of those guys who travel in a straight-line. My life so far took unexpected turns, went up and down at times. Maybe that is how it always will be for me? After all I am not straight. This unintended comparison to my "gayness" puts a quick smile on my face.

First Rape

Klaus and I are an item. Since we took our mini vacation things seem to be going much better. He wants to see me all the time. Many nights I now stay at his place. He cooks for me. I feel like I have a real home. I enjoy that he cares about me. I think I am happy. I want to tell the whole world about us. But who would that be? My parents? No way. My aunt and uncle? Not sure. My grandmother? I don't know about that one. My co-workers? No courage. Anyway, for now it will stay a secret.

Klaus is opening a whole new world for me. Almost every weekend we are invited to a party. He knows a lot of people who work at the theater or television. It's a happy and close-knit crowd. No one really famous. Some of the dancers I recognize from seeing on stage or at TV shows. But the majority of the people at those parties are stage managers and stage hands, make-up people, camera assistants, and ushers, students from the ballet school or box office cashiers. Nevertheless, access to their world is on a know-you-basis only. I am mesmerized. Shy as I am, I mostly observe. I listen to their small talk. No one seems to mind, as matter of fact no one seems to notice me. What's new? But I am happy to be there.

Of course, Klaus is the ultimate party animal and melts right in. He laughs kisses, touches, romps, flirts. Everybody likes him. Many men can't take their eyes off of him, and their hands. He enjoys the attention. Klaus is handsome, funny, admired, wanted. It would be awesome if I could be like him. Hugged, acknowledged, desired. I have to admit I am a little jealous. But I also feel proud that Klaus is my boyfriend. Some of his persona and looks fall on me, too. Whenever we enter a crowd he draws immediate attention, and for a split moment I get the look, too. I enjoy the few seconds in the spotlight. Being by Klaus' side gives me a little jolt of confidence.

But as much I enjoy going to these parties it also has a

downside. Naturally there is plenty of alcohol. Klaus drinks a lot, like everybody else including me. However, as opposed to me he never knows when to have the last glass. Eventually he is unable to move without stumbling or falling. It's embarrassing to me. Often I have to ask for help to get him into a cab. These are the good endings. Very often he doesn't want to leave despite his total drunkenness. Pleading with him only increases his stubbornness. I have learned to wait until he is ready to go.

Because he made it very clear to me once that I should not tell him ever again what to do. That particular evening he appeared to have reached his limit many times over. Not only was he unable to walk two steps without falling flat on his face, he also started to undress himself. I pleaded with him to get a cab to take home.

"Fuck off," he hissed at me. It took him a while to walk out of the room. I was worried but I didn't follow him. I don't remember how much time was gone until he reappeared again. He looked less drunk but had a very cold expression on his face. His eyes were squeezed to two narrow slits.

"Never *ever* tell me what to do. Do you understand? Let's go home now." He grabbed me by the arm and dragged me out the door. I felt terrible. I didn't want to ruin the evening for him. I just was worried for him. We walked in silence to his apartment because he refused to hail a cab.

He went straight to bed, no words. He faced away from me. I felt so guilty. I wanted to apologize to him. Show him how much I liked him. I didn't want him to fall asleep angry at me. I pulled the comforter over my head and slid down. I started touching him. He was soft. I started to stroke him with my mouth. He got hard. Suddenly he pulled me up by my shoulders.

"You want me to fuck you, boy? I will give it you." With full force Klaus flipped me on my stomach. I heard him spitting in his hand. Without any forewarning he lifted my hip and penetrated me. He slammed in and out of me like a madman. I never felt such pain in my life before. I wanted to tell him to stop. But I didn't dare. I wanted to please him. I wanted that he was no longer angry at me. I just hoped it to would be over soon. As soon as he came he got off of me and turned on his side. The silence was deafening. My ass was burning like hell. I felt something warm running out. I knew it was blood. I looked at Klaus' face. His eyes were closed. I could see his hands slightly shaking. A sure sign he was asleep. I got up. Every move I did hurt so much. I slid into my underwear. I didn't want to stain the bed sheets.

Klaus was never that rough with me. Was it anger, or does he enjoy inflicting pain? Whatever it was I made him come. I am glad for that. It will show him once more how much he means to me. The burning pain didn't stop. I was dead tired but I couldn't sleep. I tried every position possible to release the pain. Nothing worked. I tossed and turned until the first daylight peaked through the curtains. I finally dozed off.

I woke up to the clanging noise of dishes and the distinctive smell of scrambled eggs with bacon and tomatoes. Klaus was cooking breakfast. How nice. I stretched my arms. When he saw me wake up he bent down to me. He kissed me on the forehead.

"Good morning handsome. Ready for eggs and coffee?" I wrapped my arms around his neck. He lifted me to my feet. His hands caressed my butt. Even that little touch hurt.

"I love your little ass," he whispered.

"I know."

"Somebody is getting ready." My dick stretches in my underwear. Pain and pleasure not far apart. "Let's eat. I am starving." I am glad that he didn't want sex.

That morning as we were eating breakfast I swore to myself never again I will make any comment when he is drunk. I never wanted to feel that pain again. Ever.

Stasi, Duet Cigarettes, and Wanting to be a Spy

"Comrade Kiefer I would like to talk to you."

The deputy library director looks at me, her eye glasses low on her nose. "I hope it doesn't take long. Sit down. What is it?" Her tone is very directorial. I almost lose my courage.

"This is not easy for me. I hope you won't be too angry. I am sorry to disappoint you. I know you have placed a lot of trust in me. I really appreciate that and your willingness to become my Party sponsor. Again, this is a difficult decision. But after I thought long and hard I want to end my candidacy to become a Party member." My voice is trembling.

Kiefer lifts her eyebrows. "Thomas, I don't think I understand what you are trying to tell me." She leans back in her chair, grabs a cigarette. I light a match. She takes a deep breath and pushes out the smoke. "Thanks," she says. For a second I want to light a cigarette for myself. But decide not to. It does not feel right at this moment. I throw the still-burning match in the ashtray.

My thoughts are racing. "I don't think I understood the impact of my decision to spend the weekend around May 1 in Wittenberg and not here in Berlin to attend the march. It was foolish of me. I should have shown more maturity, a maturity that makes a good Party member, or in my case a good candidate for the Party. This became very clear to me during the recent meetings. I thank all of the comrades for their productive criticism of my actions. In the weeks after the meeting and during my conversations with Comrade Dr. Krause I realized that I don't have what it takes to be a candidate for the Party. Not yet. I need more time to be more politically educated in order to fulfill the responsibility that society expects from me to be part of the advance of the proletariat."

I admit I prepared this little speech during my many sleepless nights. I am kind of proud what I just said. It

106

sounded very eloquent, at least to me.

I give in and I take a cigarette out my pack. I light a match. Through the smoke I look at Kiefer. She presses her half-smoked cigarette into the ashtray. Knowing her I can tell that she is short of exploding. "Thomas I consider this meeting as confidential and off the record. This never took place. Understood?" I feel obligated to agree. I nod my head. "All right. I am not sure what possesses you to come to this kind of crazy decision. You are disappointing me again. Why didn't you come to me when you started having thoughts about leaving the Party? Your thoughtless decision to go to Wittenberg was incomprehensible. We discussed that at length during the meeting. I and all the other comrades forgave you with the expectation that from here on you will be a responsible and a devoted apprentice of the Party." She pauses. Takes another cigarette. I grab the matches. "Don't." Kiefer uses her own cigarette lighter. She is mad at me.

"Don't you think you created enough trouble? Don't you see that the Party has more important tasks and issues to deal with than you? The number one obligation of each and every one in the Party is Party discipline. Do you think that the achievements of our socialist society despite the constant thread and infiltration of our enemy would be possible if Party members all of sudden decide to throw their membership book on the table every time they think they have a problem? In the struggle for complete victory no one's problem is relevant. We have to keep our eyes on our common goal. If each and every one does it then each and every one will see how minute he or she is in the fight for the bright future of communism. That said I hope you see how preposterous you are with your idiotic thought to leave the Party. Comrade Thomas Schardt, you are out of line. I expect repentance. You will not leave the Party. You will not disappoint the trust the proletariat has put in you. You will not create a problem for me. The proletariat has ways and means to deal with its enemy. Am I clear?"

I am stunned. Did she just threaten me? I will not let this happen to me, no matter what. I straighten up in my chair.

"Comrade Deputy Director Kiefer." I make a point to

address her in full. "I appreciate your openness. Please let me be frank as well. I won't consider this meeting as confidential. If I am asked I will say that this meeting took place. I came to you first because I felt as my sponsor you should be the first to hear about my decision to leave the Party. However I did not come to ask for advice or permission to do so. I am not an erratic person who makes decisions, any decision in the spur of the moment. I looked at all the pro and cons. Part of the process was reading the Party statues. To become a candidate of the Party first before becoming a full member means for the candidate and the Party to see if that person has the willingness and maturity to dedicate his life on behalf of the proletariat. I came to the conclusion that I don't have that maturity. That does not make me an enemy. That makes me an honest person. Also, the Party statue allows any Party member to leave the party at its free will. And I want to enact this rule for me."

"Bastard. As long as I have a role in this you will never be allowed to leave the Party on your own. If it is your decision to turn your back on the Party, society and the government of the GDR you will be expelled from the Party. And you know what that means don't you? Therefore I am asking you one last time. What is your decision?"

It dawns on me that I am at the brink of serious trouble. Again, I was naïve to think I just could go by the rules and regulation of the Party's statue which clearly states three ways to get out of the Party. But how can Kiefer threaten me with expulsion without contemplating the other two options? I did not commit an act of treason, did not embolden the enemy of our society with anti-Communist comments? I am not a criminal either. I want out because I can't be part of the stark discipline. However, I will be still a productive member of society. I don't have any intention to be a turncoat, become a dissident or such.

"Comrade Kiefer. My decision is made. I want to leave the Party on my own and free will. Tomorrow I will submit my resignation letter."

"I have warned you. The meeting is over. Please make yourself available. Don't leave the building until further

Under the Linden Trees

notice." I am at a point where I may provoke an outburst by asking her if I am detained now, but I don't want to stir the pot. I have done enough for now.

"As you wish," I say and leave the room.

Not until this moment I realize how hot I am. The insides of my hands are sweaty. I wish I could go around the block to clear my head, breathe some fresh air. But I will be a good man and wait at my desk for whatever comes next. I know I have crossed the Rubicon. What will be on the other side? I only know one thing at this point: I will follow through with my decision and I will fight any attempts to be expelled from the Party. I go back to my office. Thank God my colleagues are not there yet. It's a couple minutes to nine in the morning. They will be here soon. I light a cigarette and open the window.

My office is in a corner of the library with tall windows on both sides. To the left I look at the Library School, to the right is the corner of the main building of Humboldt University. A streetcar rumbles by on its tracks. People walking hastily and with purpose. My eyes follow the smoke coming out of my mouth. I am lost in thoughts watching the street scene. No one pays attention to me. A moment of utterly loneliness. Is everyone struggling with or against something at some point in his life? Or is it just me? Why can't I just repent? Play the game? Do what they want me to do. Why can others do as being told or as expected? Is it an act of foolishness to be truthful to myself? What about those who act under the whatever-it-takes premise? Goal minded, calculating, following. Am I really happier when I aggravate than those who don't mind to take things at face value? The answer is no. So, what do I get out of being my own person? I am not hero material. I don't want to change the world. I am probably just as selfish as most of the rest. Maybe I just long for attention, when I do the unexpected? When I lift a finger, do I want just to be seen and heard? If the answer is yes, am I honest or sick or out for punishment?

I hear the door open. It's probably Maria. I don't turn around. I throw the cigarette butt out of the window.

"Comrade Thomas Schardt, please follow me." I don't recognize the voice. I turn around and face two men, I have

109

never seen before. The third one is Dr. Gross.

"Where are we going?" I ask.

"We have a couple of questions." One of the strangers answers. I know in an instant that both of the men are from the Stasi. "How long will this take? Can I call my mother? We meet for lunch today," I lie.

"I will call your mother. Don't worry. Let's go." Dr. Gross grabs my arm. One of the Stasi man takes my other arm. I am being escorted. What is going on? Should I cry out for help? I am very frightened but keep silent. They hurry me through the corridor. Why are none of my colleagues around? I pass by closed office doors which are usually open. We reach the library's reading room. No one here either. Strange. It's just minutes before the library opens for the public. Where is the reading room attendant? Another hallway. No one at the front desk. This is no coincidence. We reach the huge entrance door. The Stasi man swings it open. The three of us step outside.

At the same Maria comes up the stairs. She looks at me. "Where are you going?" I lift my shoulders. Try to tell her with my eyes what's going on. A white Wartburg sedan is waiting for us. As I get into the backseat I see Maria standing on top of the stairs. I see fear in her eyes. I try to smile. Dr. Gross does not get into the car. One of the Stasi men slides next to me. The one is the driver.

It is dead silent inside the car. I calm myself down by looking out of the window. We turn towards Unter den Linden Boulevard. Tourists taking pictures of the two soldiers standing motionless in front of Die Neue Wache memorial for all fallen and unknown soldiers. I always wonder how one can stand total motionless for a seemingly eternity? Every so often the soldiers change their rifle from one arm into the other one. All in synchronicity and in total perfection. I have seen people making faces in front of them to get some kind, any kind, of reaction from the two guards. I never saw any of them even blink an eye. We cross over the Schloss bridge, to the right in the distance is the State Council Building, the official seat for the head of the GDR.

Only a stone's throw away are the headquarters of the Socialist Unity Party of Germany. During the Third Reich it was the home of the Central Bank. The State Council Building on the other hand is GDR made. It incorporates the old main portal of the former Berlin Castle, which was heavy damaged during World War II. Even it had still enough building substance left to be restored to its old glory, SED-Leader Walter Ulbricht ordered it to be demolished. The historic Berlin Schloss was apparently too much past to swallow for the Party elite. It's such a telling sign of an insane need to re-write the architectural biography of a country.

Only symbols of the past which can be useful propaganda tools to establish and strengthen the power base of a new current rulers are worthwhile keeping. It happens throughout history. The fear to measure up to or, even to be compared to, must be so daunting for new dictators that breaking with the past becomes such an urgent matter. But if they are so compelled to erase parts of history don't they at the same time invite critics who will question their actions? What are these totalitarians trying to hide by getting rid of history? Doesn't it show time and time again that even the most erratic behavior cannot erase the past as it really happened? Sure it can be suppressed, defaced and lied about it until the truth will break through again.

Anyway, Socialist Unity Party-leader Ulbricht made sure that the main entrance portal to the old castle was preserved. Because it was from the portal's balcony where the revolutionary Karl Liebknecht declared the end of the monarchy and the birth of the Republic in 1918. The rest of the grandiose castle and its architectural beauty as a whole had no relevance for the Party's history writers. It had to go. However, not before a piece was cut out and declared an important symbol for the "First Workers and Farmers Country on German Soil." And there we have re-defined a new past after usefulness was separated from the uselessness.

The grinding noise of the car's stick shift brings me back to my very reality. We pass the Television Tower and the department store at Alexanderplatz. I wonder if we are going directly to the Stasi headquarters in Lichtenberg. I don't dare to ask. I try to appear relaxed and continue to look out of the window. In a split second I catch the eyes of strangers. What would I do if I recognize somebody I know? Should I bang at the window to get their attention? How about when I scream? Would anybody even care? I am trapped in a white car. Absolute nothing about that Wartburg would draw any attention from pedestrians. We blend in. I have heard before that white Wartburg passenger cars are supposedly the official unofficial Stasi vehicles. The Wartburg is one of the two models produced in the GDR. A private citizen who wants a Wartburg either has to wait fifteen years to get one or has a relative in the West who can buy the car through Genex. Wartburgs are also given as token of appreciation to GDR athletes and trainers after winning international competitions. Members of the elite and the ones in the waiting line to become eventually members of the *Nomenklatura* will get the privilege of owning a Wartburg. Waiting time: none.

Equalizing everybody, breaking down class barriers and abolishing private ownership is a good read in the books of Marx, Engels and Lenin. The class system that defines the capitalist societies is abolished in the new socialist countries and replaced by a very structured group system. Depending which group one belongs to determines which perks one is entitled to if any. I wonder if I am on the verge of joining the group of Stasi interrogatives who will be asked to spy on their fellow friends, neighbors, colleagues. Why else would I get hauled off to their office? Will they try to convince me to stay in the Party? Maybe they will ask me to work for them as an informant? What better cover would I have as a shunt Ex-Party-member to become a Stasi part-time worker? In order to get me sign on with them they will promise that I don't will experience any backlash because of my former apprenticeship for the Party, won't they?

I have heard about all kinds of scenarios the Stasi have in their playbook to get ordinary citizen to spy for them. Supposedly, it's done all the time. Those "second" jobs are either compensated with money or with help for career advancements, nice apartments or summer vacations at "special" resorts. The question is, what I will do when they offer me a spy job? How can I decline that? Isn't leaving the

Party defiance enough? Would rejecting a Stasi-job on top of that also mean the end of any realistic future for me? On the other hand, becoming an unofficial Stasi employee could also be a way out of the Party mess, couldn't it? Maybe being an informant is less stifling than being a Party member? Would a sign-on with the Stasi relieve me from the pressure my Party group is putting on me? Will Kiefer, Gross and the rest of the Party bunch back off if the Stasi wants me? Is there even a real choice between the two evils, one less bad than the other? I wish someone could help me to do the right thing. Maybe there is no right thing anymore for me? What if I am already caught between the millstones with no exit except to be crushed? Whatever lies ahead in the next few hours, I have again underestimated their overestimation of my decision to leave the Party.

Our car makes a turn into the parking lot adjacent to the "House of Travel" and stops at a side entrance to the headquarters of the People's Police.

"We are getting out here," says the guy next to me. A man in police uniform approaches my door and opens it. I am a little bit confused. Am I being taken to the police? For what? I didn't do anything criminal, did I? On the other hand Stasi and police are two of the same thing. I get out. The Stasi man is right next to me. We enter the building. A long hallway with numerous closed doors left and right. It's kind of dark. I notice the shiny brown linoleum floor. The Stasi man opens one of the doors.

"Please step in. I will be back in a minute." The door closes behind me. I am in a windowless room. The ceiling light is dim. A chair is in the middle of the room. A bunk bed is in the corner. This is a prison cell, I say to myself. I am in a prison. I feel nauseous. Oh my God, this is serious. *Gulag Archipelago*: I don't know why I think of this book all the sudden. It must be the tristesse of this room that reminds me of Solzhenitsyn's roman. Is this the start of me disappearing in the bowels of the Stasi system, and no one will ever know, what happened to me?

Maria was the last person to see me getting in the car. She will add one and one. She will tell, if I am not heard of anymore. Or won't she out of fear? Maybe she will be silenced through threats. She just got her library science degree. There was talk that she could be the new deputy manager for the book-filing department. When she talks she could lose that chance. My mother will do whatever she can, to find me. I am sure of that. Depending how long it takes until she notices I have disappeared. My uncle knows people. He is a Party member himself. He probably can find out something. I am way too nervous to sit down.

I wish I could smoke, but I left my cigarettes on my desk. I listen to see if I can hear anything. No steps outside of my cell. No opening or closing of doors. Nothing. No kind of any noise. Either no one is out there or this cell is perfectly insulated.

The absolute silence makes me sleepy. I sit down, lean back and close my close my eyes. I am not sure how much time goes by. I don't carry a watch. Hate the feel around my wrist. Suddenly the door opens. One of the Stasi men who brought me here and another person come into my cell.

"Herr Schardt, please follow us," barks the second Stasi guy, I assume he is Stasi. He looks kind of attractive. Black hair nicely groomed. The gray suit looks wool to me. White shirt, dark blue tie. His jacket is open. His pants are pretty tight. I see the outline of his dick, lying to the right. He leads our little group. I look at his neck. Even hairline. He must have had a hair cut just recently. His walk is strong. His shoes make a clicking metal noise. We turn a corner into another long hallway. He opens a door.

"After you, Herr Schardt." I am impressed by his manner. In the middle of the room is a long table. One chair on each end. At the head of the table is a typewriter, a desk lamp and a stack of paper.

I don't have to be told where my place is. The good-looking Stasi guy sits down. The other one leaves the room. I still stand. I look around and notice that this room has no window either. The desk lamp seems to be the only light source. I don't see a ceiling light. *This is like in the movies,* I think, *this is an interrogation room. Plain, grayish, stark and frightening.*

"Herr Schardt, would you like a cigarette?" Oh God, the movie script continues. Doesn't it always start polite and cordial? Breaking the ice before they break you?

"Yes, I would like to have a cigarette." He slides a full pack of Duet across the table. The most expensive cigarettes you can by. Six Marks. Sometimes I buy them; even I really can't afford them. I like the 100 millimeters length and the gold-colored pack they come in. Wherever you take them out of your pocket you get the "Wow-this-guy-must-have-some-money" look.

The Stasi man opens a drawer underneath the table and takes out an ashtray and a matchbox. With the same ease he slides both items towards me. He must have done this a million times. Ashtray and matches are coming in a straight line; stop just inches before the table's edge. I light a cigarette and take a deep breath. The inhaled smoke makes me dizzy. I let the smoke out.

"So, my dear Herr Shardt, tell me a little bit about you." I look across the table. I don't see the Stasi man's eyes. The shade of the lamp covers is upper face. I see his lips and chin.

"What do you want to know about me?"

"Let's start with your birthday, profession, and your mother's and father's name. You get the idea." I detect a slightly harsher tone in his voice. The gloves are coming off. I rattle down my biography and feel foolish doing so, because he knows all that. I am certain of that.

"So, your father lives in the Federal Republic of Germany? Mmh. Any contact lately?" What kind of a question is that? Of course I have not had any contact with him lately or earlier or at any time. I am angry because of that question.

"You know very well that I don't have any contact with my father." I say.

"Don't you tell me, what I know, Herr Schardt. Answer my questions. That is the rule for now. Do you understand, Herr Schardt?" Addressing me constantly with Herr Schardt starts to irritate me.

"I certainly understand. And I am very willing to answer any questions you have. But at first I would like to know, who you are and why am I here?" The Stasi man pushes the typewriter away from him. It catches the table lamp. With

Thomas P.W. Schardt

a loud bang the lamp tips over.

"You are not in the position to ask any questions, Herr Schardt. Who I am is not important. You are in the custody of the State Security Service of the German Democratic Republic. Again, have you had any contact with your father lately or with any other citizen of the BRD?"

I am stunned and not sure where he is going with that. He knows that I have no contact with my father. I try to think if I met any West Germans lately. My mind is racing. This is a trick question, I wonder. I can't think of any Western contact. I saw my stepfather's sister briefly about two or three months ago, when she visited my parents.

"Again, I have no contact with my father. I wouldn't even recognize him if I would pass him on the street. I saw my stepfather's sister a couple of months ago."

"What's her name? Where does she live? Where did you see her? What did you talked about? I want every detail." The Stasi man pulls the typewriter back towards him. Puts the table lamp back into an upright position. I see his hands ready to type. Of course he knows the answers to all these questions as well. Every visitor from the West is documented: Time of visit. Who they visit, etc. This is a charade.

"Her name is Hildegard Schramm. She lives in West Berlin, where she is an opera singer at the Deutsche Opera. I can't remember the exact day she came to visit my parents. But it was on Saturday. We had coffee together at my parents' house. I remember that she had to leave at around five in the afternoon or so, because she had to go back for the evening performance."

"What did you talk about? Were you and she at any time alone in the room? Did she bring you any messages from your father? Did you have any message for him? I am getting a little bit impatient with you, Herr Schardt. I expect more cooperation here."

I am in total disbelief. The Stasi thinks I used Hildegard as messenger to be in contact with my father? Where is this coming from? I pull another cigarette out of the pack.

"Don't smoke. Answer my questions." The Stasi man shouts at me. I am become very calm, because what this guy

116

is trying to imply is totally false and off the rocker. I put the cigarette back into the package and sit up straight.

"Herr Officer if you want me to answer real questions regarding a real issue I have to ask you not to yell at me. Otherwise I consider this conversation finished and you can bring me back to my cell. A loud voice or screaming never, I repeat, never intimidates me. I am obviously at your mercy, but I am not afraid of you. You are wrong with your assumption that the sister of my stepfather is some kind of a secret link between me and my father. Again, you are wrong."

The Stasi man's head jerks forward. I now can see his full face framed by the lampshade and the top of the typewriter. The white light of the lamp has taken somehow his good looks away.

"Herr Schardt, you are trying to tell me there is no connection between announcing that you want to leave the party and meeting Frau Schramm from West Berlin? You are telling me it is also a coincidence that your decision to turn your back on the German Democratic Republic and meeting Frau Schramm, which happens to be at almost the same time, exactly three months ago?"

That's it. My comrade delivered me to the Stasi to help to build an anti-socialist case against me. Involving the Stasi will save them from any suspicion that they must have seen it coming but didn't act quickly enough. By calling the secret service they will rid themselves from any critics from the Party headquarters. They will earn praise for their action. Someone amongst my former library comrades must have concocted my West-contact story. How easy it is to throw someone under the bus when they can fabricate a tale of being in the net of the enemy. Accusing me of having a secret channel to my father and being influenced by revanchist elements to undermine the Party's stewardship washes them clean. Didn't Kleinert warn me that she will do everything possible, so I could not leave the Party on my free will? Now it becomes clear why I am here in front of a Stasi interrogator. By connecting dots, as preposterous as it seems, they certainly are in the driver's seat. Do I become another one of many examples that if the state wants to blackmail and silence you they can? Intimidation as tool to herd its population — what a powerful doctrine!

I honestly tried to play by the book. I wanted to invoke the written guarantee in the Party's statue that I can leave whenever I wish. I should have known. Any GDR law is not worth even the paper it is printed on. The feeling of helplessness creeps up. I have no legal right to go by. They know and I know that my step-aunt is not my or anyone's messenger. But just the fact that seeing her for coffee at my parents house and my wish to get out of the Party happened to be at about the same time puts me in their hands. I underestimated the system and its enabler. I really thought I could outsmart them, didn't I? How dumb of me! The Stasi man is silent. He knows what I am thinking. He knows I lost that round. I look him straight in the eyes. I feel defeated.

"So, why don't we get down to business and get this wrapped up as quickly as possible? You tell the truth about everything. After that you can go home. Another cigarette?" I hate the smirk on the Stasi man's face. He thinks he has me in the palm of his hand. He is right. He won the first round. But I won't give up that easily.

"I am not sure what do you mean by getting down to business? You know and I know that my step-aunt has nothing to do with my decision to end my Party candidacy. As a matter of fact, no one has anything to do with that except me. Why don't you believe me? I came to this decision on my own. I don't feel mature enough to join the SED as a full member. It's that simple."

"Enough with this going around and around." The Stasi man jumps out of his chair. With both hands on the table he is leaning forward. His face is red. He is angry. "If you not come clean I will get all your faggot friends rounded up and delivered to this building. Someone will talk. I will make them talk. That's a promise. I know how to make you pansies piss your pants."

I am glad we have that out of the way. He knows I am gay. So what. Officially, even in the Workers State of the German Republic being gay alone can't get you prosecuted anymore. A couple of years ago the paragraph 175 of the Civil Code was voided. Another fig leaf waved in front of the world to show how good and compassionate this New Germany is. A farce in the end. Making being gay not a crime in the eyes of the law does not mean that one gains any rights. It certainly doesn't change the core of the inner workings of a dictatorial system. It softens the face directed at the world. The same was attempted when abortion got legalized against a pseudo-protest from the East Germans Christian Democrats. Gays cannot be thrown into prison in East Germany anymore just because they are gay. But it still leaves them vulnerable to blackmail by the East German authority. The Stasi man just made that clear.

Anyway, calling me a faggot struck a nerve with me. I have my composure back. "It is totally out of line to call my friends faggots. I am not sure what you try to accomplish by insulting me or the few friends I have. Again, none of my friends have anything to do with any of my decisions. To tell you the truth some of my friends don't even know that I am a Party apprentice. Again you are trying to concoct something that's totally baseless. You must really believe that the citizens of this country are not able to make decisions on their own. They either follow, or if they swim against the tide then somebody bad and devilish must behind their actions. I can't and won't speak for others. But I have my own head, and I am able to see how things are."

"Okay. You asked for that. I warned you. This can go on forever. I have all the time in the world. I am surprised how selfish and self-centered you are. Don't you want your family to know where you are? Don't you have any empathy for your mother?" Here we go again. Operating by creating guilt. Making me the villain. I am getting cynical.

"Interesting that you are bringing first my friends into play, now my mother. I can't help to draw parallels with methods of another past regime. At that time it was called guilt by association. I don't know how many hours I have been in here by now? You tried to be nice first, then tough and fear mongering. If you don't want to believe what I repeatedly told you about my reasons to leave the Party that is your decision. My decision is not to buckle under blackmail and pressure. Of course I worry about my mother and my family and my friends. They have already or will

119

soon start to look for me. I am sure you won't be helpful. But even the worries of my mother, the worries of my family and the worries of my friends won't make me say things you want to hear but are not true. I have played with an open deck of cards from the very beginning. I told the members of my Party group I that can't continue to be a Party apprentice at this point. I did not hide or create something outrageous. I was aware that it would be difficult. But I had no idea that it will be turned into political tribunal against me. I am not an enemy of this country. I am still a hard-working and determined citizen with no criminal record. Believe me I am a little bit disappointed in myself as well. My Party membership would have catapulted me into a career haven. With my decision that will be stopped, but hopefully only delayed. I am not a hero. Don't forget, I am gay after all. But I am trying to be honest."

Total silence followed the last clang of the typewriter. The Stasi types every word I am saying, or so it seems. He is a fast typist. Every time I stop talking, a split second later he hits the last key.

"Who was the older man you were walking with last Thursday at around noon near the Friedrichstrasse train station? Was this someone who paid you for sex?" The Stasi man's voice is calm and all business. No emotion at all. Another twist. Now I am accused of hustling around the train station. It's bizarre. This nonsense has to stop. Last Thursday I had lunch with my uncle Ernst who was in Berlin on a business trip. He had picked me up at the library and, we were trying to find a place to eat. Dr. Gross had passed us. So he must have reported us to the Stasi. How ironic.

My uncle is a Party member, a very loyal but also critical one. Nevertheless, he believes in the cause of a brighter future under the "Hammer and Sickle" symbol. He was sixteen when Goebbels rounded the youngest citizen up to fight the total war. My uncle was severely wounded in the head and shoulder, but was lucky to survive the madness at the end. He came from a blue-collar family with strong socialist convictions. His parents were Social Democrats. My uncle was one of the first members of the new youth organization FDJ, became one of the first to joined the Socialist Unity Party and as such was sent to Humboldt University to start an "educated new generation." He was a member of the Party militia securing the border when the Ulbricht government decided to erect the Berlin Wall between West and East Germany. After the university he worked at the ministry of education and in the Sixties started to work at the Museum for Ethnology in Leipzig.

How stupid is that accusation to turn my uncle into a dirty old man seeking gay sex? *If the surveillance of the Stasi apparatus is so flawless and perfect how can that happen*, I wonder. Or is this another trick to lure me into a trap? The Stasi man's face is stoic. His fingers hit the keys. No reaction, when I tell him with whom I was this past Thursday.

He pauses. "Why don't you tell me about your recent visit to the Office of Interior Affairs at Pankow City Hall?" I can see the smirk around his mouth. He is again in the driver's seat. In my search to get out of this Party mess and be still on the winning side I came up with this brilliant idea to offer my service to Stasi. Not only was I going to sell my soul to the devil in hope of a reward and forgiveness. I wanted to go to the devil's place. Taken on the wings of my optimism born out of stupidity I went one recent afternoon to the interior affairs office.

Even the name of this department doesn't say it but everybody knows it is the local branch of the Stasi in disguise. The office is on the second floor of the town hall. A simple plaque at an unassuming and locked door tells you that you are at the right place. You slide your ID card through a small opening at the door and wait. Guessing that somebody behind the door will check your ID against your "Second File" as it is unofficially called. The first file is kept at your place of work and follows you from work place to work place, filled with evaluations and such. This file you can see after you ask in writing for to do so. It will be handed to you in the presence of the HR person. And you have to read it in her or his presence as well. You can't take anything out or make any notes. Since every piece of paper in there is numbered consecutively you will see if any files were taken out or not.

The "Second File" is a totally different story. It will record whatever the Stasi wants to record about you, fed by informants. Officially these files don't exist, but everybody knows they do. You are never allowed to see these. Rumors have it that even for some of the highest Party elite such files exist, kept in personal safe of Erich Mielke the head of the Stasi. Blackmail and scare tactics as part of the control and power goes all the way up.

Anyway, after about an hour's waiting time the simple door with the simple plaque with the small opening in it opens. A middle-aged man greets me, shows me where to sit. Two massive tables are arranged in an L-shape. He sits in the middle of the horizontal one, I on the vertical bottom. He asks me about my name, birth date, residence and work place. He is repeating everything I say. There must be a microphone someplace.

"Why are you here?" I tell him about my plan to leave the Party and that I want to still be a good and responsible citizen. As such, wouldn't it be a great opportunity for the German Democratic Republic to let me move to West Germany? In exchange for that I will become an informant for the Stasi. Since I will be let go — out of the Party and the country — no one would ever suspect that I'm leading a double life. As I make my case to the Stasi man, I really can envision living someplace in the West, spying on something and reporting it to somebody. Again: Thomas' dream to live a movie script. I feel very excited, convincing and confident. That is a spectacular plan with a spectacular future, I think. Dream and reality melting into one: My new life.

"You seem like a very nice and intelligent man with a bright future the GDR is providing you with. I suggest you talk to your Party comrades to help you to make the right decision. I consider this meeting has never happened. I expect the same from you. Here is your ID card back." The Stasi man comes around the table towards me. He shakes my hand. I am dismissed. It is a short, a very short meeting.

They don't want me, I think as I leave the building. Outside I sit down on the wide granite steps leading down from City Hall. It is now that I start to shiver. My legs shake. So do my arms, my torso. I can't even control my upper teeth from hitting my lower jaw. It's not the temperature. Something in my body gives way. What a stupid, stupid idea to come here? Why did it seem at first so possible when I dreamed up my plan to join the Stasi and now, after I really took action it seems so ludicrous? Now it becomes crystal clear that it was the wrong thing to do!

Before I came here today I was so sure that I would be the perfect candidate for a covert operative. But as soon as I told my plan to this Stasi man I knew I made a big mistake. Did I dig my hole even deeper? Where was my right mind to stop me in my tracks? Where does my desperation come from to turn my life not only upside down but also on a dangerous path? What is wrong with me?

I try to concentrate on my breathing. I count to ten. It helps to slow my panting down. My body tremors are almost gone. I am able to get up from the cold granite steps. Slowly I reach the street level and I join the pace of the pedestrians. The Stasi man said he would not tell anybody about my visit. I lift my shoulders. Maybe I dodged a bullet this time. It's a comforting thought. For a moment I toy with the idea to cross the street to sit down for a cup of coffee. I decide against it. I just want to keep walking.

"I am not sure what you are referring to." I look up, thinking I will keep my end of the bargain, that my visit to the Interior Affairs office never took place.

"You are a liar. I know and you know that you went to the Department of Inner Affairs to offer your services. Did you, or did you not?" No sense in denying it anymore. The Pankow Stasi man lied to me, broke his promise. It's all in my file. How else would this Stasi man know about it?

"I have nothing else to add," I say.

"You have nothing else to add. You can't be serious, young man. Did your father tell you to leave the Party and the GDR to live with him?" Here we go again. Why does everybody does brings my absentee father up? I never met the guy. There is vague memory going way back. I am in the bathtub, my mother soaping me and, my father is sitting on

123

the toilet watching us. I must have been one or two years old at the time. I have no other memories except for this one. My parents' divorce was very messy. My Communist father left the Worker's Paradise just before the wall went up to go back to his hometown Düsseldorf. The little I know about his life after the divorce I know through my distant Western relatives. I have no contact to my father whatsoever. So why then does the Stasi man accuse me otherwise again and again that my father has anything to do with any part of my life?

"You know and I know that I don't have any contact with my father," mocking his earlier phrase. He is typing. I feel tired. I want this to end. As if he was reading my thoughts he pulls the page out of the typewriter and adds it to the pile of the others. By now he must have filled about twenty pages.

"I want you to read your testimony and sign every page with your full name." The Stasi man comes around the table and puts the stack of papers in front of me. I don't have the concentration to read that. He knows that, too. I sign every page, mechanically.

"Who can we call to pick you up?" I am somewhat surprised that it's over.

"Just in case you don't know, there are only very few GDR citizen who have a private phone line. I am not one of them nor my family. Besides that, I don't even know what time it is." The Stasi man looks at his watch.

"Ten minutes to eleven." That means I have sat in this office and answered questions for over twelve hours. My head aches. I feel dirty. The ashtray is overflowing.

"Maybe you can drive me to the closest night bus stop. I take it from there." Then I realize I don't have any money. And my apartment keys are on my desk at the library. I have no clue how to get even into my apartment building since it will be locked. I have to spent the night on a park bench and sneak into the library very early tomorrow morning before anybody else comes to work. I am close to tearing up. I really don't have anybody to call or knock at the door at this hour. My parents. Impossible. My stepfather would have a fit. Friends. I don't have any close ones I could bother at this hour. My grandmother is out of town. My uncle Paul who lives with her is an asshole. I don't like him. And I certainly won't wake him up.

"I will drive you home," says the Stasi man. My first impulse is to reject that offer. A white Wartburg in the middle of the night stopping in front of my apartment building. Somebody would notice that and the word would spread. "The young man who left on the first was driven home in a white Wartburg last night. He must be Stasi."

"I don't think that I want to be seen in an unmarked Stasi car. Thank you." The Stasi man smiles.

"I drive a Polski Fiat. So, you don't have to worry."

"I hope it's not white," I reply. For a moment I find this Stasi man likeable again.

"My car is beige". He opens the door to the hallway. Again, no sounds, dim lights. Only the echo of our steps. How can this evil place project so much calmness? How many people are held right now in one of those cells I was locked in earlier? How many people are getting interrogated at this moment? Whose career is ending right now? Whose is beginning?

We step out of the building. The night sky is foggy, indiscriminatingly spanning over our lives. Whatever happens from here on, my life has changed forever. I have been in the inner sanctum of the East German dictatorship of the proletariat. I got a peek into the grinding and processing of its out-of-line citizens. If they have the capacity and time to turn on a small light like me what must they have in store when someone or something is really rattling their cage? Why does fear produce so much insecurity? How about joy as a common denominator, for a change? I guess happy people are hard to scare, aren't they? The Stasi man drives through the silent and almost empty streets. He must be exhausted too. I make a point of looking out of the side window. I don't want to talk to him. I don't want to like him.

125

"You Are my Angel"

Klaus and I walk along the Havel River. The path is lined by thick rows of trees and bushes. Sometimes they open a beautiful view of the river. It's very peaceful. We encounter only few people. We are holding hands. A soft breeze from the water adds to the moment of good feeling and serenity at this late afternoon. Klaus likes the outdoors as much as I do. I am happy. But I also have to find the right moment to let him know about my imminent move to Leipzig. It's hanging like a dark cloud over my head. I am afraid because I fear this will be the end of us. I don't want this. I take a deep breath and squeeze his hand.

"I have to tell you something". I stop and turn towards him.

"That sounds pretty serious. You have found somebody else, don't you?" He pulls me closer and takes my other hand. "But you know, I won't let you go." Klaus kisses my forehead.

"No, there is nobody else. However I never told you about my horrendous last year I had to live through. It was all my fault, but nevertheless it was like living a nightmare. It's kind of over now, but part of my recent past is the reason that I took a job in Leipzig at my uncle's museum."

I am glad it's out. Klaus lips are still on my forehead. I feel his warm breath. His grip gets very tight. "How long have you known about that job?"

"Since before I met you." Our surroundings disappear. It's only him and me. Right now I wish I would not have to go to Leipzig. Period. But I can't. It really seems the right thing to do. But what is the right thing to do in the face of a man I am starting to love. He is the first man who seems to care about me. Why is life never uncomplicated and a straight line from one point to the next? Klaus pushes me to the nearest bench. We sit down, close to each other, our bodies touching, and my hand still in his.

"Tell me about this last year of yours." His free hand is

on my zipper. His index finger makes circles, presses down, and finds his way between my legs. I don't want to get excited right now because I want to tell him about all this Party shit that happened to me and what followed. He doesn't appear to care to hear about it. It's certainly not the first time that he is so nonchalant about things. He can be sweet one minute and, the next moment he is very aloof. Sometime he can be mean. Whatever mood he is in he can switch from one to the next in an instant.

"Please, Klaus stop that. I am really not in the mood. We are also in public." I move a couple of inches away from him. His expression becomes stern. His eyes and nose turn into an eagle-like face. This is the same expression before he went into a tantrum in the pizza place or when he ridiculed me in front of his dance buddies. I don't want him turn on me. Not now. Why did I choose this beautiful afternoon to tell him about Leipzig? I hate myself?

"I am so sorry to have brought this up. I should have waited for a better moment. Let's forget about it. I don't want you to get angry at me." I inch towards him.

"Too late," is his cold response. "Let's go back to the train station. You probably have to start packing. I am invited to a party tonight anyway."

I try to get in his way. He lifts both arms and his flat hands hitting my chest at once. I almost fell backwards.

"Leave me alone." Klaus starts to run. My chest really hurts. Even if I wanted to, I couldn't catch up with him. I am back in my surroundings. I see people walking by. A boatful of laughing people on the river. It's Saturday. It's summer. The welcome ingredients for a carefree time. And I have just ruined mine.

"So, what makes you move to Leipzig?" I am perplexed. I did not notice Klaus come up to me. I stop and turn around. I am on my way to the department store at Alexanderplatz.

"It's been almost three weeks since I've heard from you. And here you are acting like nothing? I think that's not working. Why don't we just end it?" I really don't believe I am saying that.

"Wow, Mr. Tough Guy has spoken. Seriously, I want to

know why you are moving to Leipzig. When we are having sex again? Do you want to have it tonight?"

"Klaus, you can't just move in and out of my life pretending everything is just great as long it's played by your rules. We've known each other for three months, and you have hurt me at least that many times. That's not a good beginning." I keep on walking. "Talk about a good beginning, who is leaving whom?"

Klaus grabs my right arm and pulls me around.

"Don't do that," I tell him. I pull away from him.

"Young man, you answer my question here and now. Why are you moving to Leipzig?" Klaus is almost yelling at me. We are in the middle of Alexanderplatz, a pretty busy place. I don't want to argue with all these people around us. I don't want to argue, period. I wonder if it is a coincidence that Klaus run into me here of all places? I wanted to do some window shopping at the department store. I like to do that. Apparently that won't happen today.

"Klaus can you lower your voice? I can't believe that you are yelling at me. Let's sit down someplace and act civilized."

"Okay. You are right. Why don't we go to the Grill Restaurant here at the Hotel Berlin? I'll buy." I have a flashback at our first dinner, when Klaus had a fit and I had to ask Henry if I can pay him back the next day since I didn't had enough money on me. I think I have about ten Marks with me now. The restaurant Klaus is suggesting is very expensive. I have never been in it. But I have heard that it's a favorite hangout for Westerners and their East German girlfriends.

"Klaus I can't afford this place. Let's have a coffee someplace else. I don't want you to pay for me."

"For God Sake, what is wrong with you? You don't get it, do you? I love you. I have never felt anything like that before. I want to be with you. I want to take care of you, and you are playing little poor baby."

Did he just tell me that he loves me? I look at him. His eyes are sad. His face is that of a boy who just was told he is grounded. What is it between us? I feel a wave of emotions going back and forth. He is the first man who was nice the first time we were together. He is the first man telling me he loves me not in the heat of passion. But in the most unromantic setting. It's rush hour. People walk fast. Others, some of them not very trustworthy looking, are just hanging out. I noticed some drunks. So Klaus must mean it when he tells me how he feels. Maybe I am reading him wrong when he is abrupt and rejecting? Maybe I am the one who should control emotions and reactions? I am certainly the less experienced when it comes to relationships. But where in the world do you learn to do the right thing with another person? Who can tell you to do this at any given moment and do that at another? The relationships I have witnessed so far are those of my mother's, my aunts' and my uncles'. All of which I think are totally fucked up. Nothing like what I want for me. My Uncle Paul's marriage ended in divorce a couple of years ago. Aunt Thesi and Uncle Ernst's is as horrid as it comes. My mother should have never married my stepfather.

The joy and warm feelings right now are not erasing the pain of looking back at the last three months with Klaus. There is a side, or even sides, of him which frighten me. Maybe the human interaction is structured by roles we each are born into. Is my role the role of my mother or my uncle Ernst, which seem to take it, to smooth the waves, to harmonize and to forgive? How far can one be pushed? I don't want that role, but do I have a choice? I also have learned nothing will be perfect in life. I know my heart wants another heart. Here is his. Why not follow my impulse and try to make it work? It must be only in the books and in dreams that the beginning of togetherness is a ride on happy clouds.

I don't know how long we have looked at each other. Again the magic of shutting out our surroundings works. We are each other's center right now. "In so many ways you are the first man for me. Saying that you love me adds to that. I can't express how good that feels to me. I want to try. I want to be with you. But let's be caring and careful with each other. My heart has so many scratches already." I put my arms around Klaus.

"You are my angel," he whispers, "Thank you." I feel his

tears on my cheeks. "Let's walk home. It will give us enough time to talk." We cross over to the Prenzlauer Allee. I begin to tell him about my past year.

Mail Room Assignment

My employer is relieved that I am leaving. The time in the mailroom the last couple of weeks went better than I thought. None of my co-workers there are really interested in my story. They are not interested in anything period except to let everything go as soon the clock hits five p.m. Wrapping big bundles of books to send out to other libraries is kind of an art I mastered after a couple of mishaps. But the mailroom supervisor is patient and passionate about knotting the strings around the packages. She's been doing it since the late forties. Day in and day out. And she is still passionate about it. Renate is very bony and probably in her early seventies. She is a lesbian and tells everybody that she is one. She doesn't live with a woman but she has her share of fun, so she always tells me with a little twinkle in her eyes. I will miss her optimism. My four years at the library come to a silent end. No goodbye party. I leave my locker key at the front desk and leave through the big iron front gate for the last time. It's Friday early evening. Tomorrow I will take the train to Leipzig to start over again. I have very mixed feelings about it. I am looking forward to the new but I also will miss Berlin. Against the wishes of my aunt and uncle I will not give up my apartment. No matter what the future brings I want to have a place to come back to.

* * *

Klaus went away on vacation with three of his friends to the Baltic Sea. Our goodbye last week was romantic, teary and full of promises. I write him a postcard every day. I miss him. I have not gotten any mail from him as of yet. Lost in thought and ambivalent to the warm summer air I decide to walk home. It will take about two hours. I like the exercise. I also like the fact that it will shorten my long evening by two hours. I may stop at Burgfrieden pub for a beer and some memories. I wish I wouldn't be alone tonight. Friday evenings feel always different from the rest of the weeks. Everybody seems to have plans. Couples promenade. The

131

terrace of Opern Café is filled with laughing patrons. I walk fast. I am sad. I don't want to see happiness.

The fountain park at the basin of the TV Tower is filled with people. Kids trying to run to the top of the slanted cement wings attached to the bottom of the tower. They never were intended as some sort of a playground. Regardless, they ask to be climbed. As soon as I cross Alexanderplatz the sidewalks are empty. I encounter only a few pedestrians passing the House of the Press. From here on until the bustling Schöenhauser Allee there is really no reason for promenading. Some of the dingiest pubs and neglected apartment buildings line the way. The Senefelder Café, part of the trist line up, is a rumored hangout for gays. I have never been there, and have no intention to change that. Where the subway comes out from below street level to continue as an overpass train is a well-known gay cruising area. Anonymous sex happens either in the pitch-dark *pissoir* or across the street in the unlit parking lot. Thick shrubs and cars create a shield which makes the quick encounters invisible to others. Only the knowing eye will notice the commute between the public bathroom in the middle section of Schöenhauser Allee and the parking lot across the street. I am certainly not proud of the fact that I have cruised here, too.

At that parking lot I met Bernd, a dentist and much older than me. He had watched me pull my pants down. He came over, checked out my ass and dick. "Get dressed and come with me if you want." I did. Our affair lasted on and off for about two months. He was nice to me. But it was clearly it was only sex he was interested in. When it was over I didn't miss it. I also visited the public bathroom. It is a revolting place. It stinks in there and you can't see a thing. You only realize that you are not alone in there because of the many hands that came out of nowhere. Afterwards I always hated myself for going there. Anyway, on the other side of Schöenhauser Allee is Schoppen Stube bar, a more sophisticated place for men with a bouncer and control. Mostly wine, champagne and mixed drinks are served here. I like to go there to have a glass of champagne. Six Marks for a glass is hefty. I never can afford more than one glass.

132

But I enjoy every sip of it.

All in all Schöenhauser Allee is one of the busiest streets in Berlin, a mix of shops, restaurants, movie theaters, hairdressers — you name it. Nothing here seems to be staged and artificially grown like so many other places. You walk Karl-Marx Allee and it feels cold, stark and uninviting, designed by men who are first ideologists and second architects. The same heartlessness can be found in the Pragerstrasse in Dresden. The Schöenhauser Allee is one of the very few urban settings that grew into its own starting at the turn of the twentieth century, survived the turbulence of the Weimar Republic, escaped the Nazi re-city-planning gigantism and made it through the bombing raids by the allies during the Second World War. The new rulers so far have not "Communistized" the street. Many shops are still in private ownership.

It's a buzzing place. Subway and S-Bahn stations, streetcars, pedestrian and cars seem to be at the same place at the same time. My aunt Hildegard from West Berlin once told me that when she was on tour in Tokyo one morning she was in total panic. She had stepped out of her hotel and wanted to turn to the left. But all of the pedestrians came from the left going in the right direction. She was not able to go against the flow. She had to become part of the people stream until she reached a corner. I always remember her story when I walk the Schöenhauser Allee. I just imagine it to be Tokyo.

Before the Schöenhauser Allee turns into the Berliner Strasse you pass through another dead spot. The subway goes underground again. Shops become fewer. A set of apartment buildings from the sixties change the landscape. I am almost home. I am hungry; my feet start to hurt from the long walk. I will visit Tata. She is worried about me, I know. I will miss seeing her. I offered her my apartment when I am Leipzig. My Uncle Paul, her son, is just a pain to live with. Mother and son are constantly bickering. He is very selfish and spoiled. I think, Tata feels somehow guilty that she couldn't provide better for him when he was a child. He was supposed to be the heir apparent of my grandfathers' carpentry business back in Silesia. But the

Yalta agreement amongst the war allies voided that plan. Instead of prosperity and a settled future for my grandparents and her three children the loss of everything and the long track into a much smaller Germany after the war defined their new life.

Move to Leipzig

My heavy and huge suitcases slow me down. Climbing up the stairs to the platform of the train station is a struggle. I am here to catch the train to Leipzig and to a new beginning. I wish somebody would be with me to send me off. I kind of had hoped my mother would come, but she is busy with her family. I am not in a good mood. And that Schöneweide train station is as inviting as a state-run HO-Restaurant does not help to lift my spirits, nor does the cold wind blowing in my face. The cloudy sky looks like it's ready to break open in a downpour. Of course the waiting room is locked. This is a sad afternoon. The train is two hours behind schedule when it finally pulls in. Without any order, people pushing each other out of the way. No one seems to be happy to arrive or to leave. I manage to get a seat at the window and an overhead space for both of my luggage pieces.

I get lost by looking out of the window as Berlin's backside passes by. I can't count how often I have taken the train to Leipzig. Only a couple years ago, it would take close to five hours to get to Leipzig. It was still the time of monstrous steam locomotives. Half way through the journey the wagons that would hold the coal had to be refilled. In the winter the passenger cars were rarely heated, the bathrooms were unplumbed and the waste would go straight onto the tracks. Signs warned not to use the latrines during stops. The trains are now a little bit more updated and pulled by diesel-run engines. But it doesn't mean that train rides are more comfortable or offer any convenience. One has to bring sandwiches and drinks because food cars are not the norm. Toilets are more out of service then not. However, the state of the workers and farmers subsidizes the train tickets. I personally don't like trains or buses. But what is the alternative if you want to get from point A to point B?

I have a very ambivalent attraction to Leipzig. I always like to visit my aunt and uncle. Their apartment is across from a large and well-maintained park. Since Leipzig has been an international trading place for ages the city has the feel of worldliness. The train station is the largest in Europe, Bach was Cantor here, and the University is one of the oldest in the world. Auerbachs Keller restaurant plays a role in Goethe's Faust. Herder Institute has students from all over the place. They learn German there before they go to other East German universities. My aunt teaches at the Herder Institute. Many of her students — from Indonesia, Vietnam, Cuba, Nicaragua and Angola — are often guests at my uncle and aunt's dinner table. The first Party boss Ulbricht was born in Leipzig. He liked opera therefore Leipzig got a brand new opera house, including a private elevator to Ulbricht's private box. I have never seen him and his wife Lotte at the Leipzig Opera House but numerous times at Staatsoper in Berlin. The Leipzig Trade Fair is held twice a year. Until now, I considered this city as a place to visit not to live. Well this is about to change.

I hope I like my new colleagues at the museum. Some I know from my earlier visits, even my future supervisor, and the manager of the museum's archive. He is kind of a dorky guy with a total fascination for Native American Indians. He is even part of a reenactment group. On weekends he lives in wigwams and dressed in Native American regalia. Kind of funny. I have seen picture of him. This overweight, pasty-skinned guy in featherhead gear. Anyway, I hope it will work out between him and me. He dislikes my uncle as well as all people who have a higher education. He is self taught. The high school diploma was all what he was allowed to achieve, educational advancement cut short because of his social background. Born out of wedlock, a grandmother in West Germany and his refusal to join the DDR-youth organization disqualified him for a spot at a university. Playing Indian is his escape from the proletarian reality. As a kid when I visited my uncle at the museum I could feel his resentment towards me. I knew for instance from early on about his hobby. Once I asked him if I could visit him in his Indian village. Without a blink he said "No." In his view, a nephew of a Party member is pretty much a Party member himself.

If everything goes according to plan, I will do my time at the museum in order to earn a sponsorship to go on to the university. My uncle has already secured the museum director's promise to support my application process which I can start in three months. My uncle convinced me to get a degree in Ethnography, specializing in early European tribal history. His specialty is the native history of Borneo. The tragedy is that he is researching everything from his desk. So far he never had the chance to go there to see it with his own eyes. He almost did once. He and my aunt were all set to go to Indonesia for three years. They literally had their suitcases packed. But the pro-Soviet President Suharto was ousted, my uncle's dream with him.

I kind of like the idea of going into Ethnography. I do not know much about pre-historic tribal life. My work at the museum will help me broaden my knowledge about that. Maybe I will stand a better chance than my uncle and I will be allowed someday to travel to the places I have studied about. Europe seems more likely than some other distant and hard-to-reach continent. The territory of the Soviet Union is rich and diverse in tribal past. I shouldn't have a problem being allowed to go there for some field research. The only down side is if and when I get accepted for a study program I have to continue to stay in Leipzig, because the Karl-Marx University there is the only one that offers the course. But, maybe by then I will like the city and won't mind staying here for another four years. It's only a three-hour train ride to Berlin, easy to manage for weekend visits. If everything works out Klaus could even try to get a job at the Leipzig Opera.

I'm getting ahead of myself. Nothing new. But making plans and mapping out solutions to get where you want to be seems always an easy process. As soon as realty sets in things lose the lightness to reach an anticipated goal. My life so far is a shining example of that. I am the unrivaled planner of my future. I only forget the real world I am live in. But I know I have to continue to make plans. I need the structure of hope. Even when and if I fail soon after I will start to plan again. Or should I say, dream again. Yes, that keeps me going. I hope I will never lose the ability to look

137

ahead. Thank God, hope is the last thing that will die. Leipzig is my new hope, dream, plan. Maybe now it will all come to together for me?

"Today is a Sad Day"

"Comrades, today is a very sad day. The Central Party office of the University has decided to expel Thomas Schardt from the Socialist Unity Party of Germany." I am stunned at the words of Dr. Gross. Not only does the announcement come as a total surprise for me. He already has stopped addressing me as comrade. I couldn't care less about it. But to extradite me without any prior notification makes me dumbfounded. No one says a word. I try to catch someone's eye as I look around.

"Herr Schardt, please hand over your Party membership book and leave the room." Dr. Gross not only has dropped the comrade in talking to me. He makes clear that the time of the first name basis is over as well. I take out my Party ID and put on the table.

"I am probably the only one in this room who didn't know what was coming at today's Party meeting. I guess that shows the very human, or should I say the very inhuman side of you all. My conscience is clear of any wrongdoing. I played with open cards right from the beginning. I let you all know the moment I decided I can't continue to be a pre-member of the Party. I was threatened. I had to defend myself during countless meetings. I was dragged to a twelve-hour interrogation by the Stasi."

"Herr Schardt, that's enough. Please leave the room immediately." Dr. Gross gets up from his chair and comes towards me.

"Or," I ask, "I hope that you don't lay a hand on me, Herr Dr. Gross." My voice gets louder. "This is not ending here and today. I will demand an explanation for the extradition. Nothing, absolutely nothing, warrants this decision to invoke the extradition clause. I have done nothing wrong. I have not harmed the reputation of the Party, the society or the government of the German Democratic Republic. Your inability to take my word and decision at face value is an outrage."

Everybody is looking at me. Dr. Gross did not move another inch towards me. I push my chair away from me. I have to get the tremor in my voice under control. I am so mad.

"Dear ladies and gentlemen," I am being deliberately cynical by addressing the group in front of me that way, "you thought you have cleansed yourself of me. But I still consider myself a Party apprentice until my resignation; I repeat my voluntary resignation based on the Party's rule until it will be accepted in writing. You will not make me an outcast and ruin my future by expelling me. Herr Dr. Gross, will I be excused from the remainder of the meeting?" I look him straight in the eye. He looks back. He nods his head. I leave the room.

I feel so wrongly treated. I have to fight their decision. I will petition it at the Party headquarters for Berlin. And I will bring my case directly to the office of the Secretary General of the Party, Honecker. If the extradition verdict stays my professional life is over. The next thing that could follow is a ban to continue living in Berlin. The only job I would ever get is in some nasty factory in some godforsaken place outside of the capital. I am just a nineteen- year-old gay man; almost no one would give a dime if I was made into a fringe. Nevertheless, I will fight tooth and nail not to be extradited from the party.

Out of the Closet

I slowly fall into a new routine. My day starts at seven each morning at the museum. I work closely with three other guys who began the same day as I did. Right now we are checking catalogs against the actual objects in the large glass-walled storage bins. It's kind of a tedious job but not too bad. I am glad that no one knows about my past. And I miss Klaus who is still on vacation, I write him a postcard every day. So far I have not heard from him. But he should be back in Berlin from his vacation in a couple of days from now. Hopefully he will call. He has my aunt and uncle's phone number.

It's Friday early evening. I am at my aunt and uncle's apartment. We are all settled in comfortably to enjoy the upcoming weekend. My third week at the new job ended like the previous ones: good. All of us are in a very relaxed mood. The phone rings. My uncle hands me the receiver. "It's for you."

"Hi, this is Klaus. Just wondering which train you are taking tonight to come to Berlin?" My heart takes a happy leap, hearing his voice after four weeks for the first time again.

"I didn't know that you are back from your vacation. How was it?"

"I will tell you when you are here. Are you coming tonight?"

"I didn't plan on it. I have to check the schedule to see when the next train leaves," I say.

"I miss you. I want you here as soon as possible. I checked the schedule. It is still time to get the train at nine tonight. You can get off in Schöeneweide. I will pick you up," Klaus says.

"That's in an hour. I have nothing packed. I don't even know if I have enough money for the ticket."

"You don't need anything to visit me. Ask your relatives to give you the money for the ride. See you at midnight."

141

Before I can say anything the line goes dead.

I am not sure how much my aunt and uncle have heard. I must have had a perplexed expression. "What happened?" my aunt asks.

"I think I should take the next train to Berlin."

"Oh, do you really have to go? We were looking forward to spending time together this weekend. Can't you go next weekend?"

I say "I am sorry. But I have to go. Can you give me 20 Marks for the ticket?" I feel a bit embarrassed to ask my aunt for money. I can see at her and my uncle's expression that they don't know what to make out of this sudden change of situation. I wish I could tell them that I have a lover in Berlin. That I am gay. A couple of weeks ago I was very close to coming out to my uncle, but I lost the courage. Now it's not the right moment either.

"Who was it on the phone?" My uncle asks.

"A friend."

"What kind of a friend calls out of the blue, and the next thing you have to catch a train to Berlin? Did something happen? Can we help? Are you in trouble?"

"No, I am not in trouble. Maybe we can talk about it after the weekend? But I really should get to the train station now." My uncle hands me the money. I grab my duffel bag and throw some clothes in. "Thank you. You are the best. See you Sunday night."

"Is there a phone number we can call you in Berlin?"

"No, not really. I will try to call you." I hug them both and run out the door. I have about forty minutes to get to the train station. It will be close. But for some reason I can't stop wondering how I will explain my rushed trip to Berlin when I return on Sunday. I am certain my aunt wants to know. I guess I have to come clean. I want to come clean. I think it's time to let them know that I am gay. Having Klaus in my life will help to tell my family who I am.

The ride to Berlin goes without a hitch and we are right on schedule. There are only very few passengers with me on the train. I smoke one cigarette after the other. My reflection in the window fades in and out with change of the passing lights outside. The closer the train rattles towards

Berlin the more excited I become to see Klaus again. My
worries about how to deal with my aunt and uncle after the
weekend are gone for now. Sure I am a little bit irritated
about the tone of Klaus' call. Maybe it's his way to let me
know how much he wants me.

At the Schöeneweide train station I get off. The platform
is almost dark. Only one of the lights works. I look around.
Not one soul is there. I walk the length of the platform to
look for Klaus. Nothing. Maybe he is late. He didn't expect
that the train will be on time. I feel tired and cold. I huddle
on the bench, the duffel bag in my lap. Time creeps slowing
towards one a.m. Still no Klaus. I look for a phone booth. I
feed the slot with a 20 Pfennig coin. On the other end the
phone rings. No answer. Where is he? I start to worry.
Maybe something happened? Maybe he got into an accident
on the way to the train station? I don't know what to do?
Should I go to his place or mine? Either way I have to take
a night bus. I don't have enough money to pay for a taxi. I
am also on my last cigarette.

I take my bag and walk down the stairs to find the bus
stop outside the train station. The street is totally deserted.
The only noise comes from a nearby pub. The night bus that
stops here will bring me very close to Klaus' apartment. I
am lucky the bus arrives in a couple of minutes. The bus is
full of loud people, many of them pretty wasted. I am always
afraid of loud and drunk people. But no one pays any
attention to me. The driver jerks the bus along the barely lit
streets. I am getting anxious to get to Klaus.

Thank God the lights in the staircase hall are working.
I take two stairs at the time. As I get closer to Klaus'
apartment door I hear music. No doubt it's coming from his
apartment. Weird, I think. I push the buzzer. No answer. I
hear voices. I knock. Nothing. I knock and push the buzzer
again. The door flings open. I look at a completely naked
Klaus. His eyes are glassy. He is drunk.

"What are you doing here? I have friends over. Come
back tomorrow." Behind Klaus I see two guys. Both naked
with hard-ons. "Hey, Klaus come back. Let's fuck." I have a
moment where I am not sure if this really happening to me.
Klaus' face is expressionless.

143

"I waited at the train station for you. You said you would pick me up. I tried to call you." I have to lean against the wall. I feel like I have to throw up. I slide down, my back pressed against the wall. The door slams shut. The hallway lights shut off. I want to cry but my eyes refuse to tear up. The voices behind the door become one. Undoubtedly, the sound of sex. I get up. I don't bother to push the switch for the hallway lights. I hold on the railing and make my way down. The temperature outside must have dropped further since I arrived. The cold air needles my face. But somehow it doesn't penetrate my skin. I don't want to wait for the night bus. I start to walk. I will walk towards Pankow.

I open my eyes. For a moment I have to think where I am. It's all coming back. I feel very rested. I must have slept like a baby. I am not upset anymore about last night's events. Klaus is Klaus and never will change. Maybe I should have been bold and joined in on the group sex? The thought brings a smile to my face. I never have done a multi-some.

Come to think about it, I am not sure what I would do. The thought of having sex with more than one man at once gets me excited. I push the blanket off of me and look at my erection. My right index finger circles around the top. It's getting wet. I go to the hallway and look at myself in the tall mirror. My right hand goes back and forth. With my eyes on me I go down on my knees and spread them as far as I can. I lean backwards. My ass touches my ankles. I am close. The sensation reaches my dick. One last stroke. I feel the warmth on my stomach as it runs down into my pubic hair. I roll to the side and enjoy the aftermath. I am relaxed. What's my plan for the next 48 hours? Alone and without money.

"Precious Time Taking from Comrade Erich Honecker"

I have two letters in the mail. One from the Central Party Office of Berlin. The other one from the Office of the Secretary General of the Party. Both acknowledge my letters in regards to overturn the decision of my extradition from the Party. Almost identical in tone and word. "The matter will be looked at. The Party office of the Humboldt University will handle the issue at hand. An answer will be given by ways of your Party group." I had hoped for a different message. That for instance the decision of my Party extradition decision had been reversed. Instead I have to continue to deal with my Party group at the library. On the other hand neither of the letters confirms my Party extradition. That makes me a little bit optimistic.

Two days after having received the mail a very grim looking Dr. Gross fetches me in the hallway of the library. "Thomas, we have to talk. Do you wish it to happen with all our comrades present or just the two of us?" Interesting, I think. Dr. Gross addresses me by my first name again. Well, I can be very distant if needed. "Dr. Gross, whatever the reason for this talk is it should be out in the open with all the members of the Party group present."

"We will meet in an hour." Dr. Gross turns around and walks away. That will be an interesting meeting. I can't wait for it to start.

I make a point of entering the room five minutes after the scheduled time. The chatter stops as soon as I approach the u-shaped conference table. An empty chair in the center of the setup tells me where to sit. It is not lost on me that everything is intended to be to look like some sort of a tribunal. "Dear comrades, Herr Schardt. This is a meeting I am not looking forward to conducting since we again have to discuss the matter related to Herr Schardt. We all have better things to do. Speaking in the name of all of us, I hope this will be the last one regarding this unfortunate matter."

Dr. Gross goes on to tell everybody about my complaints to the Party office in Berlin and to the office of the SED, Secretary General. "It shows Thomas Schardt's total lack of understanding how to and where to address his misguided complains. This action is his latest attempt to paint a picture of self-importance again. He did cost and still is costing distraction on all levels. He is taking precious time away from all of us including from our dearest General Secretary and head of the DDR, our comrade Erich Honecker." Gross looks up from the piece of paper he is reading off. What pompous asshole, I think. If he really believes what he just said about me and my actions than the GDR is built on very thin ice. Who I am apparently is able to distract not only the comrades here at the library from their daily fight against imperialist and revanchist elements but also their dearest Party leader? It is just laughable.

"Herr Schardt, what is your response?"

"What is this meeting about?" I ask. I can see at the reaction of my former comrades how they despise me. Kiefer makes a point by dropping her pencil very loudly on the table. Others sit back in their chairs, roll their eyes at the same time. Some lean on their elbows and shaking their heads. "You see comrades, how the enemy still can infiltrate our rows? Herr Schardt, I will spell it out for you. Don't you think it's finally time to show remorse? Don't you think it is time to apologize to the Socialist Unity Party of Germany? This is your very last opportunity to admit how wrong you are." I try to catch Gross's eyes. But he deliberately avoids me. He addresses me, but looks at the others at the same time. And they nod their heads in total agreement.

"I didn't know that this meeting, a meeting by the way I have not asked for, was about an apology. I thought this meeting was in direct response to my complaints, send to the Central Party Office for Berlin as well as to the office of SED Secretary General. I did that after you had decided to throw me out of the Party. A clear violation of the Party rules. I don't want any more meetings than you do. I also honestly hope this is the last one and that it will end with a just verdict. My question again is: Will you reverse your

146

decision to expel me from the Party? Will you now accept my voluntarily leave of the Party?" Again, I try to look into the attendees' faces. Still no luck.

"Comrade secretary please take to protocol: at today's Party meeting Herr Schardt has refused again to apologize for his action and damage he has done to the Party's reputation. By showing the democratic and truly human face of the Party we regret that Herr Schardt wants to terminate his Party apprenticeship. It is our decision to cancel his membership. An earlier decision in this matter will be voided. We wish Herr Schardt all the best for his future, and hope that he will over time become again a productive member of our society."

I am flabbergasted. And so seem the rest in the room after Gross told the secretary what to record. I am stunned that my Party extradition was revoked. Voiding my membership is still not what I wanted. But anything is better than the extradition. I can live with this decision. I have won a half victory. With that my professional and personal future is less threatened. It has taken almost six months to come to this point after I told them I wanted to end my Party candidacy. What followed was a lot of wasted time, hate and strained relationships. My life was in peril. My family had to live in fear being blacklisted. But I also have gained a lot. I was given an unwanted view behind the curtain of a system that otherwise fig-leaves itself with democratic laws and humanity. I experienced that the creation of a classless society short circuits as soon as one tries to invoke the ideals, manifestos, teachings and rules it's based on. I have learned more in these past months than I have lost.

It is still very quiet in the room. My former comrades' stare is blank. I wish I could read their thoughts. All of them had vehemently pleaded and argued for my extradition. Some based on their personal conviction I am sure. Some of them because they thought it was expected from them to act in unison. Somebody somewhere in the Party pyramid overruled their decision without letting them know beforehand. It seems like someone would like to say something. But Dr. Gross keeps it all together and ends the

147

meeting. There is nothing more to say, really.

It's an awkward atmosphere in my aunt and uncle's house since my return from Berlin this past weekend. We have not touched on the subject of Klaus' phone call and my abrupt travel to Berlin. I know at some point I have to say something, because I want to. I think they will understand and be supportive. Both of them are educated. My aunt is a teacher. She must have had gay students in her classes at some point or other, in fact she is still in touch with one of her former students. Assuming that she is aware that her former student is a man's-man should make it easier to accept my coming out. My uncle is like a father to me, he definitely will understand.

"Thomas, we have to talk. Your uncle and I are afraid that you are on the wrong path." I don't say anything because I don't like my aunt's introductory remarks.

"What do you mean by wrong path?" I have to clear my throat.

"You are clearly under the influence of a criminal. Is this man who called you last Friday blackmailing you? Is he threatening you? I think we should call the police?"

"What are you talking about? I am under no one's' influence. I am not blackmailed either. Where do you get this from?" My uncle does not say a word. He scratches dry skin off his right elbow. He always does that when it gets serious.

My aunt continues. "I know what those men are capable of. They pray on the young, lure them with money to exploit them. Because it's so dirty they threaten their victims not to talk to anybody about it. They make them feel ashamed. And when they are done with them they throw them away like a rotten apple. They sometimes even murder their victims. That's how these men are. We are worried about you."

"Okay. I am gay. For a long time I wanted to tell you that. But it is not that easy. It took a while to figure it out for myself that I am attracted to men and not to women. It made me an outcast in school. I tried to have relationships with girls but it didn't work. Klaus is the first man I met

148

who is nice to me."

"So his name is Klaus. Is he still nice to you?" I don't want to answer this question. "So, he is not nice to you anymore. Didn't I just tell you that's how these dirty men work. Always. What is he doing to you? How old is he?" I can tell my aunt is talking herself into a rage. Not a good situation.

"He is in his thirties."

"Oh, I knew it. Ernst say something. We have to stop this right now." My aunt is addressing my uncle for the first time directly.

He clears his throat and takes a sip from his drink. "I don't understand how this could happen. Tell me, where did we go wrong with you so we can fix it?"

Fix it, I think. "You didn't do anything wrong. You must know other gay people. This is not happening to us because somebody did something to us."

"Yes, we know such people. And we know what they are able to do. They are criminals. They are ruining families. Yes, and they are killing people." My aunt is jumping out of her chair. She is yelling now.

"Thesie, please keep your voice down." My uncle gets out of his chair, too. He knows and I know what is going to happen pretty soon. My aunt is a hysteric. If and when something is going against her grain, she starts to scream. Her face gets an almost insane expression. When she is all worked up she will start hitting whoever is next to her. I have seen my uncle going behind her wrapping is arm around her like a straight jacket. She will yell until she is exhausted. Then her body will collapse. Her demeanor changes to childlike manner. My uncle will undress her and bring her to bed. He will put hot towels on her forehead and stomach. She will whimper for a while. Soon after, she will be sound asleep.

Anyway, I get up now as well. My aunt's index finger is only inches away from my face. My uncle goes into position behind her. She lifts her hand. He grabs her arm. It's like as everybody follows a script. She wrestles her arm free and turns quickly towards the dining room table. Both of us, my uncle and me, know immediately what will happen. Above the table on the wall hang very expensive hand-turned and hand-painted plates from all over the world. A very nice collection. My aunt grabs the first plate. But before she can throw it onto the floor my uncle takes it out of her hands. He gives the plate to me. She grabs the next plate. He takes it. I get it. We are forming a conveyer belt. This goes on for way too long. After the fifth or sixth plate, my uncle raises his voice. "Theresia, stop this right now." When he uses her full name that means he is angry, very angry.

It's like something snaps inside of my aunt. She stops and sinks on the chair. We all sit down. The drama is over. You can feel the tension slowly leaves the room. I notice that their dog stares at us from his favorite corner on the couch. We all sit in silence. We don't look at each other. "I think we have said enough tonight. We all should go to bed." My uncle's voice is calm and relaxed. My aunt comes out of her funk. "Yes, we should." I go to my room, whispering "Good night." I close the door behind me. I am confused and still surprised. I had not expected this kind of reaction from my aunt and uncle. I look out the window into the dark night.

Breakfast the next morning is very quiet. We sit in the kitchen; the gas kitchen stove is on full blast to heat the room. I can't wait to leave for work. My aunt gives me hug. She is not a hugger at all. It feels weird. She is not a touchy physical person. She shows her love by doing things for you. If you give her kiss on the cheeks there is almost an immediate stiffening of her body. My uncle on the other hand is a very warm and has no trouble to show it. How they made it so far without breaking up is a wonder to me. Sure, they are more partners then lovers. I guess it's the past that keeps them together.

I really believe that they dread their everyday present and, that they both can't wait until that quickly becomes their past. I think they don't like the future. Because that would mean they have to make the present work. Looking back, realizing they have lived through another day, makes it bearable easier for them. Anyway I don't look forward to another talk about my gayness with them. I take one more sip from my coffee cup and leave the apartment. I run so I won't miss the next streetcar. Another day at the museum right now seems very attractive to me.

The scent of roses greets me as I enter the side door to the museum. The porter's room door is wide open. I can see an enormous bouquet of yellow roses, stuffed into a bucket. That must be hundred roses, I think. "Good morning. Nice roses. You must have a great admirer," I greet Hans as he steps out of his room. "No, they are for you. I already have a headache from the scent. Take them away from me." I look at him in disbelief. For me?

I open the little card attached to one of the roses. "I want to see you. K." At first I don't understand. Who is "K"? Then I know, of course the flowers are from Klaus. I don't know what emotion is stronger? My embarrassment to have received the roses? It is out of the question to bring them to my aunt's apartment. No way. Since I don't have an office at the museum or even my own desk, I can't keep the roses here either. The only alternative is to throw them out.

"I always thought men sent girls flowers and not the other way around. Must be some girl you have there. You must be a good fucker. I am pretty good in bed. But no women have sent me flowers afterwards." I am blushing. If Hans only knew that these flowers are not from a girl. He is as straight of a man as it gets. He always talks about the women he picks up in bars, on the street, anywhere. Most of the stories are lies, I am sure of it.

"Maybe I can find a large vase for the roses. Do you know who has one?" I ask Hans.

"Try in the director's office. They might have one." I lift the bucket. It's heavy. The thorns scratch my face and my hands. I maneuver the bucket down the hallway. The roses blind my view.

"Are these for me," Charlotte the directors' secretary giggles. "Do you want them? Here" I put the bucket down on her desk.

"Are you serious?"

"Yes, I am. I don't know what to do with them. But you have to promise me not to tell my uncle where they came from."

"I can't believe it. You really give me these gorgeous roses. Sure, I will take them. Where did you get them from?"

"A friend." She looks at me. She gives me a hug. I think

she knows that I am gay. She told me ones that her son lives with a man. "That must be a very nice friend of yours." Charlotte is your typical middle-aged secretary. Always dressed nicely, big hair, long nails. Always friendly. Always helpful. I am glad that she will enjoy the flowers.

What a morning! One part of me would like to tell my aunt and uncle about the flowers to show them how wrong they are about Klaus and gay men in general. But are they really wrong with their opinion about gay men? Maybe there is a little truth to it? My experiences with men so far are not all that great. My hope that Klaus will be different was more than once shattered.

Yes, Klaus. I have not heard a word from him since last Friday night when I went to his apartment. I only hope it was the last time that I saw him. I really, really don't want have anything to do with him anymore. Our relationship, if we can call it that, is totally fucked up, almost from the beginning. I don't want to be subjected to his insults and humiliations. As much as I like his caring and gentle side, but his other side is voiding everything good down to zero.

I force myself not to think about him right now. I need distractions. Later I apparently have to decide if I should even acknowledge the flowers and thank him for that. They must have cost a fortune beside the fact that he has to have some connections to order so many roses. I have never seen so many roses at the same time even in a flower shop. He must have gone to some effort to get them. This is the nice Klaus I love. But the ugly Klaus is just not tolerable.

I label silk scarves. They feel stiff and almost scratchy in my hand. The colors are brilliant, mostly red. The scarves are part of elaborate ceremonial oversized dresses of former Chinese royalties; more than 500 years old. I hate to push the small safety pins with the round metal framed tags attached through the material. Making tiny holes in these ancient fabrics seems a sacrilege. But that's what I am being told to do. I try to be as careful as I can be. The smell of mothball lays heavy in the air. Copying file numbers from old labels onto new ones is boring. Therefore it's easy to separate my mind from my hands. My thoughts drift to last night's drama at my aunt and uncle's house. I feel like moving out. But where would I go? The way they reacted was so unexpected. I consider both of them my surrogate parents as well as my friends. If I needed advice, help or support they were always there for me. But now they calling me who and what I am wrong. That is wrong!

In the distance I hear the telephone ring. A muffled voice answers I hear the echo of steps. The enormous glass cabinets in the museums archive seem to vibrate louder and louder. "Thomas, are you here? There is call is for you. It sounded like a long distance call. Hard to understand." The director of the archive comes down the aisle. "Make it quick. Private phone calls are not allowed."

What an ass, I think. Everybody here gets personal phone calls. Because it's me, the nephew, he feels obligated to make a point. "Thanks for letting me know." I run down the aisle. It must be Klaus. No one else would call me here. "Hello, who is it?"

"Klaus. How are you? Did you get my flowers? Do you like them?"

"Yes, they are beautiful. How did you manage to get so many roses? Thank you."

"Oh that's a long story. How is the man I miss so much?"

"Not good. My relatives found out about you and me. We had a big fight last night. It's terrible."

"Take the next train to Berlin. I will make it up to you."

"I can't. I have to work. I can't just leave. But thank you for the offer. This is all too much." I tear up. "Klaus I can't talk much longer. I haven't heard from you in ages it seems. You treated me terribly last Friday when I came to your door. You always do these unexpected and bad things to me. And now I have my family on my back. My aunt and uncle think I should see a doctor to get cured from being gay. I don't like my job here. Things are really as bad as they can be."

"Wait. You are my angel. You know that, do you? Do you?"

"I don't know that, Klaus. Remember just last Friday night."

"But I am telling you. You have to believe me. If you can't come right today, I understand. But can you come this weekend? Please. I want to see you. I want to hold you. We need each other. We have each other. Right?"

"Oh, I want so much to believe what you are saying. But..."

"Angel, no buts. Come Friday night to Berlin. We will have the most wonderful weekend. We will talk. Promise?"

"I will call you and let you know. I have to go." I put the phone down and look out of the window above the desk. All I can see is the roof line of the opposite museum's wing. As it happens so many times before when I am in distress I feel like I can't move my arms and legs. There is the urge again to throw up. In my fingertips is this tingling. Everything around me shuts down into total silence. I am alone. But I also know I have to control myself. I move my hand away from the phone I still hold on to. I close my eyes and put the hands on my chest. I breathe in through the nose and out through the mouth. Over and over again. Slowly I gain back my reality. I feel safe enough to let go of the support of the desk I lean against. I start to move away from the desk. I can walk again. My body feels still very heavy. I reach my workstation. I unfold another silk scarf and copy the faded archive number to a new tag.

How can life produce so many seemingly opposing events in a matter of less than twenty-four hours? Just when things were becoming my new routine almost everything connected to it implodes. I had to be witness to Klaus' sex orgy. My aunt thinks gays are criminals. Then a bucket full of yellow roses arrives and, Klaus tells me I am his angel. Wasn't I sure after this past weekend that Klaus and I are no more? Wasn't I hoping my aunt and uncle would still embrace me after I told them I am gay? Wasn't I looking forward to a new beginning? No, no and no is the answer to all these questions. Again, I am the one who has to take a stand. Again, I have to fight to be accepted who I am and, what I want. Why has everything in my life to be a confrontation? Why can't the dice land in my favor? Will there be ever a time for me not to make down payments for future luck? When will I receive without pre-conditions? Questions and more questions tumble in my head like laundry in a washing machine. At the same time I push safety pin after safety pin through centuries-old silk.

I dread going home. I don't want have another outburst from my aunt, nor do I want to discuss my homosexuality. Not today. My brain needs a rest. The streetcar rumbles along its track down Ernst-Thaelman Street. Every bump in the uneven tracks pushes me from one side to the other side. My tight grip on the handle does not always absorb enough to counter balance the uneven ride. The streetcar takes a sharp turn to the left. I have taken the ride countless times. But every time I expect the car would jump out of the tracks and turn over. But never has happen. The wheels of the streetcars produce an ear-hurting screech during the turn. We cross the bridge that spans over railroad tracks. Another violent turn and I can get off.

The walk to my aunt's house is nice. The street is lined with Linden trees and three-story apartment buildings erected in the thirties. Despite the peeling mortar the buildings still show the pride of past middle class living. They were erected across from the vast Schönefelder Park which stretches for miles with wide alleys under the shade of tall trees. Here and the there they give away to lawns, fountains and flower beds. Somewhere in the midst of all runs the river Parte. In the past people would swim in the river. Today it's almost black from industrial pollution. On hot summer days you can smell its dead water in the apartment of my aunt and uncle. It mixes with stench from the nearby coal-fired power plant. There are days when fine brownish-blackish ashes cover the entire neighborhood.

I unlock the front door and step into the small foyer. I feel a pressure in my upper stomach. I hope the evening will be without an air of tension. I hear some voices from the living room. Bojar is the first one to greet me. He jumps up on my side trying to reach my face to slobber his tongue all over me. I like dogs; I don't like to be licked by them. I hang my jacket up and look in the mirror. I see my mother. It's just a mini moment that I feel I stepped out off reality. I turn around. There she is standing in the door frame. "What are you doing here?" is all what I can say. She puts her arms around me. I don't move. "Your aunt called me. She told me what happened." I can't take any physical contact right now.

I loosen my mother's arms still holding onto me.

"This is crazy. Is Heinz here also?" She shakes her head. So, my aunt called her sister, my mother, to take the next train to come to see me, and then what? I am angry. The grip of my family never lessens. It's not love or care that has motivated my mother to contact me. It's another insane variation to push the guilty button in me. My mother's see-what-have-you-done-now-I-am-having sto- mach-pain-again-method, my uncle's where-did-we go-wrong-with-you question. And now my aunt's you-have-to-come-immediately-to-Leipzig-order. I wonder what my mother told her husband about why she had to go to Leipzig on a short notice. She probably lied to him about the real reason. I can't imagine she would tell him: "Thomas is gay. I have to see him." In my family it's always the others who do something to them. Perfection creates perception creates reality. I feel like I am in a middle of a nightmare.

My aunt comes into the foyer. "Why don't you and your mother go into the study and talk? In the meantime I will prepare supper." What in the world is there to talk about, I think as the both of us basically get pushed in my uncle's study. The door closes behind us. My mother and I look at each other. "I don't know what to say, mother. Yes, I am gay. But that's not the end of the world, or is it?" I am tearing up.

She steps towards me and takes both of my hands. "I don't care. You will be always my son, my big son. Yes, I have two sons, but you are the most important one to me." Tears running down her cheeks. Never before she has she said that to me. I sit down.

When my brother was born I felt like I wasn't a son anymore. I became an adult overnight. Expected to be good and not to cause any trouble. I look at my mother and think, why does it take a drama situation like this to verbalize love and care? I will never understand why my mother would not stand up for me when it comes to my stepfather and his hatred towards me? And here she is and accepts me how and who I am. Will she tell her husband what I just told her?

"So, you won't send me to a doctor to fix me? Because I never will do that. I am gay and I believe that the way I am was born. I really don't get your sister. She honestly thinks I have to be treated." My mother takes my hand. "Of course I won't pressure you to do anything you don't want to do. I will talk to her about that." I can't control my tears. They form a small stream running down to my chin. Dripping onto the front of my shirt. I am embarrassed. I can't remember the last time I cried in front of my mother. She puts her arms around me. "Everything will be fine. You are my son. I always have trusted you in what you do. Let's go back into the living room."

My aunt, uncle and cousin are sitting at the dining room table. We join them. I don't feel hungry. I feel tense. Only the clanging noise of our silverware fills the room. *What can we talk about?* I think. The silence stresses me out. I don't want to be here right now. "What time are you taking the train back to Berlin?" I look at my mother.

"I have to back tonight. I have to work tomorrow."

"Can't you call the office and tell them you held up by a family emergency?" My aunt asks.

"No. I also have a son and husband at home. They need me too." There is tension building between the two sisters. My mother the dutiful wife and mother. I wonder again how she has explained her sudden trip to Leipzig. And what she will tell him when she is back? The turmoil of the last two days is all because of me. And my family certainly won't diffuse that. Projecting guilt is part of my family's dynamic. I feel guilty.

"Hi, it's me. Sorry to bother you at work. But this is the only time I can call." I put my hand over the phone to muzzle the echo of the long halls of the archive. "Klaus, I had the most awful two days."

"What happened?"

"My aunt and uncle found out that I am gay. They ordered my mother to come to strategize my change. It's totally absurd. I don't know what to do. I don't want to be here."

"Tell you what. Take the next train to Berlin. We will talk."

"Thanks for saying that. But I can't just leave. I also have no money."

"Ask someone to loan it to you. I will give you the money for the train ticket."

"That is very nice." I am tearing up. Klaus just offered to pay for my ticket. He wants me to come to him. My chest almost can't take the pressure of the happiness and relief I feel. My eyes fill up with tears. I want so very much to be with him right now. Feeling his arms around me, his kisses, and his hands.

"Even if I want to come right now I can't. We have to wait until the weekend." I hear the pounding of steps. Somebody is coming down the hall. I have to finish the call. We are not allowed to make private calls on business phones. "Klaus, I have to leave. I will try to catch the five o'clock train on Friday. I will try to call if anything changes."

"I think you should come tomorrow. But that's your call."

"Yes, I know. Please understand. I really have to get off the phone."

"Ok. I love you; you know that, do you? Everything will be fine."

"Yes!" I hang up. I turn away from the desk to see who is coming closer. It's my uncle. It's the first time that I have seen up here in the storage area.

"Hi, are you busy right now? We have to talk," he says.

I look at him. "No, it's not about that." He must have read my mind. I am relieved. Because I don't want to talk about what he calls "that."

"Can we talk here?" I suggest.

"No let's go down to the cafeteria."

"You are the boss. But I don't know if I can just leave for a break," I say.

"I talked to Erler. So he knows."

"Good." I take off my smock. I hate that thing. It makes me look so foolish. But it's so dusty here that you need protective gear.

Leningrad, Looted Artifacts, and Gray Longjohns

The cafeteria is on the second floor of the museum, right at the entrance to the exhibition hall. It's not only for visitors but also for the employees to use during their lunch break, thanks to my uncle who had fought long and hard to get a coffee shop opened. The former museum's director thought it was a waste of space. A museum's sole purpose is to display objects, not to offer pastries and coffee. He hated that "modern nonsense" as he would always say.

My uncle and I take the table farthest from the door in the corner opposite of the window. Most of the patrons are museum employees. Everybody takes note as we make our way to the table. For a couple of seconds all conversation dies down. My uncle has some clout among the staff, he also comes across as very grumpy and unapproachable. I am still a little bit disappointed how he reacted to my coming out. I never ever would have expected that he would suggest that I see a doctor to treat my homosexuality. As an educated man he should know better. But truth be told, maybe he just wanted to please my aunt when she went berserk about gay people. When it comes to her he is a little puppy dog. He will do everything and anything to accommodate her. That this is never enough is another subject.

My uncle and I face each other. The silence seems endless. "What would you think about a three-month work duty in Leningrad?" he asked.

"What do you mean?" I ask, fully understanding what he just had said. But I need time to think and react. Of course, I would love to go to Leningrad. Any place for that matter, just to get me out of the mess I am in. "Wow, do you really think I have chance?"

"Koenig asked me if I think that you would like do to that. You must have told him that you speak Russian." Indeed, I remember a talk with him about my Russian. I think he studied at the Lemonosov University in Moscow

Thomas P.W. Schardt

before spending some time in Mongolia. He seemed very impressed when I told him that I liked Russian, and that has to do with my former Russian teacher in high school.

To learn Russian is mandatory starting in the fifth grade. Most kids I know hated it. I think it has something to do with the fact that anything mandatory produces opposition. Russian is also not an easy language to master. And, where can you use Russian other than in the Soviet Union? The litmus test to love the Big Brother unconditionally is crazy, too. The truth is that most East Germans don't have a high opinion about the Soviet Union. Of course, officially, every citizen in East Germany has to constantly express his gratitude towards the Russian people. They liberated us from Fascism and set us on the course into the Worker's Paradise. My uncle's favorite but secret saying is: "They don't have any real culture. Peter the Great went to Holland to learn about civil lifestyle, Western craftsmanship and culture in general. The Russian Court spoke French, for Christ's sake. Lenin would have been a nobody without German help."

I am very ambivalent about that. I don't feel any animosity. I think it is ridiculous to put the Soviet Union and its people as a whole on a pedestal to be adored by the rest of us. Growing up with phrases like "Learning from the Soviet Union means learning to be victorious" is such a humbug only brainwashed Party midlevel officials can believe it. The blind following of the Soviet propaganda has also had a disastrous impact in East Germany. I remember in grad school that we were told that the best way to raise cattle is in open barns even in the cold of winter. As kids we had to build circular barn-like buildings without any walls out of paper cutouts. The whole East German cattle corporations dismantled traditional stalls and build wall-less stalls. It had a devastating result. The cattle froze to death in the winter. The whole thing was abandoned.

Recently, under some international pressure, the Russians decided to return all the artifacts still in their possession, among them the countless objects that belonged to Museum in Leipzig. Since the Soviets portrayed themselves as a shining star, the moralists and protector of

160

the good and better, how could they explain away the fact that their archives and depots still were filled with stolen objects? Nazis and Imperialists are by nature looters and suppressers, but not the Soviets as torch holders and self-anointed enforcers of the ultimate purpose of all human history: the Communist paradise. Therefore it was decided to return the stolen objects, but under cover and in the dark of night.

A detailed schedule was worked out between the Museum for Ethnology in Leipzig and its counterpart in Leningrad. According to the agreement, it was determined that three museum employees in three-month cycles would go to Leningrad to prepare the artifacts for secret shipments back to the GDR. The shipments would always arrive in the middle of the night. Big trucks being unloaded in daylight could harm the secrecy of the operation. I would be part of the second of the three-month cycle, living in Leningrad from the middle of December until February. That was just two months away. I am very excited about that trip. Not only will I work and live in another country. At the end of my stay I have something extraordinary to add to my resume: living and working abroad.

I look at my uncle with my head spinning with thoughts of a possible send-off to Leningrad. That would not only clean my bio, I would improve my Russian. I will live and work in a foreign country. I will meet new people. Upon my return new career doors will open. A brand-new beginning. "Do you think I have a chance to get this assignment?" I ask him again. "Wouldn't I need a security clearance for this, since it's kind of a secret mission?"

"Koenig knows your Party past. I talked to him about it. Told him, that you were immature and misguided when you made the decision to leave the Party. He understood. He likes you. And he thinks everybody deserves a second chance." I almost started to argue with my uncle about his comments to Koenig about my immaturity and being misguided. Even he doesn't seem to get it why I did what I did. But it's moot. It's over. I moved to Leipzig to start anew. And what an opportunity Leningrad will be for me. I will be golden afterwards. Working in the Soviet Union —even it's

161

only for a limited time—will legitimize me again. No question that I will get a spot at the university.

"If you really think I have a good chance to be part of one of the future teams I think I would love to do it. Thanks for your help. I am sure I wouldn't be considered without being your nephew. Do you know what the time frame is?"

"Yes, in two weeks."

"In two weeks. That's kind of a short notice."

"I know. You are a replacement. The guy who was going to go canceled because his wife is pregnant and he wants to be around her the whole time until she gives birth."

I am a replacement. A second choice. I feel a little bit ticked off. Just because somebody else didn't want to go they pulled me off of the top of their head. Oh, well. That what happened when you have a blemish on your bio. In two weeks. That means I will leave the beginning of November and stay over Christmas in Leningrad. Not only that. It's very, very cold over there. *Sent to the Gulag*, I think. The real reason that they couldn't fill this slot has probably something to do with both the bitterly cold winter and the holidays. No family man wants to be away during that time. For a second I want to tell off my uncle. But I decide against it. I am single, without any family or kids. I am a natural choice to be assigned this time of the year.

"You need to buy some warm clothes. I mean real warm. Not fancy looking but useful. It's cold over there." My uncle must have read my thoughts. "Human resources will give you 200 Marks to buy warm underwear, gloves, you name it. I talked to your supervisor. Take the afternoon off and start shopping." My uncle puts his hand on my shoulder. "I am really glad that you have this chance. It will help you afterwards."

I arrive at my aunt and uncle's house with bags of unattractive looking undergarments. Gray, shapeless. But the stuff is extra thick. The saleswoman at the department store encouraged me to buy these after I told her the reason for it. The thick socks are equally ugly. I couldn't find any fur-lined hats or gloves. I was told at the Konsument Warenhaus department store that there might be a delivery of hats, scarves and gloves the day after tomorrow. The shipment comes from Poland. I should come first thing in the morning because a lot of people wait for the warm winter clothes. I envision myself fighting with other customers over the stuff. Maybe my aunt and uncle can come with me, so one can grab a hat while another one fights at the table with the gloves. All part of the birth pains of a glorious future, I guess, to elbow for necessities. It is so ridiculous to think that you have to stay in line for warm clothes. Except for the gray long johns, no one buys them anyway.

"So, you were successful." My aunt greets me at the door looking at my shopping bags.

"I guess so. I have to go back after tomorrow for more."

"I am so happy for you. What an opportunity for you." She gives me a hug. Kind of a hug. I know my aunt. She wants to make good. Two days ago I was some sicko who needed to be cured. Things really can change very quickly. "Have you called your mother with the news?" she asks.

I haven't even thought about her to be honest. I should also tell Klaus. Maybe that can wait until I see him next the weekend. All the sudden I have a knot in my stomach. I promised Klaus to spend the weekend with him. That means I have to ask my aunt for money for the train. She will have a fit. Somehow I have to find the right moment, I think. Dinner is ready. My cousin comes running out of her room and gives me a big hug. "You have to bring me a Matroshka. Promise?"

"Yes, I will." We all sit down. The dog places himself across my feet. He seems to know as well that I am going away. If some stranger would walk in right now he would think, what a happy family. A farce and a façade. Keeping up appearances. Maybe my aunt and uncle came up with the plan to get me the assignment to Leningrad to have me as far away as possible from the bad influence of men? I have to smile just thinking about that possibility. No matter what, right now I feel a warm wave of happiness rolling through my body. I load up my slices of bread with cheese.

The overcrowded train enters the station in Schöeneweide. Over three hours of standing room only. People push to get to the bathroom. Drunken soldiers on weekend leave yelling. Some of them throw up before they could reach the train latrines. The sour smell of the vomit and urine stink from the toilets mix with the sweat of other passengers. I am glad to get off. The evening air is cool. People stream out of the wagons onto the too-small platform. I have to box myself away from the train out of fear to be pushed on the tracks. The train starts to move again. I look around for Klaus. At the moment there is no chance of recognizing anybody. The mass of people roll in unison towards the stairwell. I step aside to get separated from the rest. I still can't see him. Maybe... I don't want to finish my thought. He had promised to meet me. I pull a cigarette out of the box. I exhale a long line of smoke. It makes me a little lightheaded. I like the feeling.

"Hi handsome," I don't have to turn around. It's him. His arms slide through mine, crossing over my chest. His chest presses against my back, his hips against my ass. His warm breath runs down my neck. We don't move. We just enjoy our bodies touching. I drop my cigarette and turn around in his circle of arms. I look into his blue eyes. His blond wavy hair covers his forehead. He is so beautiful. There is no space between us. I put my head on his shoulder.

"It is so nice to see you. Thanks for coming, "I whisper. His lips seek my ear. His tongue circles the inside of my ear. The tip of my dick is getting moist. "Please stop," I say but wish we could do it right now and here. "I missed you more than you can imagine." Klaus grabs my shoulder. "I really mean it. Let's go before I come." He laughs, his white teeth showing. Everything seems so perfect on him. For a moment I feel un-equal to him, much less attractive.

Klaus takes my bag. "You have to start smiling more," he says looking at me. "You are always looking so serious." I know. I blush.

We run up the stairs to his apartment. We have the same thing in mind without saying so. Klaus slams the door in its lock. We are breathless. He pulls his pants down. "Show me your dick. I want your dick." With one hand he unbuttons his shirt and with the other he undoes my fly. We are both hard. I can see the tip of his dick peeking out of his underwear. It is so hot to see that. My jeans fall down to my ankles. I am on my knees. I pull his briefs to the side. His dick jumps out. I take his balls in my mouth. My thumb slides over his tip. He is wet. Wait, he moans and turns around. He bends down. The inside of his ass opens. "Fuck me. I want that you fuck me now. I want you hard and dry." He steadies himself with his hands against the door. My tongue circles his hole. "Don't wait. I am almost ready. Take me. Please."

I put spit on my dick and stand up. I also feel that I am close to coming. My hands grab his hips. I look at his ass. Smooth, no hair, no pimples. I guide myself towards his hole. We are the perfect height for each other. "Why are you waiting? Fuck me." I push my hips away but he pulls me back. I slide right in. His softness makes me crazy. Klaus erects himself. "Please stay in."

His hand goes between his crotch, touches my ass. One of his fingers goes in his hole, stroking my dick inside of him. I am going out of my mind. He bends his head back. "I want you to fuck me in front of the mirror. I want to see you." "Yes, yes," is all that I can say. We move slowly towards the living room. His finger is still on my dick inside of him. Even though I am motionless in him, I am ready to explode. Klaus opens the armoire door. We both are in front of the mirror. I see his stomach, his chest, his strong legs that slightly bend to keep me inside of him. My head is next to his. "You feel so good. You are the perfect size for me." He leans forward. I stay with him. Our eyes lock. The slapping noise of our bodies make me ecstatic. I push harder and harder. The look on his face is so serene. He grabs his own dick. He pushes a second finger in his hole, reaches the end of my dick. I hear myself screaming like never before. I feel his body shake. He is ready to come, so I am. "Come, please come."

"Yes, I am ready. Spray it in my ass. Now, now..." He straightens up, grabs my ass. His hips push forward. It is floating out of me. He comes all over the mirror. We look at each other, silently, just listening to our breath.

He pushes me out of him. Turns around. I see his perfect backside in the mirror. "This was incredible. I have never had such hot sex." Klaus looks at me. "We can have this all the time. You just have to move in with me. Will you?"

I put my arms around him. I seek his mouth. "Yes, I want to."

"Don't go back to Leipzig. I make enough money. You can take your time and look for a job here. I don't want to lose you." I don't know what to say. It's like a dream come true. I pull him tighter. If what I feel right now is happiness than I am happy.

"Let's have a shower."

"Can we stay like this for a little bit longer?"

"You are so sweet. Sure." I kiss his eyes, forehead, the rest of his face, neck. If I could I would crawl inside of him and stay there forever. Silly. I let go of him. "I wish I could make this last forever," I say.

"It's up to you," he says.

"Let's not hurt each other anymore."

"I don't want to, honestly."

"Good."

"You are so different from all the others I had. I want to make it work this time."

"That would be wonderful. I am so tired of being alone."

"Me too."

For a while I forget that in a couple of weeks I will be working in Leningrad. Do I really have to decide between him and working abroad? Couldn't I have both? I fear Klaus' reaction when I remember what happened when I told him I would move to Leipzig, just three hours south of Berlin. Leningrad will be two countries over to the East. Why must be a decision for something includes a decision against something by default? I know I have myself already committed to this great opportunity. Now I have to be man enough to tell him before I take the train back to Leipzig on Sunday. I feel like I am on cloud nine. I am officially gay, I have a man who declared his love to me and I will live and work for three months in another country. I bottoming out. I am climbing.

Our weekend together is all holding hands, not letting the other out of sight longer as a trip to the bathroom lasts. We act like a couple. He cooks. I watch. We eat. Long walks through the Friedrichshain Park. Most of the time we don't even talk. Each of us is in his own world. The dream we are dreaming shines through our eyes. A squeeze of the other ones hand affirms we are on the same wave. I feel at home.

And then comes the time when I tell him about the job in Leningrad and how much I want to do it. Klaus listens. Calmly. I can't see any emotions. But he holds my hand throughout my monologue. "Can you say something?" I step in front of him. He pulls me towards him.

"How about celebrating New Year's Eve together in Leningrad?" Klaus looks at me. If there is a moment that I can pinpoint to say I was falling love, that's the one for me.

"Yes, let's do that." I start to cry. I feel his tears on my forehead. "I love you, Klaus." His lips on my cheeks are his answer.

"I am proud of you. You will make it in life. I know it. The first time I saw you I knew you would be special to me. Let's take the life we have left together, yes?"

"Yes. Let's have a life together."

I am still in awe that I will be leaving for Leningrad in a couple of days. I have all my warm clothes to face the cold time ahead. My family and I don't talk about my coming out and Klaus. The family protocol at work: if we don't talk about it, it doesn't exist. Klaus and I are very good. We talk every day on the phone hidden in the vast archive of the museum. I don't even think that my supervisor knows about that phone. Most of our lunch hour Klaus and I talk, reassure each other, and plan the future. Klaus is trying to get a visa and an airline ticket for Leningrad. Kurt, the artistic director of the ballet ensemble had studied choreography in Leningrad. He still has many friends there that Klaus could stay with. I feel in balance for the first time in the longest time that I can remember. Love can turn bitter into sweet. It's not just a saying. I am living it right now.

Candles, Sekt, and a Declined Travel Visa

My flight leaves from Schöenfeld, the only major airport in East Germany. Therefore I can spend the last night with Klaus before I will go back to my apartment to get my huge and heavy suitcases the next morning. Klaus has prepared my favorite dish: beef with red cabbage and mashed potatoes. Candles and Rotkäppchen Sekt. He and I are hopelessly romantic. We hold hands across the table. It is the incredible mix of sadness and happiness that made our hunger disappears. No words are needed. The knot in my stomach does not hurt. Without letting go of his hand I get up and sit in his lap. I smell his hair, his lips are on my neck. I put my feet on top of his. He gets up and walks us over to the couch. It is so peaceful. His arms around me, my head on his chest. We both slipping into sleep. Harmony carries Klaus and me. We have found each other.

I rush up the stairs to my apartment. I have about thirty minutes to pack the last things before going to the airport. I slid the key in the door. But before I can turn it, the door opens. My uncle is on the other side. "Where were you? I've been here since last night."

"What are you doing here? I was at Klaus' place. I know I am kind of late." I try to get by him into my apartment.

"There is no rush. You are not going anywhere. Your visa was denied. That's why I am here."

I stopped. "What do you mean? I was told just yesterday that it will be ready at the airport together with my ticket."

"No, it won't. The Interior Department called the museum yesterday afternoon to let us know that you are not going. I tried to find out why. Even Koenig went ballistic. But the decision was made higher up." I look at my open suitcases. The fur cap, bundles of long johns and ugly thick socks, the black scarf my grandmother had made "for Russia" as she always refers to the Soviet Union, the shapeless gloves. It all glazes over. Tears are gushing out of my eyes.

"Why always me, why? What have I done that I never get ahead? Tell me. You always have an answer. How do you answer this one?" Through the tears I only see the silhouette of my uncle. I feel his hands on my shoulders, trying to pull me towards him. "Don't." My stutter drowns out my words. I think of Klaus. He will now think I am a loser and I will lose him. What about those I had said goodbye to? Now I have to say hello again. Sooner than I had thought. What about the people I worked with in Leipzig? I am such a fraud.

Without a clear thought I start to close the suitcases. I don't want to look at all the stuff that only makes sense in Leningrad and not here. The tears mix with the snot running out of my nose. What am I going to do? How can I pick up the pieces from here on? I remember the words that Kleinert had thrown at me when I told her I will leave the Party. They really follow through with their threats. You turn your back on us and you will never get up again. I had started to walk again, thinking Leipzig is far enough away from it all. Klaus and I had overcome the odds from the beginning. My mother told me she loves me and, I am special to her. All in a couple of months time. Do I really give up my dreams when I decided to return the Party book? I look at my uncle hovering over one of the suitcases.

"What should I do? Here I am, twenty-one years old with an impossible future?" My uncle offers me a cigarette. We smoke in silence. I am lost. He looks for the right words. I can feel it. He always knows the right words, has a plausible way out.

"I think we should take the next train back to Leipzig. You go back to work tomorrow. Within the next six weeks you have to apply for a spot at the University. I think that you should do. Focus forward," he says.

"Do you really think I have a chance to get accepted at the University? After all of this here? I think I am done."

"No, you are not. The job in Leningrad is highly sensitive as you know. They probably didn't want to take the smallest chance of any problems, leaks or whatever." I look at him.

"So, you also think I am a risk? Could cost a problem? When my own uncle thinks that how can I be surprised that some Stasi asshole denied my visa?"

"You know I don't mean that. I was just playing devil's advocate."

"Please don't be the Stasi advocate in order to make me feel better."

I get up into the kitchen to wash my face over the sink. I feel hot. I hear my uncle using the bathroom. Human basics don't give a shit about life's jokes. "I feel like I should quit my job and move back to Berlin. I can be miserable in both places. Here at least I have my own place."

"I think it's a bad idea," my uncle said. "Come back and we will work on your University application. I know people at the Ministry. They owe me. They will help."

"Well, your connection didn't help me to get a freaking visa to freaking Leningrad to get freaking stolen objects back. All right, let's go back to Leipzig. You are right; I should give myself another chance." I say it but I feel inside of me, that I have already made a decision against Leipzig. As I close my door I know I will be back for good very soon.

I called Klaus. "Hi. It's me."

"Well, how did you find a phone that quickly? Or are you still at the airport?"

"No, I am back in Leipzig. I didn't get a visa."

"What? What happened?" he asked.

"I don't know. They won't tell me why. But I didn't fly out."

"Oh my God. I am so sorry. How are you? Why are you in Leipzig again?"

"My uncle made me. I don't know what to think or do anymore? I feel so trapped."

"I wish I could hold you right now. Whatever it is, let it go. You can't fight these idiots. The only way to show them you don't need them is to be strong. I can be strong for the both of us."

"Klaus, I am at a loss. I am so helpless."

"Don't. Come back. Come to me. I will help you to find a job here. I make enough to support us until you figured it out. Trust me."

170

"I wish I would have the strength and just leave. I need to calm down."

"Take your time. But I think you better of here with me."

"I love you. Thanks for saying all that. It will help me to clear my head. I wish you could be here and just hug me."

"Do you want me to come? I can take the next train."

"No, I don't know. Thanks. I will call you. I am shaking. Klaus I feel like this is not really real. I am so ashamed."

"What are you ashamed off? That the Stasi didn't give you visa to help the Russians to return what is ours? Are you kidding me? Be proud that you won't be part of their dirty business."

"It's a funny way to look at it. We should be careful because the probably listening to our conversation. I don't need more trouble."

"Listen if we start to be afraid of them, than they have won. I don't care if they are listening and you shouldn't either. Fuck them. We don't need them to be happy. We have each other."

"I know, you are so right. I already feel a little bit better. But I am so angry right now. How can these bastards rule my life? Why are we at their mercy?"

"We are not. They want to make us believe that they rule our life. But only when we allow them to do. I hate these fuckers. But I don't think of them every day of my life."

"I guess I can learn a lot from you."

"Nothing to learn here. Just follow your own gut. Please pack up your things and come back to Berlin."

"You are right. I kind of feel this is exactly what I should do."

"Then do it. Don't make yourself sick over this. You know, someday we will travel to Leningrad. I hear it's a great city. You and me. Come. See the light. I love you."

"I am so glad I have you in my life."

"I love you, Thomas, with all my heart."

"I love you."

Its two months since my Leningrad debacle. No one really said anything to me at the museum after I came back from Berlin. Most of my co-workers are probably not interested in me and my misfortune. They have enough problems getting through their own life. Others may take joy. I am the nephew of one of the department heads. The system has worked, even they don't like it, but if it produces setbacks for somebody else that creates malicious pleasure.

Director Koenig pulled me aside once to tell me that this whole last-minute decision to reverse my earlier granted visa came as a complete surprise to him. "Honestly, I was very skeptical right from the beginning. The guy from the Interior Department had told me of your visit to his office way back asking to leave the country. But he still went ahead to process your visa. A day before your departure somebody higher up double checked everything, and the shit hit the fan." Until then I thought my Party mess was the reason for me not getting out to Leningrad. But that my stupid visit to the Interior Department made me a risk surprised me.

"Does your uncle know about your contact with the Interior Department? Whatever it is I won't tell him." Koenig gave me a soft slap on the shoulder. His eyes had this you-and-I-have-a-secret look. I have nothing against Koenig. He is the director and a friend of my uncle. That he has a little Napoleon complex because of his height does not faze me. When he is enraged he looks a little bit like Rumpelstilzchen. Kind of comical. He never ranted at me. He has no reason for it anyway.

My application for acceptance is not only at the proper department at the Karl-Marx University. A copy is also on the desk of a friend of my uncle at the Ministry for Education. She is kind of the supervisor for all the application departments of all the universities in the country. Funny enough, she was my seventh-grade biology teacher. She left in the middle of the school year. She and the school's principal were openly dating shortly after she got divorced. Her ex was my chemistry teacher. Somebody didn't like the whole situation and she had to leave. I didn't know that she was promoted to a job in the Education Ministry and, that my uncle knew her from their university time together. When my uncle introduced her to me at the museum Christmas party I immediately recognized her.

She did not remember me. She was very polite and promised to look favorably at my application. She seemed sincere. Somehow our little conversation made me very hopeful. In a couple of weeks I should know if I will start my studies this upcoming September.

I am in Koenig's office. His secretary had called me to come to see him. I am nervous not knowing what he wants from me. Mrs. Eberhardt is very nice. The perfect right hand to a boss. Her job is to put everybody at ease. Being called in by the boss can be disconcerting. She is distraction by default.

"How are you this morning? You see the rose over at the window?" I see a slightly shriveled long stem adorned with a bright yellow bud. "It's from your bouquet you gave me. Remember. Just this one never died. It almost looks still alive, doesn't it?"

Sure, I remember the morning I was handed a bucket full of roses by the porter, surprised and not knowing what to do with it. Indeed the stem in the crystal vase on the window sill without water looks pretty good. Something can survive on nothing. I should tell Klaus about the rose. The door flings open. Koenig bustles towards me, right hand stretched towards me. He puts his left arm around my waist. "Come on in Thomas. Sorry I couldn't get off the phone."

The door shuts behind us. His small frame is totally out of proportion with his ornate and humongous desk. I sit down opposite of him.

"Listen I have good news and bad news. I start with the latter." I feel pain shooting down from my left chest into my left arm. My fingertips tingle. I know. "All the spots at the University are taken for this year. But your application will be considered for next year. So the good news is, you don't have to apply again. You will be on the top of the list for next year."

Koenig hands me the letter. My eyes are out of focus. I only see the bold letter head: Karl-Marx University Leipzig. Everything else blurs into little tiny lines. Without even trying to read the denial I hand it back. Next year! It will be always next year! I look at Koenig but I am really looking through him. My surroundings vanish. My head is pounding. The pain brings me back into my chair across from Koenig. I see clearly.

"Sure, I had hoped for different answer. I really appreciate that you have sponsored my application. I am not denied because of the numbers of applicants. I am denied because of my former Party affiliation as I was denied a visa to Leningrad. I have to face the fact that I am blacklisted. There is no next year for me ever."

"Oh, I wouldn't say that. Everybody has a future. We need young people like you. We need everybody to build the future. I know it must be disappointing for you. I mean you can challenge the decision and maybe they will give it a second look. I will write you a supportive letter," he tries to reassure me.

"That is very nice of you. But I think there are only so many rejections I can take. I have reached the limit for now."

"I was also thinking if you want I definitely can get you in an undergraduate program at a college here in Leipzig. It takes three years and with that degree you will be able to start out in a smaller local museum. What do you think?" He is really trying to help me, I think. There are decent Party members after all.

"I am not sure if that is a career path I want to follow. I think I want to go back to Berlin. It was a great opportunity for me to work at your museum. But the deck of cards is stuck against me. I need to revaluate my life. Berlin seems the natural choice."

Koenig leans back and grabs a cigar. "I tell you what. Take as much time as you need. Go to Berlin and find a job. If you have one you can quit here. But it's not a good idea to leave the job here before you have another one."

"That is wonderful. I didn't expect that. But I will take you up on that offer. Thank you so much." I get up from the chair.

"I don't agree that you left the Party. You should have sought advice. But I also don't agree with what my comrades in Berlin do to you. That's why I want to show you that most of us are passionate and care about our young people. You are bright, smart and thoughtful. I know you will find your way. And I want to help you. Let me know how it goes." I look down into his eyes. My tears bubble up. Our hands lock longer than it would take normally to just to say goodbye. "Thanks!"

Fresh Fruits, Ceiling Mirrors, and a Long Way Home

I weigh my options. Who would hire me knowing my background? What should or could I do? I make a point not to consult my aunt and uncle. This is a chance to cut the umbilical cord. I saw my mother marry Heinz not because she wanted to. My aunt and uncle said to do it. I saw my mother's brother not to follow his dream to do whatever it was. Teaching was his vocation according to my aunt and uncle. I have never seen Paul happy. I have heard the story about my grandmother moving from West Germany to East Germany in 1960 so that my aunt and uncle could have a Communist career. She still regrets it. My aunt and uncle made me to go to librarian school. I was ashamed telling others. They almost had me reverse my decision to leave the Party not so much for my own good but more out of fear of backlashes in their lives. But I agreed to take a job in Leipzig. For the first time my aunt and uncle had miscalculated their own judgment and the strong arms of the Party aficionados. I believe they are surprised how unapologetic the Party hammer came and comes down on me.

But they also must see by now that their Communist affiliation, their friends in higher places and their honest conviction for Party and country, that all of that does not make them or their family members immune and untouchable. In their head they are East German hierarchy. In reality they are not much more than foot soldiers at the *Nomenklatura* service and mercy. They are part of the herd. Nothing more. I think that they should reevaluate their conviction for the Party and country now that one of their own relatives has been made an outcast.

As the self-declared head of our family my aunt and uncle never intended to do harm when they pressed each and every one of us to follow their beliefs. But their authority and aura was self-serving. They made my family into a mini East Germany: ruling with a strong hand and making decisions without considering individual hopes, dreams and aspirations other than their own. They have miscalculated their influence and wisdom. Their twenty-one-year-old nephew's future is in jeopardy because he did not turn into a mindless follower. Their Party comrades have shown them how little they are really worth.

My aunt and uncle have dedicated their lives to the Socialist future. They were rewarded with good jobs, a nice apartment and the illusion that some day they also will move behind the wall of the inner circle. But unwillingly I was the one to show them the mirror: you only gain acceptance when we grant it. You have lost because you couldn't keep your nephew from stepping out of line. You should not have allowed it. You lost control. And now you lost our confidence. The all-present power of the Party has put my aunt and uncle in their place. Bonus points no more. You have to start all over again. I feel sorry for myself and for my aunt and uncle. But I also will turn the page. I am determined that from now on I will not rely or even listen to my family. I have my own head. I am old enough not to achieve goals set by others. From now on I will travel on my own road.

Klaus and I get ready for the premier party. His dance group had his first performance of a new ballet. It had opened at the Volksbühne Theater at Rosa-Luxemburg-Platz. Kurt Klein adapted a God-awful story into a two-hour dance performance. Optimism and socialist rah-rah built the frame for a love quadruple surrounded by groups of happy soldiers, sailors and workers. Some of the dance solos were not bad. But Klein favored choreographic elements are just circles and diagonals. Very repetitive and boring. Some Party underling composer had written the music. Klein, under the tutelage of the head of East Germans youth organization FDJ Egon Krenz, has delivered in the past, did so this time and will do it forever. He is the willing choreographer to translate propaganda into socialist art. His newest work earned him a certificate to buy a Volvo sedan. The hefty price tags about 30,000 East German

Markss. An amount only few could pay like Klein and other parvenus.

Anyway, the choreography as well as the story of the ballet is forgettable. Nevertheless I watch with pride in my heart. Klaus is one of the soloists. I can't take my eyes off him as soon he enters the stage. He is the best looking guy of the troupe. I have to pinch myself to really assure me that he is my boyfriend. I don't think he is a very gracious dancer, but his sculpted body shows perfect dimensions. The hourglass torso sits atop manly hips and strong muscled legs. With ease he lifts his partner and carries her through their routine. I can see that dance is his passion. Once he told me that he would have loved to become a professional dancer. But he never dared to follow his dream because of his mother and stepfather. They regarded male dancers, like so many others, as not truly men. How fortunate for Klaus and all the others on stage, who for various reasons didn't pursue a professional dance career, to have found an outlet for their dreams. Only it's too bad that their passion and talent is being exploited by the ideology who think that these kind of propaganda pieces will rally people to the Party's cause.

When the final curtains falls the applause is friendly. Most everyone in the audience is somehow connected to the performers and the behind-the-scene workers. I doubt that even one ticket was bought by an ordinary citizen in sick need to sit to a flawed agit-prop ballet. We all came to see our friends, lovers, brothers, mothers, fathers, daughters or sons on stage. And most importantly to enjoy the after party.

Klaus and I are invited to Kurt Klein's private premier fête at his apartment. The place is crowded. I recognize dancers from the TV Ballet, the Metropol Theater and the Friedrichstadt-Palast revue theater. I am in awe that I am amongst them. I am speechless shy as always. Klaus on the other hand works the crowd. I drink champagne and eat sandwiches with salmon and tenderloin. Mountains of fresh fruit including oranges and bananas are placed on huge plates throughout the apartment. I start to wonder if Klein also has access to the special Government shops. Because this stuff does not come from the store I go to. I can't stop eating and drinking. I have never been to party like that. I feel special and increasingly drunk. And when I reach that stage my face gets all red down to my neck. I decide to take it easy on the Champagne. I need some water instead. That usually helps to get me back to my normal skin color. However, there is no water to be found. Soda, beer, hard liquor, wine and tons of Rotkäppchen Sekt is all what I can find. I have to try to walk my tipsiness off and wander around the place. I also haven't seen Klaus for a while.

Klein's apartment is filled with all of the desirable goods a normal East German wants but doesn't have: crystal vases and arrangements of all sorts of colored glassware. Ornamental and huge mirrors on the walls. Leather couches, an enormous dining table, a color TV. I feel like I am in one of the Intershop stores. In his bedroom is a huge canopy bed, mirrors on all four sides and on the ceiling. I look at his carpets. All handmade and huge. His bathroom is decked out in black marble. His sink and toilet are rose colored. This is definitely from the West as well. I pass another door only slightly open. But I hear voices from the inside. A guy I have seen on TV before passes me and goes straight into the room. I follow him. The light is dimmed. Again mirrors everywhere, in the middle a monstrous bed with naked guys kissing. The guy who had just passed me is undressing. I am kind of shocked and want to leave. But I am also intrigued. It's the first time that I have seen multiple guys naked. I realize that I am not the only one watching. My eyes adjust to the semi darkness and, now I can clearly see what these guys are doing: it's group sex.

I feel a sensation in my throat. Some lick asses, some fuck, and some suck dicks. One guy kneels on the edge of the bed and is masturbating. A hand stretches out to him and pulls his penis into his mouth. It's Klaus. He lies on top of a guy. Another guy is on top of Klaus. I inch closer. Klaus is getting fucked by two guys at the same time. It's almost as if I have an out-of-body experience. I have never seen such a thing. I never thought to this moment this is even possible that two guys can penetrate another one at the same time. It must hurt tremendously, I wonder. Maybe these two were forcing themselves into Klaus. Klaus doesn't want that. But then I see him sucking the third one's dick. His facial expression I have to come to know by now. Klaus is drunk. Judging by the groaning all three guys are coming at the same time into Klaus. They all pull out. Klaus rolls on his back. I see sperm coming out of his ass and mouth. I have to gag. I need to leave the room. I am sure Klaus has not seen me. My champagne-heavy head is suddenly clear. I slip out of the apartment. Unnoticed.

It's pitch dark outside. Not a single street light works. I am not sure where I exactly am and where to go. I have no sense of direction. This part of Lichtenberg district is totally unknown to me. I take the middle of the street. It feels safer that way. I pull my jacket up to cover my ears. My hands are deep inside of the pockets. I am scared. I want to get out of the maze of dark buildings and the echo of my steps. Then I hear a distant hello. I don't turn around. I don't know what to do. I shouldn't run. Isn't that what they always say? Pretend you know where you are going. Never panic. Otherwise you are fair game.

"Hey, wait. Don't be afraid. I just left the same party as you." I turn my head in the direction of the voice. As the guy comes closer I recognize him. Not from Klein's party. He is one of the soloists at TV Ballet. I stop. He catches up to me. "I am Roland. You must be Thomas, Klaus' lover." He offers his hand."

"Hi. How do you know my name?"

"Well I asked a friend if he knows who you are after I saw you alone wandering around Klein's apartment."

"Yes, I am Thomas."

"Where are you going? Can I walk with you for a little bit?"

"I am trying to figure out how to get home. If you can point me in the right direction would be great."

"Why did you leave the party alone?"

"I could ask you the same?"

"I am not a big party guy. But Klein had invited me. And you really don't reject his invitation. He has a lot of friends. As a dancer that's pretty important." Roland laughs.

"Klaus was busy. And I had enough." My lie sounds like

a lie.

"I know what you mean." Roland touches my shoulder and gives me a light squeeze. "Did he see Klaus on the bed? For some reason I feel embarrassed. We walk in silence. I notice the bright stars.

"I watched you all evening. You looked like a kid in a candy store. You were taking it all in. Watching people and all. But you also looked so serious."

"I got pretty tipsy very fast. I had too much champagne. You were watching me. Did I look that odd?"

"No, I was watching you because you are very handsome." *Why is he saying that*, I think? Is he making fun of me? Handsome. What is the guy up to? I look at him. But don't say anything. "Sorry, did I make you uncomfortable? I shouldn't have said that."

"No, that's okay. Sometimes to hear a lie feels good."

Roland steps in my way. "What do you mean by lie? I was attracted to you the moment you arrived at the apartment. You didn't notice me all evening. I was asking my friend how I could get your attention. He said, just talk to him. Several times I was very close, but then you looked so uptight." What is this guy saying? He is the more handsome of the two of us. He is a star and can have anyone he wants. And he is telling me he finds me attractive.

"I am sorry. I didn't see you at the party but certainly recognized you from the TV."

"Does that work for me or against me?"

I smile. "This is a little bit confusing."

"You can smile. Please keep smiling. It makes you even more handsome."

"Please stop that."

"Why? Do you want me to leave right now?"

"No, please not now. I still have no clue where I am."

"Oh, I am just a guide."

I laugh. "No, I didn't mean that. But I don't get compliments very often. You are great looking, famous. I am just Thomas. And I am not handsome. And I don't say that to fish for compliments."

"Can I give you a hug?"

"In the middle of the street?"

181

"Can you stop questioning me all the time?" His sweater touches my jacket. Roland is almost one head taller than me. I put my head on his chest. He puts his arms around me. It feels so good.

"Oh, man I needed that."

"Me too." We separate. "Are you and Klaus an item?"

"I guess so. But it is also a complicated story. Every time when I think we are close he does things that hurt me. I just moved back from Leipzig. We live together. Now I have to find a job. On and on." The tip of my nose starts to tickle. I feel tears building up. Roland takes my hand. His is bigger than mine and very soft. We keep walking.

"I am such a downer. I am sorry. Tell me a little bit about you."

"There is not much to tell. I am from the South. Always wanted to be a dancer and I was always teased about it. Even by my parents. But I kept wanting it. I got a spot at the Palucca Ballet School in Dresden. I was lucky. The TV Ballet hired me right after my graduation. That was two years ago."

I like him. He talks so naturally about being a pretty famous dancer. I like his demeanor. He is masculine. Sincere. We are still holding hands. "I have a partner, too. We are almost five years together. He is a TV producer. But our relationship is not going well. He wants me to be someone I am not. We live in the same building but not in same apartment. And that is good."

I don't know what to say. I feel the squeeze of his hand.

"How long have you been with Klaus?"

"We met six months ago. But shortly afterwards I moved to Leipzig. We talked on the phone a lot. On weekends I came to visit him. Two weeks ago I moved back." We reach the S-Bahn station. "Well, I guess it's time to say good night."

"Where are you going?"

"Prenzlauer Allee."

"Can we just keep walking a little bit longer? It's such a nice night. To be honest, I don't want to be alone."

I turn to Roland. He wants to walk with me. He doesn't want to be alone. So do I. "Sure, as long we don't get lost and

182

find the next S-Bahn station."

"Don't worry. I know my way around. I am so glad that you don't take the train yet." I feel the same. "Are you and Klaus happy?"

"He is my longest-term partner. No guy before was interested in a relationship with me. He is the first one."

"You didn't answer my question."

"I like him. He was there for me when I didn't know where to turn. This is also more than I ever got before. That is worth something isn't it?" I feel torn. I want to tell Roland everything. What I saw tonight and, all the other times before that. That I think Klaus is an alcoholic. That he is mean to me when he drinks. But somehow it doesn't seem right to tell a guy I just met my problems. So far, I have not told anybody about the up and downs in our relationship. Private things should stay that way. I am the one who has to deal with that. Outsiders should not get involved.

"If you don't want to talk about Klaus then don't. I just wonder if you are happy with him."

"It was really nice that you called out for me. I enjoyed this walk with you. Let's keep it that way. Tomorrow we will have our separate lives back. Sometimes the moment is all what counts. Let's make it count."

"You are so serious. How old are you?"

"Twenty-two. And you?"

"Twenty-five."

"Do you dream sometimes what and where you want to be in ten years?"

"All the time."

"Do you want to tell me?"

"I want my own family. I mean. Maybe a child. I want to travel. Sometime I even dream I want to be famous. Crazy, isn't it? I want to show my family that I am not a loser. But most of all I want a home for my heart."

"Do you believe that you will fulfill all your dreams or only some? Or do you think you never will reach any of them?"

"Yes to all three questions. But sometimes I just keep on dreaming until I get tired."

"You are so sweet. I am so glad that I followed you out of

the party."

"You followed me?" I giggle. "Yes, the moment I saw you I wanted to talk to you. I felt we have a lot in common. It looks like I am right." Roland takes both of my shoulder and pulls me towards him. He is shaking.

"Are you cold?" I ask.

"No, I am so nervous. I want to hug you and hold you. But I also think it's not right. You have Klaus and I have Ulli."

"Let's just hold hands. They couldn't scold us for that, couldn't they?" I don't know what makes me do that but I grab his hand and bring it up to my lips. Even his hand is shaking. "Life is not easy, isn't it?"

He presses me against his body. "No, it is not."

I feel his breath against my ear. "You know, I will remember this evening for the rest of my life. You calmed me down because I was so upset when I left Klein's party. Thanks Roland."

"Oh, Thomas. Why can't we be like all the others and seek forgetting in meaningless short hook-ups?"

"Because we are different, I guess. We are not looking for easy. We want the real thing. But we are also know that we have to work for that."

"I know. But honestly sometimes I wish I could be like most of the guys. But I can't. I don't want to be betrayed. So, why would I than want to betray."

"Same here." We continue to walk again. What we are saying we whisper even no one is around us. That way it makes it like our little secret for no other to hear.

On My Own

I have packed my things. It's the morning after the Klein party. Klaus has not come home yet. I decided to move back into my apartment. What happened last night was so over the top I can't even describe my torment and pain. He has humiliated me before. But getting it on so publicly fully knowing that I am in the next room means I don't know what else is in store for me. He has asked me to come back from Leipzig and live with him. He has said we will be happy together when we live together, seeing each other every day, waking up and going to sleep together. It sounded so honest and beautiful. It's only been two weeks that we've lived together. And he did it again. I really have to get away from him.

At first I thought I would leave a note explaining why I left. But after what happened last night he does not need an explanation for why I am leaving . I pull the door shut and put the keys under the doormat. The heavy suitcases hit me in the knees as I go down. How I schlep them to my place, I am not sure. I have no money for a taxi. I start to sweat. I have to pause. I hear somebody coming up the stairs. I hope it's not Klaus. I don't want to see him. Not yet, not now. But I recognize his steps. He always takes two stairs at a time.

"Where are you going?" His face looks shocked and surprised.

"I am going back to my place. Please let me pass."

Klaus has blocked my way. "Is it because of last night? It doesn't mean anything. It just happened. Come on." He is going to grab one of my suitcases.

"Yes, it's because of last night. I saw you and what you did. It was awful. How can you do this to me? You promised me we will be happy together. Is this what you mean by happiness? And it's ten in the morning and you are just coming home. Where were you? Klaus please let me go."

"I promise it will never happen again. I will not touch another man as long as I live and we are a couple. Please believe me. I love you, you know that. Do you?"

"No, I don't know that. I have to be alone, Klaus. I can't deal with that. I have to focus to find a new job. Last night was so upsetting for me. I still can't believe it actually happened."

"I am sorry. Believe me. I am so sorry. Please don't go. I need you. And you need me. Please."

"I think it's better I stay at my place. I have to go." Klaus moves out off my way. He slams into the wall. He crouches down. His hands cover his face. "Please don't leave me. You are my life." He is sobbing. My legs are shaking as I make it further down the stairs. I still can hear him crying from the courtyard. I go as fast as I can. I don't want hear him anymore. My heavy suitcases make me stumble. My ear drums are pounding. I want this over with. Everything. I don't want to go on. I wish for the end. I don't feel my suitcases. Everything merges into weightless pain. Passing people are just body outlines. Meaningless like the rest of my surroundings. Cars, buses, streets, shops: it all is reduced to shadows. And I walk and walk. Only Klaus' crying stays real. Please stop. Leave my head. Go away.

"I can offer you a job in our archive," the head of the HR leans back in its chair. "I appreciate your frankness and that you told me right away about your past membership in the Socialist Unity Party. It really doesn't matter to me. As long you are honest and a good worker. That is all what I care about." My heart is jumping. I have a job.

"Yes, I would like to work here. When can I start?"

"On the first of next month. We can do the paperwork right away. After that I see you in a week."

It seems like I am flying. I did it. I found I job, and without the help or the input of my family. My aunt and uncle had given me such a hard time when I told them I would move back to Berlin immediately. They painted a dark picture. In it, me looking for a job without success. Unemployed I would meet the wrong people etc. etc. They made my mother call me to convince me to stay in Leipzig. Everything would work out just fine as long as I would stay put. But I already had lost almost a year in hope to break with my past to start a future. I started to realize that I never can and will erase what happen. It's part of my biography forever. The Party apprenticeship was a mistake. But it would be also a mistake to think I could clean my slate.

The job in the archive of the newspaper *Der Morgen* is a foot in the door to the news desk. I toyed on and off with the idea of writing for living. So far I only filled diaries. However I always enjoyed turning thoughts, observations and reflections materialistic by putting them on paper. Even the HR guy encouraged me. The word future is written on the horizon — again.

Fig Leaf: Multi-Party System

After the war the Soviet occupants and their German Communist underlings implemented a multi-party system for the future German Democratic Republic. A scheme intended to show the West the proletarian revolution is democratic, civil and inclusive. The Socialist Unity Party of Germany as the major power broker was founded. Former Social Democrats and Communists had to give up their original roots as well as their ideology and were pressed into the newly cooked-up SED. If they had survived Nazi concentration camps, underground living and Stalin's gulags, that is. Because thousands of the German Left who sought refuge in the Soviet Union after Hitler came to power were rounded up by the KGB. Many mothers and fathers were separated from their children and either shot right away or shipped off to the Far East's un-survivable working camps. Their offspring ended up in Soviet orphanages or in the iron fists of true believers. Stalin only saved those German compatriots, who he considered as fit to be his enforcers when the time would be ripe to spread his empire eastwards.

The slightest critique of the proletarian Gods Marx, Engels, Lenin and himself was countered with the ultimate punishment. But the new power elite in East Germany were fully aware that they had to deal also with their fellow citizens who were not Communists, social democrats or Nazis. All segments of the population had to be controlled. However, creating the "Big Brother Society" had to be more settled. Replacing the just destroyed Third Reich's totalitarian system with a proletarian totalitarian system right away would have been too obvious. Four additional political parties were created: The German Farmers Party for landowners. The National Democratic Party for mostly former military personal, The Christian Democratic Union for the religious establishment and the Liberal Democratic Party for mostly business owners. The new parties, also

188

called Bloc Party's were granted independence. But it became very clear almost from the beginning their sovereignty was never worth the paper it was proclaimed on. They became known as Bloc Floeten, Bloc Flutes, mocking their leaders as just playing to the tune of the SED.

The four parties are tightly controlled by the Socialist Unity Party which itself has to report to Moscow. Democracy ad absurdum. A quota system was put in place where the major and most important positions in politic, economic and art had to be filled with "SED" members and it's deputy by members of the other four parties. The leaders of the Bloc party's were at the same time also deputies of the head of the State. Everybody knows it's a farce, but it's a farce one cannot call by its true nature without serious consequences.

Sure, the Bloc parties have wiggle room but not by its own doing. The wiggle room of course is given. An allowance in return for compliance. I got the job in the archive of *Der Morgen* because of that wiggle room that the Liberal Democratic Party has. I am happy. An interesting footnote is that my mother once worked for the book publishing arm of the LDPD.

Syphilis

As I come up the stairs I can see two bouquets of flowers in front of my apartment doors. Without checking the card attached to one I know who sent them to me. Beautiful yellow tea roses. Klaus' favorite flower. The other one is a colorful bouquet of wildflowers. I open the note stuck to the wrapping paper. "Hello, I can't stop thinking about you. I hope things with you and Klaus are working out. If you want to talk, call me. Roland!" I am surprised. I never expected to hear from him again. We had walked all the way to my apartment after Klein's party. It must have taken us almost three hours. But time was not part of us that night. He kissed me and walked away. It was that simple, clean and nice.

I open the card Klaus had left with the roses: "My angel, please forgive me. I am so sorry that you feel hurt. Nothing matters to me except you. Don't ever forget this. Come back to me. I love you, Klaus." Two bouquets from two different men. But I don't feel good about it.

I arrange the flowers, first in two separate vases. Then I decide to combine them in one. It's so colorful. The dark blue, the intense red, the bright yellow and light green buds almost glow in the dark of my living room. I just sit there and stare at the flowers. The knock at the door interrupts the quiet.

I open the door. Klaus pulls me into his arms and starts kissing me all over. I am still not back from the mindless wandering of my thoughts. His touches don't feel good. "I am so glad you are home. I miss you so much. I can't sleep without you. I called in sick for the last couple of days. Don't do this to me. Please, please." I don't move at all. I keep my arms close to my body. Images of Klaus with the guys in Klein's bed flash by. Klaus tries to find my lips with his. I turn my head every time he is close. This is so unpleasant.

"Klaus, please stop. Let go of me, please." I wish he would leave. I step back into my hallway and try to close the door

190

on him. He is stronger. He pushes my shoulders against the wall, closes the door with his foot and slides down on his knees. His hands still against my chest he opens my pants with his mouth, pulls my underwear down and takes me in.

I am limp. I don't want this. He loosens his grip. One arm slides through my legs up my back. He still keeps me in his mouth. Slowly, I get hard. He stops. "I know you want me. We belong together." I shake my head. I don't know why this happens to me. I have a boner but I don't feel any pleasure. I try to think myself away from here and now. But I can't concentrate. Klaus goes in and out of me. I am close. But somehow my body is cut in half. What happens down below is not connected with the rest of me. When I come in his mouth I don't feel any sensation. Tears run down my face.

I am glad that I have a routine again. My new job is very repetitive. The head of the archive clips articles of all the major news papers. I have to file them according to subject. All the articles of our newspaper *Der Morgen* also get archived, divided by subject as well as by author. There is another co-worker. She will leave shortly for Angola. Her engineer husband is assigned to build a water purifying plant over there. I am her replacement. Everybody is very nice to me and encourages me to explore the archive and read as much as I have time for it. More and more I think I should start to write myself.

I moved back in with Klaus. Things are going all right so far except that he drinks a lot. He finally convinced me to join his dance troupe. I have to admit I enjoying that. I am very clumsy during the training. But everybody is very helpful. That I am not the only untalented in the troupe helps me not to be too discouraged. I never have met so many people at the same time who bound together by a passion: dancing. Currently, we work on a repertoire for the Annual Workers Festival in Suhl, a small town in the South. A town mostly known for the manufactured firearms exported to the West for hard currency.

When I can, I meet my mother for lunch during the week. My family has not only accepted the fact that I am gay. They know that I live with Klaus. Living with a guy, who they have not met yet. All in all my life is as normal as it gets and I like it.

The only thing that bothers me a little is that I am in pain when I have to use the bathroom. The same when I bend down to grab things off of the floor. Some sitting positions are very uncomfortable, too. It hurts a lot when Klaus goes inside of me. But I have not told him about it. I feel a little ashamed. I hope the pain will ease up over time. Klaus never seems to have a problem when I fuck him. Anyway, once I look in a mirror to see if there is anything at the outside. Nothing that seems wrong. I now avoid cheese and bread and eat more oatmeal and a lot of yogurt. I use a lot of cream after my morning shower. I suspect I have hemorrhoids.

"We have to talk." Klaus greets me at the door. He looks very serious.

"What happened?"

"I think I have syphilis. I am not sure if I gave it to you already. But why don't you take some antibiotics a friend gave me a while ago. Just as a precaution." He hands me a little white pill.

"How do you know you have it?"

"My lymph nodes are swollen."

"And that means you have syphilis?" I've heard about syphilis. In school we learned that for instance the writer Heinrich Heine had it. I have read that soldiers and prostitutes got it. But this is such a distant world for me. Syphilis happens to others not me. And now I may have it. I take a sip of water and swallow the pill.

"Are you going to the doctor?"

"Yes, tomorrow. It's not a big deal. A hundred years ago people died from it. Now they give you penicillin and you are fine." Nothing is a big deal for Klaus. Nothing fazes him. Please God, don't let me have syphilis. I am not one of those people.

"Where did you get it from? How long does it take to develop?"

"I don't know. I think it takes a long time. What does it matter? Tomorrow I will know more." I can hear in his voice he is getting annoyed with me. I don't want to argue with him.

"Do you want me to go with you tomorrow?"

"Are you stupid? I am not a baby. I will go alone and will let you know. I don't want to talk about it anymore." Klaus clicks on the TV.

"Hi, it's me. You have to take the other pills. I think there are three left. Take them all at once." I am alone in the archive today. My boss is in a meeting, my co-worker at the doctor to get her shots for the Angola trip. When the phone rang I didn't expect it would be Klaus. "I have to go to the hospital. I didn't tell the doctor that we are together. So keep it that way as well. I think you will be fine."

"Why do you have to go to the hospital?"

"Well, I have it. To be treated you have to be isolated for a couple of weeks."

"You have to be what?"

"It's an infectious disease. They don't want you to spread it. They give you penicillin every day and run tests."

I still don't understand what he was telling me. "You have to stay overnight?"

"Yes, they say I have to be here for up to four weeks, depending on my progress."

"Four weeks? Which hospital are you going?"

"There are only two who treat it. The Charite and Clinic Buch. They send me to Buch district. I have to be there by three this afternoon. I will call you. Don't forget to take the pills." He hangs up.

Four weeks. Syphilis must be still pretty serious when they put him into the hospital for such a long time. What would I do if I got it? I can't tell anybody. How can I? He said that a sure sign of syphilis are swollen lymph nodes. I go in the bathroom and check myself. I don't know where exactly I should touch myself. I check my groin area. I can't feel anything. Under my arms. Nothing. I am relieved. I will take the rest of the pills tonight.

Its two days later and I have not heard from Klaus. I wonder if I should call the hospital. But he said he would let me know. The suspense is killing me. Every other minute I check my groin. So far nothing. Maybe I should go to the

193

doctor to get checked. I have read that syphilis can get undetected for a long time. I probably don't have it but still. I don't know anybody I could ask or talk about this. But I know also I have to ease my mind. I have to know.

The woman at the reception is very kind. She doesn't ask me why I want to see a doctor. Everybody here is here for the same reason. The clinic at the Christburger Strasse specializes in STDs. I get a number. 21. My age. I look around the waiting room. Some of the men I recognize having seen at Burgfrieden bar or just by passing on the street. Everybody pretends not to notice the others. Including me. My number comes up. The doctor is in his thirties and good looking.

"I don't think I have syphilis but I would like to get checked."

"Why do you want to get checked?"

"Well, I am gay."

"That's not a reason alone to get tested. How many sex partners do you have?"

"One."

"Are you faithful?"

"Yes."

"Is he faithful?"

"I am not sure. We had problems in the past."

"What's his name?"

"I don't want answer that."

"You have to. It's the law. If you don't tell me I can get you arrested." Is he bluffing? "Syphilis is a very serious infection that can be very easily transmitted. It's a danger to the public health of our citizens. So, give me the names of all your sex partners you had in the last four weeks."

I look at him. "I told you I have only one partner."

"Do you have sex?"

"Yes."

"How often?"

"Three, four times a week."

"Do you have anal sex. Are you the receiver?"

"Yes. And we flip." I am so embarrassed to answer his questions.

"Do you invite other men to join in?"

194

"No."

"What is your partner's name?"

I am tearing up. "Please don't make me to tell you."

"Why are you afraid? You are not honest with me. Did you have sex with other men? Are you now afraid that you got syphilis and might have infected your partner?"

"No, no. I didn't have any other partners. I only have sex with him. We've been together for almost one year."

"So, why are you here then?"

"He has syphilis. He's been hospitalized in Buch district for almost a week. I checked myself. But my lymph nodes are not swollen, I think. I want to know."

"When your partner went to the doctor he didn't tell him about you?"

"No, he said that no one should know that we are together. He wanted to protect me."

"Protect you from what? I think your partner is not straight with you. Give me his name." I tell him. I feel like betraying Klaus. "Again, you had no other sex encounters except with him?"

"Yes."

"I will believe you. I will examine you now. And we will draw blood. Here is a form for you to sign that states that you had only one partner in the past year. It also states that you are prohibited to have sex with anyone. If you break that you will be arrested. Is that clear?"

"Yes."

"I will see you here tomorrow afternoon to discuss the test results. If you don't come we will come to get you. This is serious stuff. I want you to understand that."

"I will be here tomorrow. I promise."

I return the following day. "Your tests came back negative. That's good. But it doesn't mean anything. In some cases it takes a while to show symptoms. Have you noticed any changes on you? Have you taken any medicine recently?" The doctor looks me straight in the eyes. I know I can't lie about the pills Klaus gave me. I tell him. "What pills are these? Do still have some of them?"

"A friend from West Berlin had given it to him. I didn't look at the bottle."

"You just took pills you don't know what they are?"

"I trust my partner. I also was so in shock when he told me he might have syphilis. So, I took one. When he called me that he has to be hospitalized he said I should take the rest as precaution."

"Is he a doctor?"

"No."

"You should have told me about it yesterday. Anything else you forgot to tell me?" I think about my hemorrhoids. It has probably nothing to do with it. Or? I describe the pain I feel when I go to the bathroom or bend down. "I think I have hemorrhoids."

The doctor takes notes. "I have to look at it. Undress." He spreads me." I will do a rectal examination. Tell me if and when it hurts." It hurts. He says, "I can feel a lump." He twists his finger. I wince. "Since you are gay and belong to the high-risk group that spreads genital diseases I have to commit you to the hospital for more tests and observation. Who can you call to bring you some personal items to the hospital?"

"No one."

"What about your family or other friends?"

"You can't imagine how horrible this all is for me. I feel like watching a movie. But this is so real. I have to deal with this alone. I can't get my family or any of my friends involved in this. Please." He doesn't respond, instead he opens a drawer in his desk. "Here is a toothbrush and some toothpaste. Take it."

"Can't I go home to get my stuff?"

"Don't push it young man. You will go from here directly to the hospital. End of discussion."

"Which hospital?"

"Buch district."

"Is there any way to get me into the Charite?"

"Don't you want to be in the same hospital as your partner?"

"No. This is so horrendous for me. I need the distance and anonymity."

"You are strange."

"You are not the first to tell me that." He shreds the

admission form, fills another one out. "Here. I will call the Charite in thirty minutes. Make sure you have already checked in by then. Otherwise...you know."

"Thanks, doctor."

"If you want my advice: in the future use condoms. Leave your partner. He is no good."

I have syphilis. The pills from the West just had delayed my infection. Four weeks of daily penicillin injections. Daily, groups of doctors and residents look at my asshole. The first two weeks of those in total isolation in a one-bed hospital room with no contact to any other patients. Successfully lying to my mother that I am on a month-long vacation at the Baltic Sea. Convincing my employer that I have a skin condition and can't be around anyone out of risk to infect somebody else. Four weeks of deception. I made it. My "disappearance" is over. I am discharged. Cured. With only one blemish on my medical record. I never can donate blood. Klaus and I have not seen each other for almost five weeks. Only kept in touch by phone. He was released a couple days before me. I wonder now if we can pick up where we left things before we were submitted to the treatment. To this day he never told me how and where he contracted syphilis. And I really didn't push for an answer. Living through the hospitalization was bad enough.

Realizing that my mother and the rest believed that I was on vacation at the Baltic Sea without wondering why I never send a postcard felt like a double edged sword. On the one hand they had no clue what the real reason was for me to be gone for so long, but on the other it also was so easy for me to convince them that I went off to some place and they didn't ask any more question. My boss totally believed my story as well. People are so easily fooled. Or, is it more the fact that I am not missed by any one close to me?

I feel trapped. Klaus and I live together. We never talk about our experience in the hospital. We just slipped back into our routine: work. Weekend parties. Klaus' infidelities. His daily alcohol consumption. Weekly training sessions with the dance group. Our sex is frequent without emotional satisfaction. I hope someday I can become the right partner for Klaus and we will be happy. Of course there are moments I feel good in our relationship. And the memories of those tender moments carry me through the other times when things are really bad. There is not one week where Klaus stays away for at least a night. I always worry about his safety. He has stopped apologizing for his one-night stands. I have stopped hoping that he ever will change.

Something else is happening that I am very ashamed of. Whenever I feel lonesome I also frequent public toilets and other well-known cruising places in the city: Oranienburger Strasse, Monbijou Park, Friedrichshain Park, Berliner Stadtbibliothek library. However, I am failure there too. Hardly anyone wants me in the dark or the anonymity of a latrine. Klaus must be right. In one of his rampages after he had too much alcohol he told me I should consider myself as very lucky that he choose me as his boyfriend.

"Look at you and me. Come to the mirror. Look at us. You are ugly. Others make fun of me and wonder why I am with you? So let me do what I want. I need other men. You are not enough for me. Stop being so jealous."

I feel guilty every time I go out to cruise. Because I don't want be like Klaus. Because I want to prove to him that I can be faithful. I am so conflicted about the ideal and the reality. Just by going out with the intent for instant sex puts me where Klaus is, doesn't it? How can I judge him? Isn't living by example the best way to show you can be gay and not promiscuous? I want so much to prove it to myself, to Klaus and to anybody who cares. He says that no matter what he always will come back to me. That is something, isn't it? At least it seems more than what I see in my own family. I don't think that my parents or my aunt and uncle cheat on each other. But I believe if they would have the courage they have gotten a divorce a long time ago. Instead they come home to each other every day because they have to and it is expected. Klaus comes back to me because he wants to. Isn't that how Klaus and I differ from my family? If the answer is yes, than I have to make myself believe that one day Klaus and I will faithful to each other.

First Headline, Another Party Membership, and the Permit to Study

My first article is published. It's about a guy who loves everything circus related. He lives in a dingy apartment on Linien Strasse filled with boxes and boxes of circus memorabilia going back almost a hundred years. Historians seek his advice and archives. He wanted to be a trapeze artist but never made into the circus tent. I had found a little snippet about him in the archive of *Der Morgen* written over twenty years ago. It intrigued me enough to search for him, to see if he is still alive. He was. I talked to the editor of our local desk. He gave me the go ahead.

I am so tickled. I have a byline, my first. Not counting an article I wrote years ago for a library magazine about my work as a librarian and youth organizer at Humboldt University. Anyway, I am very encouraged. The local editor told me to come up with more suggestions for articles. The deputy chief editor of the paper also tells me I have a real chance to be transferred from the archive to the local desk. The paper might even sponsor me for a spot at the Department for Journalism at the University in Leipzig.

If I can follow through I will be part of a privileged profession with social standing and perks. My press card will give me access to otherwise closed doors like the artist club Die Moewe or free tickets to sought-after theatrical or musical performances. To go under the umbrella of the Liberal Democratic Party was a wise move. My checkered past will be just that. My family will see finally I am not a loser. My future friends will respect me because I am a journalist. Just three month after I started my work at the archive I have a realistic chance for a serious professional future.

"You better go to the doctor. I have syphilis again." I can't believe what Klaus just told me over the phone. I am not even four months out of the hospital I have to go through to another nightmare medical treatment? Without saying a word I put down the phone.

"What's wrong?" My boss asks, "You look like you got terrible news."

"Oh, it's nothing. I have a little bit of a stomachache. I haven't eaten all day. That's probably the reason," I lie. I run off to the bathroom and let myself fall onto the toilet. This is impossible. How can he get that again? I pull my pants down and examine my crotch area. I can't feel any swollen lymph nodes. But that doesn't mean anything, does it? I can't go through this again. The lies, the questioning by social workers, the threats to be locked away for another four weeks, the daily doses of penicillin. The excruciating swab tests down my dick. What should I do? How can Klaus do this to me again? Maybe I should end my life? That would end it all, wouldn't it? No more pain, no more infections, no more fights with Klaus, no more defending our home against all the sex-hungry men, no more worries where Klaus is the nights he doesn't come home. The struggle for normalcy would be over. I feel so sorry for myself. I crouch over onto my knees. Why me? Why me all the time? What did I wrong to deserve that much pain?

"Are you all right?" I hear the voice of my boss. She knocks at the door. "Do you need anything? Should I call the company nurse?"

"I think I am fine. I will be out in a minute." I need all the energy that's left to speak. I get up from the toilet. Button my pants and open the door. "Do you think I can go home? Just lying down and rest will help, I think"

"Of course. Do you want me to come with you?" She is always very nice to me. My boss is in her early fifties, was never married, has no children but a boyfriend. From day one she took a liking to me. Brings me food, asks about my wellbeing. I think I am kind of a son to her she never had. Sometimes I wish my mother would be so caring. "Thanks. I grab my bag and leave. The fresh air outside helps me to breathe normal again. I decide to go straight to the Charity hospital. I want to know, now.

The nurse at reception gives me a number. It's such a farce. Everybody in the waiting room is here because of the same reason: STD. But instead of getting called by your name your number will be announced. After a three-hour wait I sit across from the social worker. She looks at my file.

"You just had had syphilis. Now again. What is wrong with you? This is criminal. The treatment is so expensive. Do you think the government of the GDR has bottomless funds to take care of you? If you would be living in BRD the health system would not pay for your treatment. If you don't have the money you would just die. I really think this time you should be paying."

I feel so ashamed. "I am so sorry. It is not my fault, you have to believe me."

"I stopped a while ago to believe your types. Not your fault. Is it the fault of the government or my fault that you have another case of syphilis? Tell me."

"I don't know if I am even infected. My partner called me. He has it again. I got it from him the first time. I am not sleeping around."

"Did you have any anonymous encounters since you were cured?"

"Only a couple of times. But it was not really sex."

"Only a couple of times? What do you mean by it was not really sex? If you had your pants down and rubbed each other that alone is enough to get infected or infect somebody else, do you understand?"

"I only did hand jobs," I whisper.

"What? Speak up young man. Or are you the girl? I see on your card that your anus was infected." I see a smirk on her face. "Did you have anal sex? I need names. If you don't give them to me I can get you arrested. But you know that already since you've become a regular."

"I only had anal sex with my partner."

"Well, you obviously were not safe. The last time we followed your wish to be treated in the Charite, one of the best hospitals in the world. Not this time. I will admit you to Buch hospital." She starts to fill out paper work.

"Shouldn't I be tested before?"

"Your friend has it. You have it. It's that simple."

"Can you please take a blood test?"

"No, the results would not be back before tomorrow afternoon. You are a high risk for the public health. I will admit you today." I don't see the logic in this.

"Please take a blood sample now. I can assure you that I won't have any sex. Even if you don't believe me but this here is very traumatic for me. Being maybe infected for a second time in a very short period is just too much to bear for me. If you can't take my word maybe I can stay here overnight until the result comes back?" She looks at me. For the first time I can see a hint of sympathy in her face.

"We don't have beds available for short stays."

"I know you have a hard time trusting me. I am sure you hear a lot of stories. Some of which are probably not true. But I am different. I grew up in an environment where alcohol use and sexually transmitted diseases were total foreign things and only would happen to others. But please take my blood and I will be back tomorrow to get the results." We look at each other.

She pulls out another form. "Please sign this. It states that you won't have any sex until the results are in. I will see you tomorrow afternoon."

My test results came back negative. But as precaution I have to go to the Charite once a week to be tested. The first time my test came back negative. But I only had delayed the infection by taking the pills Klaus gave me. I understand that they want to make sure that I don't have a delayed reaction again. Anyway, taking blood is certainly not the worst thing that can happen to me. But every time the nurse tightens the rubber band around my arm and taps with her finger on my very weak vein I am on the verge of passing out. I hate the moment when the needle stings me. I always have to turn my head away or close my eyes. But the most painful procedure is when she pushes a small metal stick with a loop on the top through the opening of my penis to take a swab sample. No painkiller or relaxant. The instrument looks way too big for what it's made for. I feel like the inside of my penis is a raw wound. Sometime I don't want to pee just because of the anticipated pain.

Anyway I dodged a bullet. Klaus has not given me

syphilis. He has it and is back at Buch hospital. I moved out of his apartment the day he called me. He begged and cried so I would stay and wait for him until his treatment is over. I told him, no way. Living alone feels like a huge relief. I don't have to worry if and when he comes home. I don't have to worry how much he is drinking. I don't have to worry being infected by him again. I also don't attend any more dance rehearsals. Anything to do with Klaus I don't want to be part of anymore. I met Klaus a year ago. What a nightmare year that was. It's over. I am out.

Also the fact that things at work are really going well for me help me let go of Klaus. I am part of the local desk at the news paper, and I did send in my application to study journalism at Karl-Marx University. My superiors at *Der Morgen* sponsored me as promised. Of course, there was a price to pay. The editor-in-chief asked me to join the Liberal Democratic Party of Germany. In a way I was prepared. *Der Morgen* is the official paper of the LDPD. It is expected that you wear their button when you work there. In deference to the SED I didn't need any sponsors to become a member. They also don't require a litmus test to the Gods of the proletariat. It seems that joining the LDPD is a win-win situation for me. Wherever my career would lead me from now on my Party apprenticeship is painted over by my new party affiliation. If there is a downside to this then it is the fact that I never can be the top dog in any professional position. That goes to a SED member. But aiming eventually for a deputy role won't be that bad either.

Back when I worked at the library of Humboldt University the director for instance was a SED-Member, one of the deputy directors was a member of the National Democratic Party of Germany (NDPD) and the personal assistant to the director belonged to the Christian Democratic Party of Germany (CDU). This model is applied to any company or institution in the GDR. Fake. Sure. Illusionist. Of course. So is the whole political system in East Germany. A fig leaf that covers the true nature of the dictatorship of proletariat. The multi-party scheme is certainly unique amongst all the Eastern Bloc countries. The heirs to Marx, Engels and Lenin and for a time to Stalin had to take into account that Germany had a history of real and functioning democracy. Other than in the Soviet Union for instance, where the brutal Czar was replaced by a brutal Bolshevik leadership its citizen never experienced freedom and political choices. Creating East Germany's society after the war had to be an adaptation of the Communist gospel that would last only for a limited time and functioning as a stage in the process of the glorious ascent of Communism.

The ultimate goal of course is to eliminate any power sharing with any one that is not part of the vanguard of the proletariat. But the creation of a semi multi-party system and fake parliament can also sooth political anxiety and opposition within the society. It gives an excuse to those who are very critical but don't have the courage to openly act for change. They can stay quiet and calm themselves by believing that the fig leaf is not a cover up of the real intent by the power elite after all. Sometimes a lie can conveniently be morphed into a truth. Even if that just is a brain exercise, bar any realty. Why else are some within the East German art elite so content like the novelists Stefan Hermlin, Christa Wolf and Heiner Mueller, or the painters Walter Womacka and Bernhard Heisig or composers Udo Zimerman and Siegfried Matthus?

"Congratulations. You have been accepted into the journalism faculty of the Karl-Marx University." The editor-in-chief Fischer hands me the letter. I am numb with joy. I take the paper and look at the official letterhead of the University of Leipzig. It's been almost two years since my professional life was parked on a dead end road. The ups and downs since then flash by as I read the admission letter over and over again. Doubted by colleagues and friends. Criticized by a family that feared more for their own careers and livelihood than mine. My ill-fated move to Leipzig to erase part of my past. The last-minute cancellation of the work-related trip to Leningrad. The rejection of my application to study ethnography. And last but not least my insane relationship with Klaus. With the admission letter now in my hands all that seems to have happened an eternity ago.

The good news to be allowed to study journalism is only slightly tainted by the fact that I am not admitted as a direct student. It means that I will keep on working except for one week per month when I will attend courses and seminars at the university. But a degree in journalism is a degree in journalism no matter how it is achieved. Sure, I kind of hoped to live and enjoy a full-time student life. But I also have to be realistic. I could not make a living on the 250 Marks a month of student tuition.

Back Together with Klaus, Again!

I can see something white sticking at my front door as I come up the stairs. It's an envelope. "To my angel!"

The writing is familiar to me. A note from Klaus. It seems ages ago that I have heard, seen or spoken to him. Sometimes I still miss him. But most of the time I am glad I don't have the agony, stress and pain anymore. For some reason I am not eager to open the envelope. I throw it on the kitchen table. "Later." I think.

I am hungry now. I open the fridge knowing there is nothing except a piece of butter way beyond the expiration date. I don't have any money to buy food. About half of my paycheck I have spent on a pair of pants. Blue and gray striped. I couldn't pass them, even the price of 160 Marks was way more I should ever spend on one piece of clothing. Anyway, I felt very sexy looking in the mirror in the dressing room of the Men's Exquisite Shop on Unter den Linden boulevard. I even had an ass in them. Good fit. Tight. So different from what you would get in the department store at Alexanderplatz. It took me a split second to decide for or against the purchase. My vanity succeeded. Walking out of the store with a shopping bag clearly stating where I just had bought something I felt I was on cloud nine and imagined that every passerby looked at me and thought: "Aw, that young guy can afford the Exquisite Laden." That alone felt almost as satisfying as the striped pants in the bag. That I had spent my entire grocery money for the next month was not relevant at this point. Because there is always my grandmother.

"How are you? I miss you so much. I can't even describe how much. It's almost year that we spoke last. But I have seen you since then many times. You never seemed to notice me. It's either from across the street or right next to the entrance to your building. Remember the bush behind the brick wall? We once made out there. It's a good place to hide, to see and not to be seen. I love you. There is nothing more for me than winning you back. It will be different this time. I promise you. Please take me back. I feel lost without you. I can't sleep or eat. I need you. Can I pick you up from work tomorrow? Please! You will not regret it. I have changed! We will make this time. Have a little bit of faith. Everything else I will take care of. I love you so much. K."

I crumple the letter in my hand. I lean back on the couch. My eyes follow the outlines of my armchair, red upholstery with black leather sides. The coffee table. Fake oak top on stainless steel legs. The gray carpet. My mother's. The inexpensive shelves, white and oak veneer. It covers most of the lower part of one wall. My white-colored portable television set with the antenna directed towards the window. The screen is always blurred and snowy looking, not matter how I turn the antenna. The built-in radio works much better. The attached cassette deck shreds my tapes. My window treatment is a too-short curtain with a beige-colored parsley pattern. It's from my Grandmother. The huge wardrobe on the other side of the window is real pine but stained to look like oak. I covered the middle door with the same fabric as my curtain. The walls are bare. I know I should be thankful that I have my own place. But somehow I have lost motivation to finish decorating my apartment.

I know I have more than others. How many would love to have their own four walls and call it home? I like to be on my own, but that does not supplement for loneliness. I want to be loved. I want to share a comfy and inviting home with somebody special.

I still have Klaus' letter in my hand. What I just read gives my stomach that pleasurable pain. I have not been with anybody seriously this past year. An anonymous hand job in the dark, a blowjob in an unlit entryway. Some older guy fucked me in a public bathroom. Nothing meaningful. Just a second or two of comfort. I close my eyes to remember the sex I had with Klaus. Sometimes it was really good. It made up for the other times. Waking up in the morning to the scent of scrambled eggs and fresh coffee gave me warmth, protection and content. All that did not happened this past year. Maybe Klaus has changed! Maybe I should give it another try? Maybe there is comfort in knowing what to expect? Maybe Klaus and I have a bond second to none? What I encountered this past year was an eerie repeat of what I had before I met Klaus. Dirty sex in dirty places. Maybe I am ready to face the challenge of the familiar?

Klaus and I are together again. We decided to remodel my apartment to live there. It has more space, and we have indoor plumbing. Klaus is extremely handy and creative when it comes to which wall to remove, where to find enough room to install a shower and connect a washing machine. He even created a loft-style sleeping area in the living room. All the building material we need for the remodeling Klaus gets from the Staatsoper. Of course it is officially *verboten* "to redistribute people's property for private use" but no one really cares because everybody does it. Klaus even could convince the head of the costume department of the opera to cut us some red velvet fabric for curtains and matching table cloth. The management company of my building did finally approve a kitchen stove. I am now on the waiting list to receive a certain contingent of natural gas per month to heat my apartment. The insufficient coal stove in the living room is beyond repair.

If we are not working on the apartment we are re-doing a car. It was Klaus' surprise for me when we got together again. He had purchased a half-totaled Trabant car from a colleague, who had driven the car into a tree. The damage was so bad that he was eligible for a brand-new car. He sold the car wreck to Klaus for 3000 Marks. A steal. Damaged cars are almost as valuable as new ones. Since Klaus can get all the needed metal parts from the blacksmith shop at the opera we only have to hunt for two car doors, front seats, tires and a car battery. Klaus knows a lot of people who know a lot of people who know where to get things. This is how we learned that a car part shop in Mahlsdorf at the outskirts of Berlin is expecting a delivery of batteries. Klaus and I left at four in the morning on the day of the anticipated delivery. He wanted to be the first in line. Our chances to get a new battery were also increased by the fact that we had the old but defunct battery we could hand in. Without that it wouldn't matter if you were even the first one in line. Battery owners move to the front. We were lucky and got a brand-new battery. Also four new tires.

It took us two trips on the S-Bahn to get the stuff home. We could have sold the stuff several times over during those trips. People were offering us triple of the actual sales price. The two doors we found through advertisement in a newspaper. It was a real challenge to get the doors into a streetcar.

The unexpected challenge now is to find car paint. A salesperson in the paint shop on the corner of Invaliden Strasse and Friedrichstrasse told us that next week or so he is expecting a load of Cuban beige car paint. The price for telling us: two tickets for the performance of Salome. Klaus got them because of his connection to the guys at the box office. We are also missing the two front car seats. Klaus thinks we can find them at a car salvage place.

The plane wheels hit the ground hard. My head jerks in the seat in front of me. The flat landscape of the airport rushes by my window. The rectangular shape of the arrival building comes into view. The propellers of the airplane slow down and give way to the welcoming silence. The cabin door opens. The smell of engine fuel is nauseating. We are back from two weeks' vacation in Hungary, most of it a nightmare. At first I caught Klaus fooling around with a handyman the second day we had checked into our hotel at Lake Balaton. Both were at it and didn't notice when I mistakenly opened the door to the engine room. I thought it was the door to the staircase. A very familiar lust cry made me stop. I followed the noise's direction. In a corner next to the boiler was Klaus on his knees, his pants around his ankles giving this guy in a workman's overalls a blow job. The handyman's dirty hands were resting on Klaus shoulders.

Later that day we attended a performance of the local dance group. At the end the dancers came off the stage to welcome us. One of them was a tall and blond and very handsome. He went straight to Klaus. He introduced himself as Janusz and asked Klaus if he wants to go out for a beer. He totally ignored me. I was blown away by this guy's directness. Of course Klaus said yes. He came home the next morning. Just in time for breakfast. The same happened for the rest of our stay. I only saw him for breakfast. I felt totally numb. I knew that any attempt to address what he was doing would blow up in my face. I asked once if we could spend the day together.

"You are such a sourpuss. Why don't you have fun? Just enjoy your vacation and leave me alone. We have breakfast together. Isn't that enough?""

The trip to Hungary was supposed to be our honeymoon to celebrate that we are together again. That was the plan. The trip is part of FDGB union-sponsored vacations, any member can apply for. I was so excited when I read about the Hungary vacation that I immediately applied for it without asking Klaus. We had talked about a trip to Budapest in the past and we knew that we would need to save a lot of money beforehand. Hotel and airplane tickets are very expensive. Therefore, when I saw the offer for less than 600 Marks for two persons I went straight to the union office. I was sure I would be approved for the trip. Most of my co-workers have children and cannot go on vacation outside of school recess. I also pay my union dues on time and have a good attendance record for the union meetings and their ideology classes. Two weeks after submitting my application I was approved for the trip.

I know I shouldn't been surprised about Klaus becoming the Klaus I knew and hated. But I am. If I could I would take the next available plane back home. But that is impossible. I try not to think too much what Klaus is doing. However, lying on the beach is not much of a distraction. All the members of our travel group avoid me. Klaus is not very secretive about his doings. I am so embarrassed and keep to myself. I can't wait until we will go to Budapest as part of the vacation. There I could go to the opera or immerse myself in the bustling city life.

The morning the bus would take us to Budapest Klaus was not back to the hotel yet. Our travel guide had asked numerous times if I knew where my companion was. I had no clue. "Your friend seems very busy," one traveler commented. His eyes didn't betray his disgust for the both of us. I blushed. Finally Klaus appeared into the hotel lobby. I didn't greet him. I wanted him to disappear und leave me alone. I had very much hoped he would not be in time for the bus' departure. But here he was, all smiles. The travel guide told him that we would be leaving shortly, and asked him if his stuff was packed.

"Did you pack?" Klaus yelled across the hall. I pointed at our suitcase. "Oh, good. Then let's go." We formed a line to get on the bus. Klaus in front, I am at the end. That very moment I wanted to become invisible.

The days in Budapest were not much better. We went together to the opera. One evening he picked the bellboy to come to our rooms. I watched them. One afternoon he asks me to go with him to the Gellert Bath. This old roman venue is known for gay activities. After we stripped off our clothes we put on a napkin-size cloth to be tied in the back. It covers the front and leaves your ass naked. We dip into the warm water of the shallow pool. The cloth lifts up and swims on the surface. Here are all these naked men with their linen squares floating in front of them. Very funny picture. One guy approached us. Middle-aged, balding, chubby, not bad looking. We made small talk. After a while he asked if we wanted to have a drink at his place. Klaus said yes.

The guy's apartment was on the top floor, kind of a green house it seems. Glass everywhere. The view of the Budapest's rooflines was fantastic. We started at the living room with some wine. Soon the man disappeared only to come back buck naked. Klaus and I got naked too. The guy was clearly more interested in Klaus than in me. He started sucking Klaus. I didn't know what to do and started touching his ass. The guy dropped to his knees and pulled Klaus behind himself. Without much foreplay Klaus penetrated him. The guy went flat onto his stomach. Klaus grabbed my dick and guided me into his ass. We were stacked like a sandwich and humped as good as we could in unison. I came first. Probably because I didn't had sex since we arrived in Hungary. I got up. The two were still at it. It looked more like a struggle. Not a word. Just heavy breathing. I watched them and didn't feel anything. These were two strangers.

A Death Rips My Family Apart

As we crossed Kissingen Strasse towards my apartment building I see my parents' car leaving the parking lot in the middle of the street. My mother is behind the wheel. She doesn't notice me. Somehow her facial expression seems not right as she passes. My stepfather is next to her.

"They didn't see us. That's funny," I say to Klaus. He hasn't said any word since we landed. I had told him that he should pack his stuff as soon as we are at my apartment and leave for good. Reality sets in for him. I can see the sad eyes. His cheeks appear hollow. His regrets show. I am not moved. I have seen it before. There is nothing more to say for me. I set my bag down in the hallway of my apartment.

"I will go to my grandmother to say hi. In the meantime you can get your stuff together." I can't wait to get away from Klaus. The three flights of stairs up to Tata's apartment make me breathless as always. I ring the door bell. My uncle Paul answers the door.

"Hi, how are you? I just got back from Hungary. Where is Tata?" I want to pass by him to get in.

"Don't you know? Ernst is dead."

"What?" I look at him, thinking that this one of his sick jokes he likes to play.

"He was killed in a car accident a week ago." A week ago I was at Lake Balaton. I try to remember what else I did a week ago. My brain is racing. My uncle has been dead for a week and I didn't know. Paul's facial expression tells me it's true. I can't move and stare Paul in the eyes.

My grandmother comes out of the living room. "Oh, my *jungele*, my *jungele*. It is terrible. I know how much Ernst meant to you. I am so sorry." I give her a hug. Not wanting to let go of her. She doesn't move. She stays in my arms. It's is like if I want an assurance, that my uncle is really gone.

"Come in. I make you something to eat. You must be hungry."

"I am not hungry, Tata. Tell me, when and how did it

213

happen?" I sit down.

"Do you want some tea?"Paul asks. My whole life he never has asked me if I want something. It must take a tragedy that my uncle can be human, I think and say: "That would be nice. I think I can use a cup of tea."

"I will put some water on the stove." Paul disappears in the kitchen. "Oh, *jungele*, I still cannot comprehend what happened." Tata reaches for her Rosary and let the beads run through her fingers. "No one really knows how it happened. He left Leipzig last Thursday to spend some time at the museums cottage in Bernoewe. He wanted to finish his dissertation. They found the car near Falkensee crashed into a tree. He was dead when the ambulance came. He had the dog with him. Bojar was supposedly leashed to the back seat. But when the police and ambulance arrived the dog was sitting next to the car. The way the car got off the street and drove onto a field and finally bumped into a tree suggests that he was not speeding."

Paul brings a tray with the tea, two glasses and a sugar bowl. "I filled the bowl up. I know you don't like half-full sugar bowls." He sets the tray on the glass coffee table. I get distracted by his remarks about the sugar. It's true I don't like sugar bowls with not enough sugar in it. I use a lot of sugar for my tea. If the bowl is not full I feel I can't take my normal four spoons of sugar. Therefore I can't enjoy my tea because it's not sweet enough. Amazing, Paul remembers my kookiness in the worst of circumstances. How odd? Silently I pour the tea in the two glasses and fill mine with sugar. The spoon clangs against the inside of the tea glass.

"I went with your aunt to identify the body. There were no visible signs of injuries. We couldn't see the police report. They wouldn't tell us where exactly the accident happened. It's all very mysterious." Paul lights another Caro cigarette. The smoke and smell are nauseating. He offers me one of his. I take one of my own. It still sounds like something that happened somewhere else to somebody else.

"How is Tuntel holding up? How is Pinni?"

"I don't know? Your aunt is impossible to take right now." Tata blows her nose into her handkerchief. "It's awful to say. But Ernst left us with a terrible inheritance. My daughter."

I am not surprised at what I hear. My grandmother and her oldest daughter have a very complicated relationship. Their love and hate for each other always irritated me. But to say this in a moment of such a loss seems so matter of fact and void of any emotions.

"Your mother took the next train after she got the call. I followed two days later. Bad timing. My daughter thought I should have been with her immediately. I thought let the two sisters be together for a while. Anyway, the minute I stepped into her apartment all hell broke loose. There was nothing I did right. I didn't cry enough. I didn't give her enough money. I wasn't supportive in any way. She was cursing at me without any breaks. I couldn't take it anymore. On my way out of the door she screamed she doesn't want to see me anymore and shouldn't dare to come to funeral. I came home yesterday."

"How is Pinni?"

"She is quiet and consoles her mother. I don't know how she will hold up? You know your aunt. She is crazy. Now she lost her husband who always could tame her. I don't know who can take care of her now Ernst is gone. I am worried. I am worried that she will harm my granddaughter and herself." Tata still has the Rosary in her hand. "You know, Ernst's death doesn't make any sense to me. I don't understand why the Dear God did that to us. It doesn't make any sense."

The Rosary runs now faster through her fingers. My uncle stares at the floor. Chain smoking. Silent. Tata is right. Who will take care of Tuntel now that my uncle is gone? And then like a bolt strikes through metal I realize it's me. I am the closest to my aunt. She and my uncle are my surrogate parents. It's them where I could always go for help and advice. It's me who lived with them for while. More than once I was the mediator between them, when they fought like dogs. I looked after my cousin when she was a baby and her mother had one of her tantrums and ended up sleeping for hours afterwards. My aunt and uncle were the rock I could lean on when my stepfather treaded me badly and my mother would let it happen. Now is the time for me to give back. Just the thought makes me uneasy.

"You have to go to Leipzig. You must calm her down. You are the only one she would listen to." My grandmother must have read my mind.

"Of course I will. But I just came back from vacation. I don't know if I can get more time off."

"Your mother has already talked to your boss. He agreed to give you a couple more days off." That's my family. It's always someone making plans for the other ones without consulting them. "Maybe you can take the night train? I will give you money." Tata goes over to her credenza to get the money out of a small safety box.

"You can go to the neighbors and call your aunt. She is waiting for it."

"I will. But first let me go down to my apartment. Klaus is probably wondering where I am."

"Maybe he can go with you to Leipzig?"

"No, I don't want him to get involved. Our trip was not good. I won't ask him for any help. I can handle this alone."

The death of my uncle turns into an absolute nightmare. It's two days before the funeral and my aunt has alienated everybody in the family except for me. Right now I am the bridge between her and my cousin and the rest. My aunt rides the guilt trip like a good Catholic. No one mourns enough. No one remembers him the right way. No one should just go on with his or her life. My aunt was always selfish but she also had a very caring side. She would and will give you her last shirt but with a price: "Do what I tell you to do." The deadly car accident of her husband separates time now to "before" and "after" his death. In my aunt's mind the untimely end of my uncle is also the end of everybody's personal life. There is only one concern for all of us: The widow's being.

I wish I had time to sit back and think about my uncle, who was my father, friend, adviser and my rock. But I feel like I am not allowed to mourn my way. What keeps me going is the loss, the genuine pity for his wife and daughter and the mysterious circumstances of his death. They are for some reasons secrets that are kept secret that shouldn't be kept. There are inconsistencies about his car accident, it seems. Maybe not. Maybe it is the undeniable fact that my uncle is dead and so many questions will be unanswered forever. Maybe it's my wish that the circumstances surrounding his death appear suspicious. It would be so much easier to blame something or someone for his untimely and totally unexpected passing. There is so much unsaid, unexperienced, unlived together. My uncle and I were not done. There was present and future until he ended up at a tree. Now, that "us" is past. Unconceivable. Incomprehensible. Nothing comes easy to deal with after death. He was not old enough to go. Not sick enough to leave us behind. Not accomplished enough to let go. Then why?

And my aunt fuels the doubts by throwing in so many seemingly unrelated details. I can't help but wonder if she is right with her suspicions and conspiracy theories. There is this small round marks on my uncle's forehead she and her brother saw when they viewed the body. She would not say it, but implicates that it could be inflicted by a shot. The coroner declares the reason of death as undetermined. According to the portion of the police report that my aunt is allowed to read, there are no eyewitnesses who saw the car careen off the highway and roll in a straight line into a tree. The leash that the dog was tied to in the back seat was unbroken. The police say the dog was sitting outside of the car. Even weeks after it happened, the dog, the only known witness of the accident, shows moments of high anxiety. I have seen it several times. His barking is suppressed, his breathing labored, his eyes locked onto yours. He is telling us the story only we cannot understand it. Heartbreaking and frustrating. The repeated demand of my aunt to get the totaled car released to her remains unanswered. If there is an attempt of cover up, then why? If the death of my uncle was just caused by a car accident why not given his widow access to the full police report? Even the exact location of the crash is withheld.

My aunt has hired a lawyer to find out as much as she can surrounding the events of her husband's deadly crash. That is pretty gutsy. Engaging legal counsel is really not very common. There are less than five hundred practicing attorneys in all of East Germany, most of them involved in divorce cases. Citizens don't need a lawyer in the workers' paradise! The law is the people's law, the courts are the people's courts, the judges and prosecutors are the people's judges and prosecutors. Criminals will get legal services assigned. Otherwise, so goes the official doctrine, no one in his right mind has to seek legal representation. Attorneys are seen as something very bourgeois. This kind of a profession may have its justification in a capitalist society where everybody is everybody's enemy. It's there where humans degenerate to wolves because of a wolf's system. Socialism on the other hand is the tent in which everybody blossoms with the guidance and tutelage of the Party. The Party is self-anointed protector of all.

Anyway, my aunt wants to see the police report. She wants to know why things are covered up. She wants to know where exactly her husband died. She wants the wreckage of the car. But she is running into walls and silence. She realized she needed to be more aggressive since no one involved in the case would give her the time of the day. She thinks that with the help of a lawyer doors will open, files will get handed over and what's left of the car will be hers again. What the wrecked car is concerned, for instance, it's pretty important to get it back. Only she, as the owner, can turn it over to a demolition yard. There she will get a piece of paper stating that the vehicle was destroyed. With that she can go to the car dealer to apply for a new car. Since she had owned a car before she now has to wait only a couple of months to get a new one. Without a wreckage certificate she would be at the very end of the waiting list.

That she hired an attorney does not sit well with her colleagues and Party comrades. Some of them have turned their backs on her in openly displayed disdain. Others just avoid her. The same with the former colleagues and Party comrade at my deceased uncle's work place. My aunt is very upset about it. But that does not diminish her determination to get to the bottom of things. I am impressed with her feistiness and her willingness to challenge the status quo. I am not surprised about the behavior of her co-Party members and co-workers.

Fear determines almost everybody's life in a controlled

environment. It is that fear that dehumanizes many, including most of my aunt's circle of acquaintances. Their action is simple a sign of survivor instinct born out of raw pragmatism. A man is dead. Why look for the why? Nothing will bring him back. Asking questions stirs things up. And that may shine a light on them. Who knows where that would lead to? My aunt's loss is not their loss.

It is widely known that in a society plagued by notorious shortcomings ranging from daily necessities to specialty items the elite has paradise-like access to everything that their heart desires. In order to stay in the elite class its members are willing to give limited and controlled access to their goodies. The price can be monetary but in most cases it will be devoted loyalty and lifetime subordinance. But I have to confess, I was not aware how sick and perverse the Party's generosity can be.

After visiting Leipziger Zentralfriedhof cemetery my aunt is determined to bury my uncle's remains in the old part of the cemetery. She and her daughter don't like the newer part. To them it looks like a heartless landmass. No trees, no lawn, no bushes. Just lines of gravestones in a field of dirt. Their request to buy a plot in the established part was strictly denied by the manager of the cemetery. "It is closed to newcomers," was his dismissive answer. Luck had it that when the Party boss of Herder Institut, where my aunt teaches, asked her if he could help her with anything she told him where she wanted her husband to be buried. She also told him that she would like to buy natural sandstone as a gravestone, because she also had learned from the manager of the cemetery that one can only buy a gravestone made of granite and cut in a very symmetrical and square shape. It seemed so absurd to her that there were even regulations for the type of gravestones in place. The mid-level Party boss made sure that both of my aunt's wishes came true.

I suspect my aunt wants to make my uncle's death a public affair, again defying common sense and Party rule. My uncle had for years worked with some researchers in Australia. He was never allowed to visit them, but they could visit him. Over the years a casual friendship grew between them. My aunt doesn't want to send the announcement of my uncle's death to Australia via postal service. She thinks the mail will be stopped by the East German authorities. She insisted that her brother and I deliver the death announcement directly to the Australian Embassy, a risky undertaking with possible consequences. International law guarantees that the host country's citizens can visit embassies for various reasons, even East Germany has to respect that. However, policemen are posted so close to the entrances that it is physically almost impossible to pass without touching them. Then there are plainclothes guards all over the place to further intimidate and scare away potential visitors. I have heard stories where people got through the People's Policemen protection but when they left the embassy building they were followed. When they were far enough away from embassy plainclothes policemen would interrogate them about the purpose of their visit.

With that in mind, my aunt's brother and I braced ourselves on a Sunday morning to make the trip to the Australian embassy located in Pankow district. There is a streetcar stop almost across from the entrance to the embassy so we jumped out of the car, darted straight to the entrance, gave the porter the letter and turned quickly around. This was all done in mere of seconds. The policeman was so caught off guard by our quick actions that we got away without incident, but our hearts were pounding.

I have a hard time accepting the death of my uncle. It's the first time in my life that I am confronted with the death of a very close person. To deal with the emotions and the finality are so heart wrenching as well as mysterious. One minute alive, the next gone. Where did my uncle's personality go, his wisdom, his thoughts? The body that moved, spoke, hugged and enjoyed life becomes just a piece of lifeless material eventually disintegrating to nothing. They say the death of others makes you aware of your own limits. Factual it may be but we don't live by that.

Isn't all that we do totally ignorant of the fact that we die some day? How else can one stay motivated to strive, buy things, and build stuff, save money for some undetermined future? If we woke up every morning with the first thought of our own mortality how much would we accomplish? Would we even get out of bed? What happen to all the things that made him my uncle, my aunt's husband, my cousin's father, my mother's brother-in-law? When he crashed into that tree where did all those personal attributes go? Why him, why now? Is being a human more a curse than a blessing? Animals live to keep their art alive. We on the other hand go a step further and spend so much time to prepare for an unlimited life. We conveniently deny the unavoidable end and hope somehow deep down we never will die. Just the others.

When I saw my stepfather's mother for the last time she had shriveled to an unrecognizable half of her original size, helpless whimpering in a hospital bed, surrounded by metal guards so she would not fall out of bed. What has this do to with the woman who treated me better than her son? A woman I spent weekends together with, took trips to the country with, listened to her stories. What had this object in the bed to do with the woman who until recently could laugh until tears were running down her face? Did she even acknowledge me when I looked down on her lying in a bed that seemed to be made for babies? Was her whimpering real words that she was unable to articulate so I could understand them? Or was this just something totally meaningless for those left behind as part of fading away to some other place? When did her strong will, cooking skills, survival instinct leave the body and where did it go? A life of work and savings, the knowledge about war, the struggle through hunger and rebuilding. What happened to all of it?

And now the same questions arises in the face of my uncle's death. Where did he go when his dog sat outside of the crushed car guarding a body that now was not special anymore, no different from any lifeless skin, bones and water? What is nature's intention when it lets the mind disappear, leaving behind something that will start decompose and stink? Is this repeating cycle that's called life nonsensical by design? If so why can't the living men cope with the loss? Why does grief hurt so much? Why is it so hard to accept death right then and there the first

221

moment a death occurs? Why do we have to cry and question? Is it an invisible wagging finger reminding us that someday we will become that lifeless mindless mess as well?

The void I am left with after my uncle's death becomes almost unbearable. My memory of him turns into cruelty. Stepping into the past is joyful. I can see him so clearly, hear his voice, feel his kiss on my cheek, the ends of his goatee hair moist from his breath. But how deceiving. It's not real anymore, just virtual. To return to reality is so painful. The pressure in my chest so intense. But is also so immaterial. I can't grab the pain and hurt with my hand and make it go away.

The cemetery in Leipzig is like a park with tree-lined avenues, high shrubs, intersections, paths going off left and right. The only noise is birds chirping and the scratching of the sand under the shoes of the visitors. It's the first time I've been back since the burial. So much has changed since then. I am now a student at the University of Leipzig where once a month I come to attend classes and lectures. The rest of the month I work as a reporter. In addition to my salary the newspaper reimburses me for my travel costs to Leipzig, plus an allowance for lodging. When I got the admission paper from Leipzig my aunt offered for me to stay at her apartment. But the summer before the semester started turned into a family nightmare.

Shortly after the funeral for my uncle everybody in my family had severed any contact with her and my cousin, including me. My aunt's demands and expectations were not only overwhelming to each of us, they were unbearable to the point where her own mother declared her insane. Both mother and daughter even became physically abusive. It took my uncle's death to reveal the buried hate between my grandmother and my aunt. At some point my aunt even questioned if her father was really her father. The status quo became totally ridiculous.

My aunt's inability to come to terms with the circumstances of my uncle's death did lead her more and more to the most outrageous accusations. She became convinced my uncle was murdered. Several times she had called my mother at home and me at work to tell us about mysterious phone calls in the middle of the night with total silence on the other end. She was also certain that her apartment was bugged and that she was followed.

In the beginning, we were inclined to believe her. It didn't seem unlikely that something unnatural had happened to my uncle. It certainly didn't help to erase our suspicions since the police was not very forthcoming with the results of their findings. In the end we all got caught up in my aunt's web of conspiracy. After phone calls to the coroner's office and towing company, for instance, my aunt thought she had figured out the exact location of the car accident. In her very demanding demeanor she made some of us to drive to that location to take pictures of whatever we would find. She thought at least the tree would show damage from the impact. It was another risky task she asked us to do since walking along the Autobahn and taking pictures is against the law.

Nevertheless, one Sunday morning my mother, her brother, a distant cousin of my aunt and I got in the car to drive to the location of the accident. Or rather, the location my aunt had decided to be the place. She didn't come. She thought it would be too traumatic for her. We parked the car at the first rest stop after the exit ramp into Falkensee and set out by foot. We all felt so uneasy but we did it anyway. We started taking pictures of spots where we thought it might have been the right one. At one point we discovered freshly broken brush at a downhill area. I followed it until I reached a small settlement of about three or four homes. A middle-aged man was working in the yard.

"Excuse me. Can I ask you a question?" I shouted over the fence. The man was startled to see me since it was very clear that I just had come down the hill from the highway. He did not move.

"What do you want?" he shouted back.

"I just was wondering if you have heard or seen a car accident a couple of weeks ago right here." He just looked at me, his looked at me with suspicion. "The reason I am asking is, because my uncle died in a car accident. I think it was here, but I am not sure. I would like to know." I was choking up. The man came closer. I must have been believable in the way I had asked.

His face had relaxed. "There was an accident. I only have heard about it, because I was at work when it happened. A big truck or something had lost control."

"Do you know if there was another car involved?"

"No, sorry. I don't know. What kind of a car did your uncle drive?"

"A Wartburg station wagon."

"No, I really don't know. I can't help you. How did you get here?" I told him. "You know it's against the law. You can get arrested for that. You better leave now. I don't want to have anything to do with that. Leave. I don't want that my neighbors see me talking to you. Leave." His demeanor was a mixture of fear and threat.

"Can I give you my name and phone number just in case you hear anything more about the accident? I really want to know if this is the place where my uncle died. Please. He was like a father to me."

"Leave now or I call the police." I became fearful and ran back up the hill to meet up with the rest of my family. I told them what I had learned. Later I had to repeat it again and again for my aunt.

A day or so after our search she called me at work. "I know now what happened to my husband. He was killed by the Russians. That's the reason why the police won't tell my anything." I was stunned listening to her newest accusation.

"How do you know?"

"The truck, the man was talking about, was a Russian Army truck. I am sure of it. You know, the area is full of Russians barracks."

"But how do you know it was the Russian Army truck?" My head was spinning. Her theory is not that far-fetched. The Russians are stationed indeed all around Berlin. You see them everywhere as soon as you leave the city boundaries. There are always wild rumors about lawlessness of their behavior. I have heard about car and shooting accidents where Russian troops and German civilians were involved. Things were hushed away by the East German authorities. The Red Army can't do wrong.

They are our liberators and protectors against the imperialists from the West. Any rumors about amok running soldiers raping women, stealing from civilians, deserting their units are evil spirited. Seeds planted by the imperialist propagandists. No investigation is ever needed or warranted, so goes the official version. But there are also rumors that the Russians deal with their own by swift methods: death by shooting squad.

The more my aunt was venting about the car accident involving a Russian vehicle the more I found it a possibility. "You are right. But let's not talk about it anymore over the phone. I can come to Leipzig on Friday, if you want?" I don't know why I offered to go since I really didn't want to, but now I have to.

"Yes please come. But don't tell your parents, my brother or your grandmother about this. I am almost certain they knew right from the beginning what really happened to your uncle."

"I won't. I will see you on Friday." I had to cut her off. Otherwise she would go on and on complaining about the family. More than once she accused my stepfather of being a Stasi agent and my mother his willing partner. She hates her brother because he married a Jewish woman. My aunt also loathes her sister-in law's parents. She cannot stomach that they are part of the *Nomenklatura*. According to my aunt, everybody played a part "in the death of my husband." At this point, I was the only one she does not suspect of playing a role in the "murder plot." The situation is totally crazy. Sometimes I am not sure how long I can take her overbearing behavior but I feel obligated to stay with her because my aunt and uncle were always there for me. It is now time for me to pay them back. Guilt and manipulation. My aunt has that down to a T. And I don't have the strength to limit her power over me. However, I am glad that I can keep her at arm's length until Friday. A week of peace and quiet. I feel exhausted.

That same evening sitting in my favorite coffee bar at Alexanderplatz I realize again how selective my aunt's theory about the death of my uncle and its circumstances is. More and more I think about the possibility that my uncle's heart just gave out: my uncle was a heavy smoker in his early fifties who didn't believe in any sort of exercising, and his family life was a disaster. He rarely had peaceful moments. His daughter was his joy and love. Everything else must have been so disheartening for him. His marriage was just a big catastrophe. I don't know how many times witnessed their fights and the irate behavior of my aunt. I always saw his helplessness to deal with that other than with his unwavering love for his wife. My uncle was always a master of destressing the situation. I sometimes wondered if he had an affair or affairs to cope with his home life. Whatever his valve was, the fact stands that life in his home was unhealthy to say the least.

When my aunt had asked me to get my uncle's possessions left in the car wreck so it could be demolished I was hesitant to do it because I was not sure what I would find. The reason that my uncle had planned some time off to go the museum-owned bungalow was to finish his dissertation. Maybe he was not alone in the car? Maybe he was with a female companion? Maybe that was the reason the police were so tightlipped about the circumstances surrounding the accident? Maybe releasing only bits and pieces was to protect my aunt and not telling her the truth was an act of kindness by the authorities? Hard to believe, but possible. If he had a girlfriend in the car I am glad that he could look forward to a relaxed time away from his wife. Maybe the happiness was too much for is used-up heart? Whatever the answers maybe I was afraid to take on the task to see my uncles "coffin." What would I find? How would I react when I saw the car I have been in countless times myself? I certainly understood that my aunt wouldn't be able to deal with the disposal of the crashed car. But, I also knew I couldn't do it alone. I asked my stepfather if he would come with me. My aunt was opposed "to let a Stasi informant near my car." But she came to her senses when I explained my own emotions.

The car was not as badly damaged as I thought it would be. The front was crushed in, the steering wheel stuck out of the front window, kind of. But I didn't see any signs of dried blood. The passenger seat was intact and so was the rear of the car. There were no personal items left except for a couple of canvas bags that belonged to my uncle. Just before I signed off in order for the car to be demolished I took another look. Under the passenger seat I saw a single woman's shoe I had not seen before. I knew in an instant it was not my aunt's. The shoe was a high-heeled sandal, a shoe my aunt would never wear.

I was startled and unsure how to deal with my discovery. Should I leave the shoe where I found it? Or should I take the shoe and show to my aunt? How would she react? What does that shoe tell her? Would that open another Pandora's box? Would my aunt now abandon her murder theory and start obsessively looking for the other woman? I decided to keep the shoe. On our way back to my aunt's apartment my stepfather and I speculated on how the shoe ended up in the car. Was it tossed in car sometime after the accident? A possibility. The car was towed first to a garage close to the crash site, then weeks later transported to Leipzig for insurance purposes. Or was my uncle not alone in the car when the accident happened?

As my stepfather and I go back and forth all of the sudden I remembered the day of the funeral. My grandmother and I decided late in the afternoon to drive back to the burial site. The earth mound was covered with many wreaths. The fresh flowers had already started to wilt because of the sun with the exception of a bouquet of fresh flowers at the foot of the mound that was clearly laid down long after the ceremony. Somebody came here much later to say goodbye without anybody around. Maybe this somebody couldn't make it in time for the funeral? Or somebody wanted to be alone, not to be seen. Does this shoe belong to this somebody? "I think, we should show the shoe to her. Why should we alter the truth?" My stepfather agreed with me.

"It's not mine. Somebody must have thrown it in the car when it was at the tow place." It was heart wrenching to see my aunt looking for an explanation other than the obvious. Of course she could be right that some stranger used the car wreck as a dumping place, but why then only one shoe and not the pair? My aunt kept turning the shoe. She had

227

stopped talking. Her eyes glared at the sandal that did not belong to her. At that moment, she appeared so fragile, so vulnerable, so lonesome, so very lost. What was going through her mind? Does it occur to her that her husband may have died next to another woman? If so, a house of cards, so seemingly perfectly built to fool the outside world of a wholesome and happy marriage is finally falling down. I will not fault my uncle to seek moments of happiness. If it's true and he had an affair, I would only fault him to be inconsequential. It is the same inconsequence he could not overcome and admit that his political conviction had lost its footing because the political realty was a scam. He escaped by writing critical poetry. To offset his terrible marriage situation he may have found a girlfriend.

How can my aunt go on from here? How can she mourn a husband that probably sought shelter for his unhappy heart? But the most important question: how will she survive without the strength of her forgiving and loving husband? In a short period of time she has maneuvered herself into a corner. No one left to help, support, to talk to except me and her daughter. I certainly felt the sudden transfer of care from my uncle to me. I wonder if he had envisioned the day where he would step out and I had to step in? Had he actually groomed me to take over his family someday? I was the son he never had. He was the friend I never had. He took the father part that my biological father, nor my mothers' second husband, didn't want. He taught me to be critical, to ask questions, to be responsible. He trusted me, he believed in me. He created memorable moments for both of us. His whole life he gave to others. But how much did he really receive in return? Maybe at the time of his death he had nothing left anymore that he could share? His body, heart and soul were drained. His unexpected passing maybe was not that sudden. Maybe we all, who knew and took from him, did not see the beginning of his end? And maybe he knew of his limits and hoped by giving as long as he could, someone would take over when he was done?

It is he who formed and made me what I am today. Now I am on my own. I will always remember the times that he and I went on a hiking trip for a week. He constructed our tent out of plastic sheets glued together. We slept in the woods, cooked over an open fire, bathed in lakes and rivers. We seldom walked into towns or villages. It was just the two of us and nature. He made me aware of things I would have easily overseen.

One of the fascinating things he pointed out to me on those hikes through the woods was the old stone markers placed in the ground over a hundred years ago. Most of them were hidden and only a trained and knowing eye would spot them. These markers gave directions and distances for travelers by horse, in carriages or on foot. The same markers and their exact location could be found on maps made well before World War II. To this day those stone markers are reliable orientation points. Current maps are deliberately distorted by the East German authorities. The reason: to lead the enemy in the wrong direction should they decide to buy maps made in East Germany and wander through the countryside.

Hiking with my uncle felt like an adventure to me. It seemed so forbidden and secretive. I remember how people we passed looked strangely at us. Backpackers were not a common sight. Growing up in an environment where permits come before doing anything at anytime doubtless has this effect. My uncle tried to make light of it during our hikes. When I would ask: "What will we do if somebody asks us what are we doing?" He answered "I give a good impression." With him I always felt protected. He always knew what to do. He always taught me, not to be afraid to challenge normality.

In later years my uncle shared with me his political poems that he would write in the privacy of his study. They were his personal reaction to the "irrational politics of the Party." In them he brilliantly made fun of the lifestyle of the *Nomenklatura*, the blind adaption of all things made and cooked up in the Soviet Union as well as his fellow citizens who would out of fear stop using their own brains. I really enjoyed listening to the sarcasm and sharp tongue of his writings. These readings would always happen far away from the phone, mostly in the kitchen. Those were the moments where equal minds could be free. My aunt, my uncle and I felt inspired. The words that my uncle used so eloquently to capture observations and frustrations almost made us hopeful that things could be changed. Isn't describing what feels so wrong the first step that will later lead to actions? But his critical approach to current policies, ideologies and events around the world that he saw so clearly would never lead him to the apparent next act: denouncing the Socialist System. He stayed a true believer in the bright future of Communism.

Our frank and open discussions, like his writing, seemed to him just intellectual exercise without the seemingly consequential next step. I always wondered how he could fall so short. I was much more radical in my thinking and practice. When I first told him I wanted to get out of the Party he was totally against it. He tried everything to make me change my mind. Leaving was for him an easy way out. Staying in the only manly alternative. After all my trouble with the Party was over I kind of had the feeling that he was impressed with my determination. My uncle never agreed with my decision but he also never shunned me because I returned my Party button and membership book. And I stopped short of criticizing him for his "inner immigration."

Now that he is gone I sense the burden I am under. I have to be good and do the right thing. I have to try. I know that I never can do what my aunt expects from me to do. I can't be and I won't be a stand-in for her dead husband. I will support, help and listen. But I will not allow anybody to put me into the family harness.

By late August, just three months after my uncle's death my aunt seems to reach a melting point. Everybody around her are suspected liars, spies and lowlifes. Even her attorney became "a bastard." I sense that I am very close to joining the group of "heartless and despicable human beings." It was hard to listen to my aunt's tirades. Now it was her against the rest of the world.

I wanted to help and at the same time get some distance between us. Maybe if she would leave her current surroundings for a while that would distract her? However, the possibilities are limited. Finding a hotel somewhere will be fruitless since dogs are not accepted. Period. The same with any short-term vacation homes. Than luck was on my side. Coincidentally, Kurt Klein was looking for somebody to take care of his *datscha* in Schildow. The housesitter only had to feed his geese and ducks. Klein had asked Klaus and me to move temporally to Schildow. It's not impossible but the daily commute to work would have been a schlep. Therefore, getting my aunt and cousin to housesit was a much better and welcome solution. The *datcha* is well equipped and offers all conveniences she would require. Klein was quickly convinced to let them stay there. My aunt was at first not open to the idea to live in a house that belonged to a member of the *Nomenklatura*. I think the real reason that she hesitated to stay in Schildow was the mere fact that not the whole world was against her. Being the wronged and suffering widow was a role she wanted to continue to play rather than accepting help. In the end she reluctantly agreed to spend a couple of weeks in Schildow. I could tell, as soon as I opened the gate, she was very impressed with the property. My cousin fell instantly in love with the park-like setting and the swimming pool. In an eye blink their dog ran off to chase birds. And I was relieved to have delivered them to a spot where there were enough distractions that they would leave me alone for a while.

For the next couple of days I didn't hear anything from them. There were even moments I totally forgot about my aunt. Well, it wouldn't last for much longer. One evening my uncle Paul rang my doorbell minutes after I came home. "Your aunt called our neighbor. She can't take it anymore. It's too isolated there. The geese make a mess everywhere. They can't enjoy the pool because leaves fall into the water. She wants you to come and get her."

I looked at Paul in total disbelief. "She wants me to get her? What do you mean?"

"She wants to go back to Leipzig. She hates the *datscha*. She expected that you would come every evening to check on her. She says that you are selfish and don't care about her." I looked at my uncle. Why couldn't he step in and help his sister? Why does he expect me to deal with that? He is as useless as he is as self-centered. I never felt any deep connection to him. But right now I really hated him.

231

"What should we do? It's ten o'clock at night. I can't drive her to Leipzig now. I have to work tomorrow."

"Why don't you pick them up tonight? They can stay at your apartment. Tomorrow you can ask your boss if you could take a couple days off so you can drive them back to Leipzig." I stared at my uncle.

"Why is it just me that has to take care of her? It's you sister. Can't you do something?"

"No, she drives me crazy and I will stay away from her as far as I can." It was clear to me that my aunt's brother was not going to lift a finger to help the situation. I lit a new cigarette with the previous one. "Paul, I can't do this anymore. I feel like I have turned my life over to her. And even that is not enough. Where will that end? Tata is right. Her son in-law has left us a terrible inheritance."

I could have spoken to a wall. Paul's facial expression was totally blank. He was disengaged. He just sat there across from me, smoking his stinky Caro cigarette. Expecting any support, suggestions or even help from him was pointless. He had given up on the world a long time ago. He lives in his own, egotistic world as ever. Everybody in the family has resigned to not to expect anything from him.

"What are you going to do?" A typical Paul question.

"I guess I have to go to Schildow now. Can you come with me?"

"If you want to, sure. We can take my car, but you must drive. I don't know the way." His offer surprised me. But at that moment I didn't have the energy to wonder why, I just wanted to get it over with whatever laid ahead.

We drove to Schildow without speaking one word. I didn't have much to say to Paul anyway. I needed time to collect my thoughts and gain the strength to tell my aunt off. If I did not set the boundaries now it will go on and on. I really don't know how it feels when one is on the brink of a nervous breakdown but I felt somehow that I would have one very soon.

The gate to the property was locked. I knew the bell was not working. The only way in was climbing over the fence. What a scene: two men in the dark of the night trying to get into one of the biggest estates in Schildow by jumping over a two-meter high fence. Hopefully no one was watching. My body trembled out of fear I would hurt myself. Paul was in better physical shape than I. Finally I managed to land on the other side as well. We crossed the vast garden towards the bungalow my aunt stayed in. We could see the lights. As we got closer her dog started to bark. My cousin was first at the door.

As soon she recognized me she ran back into the house "Mami, mami, Thomas is here." She sounded excited.

My aunt greeted us at the door. "What are you doing here? I didn't expect you this late. Come in. You must be hungry." She hardly acknowledged her brother. She went straight into the kitchen.

"Tuntel, I don't want to eat. You called and told Tata's neighbor that you want to leave. I am here to get you. Please pack your things." She turned around. She looked surprised. "I am sorry. But I felt so lonesome this afternoon. That is the reason why I called."

"Tuntel, I am sorry, too. I can't take this anymore. I feel like I can't give anymore. Nothing is good enough. Please understand. I will bring you to the train station tonight. Then you will be on your own."

"Is this how you thank me for what I and my husband have done for you? What little have I asked you to do for me? It's nothing compared to what I have done for you. You are the same as your stepfather, your mother and the rest. Thankless, thankless. I should have known that I cannot rely on you. Not one minute have you grieved for my husband! You couldn't wait to leave me and my daughter."

Her voice has reached a screaming pitch. "Mami, stop. Please stop. Let's go back to Leipzig, please." My cousin tried to hug her mother. She pushed her away.

"Pack our things. We don't need your help anymore. We can get to the train station ourselves." White foam was building up around her lips. She was in a state of hysteria. I started to shake. All the sudden I felt freezing cold. I couldn't say a word. Paul had stepped outside to smoke. My aunt and cousin were packing. The dog sat in the corner. His face looked concerned. It was surreal. My cousin was in the kitchen and started to cut bread in small squares.

"What are you doing?" I asked.

"I have to feed the geese." Tears filled my eyes. I wanted to hug her but I couldn't' move.

How we got all their stuff in the car is a blur. It was little after midnight when we finally left Schildow. Paul in the front. My aunt, cousin and the dog in the back. The streets were pitch black. I had to lean forward to keep the car on the road. The tires couldn't absorb the cobblestone surface. We all were bouncing up and down in our seats. "We should have done what my daughter said after we got the news about my husband's death. We should have joined him." Since my uncles death my aunt speaks about her family as the rest of us were total strangers and not related in any way. My dead uncle became her husband, my cousin her daughter. It sounded always so weird. Anyway, it was not the first time she talked about suicide. I didn't respond.

"Please stop talking about that. If this you really want than do it." I am astonished how cruel Paul sounded. I should say something to melt the hatred of his words. But I was too exhausted. I wanted to get to the train station as fast I could. Driving in the dark always stresses me out.

"You are so thankless. After, what my husband and I have done for you. Now you tell me to commit suicide." My aunt's voice was on high volume.

"Please Mami, please. Stop," my cousin whimpers. The tension in the car reached explosive status. I could barely see my aunt in the rear mirror but her face screamed insanity. How this small and fragile looking frame of hers could produce so much negative energy was mind boggling.

"I have not told you to commit suicide. You are threatening us with suicide since the day Ernst died. It is so selfish and irresponsible of you. What is it you want from me? Tell me, how long is the payback time for me until you are satisfied with my thankfulness?" Paul screamed now as well.

"You are not my brother anymore. I don't need you. I don't need anyone. My daughter and I have no family anymore."

"That's it. Thomas, stop the car. Let me out." I was on autopilot and slowed down the car. Paul didn't even wait until I stopped the car. He opened the door and jumped out. He didn't close the door and ran off

I had to stop the car and reach over to pull the door shut. What just occurred didn't seem to really be happening. I stared out of the window to collect my thoughts. My vision came slowly back into focus. I recognized where we were. A subway train just drove out of the tunnel onto the elevated tracks. Very few people were walking down Schoenhauser Allee. To my left was the public restroom. Two men just came out and hastily walked in opposite directions. I saw a streetcar approaching us. It's now that I realized that I had stopped the car in the middle of street. Quickly I released the handbrake and put my foot on the gas pedal.

The dog's heavy panting was the only sound in the car. I felt there was nothing more to say for me either. I separated myself from my aunt. Her actions and words have alienated everybody, one by one. I am sure that was never her intention. Being the way she is my aunt wanted to control and manipulate. Her way of grieving was to induce guilt and rally everybody around her, but all of her unreasonable and crazy behavior resulted in the opposite of what she really wanted. She failed. She lost. She isolated herself. Not for one minute did she acknowledge that we *all* had a terrible loss the day my uncle died. With her relentless demands and omnipresence none of us had enough time to cry and mourn him. She would not allow it. It almost seemed like she didn't want us to grieve but only pity her. She knows her doting and forgiving husband is irreplaceable, but instead of seeking support she turned into a monster. Why? I am not sure but I suspect her own guilty conscience must overwhelm her at times. The only relief she can find is to lash out instead of reaching out.

She is the only one who knows what the last words were that she and her husband exchanged before he set out what would become his last ride. One only can assume it was not a nice loving goodbye. Now she is left with all the what-ifs and the unsaid words. Like the rest of us. How do you reconcile when your last moments together were filled with anger and unhappiness? How can you overcome the loss when the last time of togetherness ended without a hug or kiss? Therefore grief without the memory of a tender moment before parting for the last time must be maddening. Maybe that explains why my aunt is so incredibly rude and aggressive towards all the people around her? It's her guilt that no one can ease for her. She has grown into a black widow. I hope someday she can change from turmoil to balance. Only she can make that transition. And it has to be on her own terms. She has rejected the comfort of friends and family. Now I am the last one in my family to cut the cord. It hurts. But there is no other alternative for me.

"Can you drive us to Leipzig? I don't know when the next train goes. Katrin is very tired. We have so much luggage." My aunt is being my aunt. She wants me to drive through the night for three hours. She does not consider that I worked all day and that I have to work tomorrow. The way she asked puts me right on the spot. However, I had no intention to drive her all the way to Leipzig but telling her that makes me the bad one, the heartless one. I think by now she must realize that all she has to hold on to is me. Her desperation and loneliness turns her once again into a bully. Even if I would drive to Leipzig she won't appreciate it. It would be just a continuation of what she always has done: I want it and, you will do it. Except things are different now. She lost the spell over me as well. I kept on driving without saying another word.

We finally reached the main entrance of Ostbahnhof train station. I stopped the car, but left the engine running. I piled all of the luggage on the sidewalk. I felt terrible and on the verge of giving in. "I can't give in. I can't give in." I thought over and over again. "I am so sorry." For a split second my aunt and I lock eyes. She looked again so vulnerable. I saw fear in her eyes. I rushed back into the car. I avoided looking in my rear mirror as I drove away.

I have no trouble finding my uncle's grave. It is perched between a woman who died in her late eighties and a husband who passed away five years ago. His wife's name and birthday is already added on. When she dies it will be less time and money to just engrave her last day. It's such an odd habit seen on so many gravestones. For the onlooker with a sense for the aesthetics it seems unfinished. What must one think whose name is already engraved in but is still very much alive? I crouch down to be closer to my uncle. Low-grown shrubs frame a fresh bouquet of flowers. The earth in between is raked. I don't see one wilted leaf or brown flower petal. It's a perfect miniature garden. The afternoon sun completes the peacefulness of the place. My eyes fill with tears. I touch the plants. Their tops feel so soft and soothing to my hand. I miss my uncle so much. I want to talk to him. I want him to talk to me. Not that my uncle had all the answers to my questions nor did I asked him all the questions I had but not having him anymore to talk to is hard. I am overcome with self-pity.

Is the place where he is the happy one? I feel the urge to know right now. Losing somebody close seems to magnify one's own struggle, doesn't it? Is there attractiveness to death? Or is it just pure jealousy because the dead know already the answer to what comes after and the living has to wait until his time comes? To grieve does not just help to let go. It is also so depressing because I don't know where and what the place supposedly is I should let my uncle go to? The cemetery is an artificial comfort zone no more useful than a picture of my uncle at home. My visit here brings me less closure and calmness then I had hoped for, I am as confused as I was the day I learned about his death. My feelings are still raw. Pretty plantings and an impressive gravestone present just an illusion not a solution to deal with the emptiness. Nothing material will make it easier to accept. If I ever find closure it will be over time and in my heart. I have to leave this place. It opens wounds anew. My uncle's grave does not give me rest. I get up and smooth out my pants. One last touch of the stone. A whispered goodbye knowing I will never come back.

Christmas Ornaments Are Now "Year's-End Decorations"

I love my job as a reporter. It gives me status and access to seemingly important people. It sometimes opens doors otherwise closed to ordinary citizens. But best of all, my ego gets stroked every time I see my byline printed under my articles. Being a journalist provides me with a certain aura of achievement. Only a relatively few have the opportunity to become journalists. In a society that only values workers and farmers more "brain workers" are clearly in the minority. That they are allowed to do what they do is due to a privilege issued by the authorities. Some see that as an honor. Others use it for just personal gain. Some use their elite status to challenge and question the status quo. Others keep the privilege by doing the constant athletic-like brain split to stay under the radar of detection. If I belong with any, it's with those who hold on to the special status by playing the Party's game as skilled as possible.

Writing for a daily newspaper puts me sometimes in the uncomfortable position to massage reality. What we see, smell, eat and experience is very rarely the reality that is officially baptized. It needs therefore a propagandist such as journalists that will put things in a Party-driven context. We are there to reproduce doctrine perceptions which then will produce reality. Obscene? Yes. Weird? Yes. Perceived reality created by ideology. Personal experience is declared invalid. How do I manage that split? Being special compensates for a lot.

Der Morgen has the task to capture the liberal democratic niche of East Germans society which includes mostly small business owners, intellectuals, artist, actors and entertainers. Not a bad target group to write about. It only becomes tricky when I have to interview owners of newly opened restaurants. Describing menus is off limits since we deal with a shortage of certain food items on an almost daily basis. Mentioning dishes being served in a particular restaurant may cause a stampede of the desperate. Our reporting has to mirror self motivation as well creativity of the entrepreneur in a Socialist dimension. Whatever we report cannot and should not stimulate desire. Especially when it comes to daily necessities such as fresh vegetables or lean meat. Lines at the country's butcher counters are long. Exotic fruit such as bananas and oranges are only plentiful during Party congresses, around Christmas, elections or special occasions like the anniversary of the GDR or the birthday of the Secretary General of the Party.

Reporting on a new restaurant is reduced to writing about the interior. The owner gets profiled by deeply emphasizing his motivation to join the Liberal Democratic Party of Germany. Sometimes it has to be a little tweaked. We always want to report that the LDPD membership was solely motivated by being a productive and active member of the society. But quite often potential entrepreneurs seek membership in order to secure help to get all relevant permits. The East German authorities encourage the creation of a small private business sector. But they don't want have any "loose cannons" open-up businesses. Therefore it is the task of the so called Bloc Parties to get small business owners to join their ranks. And a lot of them don't mind. Other than a membership in the SED, where the litmus test to Communism is mandated, the other parties don't require such oath. Here one is only asked to acknowledge the undisputed leading role of the SED.

The semi-private sector in East Germany has gained in size in recent years after in the sixties and seventies the Party wiped out almost all private businesses except for some bakeries and cobblers. But with Honecker's rise to Secretary General a limited private, but heavy controlled and regulated, sector was encouraged again. Not because, ideology was being altered to allow individualism. The purpose is to counter balance the notoriously badly run state-owned grocery stores, restaurants, repair shops or any customer-service oriented businesses.

Recently I was sent to write about the opening of a private bakery. Its pastries looked freshly made and attractively displayed. The bread was visibly stored in nice and oversized baskets. I wondered where the owner got the baskets from because nice and big baskets are on the shortage list. Fresh flowers were arranged on the counter. I learned that the owner grew them in his own garden. The staff, all member of the owner's family, was very friendly and attentive. Small tables were placed in the back for the bakery. A stack of dishes with the highly desirable blue-and-white onion pattern ready to be used for potential guests, who want to enjoy a cup of coffee and a sweet. The combination of bakery and coffeehouse was very attractive. It also certainly was going to fill a niche.

But none of that I was able to report in my article. Yes, I could write that there is a new bakery. But the focus of my article had to be once more on the Party's great care and generosity because the flour used to produce the delicious goods is heavy subsidized. One of the many signs of the greatness of the workers' paradise is that all citizens can eat cheap bread and rolls. I enjoyed a bag full of freshly made Danishes, still warm, that the owner gave me after the interview.

Every Thursday our editor-in-chief has to go to the Ministry for Culture Affairs to get our "writing marching orders" for the next seven days. Together with the heads of the other four Bloc Party newspapers he will be given the talking points to be reflected in future articles and editorials. He also will receive a list of words to be used or not to be used in articles. If there is a shortage for instance of tomatoes in the tomato growing season the word tomato is absolute taboo, the same for onions or potatoes. Christmas decorations have to be called "year's-end decorations." And so on. It's absurd and laughable. But one learns to keep the chuckle inside.

And then there is the red leather case locked with a very visible padlock. How little the authorities trust their own people is evident when once a week the red leather case is delivered to the office of the editor-in-chief. The delivery itself is supposed to be a secret, meaning no one should even see the case. As is so often the case with secrets everybody at the paper knows about the case, only a few have seen it and only one can read what's inside: that is the editor in-chief. I am one of the few who have seen the leather case. What I have not seen is its content. It holds newspapers printed in West Berlin, among them the dailies from the Axel Springer Verlag such as the *Bild Zeitung* tabloid and *Berliner Morgenpost* newspaper.

The very existence of the papers is officially only known by the Party's appointed chief journalist Arnold von Schnitzler. He has a weekly propaganda show called "Der Schwarze Kanal" broadcast every Monday night. The title of the show alone shows pure rhetoric by suggesting everything broadcast on the Western channels is black and bad. In his show Schnitzler mocks, puts down and diminishes the West, Imperialism and its inhumane society by randomly quoting articles and news shows from the West with the only goal to praise the superiority and righteousness of the Soviet Bloc. An often repeated joke, of course only told amongst equal minds is "What defines a good GDR citizen? The one who does not switch TV channels when Schnitzler comes on." Lucky those who can receive Western TV and turn to the Monday movie, broadcast at the same time Schnitzler is on. Certainly no coincidence.

Anyway, sometimes I watch the "Black Channel" and I am always amazed that the Party's chief propagandist Kurt Hager lets his underling Schnitzler so cheaply and obviously cherry pick through the Western news media to brainwash the viewers. East German brains are the same as any other brains. There is no difference between a Western or Eastern brain. It's amusing that ideologists operate under the assumption that they can control and channel individual thinking by relentless infiltration of one approved worldview. It does not work. Nevertheless, every Monday night Schnitzler hammers away. Who can seriously believe a man, absurdly criticizing all things from behind the Wall, when he himself looks at the camera through a frame of eyeglasses made in the very West that he despises so.

Hager and the rest of the East German elite members drive around in Volvo limousines, live behind secure and high fences in Wandlitz, and enjoy the fruits produced by the devilish West (which are paid by shady companies established in imperialist countries). At the same time these "Salon Communists" deny their own people the same privileges. The chief TV propagandist Schnitzler dizzies the West every Monday night and drives home in a Mercedes. The same is true for Party-sponsored artists who willingly play, paint, write and sing the Communist gospel. After their propaganda art is sprayed onto the masses they are rewarded with the goodies made in the West. There is the Communist Chanteuse and actress Gisela May" she sings beautifully about the socialist accomplishments and is highly decorated by the Party for her praise of East Germany's uniqueness, but can't wait to get into her Mercedes and drive to West Berlin to shop. The list of the privileged is endless and even expands into my family. My uncle Paul's wife's family has bank accounts in Switzerland, enjoys beautiful homes in Berlin and on the Baltic Sea. Needless to say, they are all Party members and very stern believers in the system. I am human enough to admit I could be a convinced Communist myself if I had readily access to oranges, bananas, cars, Levi's jeans, a modern apartment and a passport that would allow me to travel to Paris, London and New York.

Humiliated and Hurt — Again and Again

Kurt Klein invites Klaus and me for a weekend at his *datscha* in Schildow. I am very excited. As a matter of fact Kurt offered us one of his guest houses to use whenever we like. In exchange he wants us to help him with maintenance work. He knows Klaus is very handy and I am a neat freak: everything that Kurt is not. I also think that Kurt likes me a little bit more than just a friend. I am fine with that as long he keeps his hands off of me. I like Kurt, too. He is very generous. He throws lavish parties at his apartment and in Schildow. Most of guests are second-tier ballet dancers. Some of them don't hesitate to share Kurt's bedroom for a night or two. Kurt has connections. I don't know how these guys do it. For obvious reasons, I don't think that men can fake it like women (maybe) can. How these lean, and for the most part, very good-looking guys get into bed and do it with him is beyond me. Sometimes he even gets straight men to have sex with him. Anyway, Kurt is fun to be with.

Fleeing the city for a weekend is something I am looking forward to. The guesthouse, the original building on the property, is kind of oval-shaped and has two stories. Downstairs are the kitchen and bathroom, upstairs is the bedroom with a huge picture window facing the pond. The building is in dire need of repair. I guess Kurt hopes Klaus could do most of the needed work. Downstairs is almost unusable because it's always flooded. We tried once to pump the water out assuming it would not come back but it did within hours. It looks like the foundation needs to be completely redone. But that is not our concern. The bedroom is all what we need to sleep. For everything else we can use Kurt's bungalow. A good-sized swimming pool is right next to it. The adjacent pool house is in sad condition but comes in handy in the wee hours of parties. It's a crash pad and dark room at the same time. The entire property is overgrown with high oak trees and thick bushes along the

243

fence, providing almost total privacy. Running around nude or having sex anywhere on the grounds is only noticeable from within. A perfect gay hangout.

Klaus will hitch a ride with Kurt to go out to Schildow. I take the bus from Breite Strasse in Pankow district. I always like to sit on the upper deck and enjoy the passing landscape after leaving the city boundaries behind its all countryside: cobblestone streets, small farmhouses, dogs and chickens running wild. If I can block out the propaganda billboards letting us know that "Learning from the Soviet Union is learning how to be victorious" and that "The party is always right" I feel like I am driving through a time capsule void of any past or present, just being. The perfect transition from the work week into time off. I make plans of what do to before Kurt and Klaus arrive. There is always something to take care of. The weather forecast predicts sun and warmth for the next couple of days. I probably should clean the pool and sweep the deck. Maybe there is time to clean Kurt's kitchen and living room? It's a mess, as usual.

The bus stops in the middle of the village. There are two ways to walk to Kurt's place. I choose the one that runs parallel to the railroad tracks. They cut through an abandoned field growing wild wheat and poppies. A breeze pushes me from the back. I love the walk. Here I never encounter anybody. The other way to get to Kurt's place is straight down the village's main street that changes from pavement to dirt. At the train station you have to make a sharp left turn that leads through a small settlement of unattractive Socialist-style houses with metal fences around them. Taking that route is faster and more direct. Taking the field path has more magic. It puts me at ease. Only a few steps and I feel balanced. The next day it will be just Kurt, Cocco, me and Klaus.

Things between Klaus and me are good right now. His drinking seems to have lessened a little bit. Lately we spend a lot of time together. We have settled into a normalcy I like. Everything has its daily routine: cooking, cleaning, grocery shopping, falling asleep in front of the TV. It all feels comforting to me. I have my own family. Even the nightmare that followed my uncle's death disappears the moment I put my arms around Klaus. In a way my uncle's accident saved my relationship with Klaus. I was so sure I would leave him for good after our disastrous vacation to Hungary. But the avalanche that hit me with the news of my uncle shifted my focus. My own pity became unimportant. And Klaus understood my grief and sorrow. He gave me the anchor to hold on to so that I wasn't tossed by the upheaval of my family dysfunction. He was after all the right man, partner, friend, lover and shoulder to lean on. This all convinced me that we not only have a present. We also have a future.

I do what I like to do when I walk alone. I talk out loud and vent whatever is on my mind. No response needed or expected. I am the speaker and the listener at the same time. I am in my own world. And today I am in my happy world. The thirty·minute walk from the bus stop to Klein's estate is over in a flash. I open the heavy gate. Every time I step through it I feel like being part of a Guy de Maupassant novel. Enchanting. It's like getting out of something real into something dreamy and distant. Leaving everything behind and just enjoying the moments of peace and quiet. In a way everything inside the gate and fences is untouched, left to itself. Presenting a wholesome and perfect surround to immerse yourself in. The guesthouse close to the gate, the pool at the end of a winding path navigating at some point over small bridge underneath the black waters of the pond, the bungalow to the right all blends into nature and is created by nature. The setting is enhanced by a layer of silence and serenity created by ancient old trees. The flapping sound of the geese's wings mixes with the breeze going through the oak branches. Except for the area around the pool very little sun can break through the tall and top heavy trees.

For a moment I stop and take everything in. It feels good to be here. I can't wait for Klaus and Kurt to arrive. A warm wave goes through my body. I wish someone would be here right now that I could hug and share my happiness with. I drop my bag in the bedroom of the guesthouse and wander toward the bungalow. I crave a cup of coffee. Kurt's living room and kitchen is in typical disarray. As usual he must have left last weekend without washing the dishes or picking up his clothes. The air is stale. Something smells rotten. Probably leftover food. I find a mug and get the coffeemaker going. The deck outside is not in better shape. Chairs and tables are scattered around. Half-full glasses everywhere. The leftovers of a party that no one cared to clean afterwards. Kurt never can be bothered with any of that. If he is here he wants fun. Party central. I wish I could be a little bit less anal about cleaning and putting everything back where it belongs.

The scent tells me the coffee is ready. I pull one chair to the edge of the pool. Take my shirt off and fall back stretching my legs, feel the sun on my face and hold the mug with both hands. Life is good. I notice the leaves on the bottom of the pool. Another task for this weekend. But not right now. I am adrift. It takes me a couple of second until I realize that the noise I hear are voices. I turn around. Kurt comes down the path, Cocco right behind him. He waves.

"Hi, guy. We are here. Let's get the grill started. And I need a drink." He is full of energy. I get out of the chair. The voices that woke me up become louder. I see group of guys walking over bridge. I recognize some of them. Olaf, one of the solo dancers at the Metropol Theater: Kurt has the hots for him. Bernd and Ralf. They are a couple but have an open relationship. Bernd is a group dancer at the Metropol, Ralf does the make-up there. Dieter dances at the Komische Oper. Peter is a construction worker and dances in Klein's ensemble. He has a steady girlfriend but sleeps with Kurt now and then. Behind him is a guy I have never seen before. Very tall, slim and very handsome. Could be dancer, I think. He is holding Klaus' right hand. In Klaus left hand I see a bottle of vodka, almost empty. My heart races. I don't have to wait as the evening will progress what is going to happen. Klaus and this guy are going to make out. Here goes my weekend. All my calm and balance is drained.

"How are you?" Olaf gives me a hug. Bernd just waves and disappears into the bungalow. So does Dieter and Ralf. Peter gives me pat on the shoulder. The new guy doesn't even look at me. He pulls Klaus past me. "Hi, handsome," is all that he says. I am left alone at the pool. I am in self-pity mode. I can't get a hold of my roller-coaster feelings. All the sudden I don't want to be here anymore. The party has not begun but I know its outcome. Maybe I should leave before I have to see Klaus doing what he will be doing.

"What do you want to drink?" Kurt yells from the door.

"I think I will stay with coffee for now. It's too early for me to drink."

"Oh, come on. It's Friday. The clock has stopped ticking." He hands me a glass. I smell gin.

I try to smile. Maybe I should get drunk. Quickly. So things won't be too bad to watch. I don't want to get inside where there is a lot of commotion. I stay at the pool and try to drown out my surroundings. The drink is very strong. I really don't want it. I toss the liquid into the planter next to me. I feel like walking. I want to relax and have fun. Why am I so anal and uptight? I am twenty-two years old but behave like an old fart. I could go inside and just let loose. Instead I get myself into a funk. My left arm down to my fingertips starts to tickle. My heart is racing. I am in pain against my will. I get out off the chair and walk down to the pond. I need distraction. I disturb the sleepy geese. Their wings flap the water before they lift off to get on the other side of the pond, away from me. I watch the water lilies sway in the small waves.

"Thomas, where are you? Come here. We have some hors d'oeuvres." Kurt calls me. I know I should join them.

Inside the bungalow the air is thick with cigarette smoke. I grab an open pack of cigarettes and pull one out. The lighter is not working. I am glad. That keeps me busy looking for matches. It occupies me so I can delay joining the group. They don't pay any attention to me anyway. The food tray gets passed between them. Klaus' eyes are already glazed over. He is drunk. The others are close behind him. The tall blond guy sits on Klaus lap, enjoying a big chunk of cheese. Klaus' hand pats his back. A cigarette dangles from his lips. No one really talks. The loud music would drown out any word anyway. Amanda Lear is on. It's a signal for Klaus. He pushes the blond guy off and jumps to his feet. He starts to dance. He twirls on one foot around and around, his arms move like snakes. It's always the same choreography. His movements are actually very nice. Except for the fact that he is in a state of trance. His eyes are totally blank. Kurt moves the coffee table just in time before Klaus bumps into it.

Klaus speeds up his movements. He pulls his shirt over his head. "Yeah, show us what you have you little whore," Ralph encourages him. The others clap their hands. I sit at the dining room table sucking on my cigarette. I want to stop what is to come. But I don't.

Klaus unbuttons his jeans. Peter drops onto his knees and pulls the pants down. Klaus grabs his head to steady himself and steps out of the pants. Then he moves closer to the tall guy and circles his hips right in this guy's face. He puts his hands on Klaus' ass. His index fingers slips under the underwear. Klaus pulls the guy's head into his crotch.

"I wish Klaus would be as good a dancer on stage as he is right now," Kurt says. I hadn't noticed that he had moved next to me. "He has great posture and a body to die for. He really could be a professional dancer. For some reason he cannot follow my choreography. He just won't pay any attention. He always does what he thinks is right. Well, that doesn't work in the ballet world." Kurt chuckles. He is right. Klaus doesn't follow any rules. He is his own man no matter what. Who knows that better than me?

Klaus is completely naked. His low-hanging balls bounce around. His dick is soft. He is way too drunk to get aroused. But his body teases the guys. One by one they touch him wherever they want. Klaus won't stop them. He has another drink in his hands. His dancing becomes less stable. The tall guy starts to undress himself. Ralph and Peter do the same. Klaus sinks to his knees and bends backwards. His head touches the floor. His back arches. He spreads his knees. He turns to the side to get his legs from underneath. He now lays flat on his back. The three guys stand directly over him. All naked and aroused. Klaus lifts his legs, grabs his feet and pulls them towards his face. I should leave. I don't want to see what will happen now. My fingertips start to tickle again.

"Why are you still staying with him?" Kurt asks. "You

know that he is not faithful. Never will be. He lets anybody fuck him. He won't remember afterwards. I even fucked him once. I am sure he doesn't know that. You should leave him. You deserve better. Klaus' world is not yours. You only get hurt." Kurt puts his arm around my shoulders. I know he is right. I look at him. I don't know what to say.

The tall guy has moved and stands over Klaus' head. Bernd and Ralf are on either side of Klaus. They have grabbed his legs and pulled Klaus' body up higher. Klaus supports himself by holding his back. Only his neck and head still touch the floor. The tall guy still stands over Klaus' head and bends his knees. He is fully aroused. Ralf and Bernd pull Klaus legs between the tall one's. Klaus ass is fully exposed and ready to be fucked by the tall guy. I can't watch that any longer.

"I am going to bed. Good night."

"I am sorry that you have to watch that. Good night." Kurt gives me a hug. I walk to the guesthouse. I am too tired to go to the bus station. I want to cry. But I have no tears. I fell onto the bed and stare at the ceiling.

The sun wakes me up. I am alone in the bed. Slowly last evening's events comes back to me. Klaus is probably still at the bungalow. I don't care. I want to go home. I am still dressed. I get up. Everything is quiet. I only hear the birds. I pee and look in the mirror. I feel so ugly. My hair is all over the place. On my upper lip is a big whitehead. I don't care. I just want to get out of here. The lock falls into the gate behind me. For a second I wonder if I should take the walk through the field or go straight down to the street. I am not in the mood for a long walk. I turn right for the street and walk as fast as I can, my eyes fixed on the cobblestones. It's Saturday morning. I am not even sure what time it is. It must be very early because there is no traffic. As I pass by homes, dogs bark at me. Not very loud. It's like if they are talking to each that somebody is coming but not to worry. I don't look at any of them.

At the corner of my eye I notice something I can't really recognize. I lift my head. I see somebody sitting at the curb of the street, the head turned in my direction. I focus my eyes. It's Klaus. For a split second I think I should go back to Kurt's place. But I don't. I keep walking. I pass him without stopping. Our eyes meet. He looks very sad. And somehow old. I take my eyes off him. I don't want to talk to him. He gets up.

"Thomas, please." I don't stop. Thankfully I hear the bus coming. I have to run so I wouldn't miss it. And I don't want Klaus to make it. The door shuts behind me. I look out the window. Klaus is still where I passed him. He seemed so lost and lonesome. I don't have the energy for any feelings.

Trained to be a Journalist Foot Soldier

I am a student, at least for three days out of every month. The six a.m. train to Leipzig brings me right on time for the beginning of the first class. Wednesday late afternoon I return to Berlin. Just the fact of being admitted to Karl Marx University gives me a sense of accomplishment. But the happiness level stops right there. Sitting through class after class to learn the economics defined by Marx, Engels and Lenin is not only tedious for me, I have no clue what the professors are talking about. I am a very practical person. Meaning, all that I hear and learn I try to apply to the real world. I am not ignorant to intellectual models just for the sake of a scientific exercise but at some point all should show some practicality, and the truth. However, the economics I am taught have to fit only an ideology. The premise: The society takes ownership of all and everything. Collective responsibility is the mechanism that drives and furthers all facets of society. The equalization of every human unleashes unlimited brain power and progress for the benefits of everybody. There is no need for individualism, desire for material things and wealth. The need for money and individual power will eventual become unnecessary. We all become one as well as our goal.

That dazzling paradise has a name: Communism. The Soviet Union has been on that path since 1917. Soviet Party Secretary Kruchev predicted the arrival around the year 2000. East Germany's counterpart Ulbricht had the same time frame and target in mind. A society where all needs and desires are met. The class system becomes just a word definition in the dictionaries. As well as capitalism, of course. But why in the world if the twentieth century is the century where all antagonism will end are we still missing essentials in stores just about eighteen years before the deadline? Why we are not allowed to travel freely? Why are we subjected to censored news and movies? And after the disastrous abolishment of private ownership of land and factories, why is there an order to create a private sector again? Why can't I report about the struggle of shop owners to fill their shelves with onions and filets or why restaurateurs have a hard time serving whipped cream on top of a cup of coffee or a bowl of ice cream? On the other hand my aunt's sister-in-law, a seamstress in West Berlin, can vacation in Mallorca, drives a car and has a telephone? But according to my economics professor, my Western aunt is totally taken advantage of by the bloodsucking West German imperialists and their corrupt government?

Do I dare to challenge him and his colleagues? No. Do I ask my fellow students during breaks if they really believe what we just get fed? No again. I sit through these classes only thinking how I will ever pass a test or the final exams? One solution could be to memorize the principles of the Marxismus-Leninismus economics. I am not smart enough for that. I know. Watching some of my fellow students I can't stop admire how they re-chew the nonsense. Most of them seem to know all the right answers, can make a sensible presentation in front of the class and always, always finish their homework.

There is one guy I am particular envious of. Good looking, slim and always dressed in a suit. The Party button prominently displayed on his jacket. He works at *Die Jungle Welt* newspaper, is married and has an infant son. His class participations appear so engaged sincere and accomplished. But is he really a true believer or, has he just figured out how to bullshit to advance his career? He lives in the real world, too. What about his fruitless attempts to buy bananas for his infant son? Is he on a waiting list for a bigger apartment? What about his wish to vacation on the Baltic Sea in the summer? Does he stay in line for a table at the Ratskeller restaurant but gets pushed back because day visitors from West Berlin get preferential treatment from the host? Or what about buying a nice bouquet of flowers for his wife on their anniversary? But all what he can get is a bunch of sad-looking red carnations? Maybe all that doesn't matter to him because he is able to see the big picture, the bright future somewhere in the future? Should I just be

252

thankful to have a spot at the university, pay only a small tuition every semester and get into the movie theater for 1,55 Marks, pay just 37 Marks for my apartment and 20 Pfennig for a subway ride? Is it just me that wants what I can't have?

I would like to discuss in class the balance between individual and collective happiness. Or how Communist's society values self-indulgence versus group satisfaction? How much personality is too much personality in order to keep Marxist ideology functioning? If communism doesn't see room and need for property ownership are thoughts and intellectual products also everybody's property? Marxism and Leninism sees history as an upwards spiral with communism as the ultimate goal of all humanity. Does progression stop when communism is reached and the whole world becomes a big dance hall? As I struggle to somehow bridge theory as taught and reality as I live it I realize that at least at the department of journalism at my alma mater I am in school again.

I am relegated to listen, absorb and repeat. The goal: a journalistic soldier in the army of puppets to create an illusion. Even Marx and Engels must have realized that their vision is just that. One wrote and published the other one footed the bill. The monumental work they produced just stroked their fancies, gave them knowingly a place in history. I can't believe that they really believed what they wrote as a blueprint for the future. Power-hungry politicians and ideologists like Lenin, Stalin, Trotsky, Mao, Kim IL Sung, Castro and all the other left wing dictators took Marx's and Engels' work as tool to manipulate society to create their own monument. They also did not care about the common goods. The most, they were just experimenters. In all honesty, I should not sit here. I can't turn myself into a believer. The overwhelming part of my studies is listening to the teachings of Marx and Engels and Lenin. Very little is spent on the art of writing. I am not sure how I ever can get my bachelor degree with this foolishness.

The end of my daily classes and seminars cannot come soon enough. Leipzig is certainly not my favorite city. But the little time I have to enjoy it I do. There is a small and intimate espresso bar close to the old city hall. I like to hang out there after classes. Ones I met a guy there. He was visiting for a day. We decided to rent a room at the Astoria Hotel. He paid. We had sex. We exchanged addresses afterwards. I never followed up with him nor did he with me.

Since I am not on talking terms with my aunt I had to find a place to sleep for the two nights I am in Leipzig every month. Ferdinand's brother Franz and his partner Torsten have a huge apartment here. They offered for me to stay with them. I gladly take them up on their offer. It's fun to spent time with the two of. Franz sings at Die Musikalishe Komoedie theater, Torsten at the Leipzig opera. Needless to say that they have a lot of friends from the theater scene. And Franz is an excellent host. Sometimes their colleagues come over to their house after the shows. Of course, they all know how to party. That alone makes my monthly trip to Leipzig bearable. Sometimes I think I should get in touch with my former co-workers at the museum. But I feel kind of funny about it. The circumstances surrounding my uncle's death and my vague suspicion that one of the women there was his lover make me hesitant to visit. Someday, maybe.

A Friend Escapes to Amsterdam and I Pay the Price

"Ferdinand wants to go out with us tonight." Klaus is working on a new lamp for us. The two halves of the wooden centerpiece lay open as he tries to pull the electric wire through the openings. "Is there a special reason?" I ask. We never plan any outings with Ferdinand. It's always just on the spur of a moment with him. He never plans anything. Ferdinand always keeps himself busy with something. "I don't know. He called when you were in the bathroom. He suggested having dinner at the Opern Cafe."

"Wow, that's a fancy place for a no special occasion meet-up."

I like Ferdinand. He is always nice to me and accepting. Once he and I had a beer after a dance rehearsal when Klaus had to work. Ferdinand talked about his two years with Klaus. They had met at a party in Dresden. Soon afterwards Klaus moved to Berlin to live with Ferdinand. Their relationship was as tumultuous as ours is. Ferdinand was more willing than I to tolerate Klaus' sexual escapades. "I was never faithful either. Anytime Klaus would go off with somebody I went to the next public bathroom. Somehow, I was addicted to Klaus and couldn't get rid of him. You know, he is a great guy. But as a lover, forget it." He and Klaus somehow managed to stay good friends after their split. I didn't have to tell him how Klaus and my relationship is. He knew. But he never offered any advice.

When I saw Ferdinand for the first time again two months ago after Klaus and I decided to give it another try, he acted like nothing had happened. It was almost a year that I had moved out of Klaus' apartment for the second time. I thought I got over him and went on with my life. My studies in Leipzig kept me busy and, Klaus somehow slipped my mind until he showed up one day at my office asking me out. A coffee led to a drink led to me getting tipsy led to me ending up at his place. I never left. Things seem okay between us.

"I guess it's kind of a going-away dinner. He is vacationing in Prague for couple of weeks." I look at Klaus.

"Isn't it odd that he wants to have dinner with us because he is going on vacation?" I wonder. Ferdinand travels a lot. His waiter job makes him a lot of money. Just recently he bought a car. A yellow Trabant hatchback compact car. Used, but in top condition. It looks like a delivery car from the Postal Service because of its color. But who cares. He must have paid a lot of money for it. These cars go for close to 20.000 Marks. Definitely more than a new car would cost. Klaus and I are sure that part of the money paid was in West Marks. Anyway, since Ferdinand was the owner of a car he always drives places during his vacation but he never wanted to get together to celebrate that with a dinner or even a couple of drinks.

"It's kind of funny. You are right. But Ferdinand is so unpredictable. I am not as surprised as you are. And the price is right. He is paying."

We are early. The host at the restaurant looks at Klaus. Not so much to greet him. He is undressing Klaus with his eyes. Needless to say that he totally ignores me. Klaus seems not to notice the shameless flirt. "We are meeting our friend here. The reservation is under my friend's name Ferdinand." The guy grabs his list without taking his eyes off of Klaus. I can see that Klaus avoids any eye contact with him. Since his blatant advances are not met he snaps back into the so-typical host attitude. He lifts his eyebrows and scans the reservation list.

"What was the name you supposedly have a reservation?" Now he looks at me. His expression says it all: you are ugly. And ugly people don't have reservations at this place.

I turn to Klaus. I feel how my anger creeps up inside me. "Maybe we should wait for Ferdinand?"

Before Klaus can answer the host does: "We are fully booked this evening. You probably are looking at about an hour or so waiting time." What an arrogant nothing guy, I think.

"I know we have a table. Please check again. The name is Ferdinand. If you can't find it I would like to talk to the restaurant manager."

"I know the manager. I always get him free tickets for the tech rehearsals at the opera," Klaus says to me loud enough so that the host can hear it. "He will let us in."

Tables in nice restaurants are valuable commodities in the same category like Hungarian Salami, bathroom tiles or now quartz watches. It is repulsive and degrading. Of course we have a reservation, Ferdinand had told Klaus that. But this host like all the other hosts plays the power game. After he couldn't get a blow job from Klaus he now wants a tip, most likely in West Marks. And in most cases he probably gets what he wants, I suppose. He wears his self-assurance on his sleeve. There are moments where I would like to be a waiter, bartender and hairdresser where tipping in hard currency is part of the unspoken job description.

All the sudden, I feel so angry. A so banal encounter with a restaurant host can make me flip out. Why is it that a host can throw you into a rage in no time and your thoughts run amok? It is not the first time that I get going just because things are not going the expected way. It's so little and has no significance beyond the fact that we just want to have dinner with Ferdinand and this underling of a host throws a wrench in it.

"You are all red in your face. What's going on?" Klaus jabs me in the shoulder.

"Sorry, but this kind of encounter put me over the edge. I don't know why, but it does."

"Calm down. This guy is a jerk. He tried to pick me up a couple of months ago. It was in the cafeteria of the opera. I ignored him than as I did today. His ego is hurt. That's all."

Is it that simple? I think. He can't fuck Klaus. Therefore he makes a stink about a table and poses as Mister All-important. An unwanted sexual advance puts me in a tirade about society, privileges and system flaws. Ridiculous!

"Hi guys. Sorry I am late. Let's go inside." Ferdinand walks fast towards us. He is always in a rush. Everything is time for him. Two things he hates to waste: time and money.

"Hi, Detlef," he says to the host. "What table did you give

us?"

"The one you wanted. Next to the piano." This guy was playing us. Asshole. Klaus and I try to keep up with Ferdinand. This part of the restaurant on Mondays is a gay discotheque packed to full capacity. A fun place. But tonight it is what it is six days out of seven: a soothing place with dimmed lights, lit candles and one fresh carnation per table. The waiter comes. Apparently another friend of Ferdinand.

"Hi, Jonas. Bring us a bottle of Rotkäppchen Sekt."

"No problem." Jonas disappears.

"What are we celebrating?"

"Nothing, really. I fly to Prague tomorrow morning. You never know. Maybe the pilot is drunk and crashes the plane. You never know." Ferdinand laughs. The waiter pops the bottle. Our glasses clink. I like champagne. After the second glass I feel already lightheaded. I enjoy the feeling.

Our conversation is relaxed and about nothing important. Ferdinand orders one bottle after another. We have filet mignon with green beans and Pueckler ice cream afterwards. We are the last ones to leave the restaurant. I have to hold on to the railing leaving the building. Klaus and Ferdinand are behind me, arm in arm.

"Let's go to the Schoppen Stube. I am not ready to go home." I am up for it. So is Klaus. Ferdinand unlocks his car. He shouldn't drive. We all know that, but we don't care.

There is a long line outside of the bar. The bouncer fills the door frame. He sees Ferdinand. We get in. I see Ferdinand putting a rolled up bill in this guy's hand. The bar is crowded and very smoky. All tables are occupied. We push towards the bar. The bartender recognizes Ferdinand and Klaus. He lifts his hand and keeps three fingers up. Ferdinand gives him a nod. We continue with champagne. Without a word we put our arms around each other. A moment you don't want let go.

"I am so happy that you are together again. Make it work this time. You belong together." Ferdinand's words are slurring. I look at Klaus. He smiles at me. "He is my angel." Klaus also slurs. But it doesn't matter. "I want it too," I say. I like to say more but know nothing more would make sense right now. I am wasted as well. My brain is mush.

We are the last ones to leave Schoppen Stube bar. We stumble to the corner of Schoenhauser and Eberswalder Strasse. Ferdinand lives just down the street. Klaus and I have to manage a much longer walk home. "Guys, take care. I will call you." We have another group hug.

It's Saturday morning. Klaus and I have breakfast. He made my favorite morning dish. Scrambled eggs, ham, tomatoes and onions. We have nothing specific planned for the weekend. Klaus wants to wallpaper the living room. Maybe later we can go for a stroll in the Friedrichshain Park. The ring of the phone interrupts our laziness. Klaus answers. I decide to take a shower. The warm water runs down my back. It makes me horny. Klaus likes when I don't dry myself after the shower. My slippery body turns him on. I shut the water off and drip into the living room. Klaus sits on the couch next to the glass table with phone on it. He is somehow lost in thoughts. I spread my legs and sit on his lap. He puts his arms around me. I feel how my wetness dampens his t-shirt. He has no underwear on.

"That was Ferdinand. He is in Amsterdam."

"What?" I lean back and look at Klaus face.

"Yes, Ferdinand is in Amsterdam since yesterday evening. He says he is fine. He wants me to call his brother Franz." I get of off Klaus and pull my underwear and t-shirt on. I don't know what to say. It sounds so unreal. Ferdinand is in Amsterdam. How is that possible? How did he get there? Didn't he tell us he will be in Prague?

"How did he get from Prague to Amsterdam?"

"He didn't say."

"That's why he invited us for dinner. He knew. He knew he will escape. Why didn't he say anything?"

"Yes, it was his goodbye."

"He wouldn't even trust us. He must have feared we would betray him. That is terrible. We are friends. We never would have done such a thing."

"He must have had this planned for a long time. Why would he tell us that he will fly to Prague? He probably had an escape helper. He must have been hidden in the trunk of a car. It's the only way to get out."

"But why is he in Amsterdam? Someone must have driven him all the way to Amsterdam? Why wouldn't he get out as soon he passed over the border of West Germany? He probably never flew to Prague."

"There is no direct way from here to Amsterdam without hitting West Germany first, is there?"

"No, but what do I know?"

Klaus wipes tears off of his face. I don't feel anything. Of course I have heard of people making daring escapes. Some made it. Some got captured or shot. But Ferdinand is the first I know who has successfully escaped. This time for real. Many years ago, even before he knew Klaus, he had tried to cross the border from Hungary into Yugoslavia. When the schlepper had left the Hungarian border control showed up. Ferdinand was immediately transferred back to East Germany's Stasi together with another man. He was tried and sentenced to prison. He never really talked about his imprisonment. "It's in the past," he would say. "I have to go on with my life." But now he had made it. What courage!

The ring of the phone makes us both jump. Did the Stasi listen to Ferdinand's call?

"Maybe we shouldn't answer."

"I know. But on the other hand it could be somebody totally unrelated to Ferdinand's call?" The ring tone hurts my ears. Klaus picks up the phone.

"Hi... Yes... Good. See you later."

"That was Franz. He wants to meet us in an hour at the entrance to the Palast der Republik."

The white marble building seems way too big as it hovers along the side of river Spree. Where once stood the Berliner Castle, imploded to rubble in the fifties under the order of Part Secretary Walter Ulbricht, this new colossus is intended to symbolize Socialist accomplishments. It is totally out of proportion with its surroundings. It almost looks like the Party architect was instructed to outdo the Berliner Dom on the other side of the street. The size is an extension of the gigantism so common for dictators. But rumors have it that East German leaders are not quite happy with the humongous size of the place. The "Palace of the People" has a balcony above the main entrance modeled on the terrace above the Lenin Mausoleum in Moscow, where the Soviet apparatchiks observe military and people parades. The crux with the Palast der Republik balcony is that it turns the Secretary General and his group into midgets. When they stepped on it for the first, and last, time to take the adulation of the masses during the May 1 rally they had to realize that despite their *über* ego they just come in human size like the rest of the population. To copy the red marble balcony on top of Lenin's tomb failed miserable.

The Palace of the Republic was never again used as backdrop for the Secretary General of the Party and its apostles. What was billed mostly as some sort of a symbol and play ground for the *Haute Volée* just steps away from the Central Party office, the ministry for foreign affairs and the House of the State Council became just a people's house with performance hall, bars, restaurants, bowling alley and nightclub. The main hall on the second floor is designed as a shrine for Socialist painters no one really cares for. But couches and tables there are inviting and used. I never mind hanging out here to read the paper or watch people. The restaurants are decent and what's on the menu is actually available. If you need to call somebody this is the place where you would find a functioning public phone. In a way the Place of the Republic is a perfect micro world of socialism envisioned by the proletariats leaders. Everything works, is pretty and somehow harmonious.

Except by building this giant palace many other needed public projects in the rest of the republic like public pools, failing streets, buildings and desperately needed housing were canceled. Like before, Berlin had priority. No wonder that most East Germans want to move and live here in the capital of the country. Berlin is the magic word for artists, actors, and dancers as well as government employees. Whoever gets the call to transfer to Berlin has made it.

Klaus and I have a very special connection to the Palace of the Republic. Our stainless toilet paper holder and towel hooks come from there. How? Our dance group was selected to perform at the grand opening of the building. The bathroom fixtures made in West Germany looked beautiful and so shiny. Klaus could not resist. I was mortified at first but got over it very quickly when he installed them in my apartment.

The meeting with Ferdinand's brother and his partner was short and very hushed. We all felt watched and uncomfortable. Franz and his partner had just moved to Berlin after both of them were hired to sing at the Berliner Rundfunkchor choir. We all were still in a state of disbelief about Ferdinand's escape. After the fact we now can put two and two together. Ferdinand hints, at the time just remarks, are turning now into bits and pieces telling us about his planned flight. We are all still not sure how he got out. Franz knew that his brother was flying to Prague. How he got from there to Amsterdam remains a big mystery to us. We speculate that his friend Frank Mieshaber must have played a role in it.

Ferdinand had met Mieshaber during a performance at the Staatsoper. Ferdinand being Ferdinand must have sensed that this guy can be useful to him and befriended him. "We had sex once. It was awful," Ferdinand told us, "I will never sleep with him again. Every time he makes advances I have to come up with an excuse." But Ferdinand was certainly impressed by this guy's profession. He was the General Manager of the Opera in Gelsenkirchen, which in the world of opera has a pretty distinguished reputation. Ferdinand, operating like a collector when it comes to meeting and keeping new friends, considered Mieshaber the trophy in his collection. His brother and I concluded that Mieshaber with his connections must have been the man who made the escape possible.

Klaus and I still feel numb. It is like Ferdinand has died. The Wall closes us in and the others out. All that's left are memories and regrets of not having spent more time together before everything changed. Our lives from now on will be defined by before Ferdinand left us. Klaus takes it pretty hard. He cries a lot and tells me how much he loved Ferdinand. I try not to be hurt too much by his show of feelings for his ex-lover. This should not be the time to be jealous.

"Your application for a visa to travel to Hungary is denied." I am stunned. I look at the policeman.

"The visa was denied? But why?"

"According to the visa law of the German Democratic Republic we are not obligated to give you a reason for an approval or disapproval. There is nothing more I can tell you." The policeman gets up from behind his desk. It's my time to leave. I leave his office and pass through the long and narrow corridor of the police station. It's filled with people waiting. I had applied for a one-week visa to fly to Budapest. Two guys from our dance group had asked me if I wanted to go with them. *What a great idea*, I thought at the time since Klaus and I are on the outs again.

I love Budapest, a city I had visited twice before: once as participant of an international summer camp and once with Klaus. Budapest has an aura of worldliness. The glorious past from pre-Communist rule seems so alive. Street cafes, outdoor restaurants and shops better stocked for the most part than here. And there is the Gellert Bath, a Mecca for gay life. The three of us would have a super time. We bought our airline tickets together. Getting a visa was the least of my concerns. How wrong! Who and what is behind the denial decision for the travel visa?

Sure, Hungary is one of the countries where if, at all, an escape into the West has a higher success rate than trying to get out of East Germany. Stories where East Germans got to Hungary somehow found escape helpers who would lead them to the border to Yugoslavia. The border is less inhumane than the one between East Germany and West Germany. You just have to know where to cross without the danger of tripping on land mines, self-shooting guns triggered by motion and touch, electric fences and killer dogs. When you made it into Yugoslavia you had to get to the West German embassy in Belgrade. After that everything becomes just a bureaucratic process. West Germany grants every East German citizenship, because it's written in its constitution.

On the other hand, if the Hungarian border control gets you they don't have any mercy. They hand you over to the

East German authorities, well aware what will happen: prison under the worst possible conditions. Every East German knows the existence of the prison in Bautzen by heart. This is where most of the captured end up as political prisoners and share cells with the worst criminals as well with ex-Nazis. If you are lucky and able to get your name on a prisoners list which will be copied to the West Germans who might be fortunate enough to get bought out by the West German government: 20.000 West Marks per head, but this can take years.

Ferdinand tried to escape by way of Hungary and was caught. He and another couple of guys had made it to the border with the help of a paid smuggler. He never ended up in Bautzen nor did he get Berlin-Ban. Both things very unusual, indeed. Many of his friends suspect that he cut a deal with the authorities to become an informant for the Stasi in exchange for less-harsh verdict. Of course, no one knew for sure. I always tended to believe he was not on the payroll of the secret service. But now that I was denied my travel visa to Budapest suspicion was creeping up in my head. Suspicion that Ferdinand, whose second attempt to leave the workers' paradise was successful and is now living in West Berlin, had something to do with that. Did the police somehow suspect that I would try to escape via Hungary with the help of Ferdinand? As I contemplate that I remember a letter I had written to Ferdinand a couple of month earlier.

Most of the male dancers in our group are gay, but there are some that are straight. They are not very gracious on their feet but most of them are of a strong build and able to lift and carry the girls across the stage without problems, and these guys enjoy the fact that they could touch the girls at their crotches and buds. Not in a creepy way but as part of our dance routine. And no matter on what side of the aisle you are, testosterone always flies high backstage.

One of the straight guys is Ralph. He is a driver for some higher up at the State Department. He has a girlfriend who is older than he is. Klaus and I hang out with them. Ralph has also a sister who has a Turkish boyfriend who lives in West Berlin. Because of that he can freely come and go whenever he wants. Turkish men are highly sought after by East German women. They are exotic looking and supposedly not bad in bed. The Turks love their East German girlfriends because they are in control. They can come and go whenever they want. Their girlfriends are stuck behind the Iron Curtain. They have to be nice otherwise the Turkish boyfriend won't be back. Nothing that their female counterpart in East Berlin can do about it. The 25 East Marks the Turks have to exchange every time they enter East Berlin are nicely spent on their devoted girlfriends. At any given Friday or Saturday early evening Alexanderplatz turns into a mating place for Turks and East German women.

Anyway, we befriended Ralph's sister and her boyfriend as well. The guy seems very polite and is always asking if he can bring us anything from West Berlin: jeans, t-shirts, razor blades, soap. You name it. He would name the price and we pay him in East German money. With that he pays his girlfriend's rent, takes her out to bars and restaurants. For all involved a pretty good deal. One day he also offered to take letters to the other side so we don't have to use the East German postal service and run the risk that the mail will be opened. Somehow the guy appeared trustworthy to me. At the time of his offer I didn't have any use for it.

But the time would come. I again had moved out of Klaus' apartment after I found out that he was seeing two other guys on a regular basis. Both also work at the Metropol Theater, one as a dancer the other one in the cafeteria. The two are lovers but don't mind a third man once in a while. Rumor had it that they were into heavy kinky sex. But most of all they liked to fuck one guy at the same time. I knew that Klaus had the hot's for them and they for him. Sure, I should have known but he was in denial once more. One day I came home from work and Klaus was in the shower. I thought it was kind of unusual but didn't give it much thought. But as soon as I opened the door into the living room I knew. The couch was pulled out and a towel was on the floor. I picked it up. It smelled of shit and I could see blood stains. Without a word I opened the shower door with the towel in my hand.

"What do you want me to say? You know what happened anyway."

"Anyone I know?"

"Not any one, any two. And you know them both."

"Tell me."

"Jens and Karl. They fucked me. It was good. Wish you were as big as the two together. But you are not. Too bad."

Klaus stepped out the shower, brushing his dripping body by my right arm.

"Sorry, that I can't make you shit and bleed. You are disgusting. Nothing that you promised matters to you. It's all about your pleasure. Why do you even want to be with me?"

"I don't know." I feel like punching him. I throw the towel on the floor.

"If you don't know, than there is not much to say, isn't there? Why do I believe you time and time again? You just trample on everything we have. It does not matter to you. You know what, it doesn't matter to me anymore as well. Have your disgusting fun. I am out." Nothing that I said seems to faze him. He put his clothes on.

"Get out," is all that he had to say.

I don't know anymore how many times we have broken up and gotten together again. I run down the stairs. This time I have to stick to it. This is not healthy. It's like an addiction that brings us back to each other, only to be hurt again. But how can I make it final with no possibility of return? To stay together boils down to a constant struggle. Our fights inflict only pain. Hope turns into disappointment turns into hate.

More than once I thought about killing him. I know it's just a thought. But what is a thought? How can he create this dark side in me? In reality I get nervous just stepping on a spider or try to swap a fly. And here I have fantasies to murder my boyfriend. Maybe having murderous thoughts are the beginning that would end with doing the unspeakable? I kind of scare of myself. I wish I just could pack up and move far away, out of Berlin. But where to? Is moving to another city really a solution to get Klaus out of my life? I should seriously weigh my options. My mind is pulled in thousand different directions as I rushed to the train station.

The day had already turned into twilight when the S-Bahn finally arrives. Lost in my thoughts I watch the outside passing by. There is this stretch of abandoned territory. It's the no-man's land between East and West Berlin, not maintained since the erection of the Wall. Unused tracks and dilapidated stations. Maybe the other side of the Wall would bring me more luck? How could I manage to escape? It is very risky. I would have to find an escape helper, money and the physical courage to do it. The reward: I would leave everything behind with no chance to be allowed back. It would be a new beginning, no baggage from the past, just me and the future. Klaus-free. At Pankow station I get off with a seed planted in my head.

I can't get the idea to leave everything behind out of my mind. The fresh start with no attachments seems the perfect solution. Not only can I shut the door on my personal misgivings. I also don't have to deal with my family anymore. The stress over my crazy relationship with my stepfather and my aunt in Leipzig; all that I would stay right here. Life on the other side of the Berlin Wall could be different and exciting. I can travel; choose what I want to do with the rest of my life. No ideology to follow in order to get an apartment, a car, phone, job. No litmus test to have a career. No ropes that hold you in one place. Alone dreaming about all these possibilities makes me jump, infuses energy I didn't know I had.

But how can I get this into motion? I don't know anybody who would put me in his car trunk to get me over the border? I have no clue how to get in touch with any escape helpers. My biological father lives somewhere in West Germany. How can I find him? He never cared for me. Would he help me if I would locate him? The only official way to get out, without doing prison time, is to apply to be reunited with a family member. It has to be a family member you are directly related to, like a father or mother, sister or brother. I could contact my grandmother's relatives in Düsseldorf to see if they can locate my father. It's a long shot. Who else is there? Ferdinand! I could ask him for advice and help. But how? It would be suicidal to call him. All calls crossing into West Berlin are listened to by the Stasi. Writing to him bears the high chance that the letter would be opened by the Secret Service. Ralph's sister! Didn't her boyfriend offer once to smuggle a letter to the other side of the Iron Curtain?

Dear Thomas, I was surprised to get your letter. I won't ask how you get it to me. You probably took a lot of risk. Anyway, I was surprised to read that you want to come to West Berlin. I know that your life with Klaus is difficult and sometimes impossible to take but this should not be the reason for you to come here. It's not that easy here. You really have to fend for yourself. There is no guarantee to get work. Everything is about money. If you have it you will make it. If not, you are left behind. This is a very competitive society. Everybody is everybody else's enemy. You need a lot of strength. Sure, I had help to get here and to start a new life. But I miss my family. I never expected how much I want to see them. My mother is very sick. She wants me to visit. But I can't. I urge you to re-think your plan.

Now regarding your question if I know someone who would help you to escape: as you know I tried it once and it failed. It was a horrific experience. To this day I have nightmares about lying in the dark waiting for the right moment to run across a path not knowing when the Hungarian border control would patrol again: and then the moment when the spot lights turned night into day. No, I don't know anyone anymore who could help you to try get over the border.

What I can do is to try to find the whereabouts of your father. This is the only thing I can do for you. But please don't do anything you will regret for the rest of your life. I miss you and all my friends. Stay healthy and strong. Ferdinand.

I read the letter over and over. I am kind of taken back by Ferdinand's notion that I would not be strong enough to make in the West and that my motives are too shallow to take such a drastic step in my life. Is he afraid I would want him to support me if I make it to West Berlin? Why does he paint such a dark picture of life in the West? If that's true why did he plot to get out...twice? Honestly, I had expected a different response from him. Help, joy, support. Instead, he discouraged me. But there is a little glimmer of hope. Maybe he will be able to get contact information for my father? And maybe my father will sponsor my family·re-union application? That would certainly the official way to get out.

I am furious. I don't know where to direct my anger. I walk down the Schoenhauser Strasse away from the police station. I want answers. But most I want a visa to travel to Budapest. First I have to call my office to excuse myself for today. Then I will go to the main police station. Maybe I will get an explanation there?

The Police Presidium is located in the same building where I was interrogated by the Stasi years ago in connection with me leaving the Party. Way back then I was led through a back door, now I go through the main entrance. At the reception I have to leave my ID card after I was asked why I am here. The *Volkspolizist* behind the desk doesn't even look at me. The waiting room is overcrowded. I wonder what all this people doing here? And how long it will take until my name will be called. I am so restless. I can't stand still. I feel so wronged. There is also this little hope, this is all a big mistake and I can travel after all.

"Herr Schardt." A police man comes towards me.

"Yes." He shakes my hand.

"Why are you here?" I am confused. He wants me to tell him with people all around us? This is not helpful to calm me down.

"I applied for a travel visa to Budapest. It was denied. And I want to know why?"

"I didn't have a chance to look into your file. But you can be assured that the authorities in Pankow came to this decision after a thorough review. According to the visa law of the German Democratic Republic..."

"Please spare me that. I came here hoping to be treated

as a human and not a case. I have done nothing wrong. I am not a criminal. I work as a journalist. All I want is to go on vacation like many thousands of other GDR citizens. What was there to review so thoroughly, as you put it? Can you please look at my file?"

I speak as loud and determined as I possibly can. I sense that people listen in on our exchange. I want that. The policeman clearly doesn't.

"Can you come back in an hour? I will look at your file."

"Of course. And thank you for your help and understanding." I feel like this guy is sympathetic towards me. I have hope. I decide to wait right here. Maybe he will be back quicker?

"Herr Schardt, there is nothing I can do." The police man seems more uptight than during our first encounter.

"But why? I am twenty-seven years old, a law-abiding citizen and the German Democratic Republic does not trust me to give me a visa to travel to a Socialist brother land?"

"Please, Herr Schardt. Calm down. I will walk you to the door." He is almost friendly. "Herr Schardt, I can't tell you why your application was denied. But I can tell you that any application for a travel visa in the future will be denied. I am sorry."

"What do I do with this information? What would you do if you were told you never can leave the country anymore?" I try to catch his eyes.

His expression is stern. "Goodbye, Herr Schardt."

I push through the door. I want to scream. My life is over. I am confined indefinitely to a tiny country. What is there to strive for? If I am denied to travel to any country within the alliance of the Socialist brother countries what is there to look forward to? Sure, there is Poland and Czechoslovakia, the only two countries in the Bloc that don't require a visa. But maybe I will be denied to travel there as well? I feel so boxed in. But I also know I have to do something with my anger. I want defy them right here and now. Next to the Central Police station is the House of Travel. What a joke. Another fig leaf with no meaning except for the outside world to see. Anyhow, I have to return my airline tickets and I will do it now.

There are no lines. That must be the only place in all of East Germany where no one has to wait to get serviced. What a telling sign! I go straight to one of the open windows. I am still at a boiling point. "I have to return my tickets. I just was denied a visa to travel to our Socialist brother country Hungary." My voice is purposefully loud. I want everyone in the room to hear me. The clerk behind the desk looks at me with a disdain.

"Fill out this form." She pushes me a piece of paper through the window.

"I don't have a pen."

"You should have been more prepared coming here." She opens a drawer in her desk.

"What did you just say? I was not prepared to come here today at all. I was prepared to receive my visa for a one-week vacation in Budapest. That I was prepared for. Please give me something to write on so I can fill out this stupid piece of paper." I sense the tension all around me. And I like that.

"Please keep your voice down. Otherwise I will not handle your claim."

"That's enough. Your job is to refund me and not to tell me how to speak. I want to see your supervisor."

"He is not here."

"You are lying to me." The woman in front of me is red in the face. I feel the heat in mine. Out of the corner my eye I see a man approaching. "How can I help you?"

"I have to return my ticket. And the last thing I need right now is unpleasantness." He takes my ticket. "Please wait here. I will handle this." It's like my anger flushes out in an instant. I want to hug this man. He seems to care. And this is all what I want at this moment. I look for the nearest bench. Lost. Full of self pity. Vulnerable. No sense of time.

"Herr Schardt. Please sign here that you have received your money back." He counts it into my hands.

"Thank you for being so nice and helpful."

I cross Alexanderplatz. What should I do? Is there anything more I can do? I don't want to let go. The policeman had mentioned that the Central State Security Office might give me an answer. Should I risk going there?

I have heard stories that when you enter the building you won't leave it again. I have done nothing wrong! Nothing that warrants the denial of a visa to enter another closed-off Socialist country. I really want an answer. I decide to go the Stasi Headquarter at Normannen Strasse in Lichtenberg. Should I protect myself and let someone know, that I am going to go there? But who? A dilemma born out of mistrust and loneliness. I just have to do it and hope, things will work out just fine.

The Stasi building is characterless bloc of cement with many windows. *Too small to jump out of,* I chuckle to myself. The visitor's entrance is surprisingly small and easy to overlook. A single, non-descript door. I have to ring the bell. A buzzer goes off. A slight push and the door open inwards. I step into a small and narrow hallway. To my left is a huge mirror. A voice from nowhere: "ID." I hear a sliding noise and just above the mirrors is now an opening. I push my ID through it. The opening closes. For the next couple of minutes total silence. I look for signs of life.

"Why are you here?" I don't know where to look. I look at my feet.

"I was denied a visa to Budapest. I am here to find out why." Another couple of minutes pass. The door opposite the entrance opens. A man in plainclothes looks at me.

"Follow me." I do, along a narrow hallway. The man opens a door. "Wait here."

The room has a window, its glass lets daylight in but you can't see outside. There is a table with one chair at each end. The man disappears. The door closes. I don't know what to think. I feel very calm and really curious what will happen next. There is nothing in the room to distract me. I look around. No visible cameras, no mirror. But I feel watched. Or is it more my suspicion that somebody is watching me? I sit down. I am bored. I lose my sense of time since I don't have a watch. I doze off. The forceful opening of the door wakes me up. A man, also in civilian clothes, steps in the room. He has what looks like my ID in his hand.

"What makes you think that we know why your visa was denied? This is a matter of the People's Police and not the office of the State's Security." I can't help but smile.

"A policeman at the Central Police Station suggested that you may know. He only could tell me that any application of mine for a travel visa now or in the future will be denied. This is a very discouraging situation for me. I want to know why."

"Again, visa matters are handled by the People's Police."

"I assume the reason to deny me a travel visa to one of our Socialist brother countries has to do with security concerns the GDR authorities have. That's where you, the State Security, come in. Am I right?"

"Visa applications are handled at the People's Police office."

I feel anger building up inside me. "For me, Stasi and Police are one. Why are you mistrusting me? Do you think I was going to use Hungary to escape?"

"You tell me." I am stunned. Did this guy just give me the answer about why I was not allowed to travel to Budapest? "Here is your ID back. I will escort you to the exit."

I walk back to the S-Bahn station, still in disbelief about what I just learned. The Stasi thinks I am a flight risk. But if that's the case why am I still free? Any person who is under suspicion would be taken off the street, prosecuted and send to Bautzen. Somebody must have snitched on me to the Stasi. A couple of years ago I got a visa for Hungary when Klaus and I applied for it. What has changed between then and now? Who in my circle of friends and acquaintances is an informant? Who would do that knowing that will cause trouble for me?

I have an inkling but I can't bring myself to form the thought right now. That would plant a seed I never could get rid of. And there is still the possibility that I am wrong about him. Maybe it's somebody else I can't think of right now. Who else would do such a thing? Who else has read the letter I had sent to Ferdinand? There is the very obvious: Ralph the personal limo driver for the State Department, his sister, her Turkish boyfriend from West Berlin and Ferdinand. It could be only one of them, some of them or all of them? No one else knew about the letter, I told no one about his answer. Interestingly enough Ferdinand's letter arrived in my mailbox. Postmarked and stamped here in

East Berlin. Somebody must have brought it over, got a GDR stamp and sent it through regular mail. My exchange with Ferdinand must have been leaked. It's so frustrating that I never will find out. I am just left with suspicion from now on. Do I really have to add Ferdinand, Ralph, his sister and her boyfriend to the already long list of people I have to be careful with? To whom can I go to now to freely talk, convey and seek advice? I hate to be consumed by suspicion and mistrust. This is not how I want to live my life.

What I knew before and learned to accept today is this totally controlled society I have to live in makes loners out of each one of us. The first step of being programmed to do the unavoidable: welcome the authority as your only caregiver, the only one who knows, the only one you can turn to for guidance. What a depressing prospect! The beginning of paranoia. The start of being manipulated from here on. It's like taking your brain out off the head and giving it to them. Does this devilish conspiracy really exist? Do they really want us to turn our lives over to them? Are they really convinced that eventually no one is left behind to be put into the pen like farm animals? And then what? When power just becomes one sided and is only in the hands of the elite then a permanent curfew is declared for us behind the fence. If that is all that carries truth or even some truth then there is only one alternative left: leaving as fast as possible. Some unknowing, indescribable thing is pulling me. I have to stop before it gets a complete hold of me. I am not only furious about what happened to me today. I am scared. Being scared can do two things to you: duck or defy. I am not sure what I am ready for.

"Hi, my name is Hans-Peter. I am told I look like you."

I look at myself. This guy in front of me is me. I can't believe what I see. Same thin hair, round face, height, reddish complexion. His fingernails are dirty and not manicured. That's about the only difference I can make out. He smiles at me, I don't. I still try to figure out if this is a prank.

"My name is not Hans-Peter." I try to be funny, not sure if he gets that.

"Oh, my God. How did your mother ever know who is who? I have never seen twins that are so look alike." A woman passing by stares at me and him. "You should be on TV. I am sorry. You must hear that a lot." This is too weird. I just was stopped by a man I have never seen before who looks like me. At the same time a random pedestrian comes out of the subway station and assumes we are related and twins.

"Do you want to have a beer some place around here?" Hans-Peter breaks the strange moment.

"Sure. But where?"

"Well the nearest place is the bar at the Hotel Unter den Linden."

We make our way down Friedrichstrasse. The rush-hour food traffic slows us. I fall behind him. I am glad that I don't have to talk to him right now. My thoughts are in free fall. I noticed his tight pants and firm ass. Strong neck. There are some more differences between me and him.

The hotel bar is full. Three barstools are empty but the usual reserved sign is placed in front of them. Hans-Peter talks to the host. The reserved sign is taken off and, we can take our seats. I am impressed. Wonder what he told the guy behind the rope?

"You can open doors," I joke.

"Sometimes. What do you want?"

"Vodka and Cola. I don't drink beer."

"A German who doesn't drink beer."

"I don't like the taste. I like sweet."

"Like you." Was that a flirt or a snide? I look at his profile. I see a hair sticking out of his nose. Disgusting.

"In a way I know you. And this was not really a chance encounter. A couple of months ago a co-worker asked me how I liked the opera the night before. I told her I wasn't at the opera. She said, but I have seen you there. I told her, that's impossible. A while after that a friend told me that he saw me on the street the day before but I wouldn't recognize him. I told him it wasn't me because I was on a business trip. But now I really got curious. Twice in a short time I was mistaken for somebody else."

Hans-Peter has a very strange look. His eyelids don't

seem to blink. I don't blink either but it makes me uncomfortable. He just stares at me and doesn't say a word. I feel compelled to break the silence.

"So, what's your story? I hope it's not the same as mine. To look alike is enough. Don't you think?" He still keeps his eyes focused on mine. He reminds me of the guy from the Stasi and his almost brutal beaming look. If I could only read his mind.

"Oh, I don't have a really exciting story to tell. I work for the theater." Pause. I am curious. But he stops. Lifts the glass to his lips not taking his eyes of off me. This is too strange.

"What do you do at the theater?"

"I am the right hand of the general manager." Pause. One question one answer. This is a not going well.

"What does the right hand of a general manager do?"

"What the general manager doesn't want to do." I have had enough.

"I guess you are not very talkative?"

"I don't like to talk about my work. That's all." Fair enough.

"What do you like to talk about?"

"You." His straight forwardness caught me by surprise.

"Me?"

"Yes, I want to know you better. Isn't it only normal to know more about your twin?"

"I guess we just killed the theory that no two things are alike?"

"Touché. You are good." I blush.

"That's cute."

"What?"

"That you blush." His eyes are on mine.

"I am a reporter at the local desk. Not very exciting. But I like it."

"I know. I mean, I know that you are reporter."

"Mmm. Do I look like a reporter?"

"When people tell me what I did last week or the day before I got really intrigued. Because I didn't do or wasn't where I was told. Berlin is a village." He giggles. "So I started to ask questions and the answers led me to you.

What do you think? Do we look as alike as people say?"

"I think I am prettier." I am surprised by my wit, and of course blush again.

"I like when you blush." His voice has this velvety undertone. I think he is flirting.

"I am not sure if I should be flattered or concerned by the result of your detective work."

"Why is that?"

"Well isn't it odd that you just asked around as you say and here I am your double?"

"I think it's funny and not odd. I like you." Oh God, why does he do that to me? My thoughts are racing again. I want to ignore what he just said.

"You still didn't answer my question what you like to do when you are not working?"

"Did you just hear what I said? I like you." His fingertips touch my knuckles.

"I am not used to hearing that," is all that I can say.

"I am surprised. I think you are lying. I think you hear that a lot."

"No, I don't. And please can we talk about something else. This makes me really uncomfortable."

"Sorry, that was not my intention. Do you want another drink?"

"No, I am good. Thanks." I rotate the glass between my hands. I wish I just could get up and leave. "What do you do as the personal assistant to the General Manager? I always thought I want to switch to a press secretary or public relations job. I like being a journalist, but that way I could combine two somehow related jobs. If I had a wish I would like to work in the press department of a theater. What do you think what the realistic changes would be?"

"Many, I know some people who made the transition from a reporter into the public relations department of a theater. But to be honest the more realistic way to getting this kind of a job is having a degree in theater science or such." I am glad we got over the flirting thing to a more interesting subject. Maybe this guy can be instrumental in me finding another job?

"So, what would you suggest if you were me?"

"Get as much knowledge about the theater and its process. Read and get as close to the theater whether it is ballet, opera or musicals, as you can. I have not read anything you've written, but you have to be good at it. That's a given. Make a name for yourself. Network. Be around. Then you have a chance."

"If I do all that there is still one big obstacle to overcome. Party affiliation."

"That's nonsense. I am not a member of any party, and I have achieved as much as I want to at this point. I followed the script as I had described earlier to you. I have a bachelor's degree in German language as well as in culture science. I always loved theater. With that I got my first job as a production assistant at the theater in Stralsund. A C-theater. We did everything there. Some was good, some was God awful. But the general manager let us do it. After that I went to Cottbus. Rural province. Terrible talent there. I hated it. But I learned a lot. We had very little money but a lot of enthusiasm. The next job was in Anklam as deputy general manager. Terrible. But along the way I made connections, never friends. I wanted to keep my independence. After all, you never know who would fall out of favor with the local Party boss."

I am surprised how easy he talks about his experiences. I must confess I envy him and his way. I start to like the guy. We not only seem to look alike and we're both gay, his way of thinking and approaching things are like mine. As he goes on about his steps through the GDR theater landscape I drift off into my own thoughts. I should do it the way he did. Go to a small theater and work on my way up from the C to the B and finally to the A-Theater, and back to Berlin. I feel excited. Something pops into my head: maybe I could use this guy to channel my career? He clearly likes me. Maybe when I sleep with him he can fast track me? So many others do it to advance their careers. It can't be that difficult. Look at Kurt Klein and the aspiring dancers. They fuck him, and he gives them solo parts. I should be able to do that, too. As matter of fact, this Hans-Peter guy is much better looking than Kurt Klein for instance. Not my type, but.

"What do you think?" Hans-Peter interrupts my train of thought. I feel caught.

"I am glad we look alike otherwise we never would have met." I wish I could take back what I just said because it sounded flirtatious. "I mean I've never met someone who takes the time to answer my questions and is willing to talk about what's important. Like careers and how to make one. To be honest, everything you said about how to start and continue step by step is the way I imagine it too. But I don't know anybody who would listen and give advice. I kind of have a little in into the scene here in Berlin. But there is a lot of shallowness. I never seem to strike up a serious conversation with someone at premier parties. Part of that is my own insecurity, and my anxiety about approaching people. I don't have the looks. So, I am ignored."

"Now, you're being shallow. Listen, first of all you are cute and good looking. And I am not saying these things lightly. Second, it's not the looks that get you ahead. It's your brain. Being charming helps a little. Don't undersell yourself." He grabs my shoulder. His clear eyes all of the sudden glazing over to what I call bedroom eyes. I stiffen up. Maybe I will sleep with this guy but not today. "You want to go to my place?"

I knew the question would come. "Not today. We just met. Maybe another time. I hope there will be another time?" I am surprised by my own calculated tease.

"I hope so. But why can't be another time now?" Hans-Peter presses his knee against my leg. I don't move. Maybe I should go with him. He is not that bad looking. Jerking each other off is maybe the beginning of something new. He is the right hand of Professor Rohmer, the general manager of the Deutsches Theater I keep telling myself.

"I really have to go home. How about tomorrow?"

"Well I can't make you come with me now. Tomorrow sounds good. I have the evening off. I can cook for us. What would you like to eat?" Wow, he wants to cook for me. Did I hit the jackpot here or what?

"I am an easy eater. Nothing too heavy. I am even fine with a sandwich. I don't want you to go out of your way."

"I like to cook. Maybe some fish. Do you like fish?"

279

I don't but say "Yes, I do."

I walk down Friedrichstrasse. The day at the newspaper was eventless. I just had to write a story about a new restaurant in one of the kiosks recently set up along Rathaus Passage. The owner is a new member of my party. She had waitressed at Ratskeller restaurant until recently. When she heard about leasing one of the three or four kiosks she applied for a restaurant license. She was very frank with me. "I knew I had to become member of the LDPD in order to pass all the other applicants. It worked." Of course I couldn't write that. Anyway, we kind of hit it off. It made it for easy writing.

I certainly think it's a great idea to break up the monumental and vast area around the TV tower, the Marien Church and the traffic-free zone along the shops at the Rathaus passage and place these restaurant kiosks. It gives it a much needed big town flair with some intimacy. Anyway, my boss liked my story. At tomorrow's morning meeting he will ask the editor-in-chief to award me with a point for good writing. Every point brings you closer to a monthly bonus. So, I had a good day. Except that I am now on my way to Hans-Peter's apartment for dinner and sex. I wish I could somehow skip out of it. I don't know if I can sleep with him! It seems too pre-programmed, and of course part of my calculation. I want to chicken out.

I am lost in my thoughts and almost was hit by the streetcar rambling with great noise at the corner of the Oranienburger Strasse. "You idiot. Are you drunk?" A mean looking passerby screams at me. I don't know what to say. I just look at the man. I shrug my shoulders. "These young people. Punks. All of you. They should send you straight into the National People's Army." His shouting makes me angry. What does he want from me?

"Stop screaming at me. You don't know me. So, please don't call me a punk." The guy didn't expect me to confront him.

"What did you just say? I'll yell at you as long and as much as I want to. Show me respect, young man. You are still wet behind your ears. You have it too easy. That's what's wrong with you people. We give you free education, healthcare, you name it." I am perplexed at this man's outburst. I see the Party button on his jacket, but that still doesn't explain his anger. He stops me in my tracks. His face is red. Now other pedestrians take notice and surround us. This becomes ridiculous.

"Mister, let me pass by."

"No, not until I take your name and address. I will report you to the *Volkspolizei*."

"What did he do? Comrade, what did he do? Do you need help?" Another button carrier chimes in.

"If you think that you can intimidate me, you are wrong. The only thing I did, was not seeing the streetcar approaching. Nothing happened, except that you are on a rampage. This has to stop. You want to call the police. Please do so. This nonsense has to stop right now."

"Do you hear that? This punk is telling me what to do. I bet he is under the influence of the Western television. That explains his disrespect for a member of the Socialist Unity Party. This is what happens when we allow the enemy to infiltrate the minds of our citizens. But the proletariat will not allow that, do you hear me?" The man's face is just inches away from mine. I can smell his breath.

"I will now pass you. If you want to hit me there are numerous witnesses here. I sure hope that the proletariat is not only protecting you, but me too." The man backs off and so do the other dozen or so bystanders. I am fuming.

A not-noticed streetcar equals an infiltrated mind by the enemy of the proletariat. This man was not some disgruntled citizen. He is allowed to be an enforcer of a one-mind ideology. Stepping in front of a streetcar is a product of successful infiltration by the enemy. Party cadres are the foot soldiers to point out, to make aware and to outcast the wrongdoers. A totally linear society where everybody functions on auto pilot. How close are we to that? Why has interaction between ordinary people been so aggressive and confrontational? The traffic light is green. No streetcar is in sight. I cross the Wilhelm-Pieck Strasse.

It's Time to Leave Everything Behind

I feel excited. Today is the day of a new beginning. I just reach Schiffbauer Damm bridge on my way to Das Deutsche Theater to sign my employment contract. I will be the new press dramaturge at this prestigious house. I can't believe my good fortune. My double Hans-Peter helped me to get a foot in the door and an interview with the general manager. We somehow hit it off right away. The interview was more like a conversation. And luck was on my side too. The job is part of the affirmative action pool. The job I will sign on today is allocated to a member of the Liberal Party. The stars are aligned. I pass the bunker on my right, opposite is the Friedrichstadt Palast. And here is my new workplace: the u-shaped theater building. It did cause quite a storm when my newspaper colleagues heard about my new job. "How did you do that? Who do you know over there?" I didn't tell anyone that I know the personal assistant to the general manager.

The HR office is to the left. "Good morning. I am here to sign my employment contract." The woman at the desk looks at me. She gets up and enters a room behind me. I hear the door lock. A couple of minutes later she comes out.

"The general manager wants to talk to you. Please follow me." We leave the office and walk down the familiar corridor to Rohmer's office. I can't help but feel uneasy about it. As soon as I enter the room Rohmer greets me. Hans-Peter is there too. "Good morning. Herr Schardt, please have a seat." It seems like all of us take an extra long time to be seated. "I am sorry to let you know that the job offer to join our public relations department is no longer valid. I want to assure you that it is not my decision. I was looking forward to having you here. I wanted to tell you that in person, and not let handle the bad news by our HR office."

I feel surprisingly calm. "Professor, you don't know what it means to me that you have taken the time to tell me that.

282

I was so looking forward to working here as well. But... I guess there is nothing else to say." I get out of my chair. I straighten myself up. I tip my head towards Rohmer and Hans-Peter. I close the door behind me. The joy from ten minutes ago is drained. The impressive theater building is now just any other structure. The brightness of the morning is turns grey. What a fool I am! I really thought I would get this job that so many others are after: a job that would bring me closer to the shakers and movers of the cultural landscape in the GDR. A job that would bring security clearance and opportunities to travel with the theater company behind the Iron Curtain. What was I thinking? I never will get off the blacklist. How much more evidence do I need to realize that? How much more can I take? How many more disappointments do I have to experience? I am twenty-eight years old and I am in a box with no way to get the lid off. I am just allowed to look over the edge. As soon as I try to get out from under the lid it's pushed down on me. It doesn't matter how good I am I never will get the stamp to enter the future.

It was not my grades in high school that was the reason I was denied access to extended school education: it was that my father lived in West Germany. I didn't get the sponsor ship to the university because of my academic ability: I dared to get out off the Party. They didn't let me be part of the secret mission to return stolen artifacts from Leningrad to the museum in Leipzig because I was not strong enough to lift heavy crates: they wanted to make sure that I never forgot that I challenged them. They didn't issue a travel visa to Budapest because I broke the law: they didn't give it to me in order to show that I shouldn't have crossed them. The job offer to become the next public relations person at the Deutsche Theater was not taken back because I was a bad writer: they wanted me to always be aware that they are in charge of my career advancements.

But then how did I get the reporter job at *Der Morgen*? But then how was I allowed to become member of the Liberal Democratic Party? But then why was I admitted to the Karl-MarxUniversity of Leipzig? Carrot and stick. Keeping my hopes alive. Whatever the reasons are, the truth is that they will manage every aspect of my life for the rest of my life. The whip and sugar approach has only one goal: total control. But here is where they fail. I will not longer be intimidated, regulated and watched. I have tried to live within the confinement of the Party society. I have not broken any laws. I am a hard worker. I am career oriented. I have been pummeled enough. They don't want me. Well, I don't want them either. My next step seems so clear and unavoidable. I walk briskly towards Friedrichstrasse train station to find a phone booth.

I look for some change to make two calls. One to my office that I will be taking the rest of the afternoon off, the other one to call Klaus. I find 4 Groschen, exactly what I need to make these calls.

"Ursula, can I skip the rest of the day?"

"Well, yes. You sound terrible. What happened?" My colleague and friend really sounds concerned. I am choking up.

"I guess, I will continue to be your co-worker. They retracted the job offer."

"Oh my, did they give you a reason?"

"They didn't. But I think I know the reason. Can we talk about it later?"

"Sure. Don't do anything out of anger. You know how to reach me. See you tomorrow."

"Thanks. See you tomorrow." Tears run down my face. I start to shake. I have the two Groschen ready to make the next call. I turn around. Two people are waiting to use the public phone. "I will make it quick."

"I hope so. You are only allowed to make one call. You know that, don't you?" A middle-aged woman shouts at me.

"It will be quick." I dial Klaus' number. "It's me."

"How did it go, Mister Press secretary?"

"I didn't get the job. Klaus, I can't live here anymore. We have to leave."

"What do you mean? Where do you want to go?"

"You know what I mean. I am tired of all the roadblocks. I am bruised enough. We have to go on. I just wanted to call you. Can I pick you up after work?"

"Sure. See you later." He hangs up before I can say

anything more. I know he was afraid someone would listen
in to our phone conversation. I am not afraid anymore. I
can't. I have to change my life. I have to get out of here.

"But what about your family?" Klaus asks.

"What about my family? Since my uncle died I don't have
any anchor left except for Tata. But she is old enough she
can visit us anytime she wants to. You know how my aunt
is! And my mother decided a long time ago who is more
important. She never will leave my stepfather. My brother
is more of a friend than family. So, there is just you and me.
That's my family." Klaus lights himself a cigarette. His eyes
follow a young guy just passing by us. I don't want him to be
distracted. I want him to talk about our future. "Klaus, can
you please..."

"What do you mean? I am thinking. As you know I don't
have anybody left here either. My only family is my cousin
in Munich and his sister in Czechoslovakia. But what are
we going to do when we are in the West?"

"I don't know. They only thing I am certain of is that I
am not a loser." I feel like I am out of my body. I have
decided for myself to leave, regardless of Klaus. I hope we
will do it together. It's better to be two going through that
instead of being alone, but if he isn't interested I will go
forward alone. I never have been so certain.

"What should we give as a reason?"

"Family reunion, of course. You with your own living
relative. I am with my father. It's phony. We know it, and
they know it. But let them to argue the opposite."

"You have it all planned, don't you."

"Yes, I have. It's not the first time that I've thought about
leaving this country. I never told you, but when I got
interrogated over and over during my Party tribunal I was
very close to submit my Exit Application but I was scared
about what they would do with me after experiencing their
unscrupulous tactics towards me in connection with my
application to leave the Party. Now it is different. I am older.
I am not afraid of them anymore. Their fear mongering does
not work with me. I am not under their grip anymore. Today
they lost me."

"I hope I can be as strong as you are."

"But Klaus, we are together. If we stay strong and together nothing can come between us."

"I have to call my cousin to see if she would sponsor me. How will you pull that off with your father?"

"I am not sure. Time will tell. At first I want to get going, make it official."

"You mean you want to start it right now?" Klaus stops me in my tracks. "Give me at least a couple of days to think about it."

"Sure, I don't want to put my application in right now. I want to take advantage of the situation while they don't know anything about it. So let's be calculating. In less than two months we will get paid our Christmas money. Why should we not take that? In January we are going on our annual ski vacation. We should enjoy that also. But the day we are back from skiing we should go to the Ministry of Interior."

Klaus grabs my shoulders. "You really have it all planned, haven't you?" I can feel his relief that he doesn't have to do anything right away. Klaus is a procrastinator. Tomorrow is always the best day to do things in his books. "Let's celebrate. Let's have dinner at Offenbach Stuben restaurant." I can see that he would rather go to a pub and get drunk but I don't want to. I want to make this day memorable and special. Gently I push him towards the streetcar stop.

It is early evening but the restaurant is already full. The owner knows us, and he signals that we will get a table for two as soon as it will be available. He makes room for us at the bar. We both ignore the complaints of the three couples who are in a waiting line. As I sit on the barstool I notice a familiar face at the bar corner: it's Juergen Walter, a well-known chanson singer. He was a fellow student and friend of my uncle Paul. He left the university and became a co-founder of the October Club, a band performing mostly propaganda material. Later he broke out and became a solo act. I remember him vividly when he visited my uncle who was still living with my grandmother. Years later I would run into him when he and our dance group performed together at a variety show at the Palace of the Republic. He did remember me, invited me for a drink at his apartment and later fucked me. It was at a time where Klaus and I were on the outs again. We saw each other more than once. Juergen even invited me to come on a tour with him to the southern part of the GDR.

I certainly liked the attention he got wherever we went and I tried to enjoy sex with him, but he was very dominant in bed and loved very long-lasting intercourse. It was too painful for me. I stopped seeing him. I think he wanted a real relationship. Juergen and I wondered what my family would think about that. I joked that it would feel like incest since he was good friend of my uncle. My grandmother liked him too. Juergen would evade my questions regarding my uncle. Once, he made a vague a reference to Klaus. I was not surprised. Anyway, to see Juergen here was kind of a wake-up call. I tip my head in his direction. He smiles. Klaus deliberately ignores him. He knows that I had a fling with Juergen. He doesn't know that I know about his own fling with Juergen, but that's not important today. Klaus and I are here to start the countdown. I feel like I'm at an imaginary train station ready to leave but not knowing the departure time. Juergen, the singer, is unknowingly the first one I say goodbye to. Kind of.

A Family Affair

Klaus and I are busy preparing our written application for the family reunion. His cousin has agreed to send a letter stating that she wants him to live with her. I, on the other hand, have a hard time contacting my father. Ferdinand comes through with his offer to help to locate my father. He doesn't find him directly but he finds a brother, which makes that man my uncle. Ferdinand convinces him to divulge my father's telephone number. In return Ferdinand had to promise my uncle not tell his brother where he got his phone number from. The two brothers are not on good terms, so it sounds. Through Ralph's sister's boyfriend I get the contact information.

I can't believe that I hold the phone number of my father in my hand: this man who never made any attempt to contact me, visit me or paid any child support. My mother told me once that my father and his parents always vacation in East Germany courtesy of the East German government. The family on my father's side is what is called "old Communists." The Communist Party in West Germany was outlawed in the fifties but as sign of internationalism and unity of the workers of the world the GDR rewards the revolutionary struggle of my paternal family with free room and board. Anyway, maybe I can convince the ex-husband of my mother to support my desire to leave the GDR. I have my doubts. But I want to try. Over and over I rehearse the anticipated phone conversation with him. I am nervous but focused.

Then one day I dial his number from Klaus' phone.

"Yes?" It's a voice of an old man or someone who was just woken up by my call.

"Good day. This is Thomas Schardt, your son." Silence.

"Oh, how are you?"

"Good. I am sorry to bother you but I wonder if you can help me."

"I don't have any money."

288

"I don't want any money. I want to move to West Berlin. Could you write me a letter that you want me to move closer to you and that you will help me to build my new life?"

"Why do you want to move to West Berlin?"

"That's a long story, but I thought when I tell the authorities that I want to be re-united with my biological father that would enhance my chances to leave the GDR."

"Well, we have to talk about it. I will be in East Berlin next week. I can visit you, let's say next Monday. Give me your phone number." I give him Klaus' phone number. "Good, how is Katharina doing? Is she still alive?"

That's my grandmother. I am surprised by his question. "Yes, she is. She is doing fine."

"Mmmh, I will call you next week to let you know the exact time I will be coming."

"Great. I am looking forward to it. Goodbye."

"Goodbye." That was a weird conversation with a man who fathered me and has not seen me since I was two years old. No questions, no interest in what I am doing. Nothing. Just asking about my grandmother. Very odd. But on the other hand there is no written protocol how to conduct the very first conversation with your father.

I am still not sure what to think about the anticipated meeting with my father. A man I have no real memory of. Klaus is the only one I have confided in about his visit. He has no opinion about it. He is too much of a realist. He does not dream about things, or gets lost in a thought process of "what if." I have to admit, sometimes his straightforwardness irritates me and sometimes it helps me to be grounded. Now, I wish he could give a little reassurance.

At the newspaper I have to ask for a day off so I can be home waiting for the phone call. I don't want to deal with messages on the answering machine. In my head I am also plan where to meet. I would prefer to invite him to Klaus' apartment. My apartment in Pankow doesn't seem to be a good idea. I don't want that my family know anything about the meeting. Bad luck would have it and we would run into Tata. I want the meeting to be low key. My father is basically a stranger to me and I have no intention of changing that. The only thing I want to get out of this meeting is a written commitment from him stating his support for my decision to live closer to him. I will make it very clear to him as well that I don't want any financial support. If our meeting ends with the wish to stay in touch I am all for it. After all, I have a whole other family I never met: uncle and aunt, cousins. I will have some coffee ready. Klaus will bake a cake. If we meet on Monday there will be no bakery open to buy any sweets. East German bakers have Mondays off.

Monday morning. Today is the day. I get up early, clean the apartment. I almost don't dare to take a shower, go the bathroom, or vacuum. I might miss the ringing of the phone. I am nervous. Would we hug, just shake hands? How would I address him? By his first name Willy, or father, or Herr Schardt? The only picture I have of him was taken at the wedding of my parents during the church ceremony. Both kneeling in front of the altar. Both looking very handsome. Everybody says I look like my mother. When I look at the photograph I also see a lot of resemblance between my father and me. His face is round. It looks like we have the same type of hair: thin. The picture was taken in 1954. Will I recognize him?

It's one o' clock in the afternoon. No phone call yet. I am bored and restless. The TV stations are on their midday break. I don't have enough concentration to read. I eat the first slice of apple pie. Klaus made my favorite cake. There is nothing else to do. The weather outside is November-like: gray. I lie down. The ringing of the phone makes me jump. I wait for the second ring. "Hello."

"It's me. Klaus. Have your heard from your father?"

"Not yet." I look at my watch. Its 3:30.

"Let me know how it goes. I will be at work until five." I hang up the phone. I hope that my father had not tried to call me when Klaus called. I go in the kitchen to make some coffee. I cut another slice of apple pie. I turn the TV on. Doubts start to creep up. Why would he call, or even want to meet me now? He has not done it so far. He never cared. The pie is now down to half its size. I feel gross. Nothing on the TV. It's 5:00. How much longer should I sit next to the phone? I call Klaus. "Nothing."

"Maybe he was delayed coming into West Berlin? Just wait a little bit longer. I will stay at work. Call me in an hour." It's too late to serve coffee and cake. I eat what's left. I know in my heart, he won't call. He never had the intention to call. He doesn't want me in his life. Not in the past, now or in the future. I shouldn't be upset. But I am. This man never had any positive influence on my life. Quite the opposite. In school I was always the kid without a father. On my application to go on to high school he was my father living in West Germany: one of the reasons I couldn't go on. When the whole Party shit hit the fan it wasn't a surprise to the ideologist. What did we expect? His father lives in West Germany. The only time that it would be really helpful for me to have my father living in West Germany is now. I could apply for family reunion. I hate this man, hate that he is in my life without my choice. It's quarter to six. I call Klaus. "I have not heard anything. I don't think I will. Can we go out tonight? I feel like getting really drunk."

For right now Klaus and I are doing well again. It seems that his sex adventures have mellowed. His drinking is still intense. I can live with one evil but not two. We are in a couple's routine: theater, friends, cleaning, and some sex. Maybe it's the terrible first seven years we had to go through in order to become closer? Or it's merely the fact that we have a secret that we cannot share with any of our friends and colleagues. The decision to get out of East Germany is exciting and disconcerting at the same time. But it also makes us loners amongst the ones who are close and dear to us. We know, but they don't. There is a feel of betrayal. But how can we know who to trust and let in on our secret?

The sad thing is that any one of them could be an informant of the Stasi. Until we make it official we have to keep quiet. We even started only talking about it outside of our apartment. There are stories out there that the phones work also as listening devices. Maybe the Stasi already knows? I talked to my father openly on the phone about my plan. As a Communist and East German beneficiary he may even have informed officials already? Certain things in life are out of my controls. And that's just some of it. A while ago I made the decision that I won't adhere to the fear that the rulers and their underlings want everybody live under. Isn't there a saying that fear clouds your view? Therefore it is better not to do anything than to do the wrong thing. I would rather do something, even if it may be the wrong thing, than nothing at all.

Klaus is somehow very fearful but not because he is afraid of any actions from the authorities. It's the uncertainty that lies ahead of us. The change. He is so much more content than I am. He takes what is and adjusts himself to it. I on the other hand always try to mold existence to my wants. Conflict anticipated.

"A Snake Amongst Us"

It's eight o'clock in morning. We all pile into the editor-in chiefs office. Time for the daily critique of our newspaper. But I immediately sense that this will be not the usual morning gathering. Not only is Fischer, the boss, there all of the second in command chiefs as well: Fahlenkamp, who is responsible for the correct ideology content of every article, Dr. Hauser, the enforcer of any Party directives, Stiegel, the direct link to the Stasi, even the HR chief, Mueller is here. My thoughts are racing. Have they found out about my intention to leave the country? I try to make eye contact with my fellow reporters and all the bosses. Nothing tells me they know. Friendly nodding as I look at them. I squeeze into a chair in the corner.

"Dear colleagues," the editor-in-chief's voice is deep supported by his six-and-a-half-foot, three-hundred-pound frame. "We have a snake amongst us." My heart is dropping. "I should say we *had* a snake amongst us. Dieter Krause has fled the German Democratic Republic. It is unconceivable how someone who was given every opportunity to strive as a journalist. He was not perfect by any means. But we supported him to become a voice of the people of our country." I look around. Most faces of my colleagues look stunned.

The expressions on the bosses' faces are stern. "As we all know, Krause was a homosexual. But the leaders of this paper have not held this against him. Looking back, we should have. Krause fled with his boyfriend, who is a medical doctor: an unbelievable betrayal as well. We don't how and where Krause escaped. We assume he fled in women's clothes." *What a stupid idiot*, I think. To think that because Dieter was gay that it should have alerted everyone that he was a flight risk, and that because he is gay, he of course wore women's clothes to escape undetected. I almost want to jump up, and say something. The news is still sinks in. As I look around. Everybody keeps to himself, eyes

293

deliberately downwards. Avoiding connection with anyone.

Maybe I imagine it but I feel Hauser's eyes on me. I never told anyone at work that I am gay but I think that everybody knows anyway. Does the character assassination of Dieter mean I will be from here on watched and under scrutiny? Fischer made it very clear, homosexuals should not be trusted.

"Dear colleagues, the security officials, our Party Chairman Dr.Gerlach and I am asking everybody to look back and see if there were any hints that Krause was planning this act of unbelievable betrayal. Any information, any detail will help us to find out how he escaped. He must have had helpers, or friends who he confided in. We cannot allow this utterly immoral and heinous act to happen again." Fisher pushes his chair and gets up. "I have an appointment with Party Chairman Manfred Gerlach to discuss this unwelcome situation. I only can hope that Krause will come to his senses when he realizes that the imperialistic West is not interested in him and does not have his welfare in mind. The single goal of the West is to harm the citizens of the German Democratic Republic. If any of you are contacted by Krause, and I am sure he will try to come back after he has seen the inhuman face of the Federal Republic of Germany, please inform me immediately or any other leader of our paper." Fischer squeezes his huge body through the rows of chairs, and leaves the room.

Fahlenkamp in his trademark checkered shirt and mismatched tie gets up out of his chair. "Dear colleagues, I am sure you are as disgusted as anybody should be. Therefore it is our duty to condemn this act of betrayal by Krause. It is natural and expected at the same time by the Chairman Gerlach and the working class of our country. I have prepared a resolution, to be signed by all staff members of this paper. It reads: we the members of the central paper of the Liberal Democratic Party of Germany, *Der Morgen*, condemn the act committed by Dieter Krause. He betrayed the dictatorship of the proletariat. We promise that we will be vigilant to stop any future betrayal of the German Democratic Republic and its leadership. With socialist greetings the staff of *Der Morgen*."

I feel terrible, but I won't have any choice not to sign it. I can't have any attention on me at this point. I never really connected to Dieter Krause. He was always very arrogant towards me. I ran into him and his boyfriend occasionally at restaurants or at the opera. He would always make a point of not seeing me. He was very well liked at the paper. He wrote mostly human interest stories. Nothing heavy. Every one of his articles always got high remarks during the morning critics' sessions. But that of course doesn't fit the picture the leadership of our paper has to create of him now. How quickly can you fall from grace? You turn your back and an effective and respected journalist becomes a villain and ill-guided moron. Whatever the reasons were that made him and his partner decide to leave has nothing to do with betrayal of trust and ungratefulness toward a country that gave him a free education. They desired something they couldn't find here and knew they never will find it here. Condemnation and vilifying are the responses by the authorities. But will they never ask why? If they would ask why on the other hand, would they know what to do with the answer?

Klaus and I set a timetable. We will celebrate Christmas with friends, take our yearly ski vacation in Czechoslovakia and then go to the authorities. We really don't know how to prepare for what will happen after we make it official. We know some people who are going for family reunion. Nothing really changed in their daily life. But that is not guaranteed. And every case is different. Klaus' relative in Munich is a cousin, not really covered by any international human rights provisions. Not that the GDR is following that rule. If they approve an application based on family reunion it has to be a family member "first grade" like a mother or father. Siblings may fall into that category as well, but certainly not cousins. Maybe Klaus has a shot because it is his only living relative.

I on the other hand have the perfect relative: my father. He clearly doesn't want to help but I still want to use him as the reason. They know and I know it is a lie. However, a father is a father and I will go for it. What we have to avoid by all means is giving them any political reasons or we would be toast. Even though everything is up in the air and we don't have any timeline when we will eventually get out, I feel already that our time here is limited. It seems so weird, but there are things I want to do before the shit hits the fan and we may be very restricted what we can do after we submit our application.

We have a car and we should get out into the country as much as we can. Klaus wants to spend as much time in his old home town Dresden as possible. He still pays for the apartment his parents rented in the early sixties. His mother and stepfather are buried in Dresden. And there are also some friends of his. I like Dresden too. Most of all it's surrounding area. The Sächsische Schweiz mountain range is one of the most beautiful sceneries I have ever seen.

I am so excited. Our ride to Dresden is uneventful. The highway built under Hitler as one of his massive public employment plans as well as his war planning is almost beyond repair. The potholes along the way are unintended speed control. It's a bouncy ride. But Klaus and I belong to the minority of East Germans who have a car. A convenience that makes up for the inadequacy of the Autobahn. I have been to Klaus' parents' apartment before but I still feel a little bit uneasy. When I look at the kitchen stove I can't help but be reminded that his mother died there by putting her head in it.

"Don't think about," is Klaus' reaction. "It's just a stove nothing else." It's weird anyway. Our plan this time is to go to the cemetery in the morning, have lunch somewhere around City Hall, and meet his friends in the early evening. They want us to come to their apartment. I don't know much about them and I don't to ask either. I am sure Klaus and they have probably slept together. All male gay friends of his were at one time or another his sex partners. Since I decided to stick with Klaus and make it work I try the pragmatic approach: no one is an empty slate. We all have a past, some more colorful than others.

We have sex in his parents' bed. I like having sex in the morning rather than at night. Night sex seems so planned, something you do before you fall asleep. I still get turned on by Klaus' body. Smooth to the touch, just the right softness. We are both not very adventurous. We kiss, suck each other. One of us will be the bottom. If I am in the right mood I can enjoy being fucked, ignoring the pain. But it always hurts afterwards, sometimes for days. Klaus doesn't seem to mind to be on the bottom. This morning he is. We both come quickly. It feels good. As I slid out of him I can smell shit. It's happened now almost every time that I fuck Klaus that it gets messy afterwards. I feel embarrassed for him, pretend not to notice. He never says a thing. We do our after-sex routine. Klaus goes in the kitchen to clean himself. His parents' apartment has a bathroom with just a toilet. The only water source is in the kitchen. I spot clean the bed sheet. I follow him into the kitchen. The coffeemaker is going. We hug. I step up to the kitchen sink.

Visiting Klaus parents' grave is short. The ivy-covered mound is in line with all of the other small plots. Many of those seem not to have had a visitor in years. "No one will care for this one after we are gone," Klaus is very matter of fact. He pulls off dead leaves. I rake around the plot. It's sad to know that we all at one point will end up like this; having neighbors we never had met in life. As we finish we both wonder how many more times we have left to come back here. Something you really don't want to know. We leave in a rush because we are already late in meeting Klaus' friends. We have to skip lunch altogether.

Johannes and Peter's apartment is in a very impressive and stately building. The façade is in desperate need of repair but what's left shows old-world grandeur. Limestone carved leaves and figurines are still visible. The hallway and staircase is in even worse shape than the outside. The fake marble wall covering is peeling off. Metal piping replaces missing wooden rods of the original hand railing. Only the massive apartment doors have somehow survived the neglect. Their flat is on the top floor. It's huge and has high ceiling with crown moldings. Off of the very long hallway are two rooms to the right, and the kitchen is straight towards the end. I can see the shower stall next to the kitchen sink. Johannes looks like an accountant, his partner like a hustler. Peter's shirt is almost unbuttoned. A gold cross on a gold chain sits perfectly in the middle of his hairless chest. His jeans are skin tight, outlining his dick and testicles. Johannes' clothes are totally shapeless. We are introduced to Ralph, a hustler type as well. We start to drink right away: cola with vodka. There is almost no furniture except for an entertainment center and a big antique rocking chair. We sit on the floor. I feel the alcohol since Klaus and I had not eaten except for breakfast. I drink fast to overcome my notorious shyness. A tape with Amanda Lear songs keeps us quiet.

After the tape is finished Peter places an empty bottle in front of us and without a word gives it push. The top points at Ralph. He takes his shirt off. It is his turn to turn the bottle. I am surprised how quickly things are going. This time the bottle neck is in front of Johannes. "You know, I am not taking my clothes off. I take pictures." He laughs. The bottle gets another push. I have to take my shirt off. I am lightheaded, and don't mind. It doesn't take long and we are all naked, except for Johannes.

Peter has his hands on Klaus dick. I feel Ralph's hand stroking my back. He starts to kiss me. To my surprise I like the way he kisses. He pushes me on my back and sits on top of me. He is hard as well. I put my hand through his legs and push my finger into his ass. He moves his behind so I can get deeper. "Give me two fingers," he whispers in my ear. I look to the side. Peter is working Klaus' ass with his tongue. I find this hot. I push two fingers into Ralph. He clearly enjoys it. I also feel I can push my thumb in too. Ralph is getting off me to change into a doggy position. I know what he wants me to do. I have heard about fisting before but always thought that was just talk. It obviously is not. I press all my fingertips together. Johannes pushes a tub of cream towards me. I slowly go inside of Ralph.

He moans, grabs his dick and strokes it. "Go slow," he says over and over. Johannes is getting closer with his camera. I noticed that Klaus and Peter have stopped and are watching us. I am in up to my knuckles. Ralph gets up on his knees and pushes down on me. My whole hand is inside. "Be gentle, be gentle," he moans over and over. I don't know what to do. I am so afraid to hurt him. He moves his ass back and forth on me. I hear Johannes' camera clicking. "That is great. That is super," he cries. The closer Ralph is getting to climax the more I wish it would be over. My arm hurts because I don't dare to move at all. Ralph straightens his back. His head snaps backwards. He comes. I moan in support without feeling anything. He slowly pulls himself away from me. I don't want to look at my hand.

"Come let's have a shower." Ralph slaps me on my shoulder. "You didn't come, did you? I will make you." He laughs. I follow him into the kitchen. I look at his ass; still in disbelief of what I just did. Ralph does not have a nice body. He is slim. His skin looks loose. With every step he takes his thin flesh shakes. Ralph leaves the shower stall door open for me to join him. "I hope I didn't hurt you. I have never done this before."

"Oh, don't worry. It felt great. You are the right size." I laugh coyly. With one hand he grabs the soap bar and rubs it over my body. The other hand cups my dick. It doesn't feel good to me.

"I think I am too drunk. Maybe later."

"Ok." He soaps me and himself. The water rinses us clean. He gives me a towel. No one says a word. We go back to join the others again.

"You are quite the fister. Where did you learn that?" Peter is laughing. "Pretty talented boyfriend you have there." He salutes Klaus with his glass. Klaus tilts his head, and takes a big gulp out of his glass. I just want to lie down, and be alone.

"Can I stretch out some place?"

"Just lay down over there." Johannes points at the open sliding door. I get up. Still naked, very self-conscious. But I don't care. I just want to get away. I collapse on an oversized bed. I doze off.

The unmistakably sound of sex awakes me. I need a couple of seconds to realize where I am. The moaning comes from the living room. Curious I get up. The first thing I see is Johannes on his stomach, the camera in front of him. It takes a little bit to figure out what I am seeing. Peter is laying on his back, Klaus on top of him, his chest on Peter's

Thomas P.W. Schardt

chest. Klaus' face it turned into my direction. Ralph hovers
behind them, his chest on Klaus back. Klaus is being fucked
by both of them at the same time. I look at Klaus' eyes. They
are unfocused. His face unmoved. I know that expression.
Klaus is totally drunk and has no clue what is going on. My
first instinct is to pull the guys away from him. But it is way
too late. Peter and Ralph are climaxing. Somehow Klaus
becomes alive again. He rolls off to the side. His dick is limp.

"Give me something to drink, you whores." His words are
slurred. "Did you like it? I have a great ass, don't I? What
do you think?" He laughs.

"I wonder if you can take three at the same time."

"I take as many as I want to, sons of bitches. I can get
two fists up my ass. What can you get up yours?"

"Let's fist Klaus." Johannes puts his camera in ready
position. I feel like I am looking and listening at the edge of
the abyss. Sure, all of the guys are drunk as skunks. It rids
them of any limits. I feel like I have to protect Klaus, that's
all. I know how willing he is when he is drunk. I also know
how easy it is to get him in this situation.

"Klaus, do you want to eat something?" My question is so
ridiculous because I don't know where I would get anything
to eat for him. I just want to end this orgy talk. "Oh, our
fister is finally awake. When will you put your hand up my
ass? You want to do it now?" Klaus grabs his legs, and pulls
them apart.

"Thomas is our fister. Fist him." Ralph grabs my hand.

"Please, guys. Stop that. Can we get something to eat?"

"Good idea. I will make us some sandwiches. Peter, can
you help me." Johannes hangs the camera around his neck,
and gets up. Peter follows him. Thank God, I broke the cycle.
I put my pants on, and throw Klaus' in his direction. Ralph
fills our glasses. He stays naked. "It's fun to have you guys
around. We should do that more often. I like you both."
Ralphs hands me my drink.

"Yeah, we should," I lie. Klaus is asleep. The worst is
over, I hope. Now I have to get sober as quickly as I can. I
did and saw things today I wish I hadn't.

I hand my ID to the receptionist. He is usually bubbly

300

but not this morning. Something is off. I am rush up the flight of stairs. The door to my office is open. My boss is already there, puffing on a cigarette. The room is smoke filled. "Good morning. The porter is not in very good mood today."

My boss gives me a little nod. His face is reddish. His hand shakes. The collar button on his shirt is ready to burst. Martinek looks more disheveled than usually. "Is something wrong?"

"Radzek is gone," he says.

"What do you mean?" Radzek is the one of the up-and-coming men within district leadership of the Liberal Democratic Party for Berlin .

"He didn't come back from a visit to Düsseldorf."

"Wow," is all I can say. Radzek fled. Who would have thought? Hallway gossip had it that he was already considered to become one day one of the vice-chairmen of the LDPD. In his forties, tall and good looking, he had a natural aura of a leader and the ear of Party boss Gerlach. He was a prince in waiting. When I needed a quote to include in an article I could count on him. He was always friendly and cordial. But as far as I know he was a strong ideologist. Nothing about him would have indicated that he was a critic with escape ambition. He was on the sunny side of things. Married with two children, car and driver at his disposal, a nice weekend home in the outskirts of Berlin. And now, he left everything behind.

"What about his family?" I ask Martinek.

"His wife and children did not travel with him. It was just him that got the permission to visit an aunt for her birthday. I am so disappointed in Radzek. He really betrayed us all." *Oh come on Martinek, you don't have to pretend in front of me*, I think. Sure, I am surprised as he is. But he must have had valid reasons for not coming back, and leaving his family here. A high-ranking Party executive chooses an uncertain future for a programmed and safe way to the top. Now some people close to him will be in big trouble, and under scrutiny. How embarrassing it must be for the inner circle who was grooming Radzek for the future! The authorities will come down hard on them and that will have a ripple effect. We will have to pledge another allegiance to the Party, the countries' leadership and condemn the action of Radzek. We have to sit through another propaganda session to be advised about our tireless diligence and alertness at all times because the enemy is a wolf in a sheep's clothing. And at the end we have to sign another petition stating that Radzek's action was evil but nevertheless was an isolated and misguided act of a troubled man. We will assure the Party leadership and the proletariat of the GDR that we will more than ever stand shoulder to shoulder to be victorious over the enemy of Socialism. I have to be part of that farce to cover my own intentions. Who will be the next to get out? How many I know are Janus headed? How many I know are hiding in plain sight? I know I am.

I am transferred to the shipping department of the Buchverlag Der Morgen. It's located at Alte Schönhauser Strasse in the formerly known as Scheunenviertel quarter. I work under the supervision of Frau Bauer. Rumors have it that she had a short-lived affair with her married boss, the head of the shipping department. It resulted in her getting pregnant. How they reconciled and can work next to each other every day is only known to them. Frau Bauer gave birth to a son out of wedlock. Later she got married to what all referred to as a real bastard. If I didn't know the alleged story I would not have guessed. They are very cordial with each other and comfortable. Their professional roles are defined and accepted. I feel some resentment and caution by them towards me. In a way I can understand them. I came with a reputation: He has an Exit Application pending. But both of them are very polite to me. Frau Bauer can even vaguely remember my mother who worked at the Buchverlag Der Morgen many years ago. However we never really talk about my pending Exit Application or politics. It's kind of an unspoken rule. My time in the shipping department is limited anyway. I know that, they know that. Not because at some point I will get the permit to leave the country, but I have the feeling that my transfer from the newspaper to the shipping department is just a delay tactic in firing me. They have not figured out how to get rid of me. Not yet.

My work is tedious and repetitive. Filling shipping orders and packing them. We also order books for the editors of the publishing house, making sure when they arrive that they will be delivered to them. A nine-to-five job without any challenges. Just regular, normal, without any stress. I welcome that. It gives me time to think about my unknown future I can't wait to begin. Klaus is allowed to do the same job minus the teaching of the locksmith apprentices. Someone who wants to leave the country is not qualified to show the young ones how to bend metal, solder or drill holes. No rational explanation to the rationale of that decision. Klaus doesn't mind. Makes his job easier at the same pay. They didn't cut it. My pay is not cut either. No complaints.

For the fun of it I try to fight my transfer from the newspaper to the shipping department. I had written to the LDPD boss Manfred Gerlach requesting an explanation and a reason for my demotion. I certainly understand that I couldn't write articles anymore. But there are other jobs within the newspaper I could do, hidden, out off the public eye. Such as the being part of the layout team of the daily pages or proofreading after the first print. All non-political jobs, all supervised, so no fear I could do any damage.

"I would like to talk to you." Dr. Klimt, the chief editor of the publishing house greets me. We never really talked to each other before, but we've met before just by passing in the hallway back at the main house. He is almost petite in stature and looks younger than he probably is considering his position. Always friendly. An intellectual, no question.

"Sure. What is it about?"

"Dr.Gerlach asked me to tell you that the decision for your transfer lies with the editor-in-chief of the newspaper, Herr Fischer."

"I am aware of the apparent line of command. I had written to Dr. Gerlach as the leader of the party to intervene with that decision since I am still a member of the LDPD. I had expected whatever the response of Dr. Gerlach is it would be in writing."

"Yes, I know. Dr. Gerlach apologizes that because of time

restraints he is not able to write to you. He had asked me to be the messenger."

"Well, I think I know why Dr. Gerlach won't give me a written explanation. But I thank you for letting me know."

For some reason I thought that would be the end of our talk. I was going to return to wrap books. "I am sorry that I can't give you a better answer. However I would like to offer you a job as assistant editor with the real possibility for quick advancement. In return I would have to ask you to re-think your plan to leave the GDR and retract your Exit Application." I am caught off guard. Not so much that Dr. Klimt had asked me to withdraw my application. The offer to become an assistant editor is amazing. How many people out there are waiting in line for such a sought-after job? And I get the offer. Stunning.

"Honestly, I am speechless," is all that I can say.

"I always liked your articles. The selection of your words, how you describe things is very interesting to me. I really believe you will make a good editor. I promise you that I will see to it."

"Thank you for your kind words. It seems like such a long time since I have heard some appreciation for my work. I am not just saying it, but I feel honored. Thanks again. But I made my decision. I don't want a future here anymore. This is the past. ."

"I am sorry to hear that. But I am not surprised. I wish you all the best. Good luck." Klimt shakes my hand. Our eyes lock for a moment. Another goodbye. Sad this one, too. But unavoidable.

I am sure that Dr. Klimt did not go out on a limb to give me that job offer. Whatever happened behind closed doors prior to this made me realize that there are humans amongst all those that have lost this qualification. I feel humble realizing that. I feel my heart beat. I go back to my work. As I tie the strings around the packages I know also that my days with a secure work will come to an end very soon. The job offer was an olive branch. Now they have a reason to cut me loose. Wash their hands clean. Settle their minds. We tried but he is a hopeless cause.

Sure enough. Two days later Frau Bauer gives me a

sealed envelope. Addressed to me. The sender: "The Arbitration Commission of *Der Morgen.* "Inside is a short notice that I have to appear the following Monday. The reason: unauthorized abandonment of the workplace. I read it over and over, and still don't understand what they mean by abandonment. When did I do that? I never missed a day since I've been in the shipping department, nor did I arrive late to work or leave before five in the afternoon. Appearing in front of the Arbitration Commission is always a serious matter. These semi-courts exist at every workplace, self-appointed through election, staffed with members of the Party, union, youth group and none affiliated persons. The commission is another controlled organ within a tightly supervised environment. This one goes after any disorderly conduct in the workplace, such as untimely, badmouthing, incorrectness, anything short of being a case handled by the real courts and the states authorities.

Decisions by the Arbitration Commission are noted into everybody's personal file at the workplace. The commission's decision is as serious as it is important if one wants to advance in the workplace, change jobs or asks for a pay-increase. Anybody who is handled by the Arbitration Commission better stay under the radar for years to come. One who has numerous notations from the Arbitration Commission can be fired and has to report to the Office of Labor in the district he or she lives in. In other words, appearing in front of the commission is no laughing matter.

It never crossed my mind that I would be ever called in front of the Arbitration Commission. But I have to hand it to them, it's a clever move. Whatever they have against me will make their case. Whatever the suggested judgment will be, every member of the commission has to openly vote for or against it. It will be a majority if not hundred percent that will follow the suggestion of the chairman of the commission. A pseudo-democratic process, another fig leaf, a farce, where the outcome is already determined way before the session. And again it's a clever process where the individual conscience of each member is clear and clean after the vote. In public it has to be a collective and most likely a unilateral vote. Personal actions and responsibilities under the umbrella of the Arbitration Commission melt into one. No one's conscience is challenged. Not now. Not in the future. It's a group action.

Blame can be easily transferred to the other member. The perversion of a seemingly democratic civil court, by invoking the notion that if you don't vote as told the others will. "It was not just me, the others, too." Democracy degenerates again and again for the only purpose: the survival of a dictatorship. It is so absurd, so unconscionable, but true. I now wonder how many pre-sessions and back alley arm twisting they will need in order to reach their predetermined judgment: instant termination of my employment. I am sure that is the decision. And that in itself shows the perversion of their ultimate goal. Ending my contract makes me unemployed, a criminal offense. Constitution and civil law make it very clear that every citizen has a right and a duty to work. Violating one or the other puts the People's prosecutors into action.

The porter who in the past always liked to chat with me treats me like a stranger. "Please wait. I will announce your arrival. Someone will bring you to the conference room." I nod my head and try to catch his eye at the same time. For a split second he looks at me. The man is nervous but he has to follow his orders. I want to say something but don't. He had told me once that he wanted to become a reporter as well. Getting the job as a porter he saw as a first step to reach his goals. Talking to me now could jeopardize his dreams. Another sheep in the herd. But it doesn't matter to me. Everybody has a choice. As I contemplate that even dictators can't take that away from each of us, Frau Meyer comes down the stairs.

"Hello, Mr. Schardt. Sorry for the wait." I am surprised at her friendly demeanor and apology. She is an attractive blonde working at the women's page of the paper. Her husband edits the weekly science page. I always admired both as the only true intellectuals at the paper. The Meyers have an aura of success without compromising independence around them. Their membership in the LDPD seems for genuine and career reasons. Their rationale for being a productive and active part within the GDR society lies in the belief that current problems are not systemic but over time solvable. We once had an enjoyable discussion about individualism in a collective structure such as socialism. They compare it with a chain where its strength comes only from the strength of each link. Is one broken or weak the whole chain loses its durability. I agreed with that point of view but countered that each link in a chain is alike in order to make it one unbreakable force. Seldom have you had a chain where links differ in size or shape and still keeps its strength. Therefore individualism is hardly desired when all have to be one and follow one future. One's interest can never mirror the group interest to a T. But a dictatorship just wants single wishes and dreams rolled into one. Of course, the big group wish and dream is only be articulated, defined and redefined by the ones in power to keep that power indefinitely. I remember our discussion vividly because it was refreshing and honest. We all enjoyed it as a purely intellectual exercise, of course.

Frau Meyer shakes my hand. As we take the stairs I wonder how she and her husband will act during the upcoming session. Both are members of the commission. We reach the conference room. It's located in the part of the building that is occupied by the party bureaucrats. Frau Meyer opens the door and shows me inside. Everybody who should be here is here sitting around a u-shaped table. Frau Meyer squeezes towards the front. There is only one chair empty on the left side, clearly reserved for me to take. I sit down and tip my head to greet the members of the commission. No one looks at me. The mood is set. No contact, the imaginary line is drawn, separating me from them. Resentment lies in the air. I am nervous, but hope it doesn't show. I lock my hands together.

"I am now opening the meeting. The reason we are here today is to review the irresponsible behavior of Herrn Schardt who had left his workplace without permit from his supervisor." As Herr Funke the Chairman of the Arbitration Commission starts his lengthy monologue I am still not certain when I did what I supposedly did...then it comes back to me. It was the day I had handed in my written request to leave the GDR to be re-united with my family. I was immediately assigned to desk duty to oversee the layout of that day's local page. I was not allowed to answer the phone or to be involved in any way with any of the other daily tasks. After fitting all of the articles but one into the layout and sending them over to the print department I had asked Frau Stack, my supervisor at the time, if she can edit the missing article and send it over to the printer. The last article was to be submitted by a freelance writer very close to the deadline. Frau Stack told me she would do it. I also told her since all the work is done I would leave for the day. She didn't object to that. So I left.

"Because of his unauthorized leave Herr Schardt jeopardized the printing of our newspaper. Because of the action of Frau Stack that was avoided. Herr Schardt failed to complete the assigned task. I, as the Chairman of the Arbitration Commission, suggest to reprimand Herr Schardt. Members of the commission what do you think?"

I spoke up, "Can I please respond?"

"No, you will have the opportunity after the members of the Arbitration Commission haven spoken." Funke cuts me short. I never liked the guy. He is the head of the culture resort and somewhat of an authority when it comes to reviewing theater plays. Sometimes he appears on the Sunday morning radio shows dedicated to theater performances. He belongs to the very few who can travel to West Berlin or West Germany to attend plays and write about it afterwards. His wife, who works at the newspaper as photographer, brags after such visits about the gifts her husband brings home. She always hopes that someday she can partake in those business trips to the West. Behind their backs the Funke's are called brownnosers because of their closeness to LDPD boss Gerlach.

The next one to speak is Stoessling. "I am here as representative of the LDPD. I have to say I am appalled of the behavior of Herr Schardt. Herr Schardt is no longer a member of the Party. However his act is a betrayal of all of us. I agree with the recommendation of the chairman of this body. But with all respect Herr Funke I would like to suggest the immediate termination of Herrn Schardt."

I almost can't control myself. I just had learned that I am

not a LDPD member anymore. I am not surprised. At least they could have told me that before. But Stoessling's accusation of betrayal is just over the top. But typical Stoessling. Everybody in the newspaper hates this guy. He is a slimeball. No one really knows how and why he is the production manager of the paper. He is always on business trips either with higher-ups in the party, works from home or visits small private factories (supposedly to recruit the owners for the party). However, everybody thinks he works for the Stasi. At a company outing I ended up at his table and after way much too many drinks he offered me to call him by his first name, Hans.

"Herr Chairman," I try to get a word in before another member insults me, "can I please respond? This is not fair. It's me against fifteen members of this commission."

"Herr Schardt, for the last time please don't interrupt this meeting. You will be given the opportunity when it is your time." Meyer, the deputy chairman of the commission is the one to tell me to shut up.

Bischoff is the next one: a known drunk on permanent desk duty in the "Party Life" section of the paper until his retirement. He is also the head of the union group at the newspaper. "Herr Schardt is not a paying member of the FDGB anymore. Therefore he forfeited his right to a union representative. However, as a former colleague, I want to express my huge disappointment in Herr Schardt. I am inclined to follow the recommendation of Hans Stoessling to terminate Herr Schardt without delay." This is orchestrated.

I am sure the next one will be the secretary of the youth organization of the paper, Van Haydn. Sure enough Funke gives him the word. "Thomas is no longer a paying member of the FDJ. His behavior is certainly a disappointment to me." Van Haydn doesn't give any recommendation. Is it scripted, or does he demonstrate his well-known independence? The next one is Frau Ziegenhagen. She is the administrative assistant to the editor-in-chief. I really don't know her. She is always very quiet, doesn't mingle with anyone from the newspaper. She is divorced and has one son.

"Frau Ziegenhagen, as the representative of the administrative office of the paper what would you like to say?" Funke asked as the rest of us noticed her nervousness. Several times by now she tried to clear her voice. "This is so awful." Is all what she can say before she breaks out in tears? We are all stunned. United for a second. This was not planned.

I see Funke, Meyer, Bischoff and Stoessling exchange glances. Someone did not condemn me. I look at her and her tears, fighting my own. This quiet and unassuming person did not follow protocol. In her own way she took my side. I want to hug her. "Frau Ziegenhagen, you are excused from further duty as a member of the Arbitration Commission. If you want to you can leave now." Funke takes control. Frau Ziegenhagen tiptoes out of the room. I sense a relief among the rest of them. This incident should not have happened. From now on things have to go as prepared.

I want to speak. The longer they try to shut me out the angrier I become. I am afraid that I will forget about all the accusations and therefore I can't point out my side of the events. Not that it matters because I am sure the result of this meeting is scripted well in advance. But I will not be a pushover and take it from them without a fight.

I lift my arm to announce I would like to say something. Funke and Meyer ignore it. "Frau Stack, please recollect for us again the afternoon where Herr Schardt left his desk and you had to take charge to finish his work." She nervously adjusts her position and takes out some notes.

She and I had a very good working relationship. I think at some point we considered each other friends. Often after work we would go out for a drink and have a bite to eat. She is in a very unhappy relationship with a guy she must have considered her last chance to get married. I didn't care for the man. All that he would talk about was his job as a policemen. He was still on a low-level rung and had to patrol the streets. He looked very tough and acted the part as well. On the other hand, Ursula Stack was a very sweet, soft-spoken and intellectual person. Most of her adult life she had to care for her mother.

Shortly after she had died Ursula met this policeman

310

during a work assignment. What brought them closer I don't
know, but she certainly dotes on him like she did with her
mother. He must have liked it. And she was the one to ask
him to marry her. Why he said yes and she wanted him is
beyond me. They constantly fight and bicker. But I have to
hand it to her, she never would badmouth him to me. We
mostly talked about relationships and what they mean and
how much work they need. However, we were never
comfortable enough with each other to go beyond
generalities and apply them to our personal lives. For
instance, I have never told her that I was gay. She never
asked me but I am sure she knows. What woman in her
forties would spend time with a guy in his twenties and talk
about relationship stuff? And vice versa? Only a lonely
woman looking for a "girlfriend" that poses no danger
whatsoever. However, the minute she knew about my Exit
Application she distanced herself from me.

"It came as a sudden surprise when Thomas handed me
the layout and told me that he would leave. No explanation.
No asking for permission to leave. I had to cancel some
appointments that afternoon to finish the work. And there
was a lot left."

"That not true, Frau Stock and you know it." I was not
taking it anymore. "Six people have now spoken and
distorted the events and smeared my personality. Herr
Funke, I am asking you again to allow me to speak." I could
see that no one in the room expected me to talk so loud and
with such determination.

"Since you already interrupted the meeting without
permission, which seems to be a common behavior with you,
you can now speak. Please keep it under five minutes."

"I will leave your remarks about my common behavior
unchallenged, Herr Funke." I got up from my seat. "You
know and I know this meeting is primarily conducted
because I have submitted a written application for the
reunion with my father in the BRD."

"Herr Schardt, we are not here to discuss your Exit
Application. If you continue with that I will end this
meeting." I never have seen Funke so agitated. He had
jumped to his feet.

"Anyway," I continue, "As you all know here I always was and I still am a responsible worker who has never ever done anything that could be characterized as irresponsible. The opposite is the truth. Please look into my personal work file where you can find several notes honoring my input and engagement for the advancement of *Der Morgen* newspaper. Therefore if I really did what you are accusing me of then the positive testimonial in my work file alone should have not warranted a session of the Arbitration Commission."

"Herr Schardt, please finish." Meyer is poking his pen on the table. I ignore him.

"It is false that there was a lot of work left for Frau Stock. Just one article was missing. When I asked Frau Stock if she could finish, she agreed. As my supervisor she did not object to me leaving that afternoon. Looking back I probably should not have done it. But that day was a very upsetting day for me as well. Me leaving that afternoon did not jeopardize the issue of the newspaper in any way."

"Thomas, are you calling me a liar? Of course there was a lot when you just shoved the layout on my desk. I demand an apology from you." I look at her hoping that she could see my disdain for her at this moment.

"Please look at the layout page for that day. As you know, the pages are kept for at least three months. You will see how much was left to finish since my handwriting is, shall we say, very distinguished." Funke looks at me. Irritated.

"Herr Stoessling can you please hand me the layout page. I can't see anything Stoessling has in front of him that looks like the layout page." Stoessling looks at Funke with an open his hand as a sign he doesn't have it. "Can we call our print office to get the page? Herr Schardt, I want you to realize that we are doing here more than our obligation. If we have the page it will clearly show that you owe Frau Stock and all of the members of the Arbitration Commission an apology."

"Let's see when the page is here for all to inspect," I respond. Stoessling who had left the room during all that exchange comes back and whispers something in Funke's ear. Another unexpected thing seemed to have happened. Funke turns to Meyer scribbling a note. "Dear members of the Arbitration Commission, it appears that the page in question is not able to be located at this point. I don't see how this would have mattered anyway. We all have to go back to work. Therefore I would like to end the meeting. We have two proposals to vote on. Who is for the reprimanding Herr Schardt for his action, and who is for the immediate termination of his employment? Please show your hands."

"I can't believe what just happened. You have not given me ample to time to make my case. You cannot produce the layout page that would show how much work was to be done before I left. And now you are going to vote. Is there no one here with a conscience?"

"You had your time. All of us here have more important things to do than sit here all afternoon and listen to you."

"Please don't forget, I did not request this meeting," I interrupt Funke. The room is tense.

"We are going to vote now. Please show your hands those who are for the reprimand." I make a point to scan the room trying to catch everybody's eye. Of course no one looks at me. Except for Stoessling, all lift their arms. "That looks like the majority. Therefore the Arbitration Commission will reprimand Herr Schardt. This will be going on record in his personal work file. The meeting is closed. Frau Meyer please lead him out of the building." Only the scratching noise of the pushed back chairs is heard. Everybody seems to want to leave the room as fast as they can. I stay in my chair waiting for Frau Meyer to get me. I guess I still have a job. But the clock is ticking.

"You are certainly in more trouble than I am." Klaus gives me a hug after I had told him about the Arbitration Commission farce. "What do you think will happen next?"

"They will find a reason to fire me. The charade with the Arbitration Commission did not go as planned. I wonder if they destroyed the layout page or is it just coincidence that it is not there anymore. It doesn't matter. But I weakened their case against me. And that caught them off guard. Touché for me. But the next round will go to them." I feel the desire to be hugged by Klaus. I slide closer to him on the couch. I can tell he's not in the mood to be physical. It

313

happens lately a lot. I always have to initiate things. Sometime I get him excited, more times than not. Right now I want it very bad.

I slide my hand in his pants. He is not moving an inch. I grab his dick. It feels sweaty and sticky. I don't care. I try to kiss him. He opens his mouth. No passion. I don't care. I kneel in front of him. Pull his pants down. His dick tastes salty. He is still limp. I am not. I spread his legs and want to lick him. He smells bad. I spit in my hand and wet him. I get up and lift his ass so I can get inside of him. His eyes are vacant. He lets me do what I am doing. I get my dick wet. I am so ready to fuck him. His boredom turns me on. As I stretch his hole open some milky stuff comes out. At first I am not sure what it is. I look at him.

He looks me right in the eyes. "Its cum. Don't act like you have never seen it." His legs slide off my shoulders.

"You had sex with someone just before you came home?" The cum makes a little puddle on the couch. I am totally grossed out.

"Who says before I came home? I got fucked just before you came home. You probably passed him in building." Klaus' words sound intentionally cruel to me.

"No, I did not pass anybody when I came home," is all I can say.

"Well, I tell you it was close. I told him to hurry because I expected you. Just in case you want to know, he lives in the building." Klaus laughs and gets up. "Don't start an argument. I am not in the mood for that. It happened and that's the end of it." I am still naked. I feel vulnerable and silly. Standing between the couch and coffee table, my pants around my ankles. How can someone be caring and genuinely worried about a person he lives with but gave himself just minutes before to some stranger? It's crazy. He will never change. The one in this relationship to change is me. I hear Klaus finishing his shower. I have to clean myself. What I smelled on Klaus was the aftermath of the sex with this other guy. What I tasted... I can't think that thought any further. I step behind the shower curtain.

I got a letter from the Ministry for the Interior that

Secretary Dickel has received my letter, reviewed it and had forwarded to the proper authority in Pankow, the district of my residency. Any further questions I had I should address there. Klaus received a similar note. No one knows how long it will take until permission will be given to leave the GDR. There are people who wait for almost ten years. What a terrible situation. If I can help it it won't take that long for us. I will be at city hall every four weeks until they get tired of me. Klaus thinks that's silly. "If they want to let us go they will do so without you being in their face or not." I don't agree with that. If you move something will move, too. That's my mantra.

However, I will give it a little bit of time before I pay my first visit. In the meantime I try to get as much information as I can to be prepared when the day arrives that they tell us to leave. Klaus and I go through our stuff deciding what we should take with us and what not. Rumor has it that you can hire a moving company that will do the East to West move. Here in the East it is VEB Kombinat Autotrans. On the other side of the Wall Kunzendorfer company will take over.

Everything is so vague. It's so hard to get specifics. There is no office or storefront you can go. It's all "I have heard there is..." But no one really is sure. You also cannot communicate with other people who have pending Exit Applications. For one, how would we know such people? And if you know them, they are very secretive about their doings and preparations out of fear to jeopardize their case by talking. Maria, a former co-worker at the library and her husband are waiting for their "family reunion" permit. Once we met for coffee. "Oh, I don't know. My husband is dealing with that stuff," she cut me right off. She had no intention to give me any inside information.

Therefore Klaus and I we are in a little bit of a limbo. We just have to keep our eyes and ears open. Anyway, in case we should hire that moving company I want to be ready. Klaus decided not to take any of his furniture, just his personal stuff and maybe the table he made himself and his tools. I would like to take my books, some furniture, dishes and such. We want to keep it small since we have no clue how much the transport will cost.

We have told all our friends what we are up to. All of them were surprised, which surprised me. Very few congratulated us for the courage to go head·on into an uncertain future. Some said they were very close to making a decision themselves.

My friend Sonia broke out in tears. "How can you do that to me? I thought we are friends. Sure, things are not great here. But as long we have friends things are manageable. Please don't do that." I was not sure how to react to her outburst. I felt bad.

"There are phones. We can write to each other. We will be still friends. We can meet."

"That's different. You won't be here anymore. Where would we meet? I can't come. You won't be allowed coming back for visits."

"We can meet in Prague or someplace in Poland." Even by pointing out all the options we have, silently I had to agree with Sonia that as soon as we were gone the likelihood to stay close friends is very slim to null. Claudia and Marlene are more pragmatic. "It's your choice. And no one can predict the future. Let's enjoy each other as long as we can." I gave Marlene a hug for that.

Others are downright hostile towards us. Kurt Klein made it clear that Klaus has to quit dancing with the ensemble. We kind of expected that. Being a member of group sponsored by the FDGB, the state union, appears impossible for obvious reasons. One who wants to leave East Germany and dances political agitation at the same time borders on mockery. Klein told Klaus that he doesn't wish any contact with us even outside the dance group. Amazing that our friendships have to pass the ideology litmus test. That Kurt drives a Volvo, changes his East Marks into West Marks whenever he can and lets his West relatives send him nylon dress shirts makes him a cynic, doesn't it? But when you have the West already in your life it's very easy to defend the East. I will miss his humor and most of all his outlandish parties. I didn't have the balls to give him the keys to his *datscha* in Schildow back in person. I sent them in the mail.

That Klein doesn't have the balls to keep in contact with us is sad. Losing friends and known comfort zones are part of decision making. There is a reason for the saying "all things have two sides." Sure, Klein is not the first one to choose sides. He is definitely the first one I feel sad to lose. He once asked me to work with him on a new libretto for a ballet the "FDJ" scout organization was going to sponsor. It certainly had to be a propaganda piece performed at the annual Workers' Festival, a show celebration of the achievements of the GDR. I didn't mind playing a part in it. I was in it for the money and the FDJ, which was led by Klein's friend Egon Krenz, paid well. The story line: a boy grows up as a positive example for his comrades first in the scout organization Junge Pioniere then as a member in the FDJ and later as a member of the Nationale Volksarmee (NVA) to protect the GDR and its citizens. The story was flat but it had some artistic highlights in Klein's choreography. It was performed only once. Anyway, the collaboration brought us close. Somehow we understood each other's approach. Klein made suggestions to put meat on the story. I gave some input for his choreography. One evening after the rehearsal Kurt and I went out for something to eat. It was a comfortable atmosphere and he started to talk about his beginnings in dance and soon after into choreography.

Kurt, the Party's Choreographer

Kurt was sixteen years old when he had to be part of the *Volkssturm*, the last crazed effort by the Nazi Regime to stop the imminent defeat. Sure enough, he was captured by the Russians and put into a labor camp in Latvia. One day the guards decided that the prisoners should be creative and put a performance on for their entertainment. Somehow Kurt was picked to do the dance part. He chose Swan Lake. The guards liked it. One liked not only his dance. They became secret lovers. Camp life for Kurt turned tolerable. He got a dance part and soon afterwards the artistic lead role for future shows put on by the prisoners. In the process he learned something else: Russian. It was his ticket for survival. His Russian lover gave him a high-five recommendation when he was released. He also told him to go back to Berlin and offer his services to the Russian Headquarters. There he was hired to be part of the renewal of the city's cultural future. Kurt did some dancing but realized pretty soon that he wouldn't be solo-material. He wanted to be a dance creator. Some affairs with Russian higher-ups landed him a spot in the ballet school in Leningrad. After three years of studying there he had his diploma. With his Soviet credential his future back home was secure. He became the Party's choreographer.

"I paid dearly for what I have today back in the camp. The guy who took me as his lover made me to sleep with friends of his. My fellow prisoners knew what went on. Some of them fucked me too. I was young and not bad looking. I used that to my advantage. But I also hated it so much that I swore if I survive this no one ever will fuck with me. I used these bastards. I earned every bit I have today." He had tears running down his cheeks. I have never seen Kurt that emotional before or after. It's probably this survival mode, he taught himself way back in the camp that still works to this day. It's still that very fear someone or something can take it all away. Even today, in his mid-fifties and with some

318

fame and accomplishment he senses his vulnerability. In a flash, he can fall out of favor.

I made a very unemotional decision. I will stay with Klaus until we get the permit to exit. It's a very calculated, I know. But I feel I can't go through it alone with all the trials and tribulations lay ahead. It will be better as two. Sleeping around is his way of life. He never will change. Promise follows promiscuity follows promise. And on and on. After so many years I learn to accept that. At least I will get something out of it. Help, strength and a shoulder when things are difficult. After we settle in the West I will leave him. It's a game with an end. And that makes it tolerable for me; I hope at this point nothing is more important than to get out of here. Everything else has to move to second place.

I have one big task ahead of me that I wish I could do without but know I have to go through with: to visit my aunt and cousin in Leipzig to tell them in person that I have submitted an Exit Application. They know. I told them over the phone. But I also think I should tell them in person. My aunt and her now-dead husband were the only real family I had and could count on when things turned unbearable with my mother's husband. I know my aunt does not approve of my plan to leave East Germany. First of all she is a Party member. She also thinks that the West is the wrong society. She sees socialism as the ultimate destiny for mankind. It is as much as an intellectual approach on her part as it was for her husband. Both were proud of being a part of the East German intelligentsia and they made their way to accepting the mishaps and shortcomings in the East German structure of society by going back to the original teachings of Marx, Engels and Lenin.

My aunt and uncle's knowledge of the theoretical work of the fathers of communism satisfied their dissatisfaction with the reality. In a way they felt like originalists. What always astonished me was the fact that they clearly saw what was happening around them. Their denial to a certain degree led them to an internal immigration. A double life not so different from everyone else, except they never

seemed unhappy with it. My uncle compensated for it with
political satire, which was not only his outlet but also his
pride: pride that he could acknowledge the dissatisfying
present. So sad because he was such razor-sharp analyzer.
He was smart enough that he must have realized also that
the society he lived in was at its core so defective that it only
can be changed by overcoming it.

I decide to take the car to get to Leipzig. It will be a long
three-hour ride on a mostly pothole-riddled highway. There
is only one section that is as smooth as it should be. The
West Autobahn was paid for by the West German
government as one of those shrewd deals that the East
Germans have with the West. To guarantee the West
Germans a smooth ride between West Berlin and West
Germany territory the GDR Party bosses made it look like
they are doing the West German imperialists a big favor.
There are three designated highways that connect West
Berlin and West Germany that pass through East German
land. "Give us the money and we build you a wide and
perfect highway between your territories." Not only does the
West German government pay in West Marks to get a pretty
high-speed ramp built, they also have to pay for its upkeep.
Along these three superhighways are also clean and modern
rest stops where West Germans can eat and refresh
themselves...of course with their money. East Germans are
allowed to use the highway but not the fine restaurants and
shops along it. They have to take their breaks at dingy and
dilapidated Metropa restaurants with matching stinky
bathrooms.

I guess it's a reminder for East German drivers that to
reach the Communist paradise there is a long road ahead of
them. The good thing about having these three smooth
Autobahn sections is that we as Easterners have the luxury
to feel for a short while what it means to drive on a perfect
road before exiting on to the bad road towards Leipzig. The
worst Autobahn is the one going to Dresden.

The East German Autobahn is an inheritance from the
Nazis who created the infrastructure in preparation for war.
Only marginal things are done to the Autobahn system
under GDR rule. Despite the run-down highways you still

feel privileged to be able to use these awful highways because you are a car owner: what most East Germans aspire to be but only one sixteenth of the population has achieved. And so you endure the brain-rattling ride because after all you are special.

My aunt's apartment is in one of the more prestigious areas of Leipzig, in Schoenfeld. Her windows face a vast park. The trees and bushes there help to filter the polluted air drifting up from the coal mining and huge factory complex in Bitterfeld. Sometime the sulfur smell is so strong you have to close the windows. There are days more often than not where your laundry hanging outside to dry is covered in black soot. But the coal is needed to heat most of the East German homes. The products produced in the factories are exported to the brother countries in the RGW, the economic organization of the East Bloc. We are also told that many plastic products from Bitterfeld are desired on the international Market where capitalist countries pay good money. Who could argue with that? Isn't that a sure sign for the superiority of "Dictatorship of the Proletariat"? The West needs what the East can manufacture. Who cares that the environment in areas like Bitterfeld gets raped followed by an exceptional increase of chronic lung disease, miscarriages and infant deformities cases?

It's all part of the birth pains of a new and bright future. Interesting enough, none of the members of the *Nomenklatura* live in theses highly polluted areas. Their homes are behind walls in wooded enclaves. Their free time is spent hunting and carousing in protected landscape where no factories, coal mines or even ordinary peoples presence are allowed. The despot and his brown noses don't want to be bothered with the structural imbalances. They lead. To offset their hard work for the populace is the reward of pure enjoyment. They also want to be amongst themselves. They don't want to smell and breathe thick yellow smoke coming out of factory chimneys or to be covered by coal dust. The citizens' task is to produce the material goods. The other function of the masses is to be background to enhance the *Nomenklatura*'s self-importance and extraordinary presence. On my hiking tours with my

uncle way back we walked through woods solely dedicated
for the use of Prime Minister Stoph and his entourage.
Other areas around Berlin are staked out for the head of the
Stasi, Erich Mielke, and his hunting buddies. A huge area
in the Thueringer Wald mountains is off limits because it's
where once a year Party Leader Honecker entertains the
diplomatic corps with rustic outdoor fun.

Our greeting is awkward. We hug. My aunt's dog nips at
my shoes. The table is set with coffee and cake. We sit down
and make small talk about my eventless drive from Berlin.
But I don't want to put off our talk any longer. "You know
why I am here. But I thought I owe it to you to tell you in
person about my decision to leave the country."

"Yes, you do owe me and my daughter an explanation."
My aunt falls into a very official sounding voice. "We have
raised you to be a responsible person. We also tried to teach
you that no matter how difficult things can be you never
should give up. With your decision to turn your back on us
you also have failed us. And something else you have done
to us. Your cousin, my daughter will not get a spot at the
university because of your actions."

Now I feel like I am sitting in front of some Party official
or Stasi member. "Yes, you have raised me. Yes, you have
taught me to not give up. I have not failed you. I am what
you wanted me to be. An honest person. My decision to
submit an Exit Application is not a fly-by-night decision. It
is a result of what has happened to me. I don't have to
recount everything. You know them. I don't see a future for
me here. I am too young to give up and give in. I want to
learn about the world and I want to see it too. Not just read
about it."

"Listen to you. It's me, me and me. What about us? Your
uncle had always hoped that you would take on his role
should something happen to him. Your uncle, my husband
is gone. And you abandon us. I never will forgive for you
that."

"I tried to live within the confinement of this system. I
can't and no one should. I can't make decisions for others. I
only can make them for me. Unfortunately, if you make a
decision for something at the same time you make a decision

against something or someone. I have not created the inhumane system we live in, a system where you before all things have to pass the ideology test. No matter what your IQ is, no matter what you want to achieve if you do not sing the Party's song you are stopped. I will not be part of a nameless, headless and docile mass. I want to be the captain of my own destiny."

"Well, there is not much more to say, is there? You are dead to us."

"Sorry that you feel that way. You say it's because of me that my cousin won't get a spot at a university. Don't you see how wrong this system is? During the Nazi era they called it "Guilt by Association." This is no different. Is it my fault if my cousin does not get an education she wants just because I, her cousin, want to live in the West? Don't you see what's wrong with this picture?"

"Well, I hope you will find the perfect conditions on the other side of the Wall. It doesn't come easy, but I wish you all the best. In my heart I know you are making the wrong decision. Over there it is a people-eating society. Only those who have money and influence will make it. You will arrive there with nothing and you will end up with nothing. And don't count on your father. He is a bad person; he never cared for you or your mother. It was us, me and your uncle, who gave you everything. Now, when it is time to give back you leave us."

I don't want to continue this discussion. She won't convince me to reverse my decision and I won't convince her that wanting to live in the West doesn't make me a bad person. "Let's not talk about this anymore. I don't know how long it will take until they let me out. Let's cherish the time left we can be together."

"Will you write to me?" Until now my cousin has not said a word. She listened quietly to our conversation.

"Of course I will. You will be always my cousin. I will never forget you."

"Well, Mami that is not so bad. Maybe he can sent me some jeans, and for you some medication that will help you with your heart?"

"My daughter, always the practical one." My aunt can't

323

help it and laughs.

The ice is broken, the cake and coffee are finished and, I can drive back to Berlin. I am sad about what my aunt said but she is always a bit dramatic. So I shouldn't take her remarks too seriously, especially the one about me being dead. It's her way to deal with our pending separation. I have to understand.

Everything I do now is divided between the day before I submitted my Exit Application and the day after. I begin to mark the the one week anniversary, two week and so on since I dropped off my application to leave East Germany. Its two months now and, I am very antsy already. I want out now. There are rumors that a group of ten people got their exit visa by going to the Permanent Diplomatic Mission of the German Federal Republic. I will try anything.

Visit to the Ständige Vertretung (Permanent Mission) of West Germany

The building of the Permanent Mission does not stand out from its surroundings except for the very visible presence of the People's Policemen in front of the entrance. His official function: Protection of the West German diplomats working in the building. But the real purpose is to intimidate any East German who wants to enter the building. . I am so desperate to speed up our exit that I suggest to Klaus to go to the Permanent Mission with the goal of not leaving the building until we secure a promise from the embassy staff that our Exit Application is granted. At first Klaus was totally against it. He was afraid we wouldn't even get into the building because of the police presence outside. He envisioned we would be arrested and thrown into prison. Even if we get in, so goes his angst, the people at the Permanent Mission would deliver us to the East German authorities. I tried to tell them that would be against international law.

"Why do you want to push our luck? We have an Exit Application. Let the process work," so goes his argument.

"I don't want to wait ten years. I really believe that when you make a move things will move," I tried to apply physics to give him a convincing explanation.

"Let me think about it." A typical Klaus answer. He is a master of procrastination. I let it go, and began to think about the logistics and a plan that wouldn't look too obvious to him. I switch gears into manipulation mode.

"I think we should start to prepare for the day when we get the permit. We should bring the things you want to take into my apartment. After that we can start to sell the rest and empty your place."

"Sounds like a good idea." I am surprised and glad to hear that. My plan of action seems to get off to a good start. The next couple of days we are busy packing dishes, artwork and knickknacks. In preparation for moving Klaus' stuff out off his apartment I inspected the attic in my apartment building and found an empty corner where we could store some boxes.

"I will start packing up some of my stuff as well and bring it up in the attic. That way, my apartment does not look like a warehouse."

"That's a good idea." Klaus doesn't seem suspicious of what I am up to because my plan is to get all of our valuable things out of both apartments and store them away in the attic. If we go to the Permanent Diplomatic Representation and be steadfast in our resolve not to leave until we are escorted to the border we won't have a chance to take some of our stuff with us. Everything in our apartments will be confiscated by the authorities except for the things in the attic that no one knows about. When we are in the West I will tell my grandmother. My family can decide if they want any of the stuff.

I bring as many boxes as possible in the attic, mostly late at night or very early in the morning. I don't want to be caught by any of my neighbors. It's a slow process. Not only do I have to be secretive about it. There are also six flights of stairs I have to climb in order to schlep up the cartons and smaller pieces of furniture.

"You really want to go to the Permanent Mission, do you?" I jump because I didn't hear Klaus come home.

"Yes." There was no sense in denying it any longer.

"But what if that is when they arrest us?"

"I don't know the answer to that. Believe me I don't want to go to prison. But other people were successful going into embassies. Why can't we do it?"

"I don't understand why you want to rush and risk it?"

"Every day we stay here is a wasted day. Maybe it is not the best idea to try to get out through the Permanent Mission. But at least let us try. I know I would not have the nerve to escape by cramming into the back of a car or jumping over the Wall. Aside from the fact that we don't have any connection to any people smuggler organizations. We both decided we want to leave this country. Then let's try all the possibilities we have without risking our lives."

"I still don't understand why we can't wait and see. On the other hand I agree that any day here is a lost day. I am not convinced at all that your plan will work, but I am willing to go ahead with that."

"We both have to be sure about it. I am. As long we are into it together the harder for them to break or scare us." I can see fear in Klaus' eyes. He hastily sucks on his cigarette.

I know I pushed him in a direction he doesn't want to go in. I feel sorry but don't say it. Instead I put my arms around him. "We will be all right. We knew it wouldn't be easy. But look ahead. Our lives will be different and better, I feel it." Klaus pushes his head into my armpit. I feel moisture through my shirt sleeve. He is crying. My hand rests on his head. Strength and willfulness has certainly nothing to do with age. I am thirteen years younger but I am the one who gives him the comfort that I need as well.

"What about our car? I don't want the Stasi to confiscate it. We worked too hard for it."

"I am not sure. Any ideas?"

"I thought that maybe Monika would want it."

"Mmh, why not." I am frazzled. Frazzled by the fact that he must have sensed that I didn't want to let go of the plan to try the embassy escape but didn't say anything until this moment. He must also have thought about what to do with our things. Why else would he mention Monika right away? Of all of our friends it's her he wants to give the car to. Sure, she is one of our closest friends. We go on ski vacations together. She is as interested in ballet and opera as we are. But... I decide not to challenge him on that. I am glad that he came around and agreed go to the Permanent Mission

But it also means that we have to tell Monika about our plan. It's risky. What if she tells the authorities? We will be arrested in no time. Her reward: a promotion within her office. I don't believe she would do it. But do I know that for sure? No. The fewer people know about what we are going to do the better. I wouldn't even tell my family... it puts them in an awkward position. They certainly will be interrogated after the Stasi learns that we occupied the Mission. The same will happen to all of our acquaintances.

The less any of them know the safer for them too. If we want to give Monika the car we have to tell her. Something. Maybe not the whole truth. We have to come up with some story.

"How do you want to do it?"

"We can tell her that if something happens to us in the next couple of days that the car is parked in front of her building. We will leave it unlocked; the keys will be inside as well as the sales contract."

"Wow, you have thought about it in detail, haven't you?"

"We also can pack the car with our things. The TV, our turntable player, the radio. She can use that as well." Monika has just broken up with her boyfriend of five years. She and Manfred danced both with the Duncker Ensemble. They looked like they would be an item forever. But Manfred started an affair with another dancer and she got pregnant. Monika moved out with just her clothes.

"Let's do it your way. It's fine by me. Monika certainly can use our things. You are right."

"I don't know what you are talking about. No one has occupied the Permanent Mission in order to gain a visa to leave the GDR." The diplomatic clerk across from us is polite but very official sounding. He knows and we know that what he just said is not true. Just a couple weeks ago about ten East Germans did just do what he is now so vehemently denying. I guess it his job to discourage anyone to self-hostage himself here.

"I don't think that's true. We are determined to stay here until we will guarantee our safe passage."

"I have to urge you to reconsider your position. This Mission is not equipped for overnight stays. Certainly we cannot throw you out but what you are intending to accomplish with your stay won't work."

I am not intimidated by his words but I can feel that Klaus is very uncomfortable. "Maybe he is right." I could kill Klaus for that.

The clerk jumps on it right away. "I think your partner is very reasonable. Here is what I can do for you. I will take your names and addresses and will submit it to the

Government of the Federal Republic. Your names will be added to the list that our government will present to the government of the Deutsche Demokratische Republik. This is your best change to speed up the permission process for your Exit Application." I don't believe the guy. He just wants to get rid of us.

"If you can do this for us that would be wonderful." Klaus waves the white flag. I hate weaklings. For the first time I regret that I thought we should try together to leave East Germany. I now wish Klaus wasn't here. I know I would not leave the building, no matter what I am told. I would put up a fight to stay here until they escort me out and directly into West Berlin. But I realize my plan is not working. There is no use now to fight both of them, the embassy official and Klaus. I feel defeated even if there was not much of a battle. After less than five minutes it is over.

"OK," is all that I can say right at this moment. The guy pushes a piece of paper in front of us. "Please fill in all your personal information." I look at Klaus. My handwriting is bad. Klaus grabs the pen.

I hear the voice of my grandmother: "Always keep your own counsel. Never relay on anybody." How right she is. My calculated handling of Klaus has failed miserably. From now on I have to be stronger and more determined no matter if he follows or not. I am furious.

"So much for the West German propaganda that they care for their East German sisters and brothers. I have learned from you today these are just words. No intention to act on it." I push my chair back and head to the door.

As I rush out the door I hear the clerk and Klaus talk. "Thank you for your time."

"I wish you all the best."

Klaus catches up with me in the foyer. "You were very rude to him. I am embarrassed."

"Don't talk to me. Let's get out of here." I push the glass door open. The *Volkspolizist* out front on the first step didn't seem to have moved an inch since we went in. Our clothes touch when I pass him getting back to the street. Klaus and I turn to the right. Just as we reach the corner of Friedrichstrasse another cop approaches us. "Volkspolizei der DDR. Your Identification Card."

"Why do you want to see it? We have not done anything wrong."

"You just left the Permanent Mission of the BRD. What was the reason for your visit?"

"Go inside and find out for yourself," I snap at him. And again Klaus is the arbitrator. He hands over his identification. The cop reads out loud Klaus' name, address and birthday. His head is slightly tilted towards the collar of his uniform jacket. I can see a little bulge. It must be a walkie-talkie. I get closer to the cop.

"We went into the Permanent Mission with the intention of staying. We have an Exit Application and cannot wait to leave the GDR." I almost scream so my voice can be heard by whoever is on the other end of the walkie-talkie. I give the cop my identification. Again he reads all the information out loud. "I hope this visit will expedite our exit." The cop does not react to any of my comments. It doesn't matter to me. But I am glad that I could give my frustration a place to be heard. The *Volkspolizist* hands back our IDs. "Is this the first time that you went into the Permanent Mission? "

"I am sure you have ways to find out, don't you?" I know I am pushing the envelope. At this minute I wish they would arrest me. Klaus pulls me away.

We walk down Wilhelm-Pieck-Strasse. I feel the adrenaline rushing out of my body. "What now?" I ask.

"We have to be patient. The guy in the mission promised us that he will forward our names. I think that will help our cause. Don't you?"

"He was full of shit. He wanted to get rid of us in the worst possible way. I think if anything was helpful today was the fact a VoPo stopped us. Now they know how serious we are. He read our names to someone. There is a record now." We make a turn onto Brunnenstrasse where we had parked our car, filled with our stuff, unlocked so Monika could get to it. Well, not anymore. We will be using the car for little while longer. For how long? Who knows? Why does it seem that always somebody else has a final say in my life? It's never you alone who can decide for yourself. It's the "but" that stops, delays or derails things even when you come to a decision a long while ago. Why convince somebody else when you convinced yourself already? Being in control, seizing the power if only for a short moment is the name of the game we all are part of it, aren't we? I am guilty, too. The crux of life: control but not be controlled. I still have not figured out how to reconcile with that. Right now I feel the East German officials steal my time, time I don't want spent here anymore. Time forever lost. I feel already cheated. Sure, no one knows how much time we have. But whatever is left for me it becomes less and less. Missing out on whatever lies ahead.

Marscha, Anton, and a Failed Life in the West

Marscha and Anton look like they had it made. She works at the Intershop just behind the Maritime Hotel on Friedrichstrasse. He is a chef at the Cafe Moskau. Their decent income allows them to live above the average of other East German families. The two-bedroom apartment was smartly furnished with a standard Hellerau-manufactured wall unit in the living room, couch and coffee table, round dining room table next to the kitchen. Their two kids, ten and twelve years old, are dressed in Western jeans and tops: perks thanks to Marscha. As an employee she can buy things in the Intershop store. Anton has access to meat and fruits like oranges and grapes by way of the restaurant he works in. Their car, a beige-colored Trabant compact car, is paid for by Marscha's parents after her grandmother was eligible for a car. She had never intended to buy a car, since she couldn't drive. But like so many other families in East Germany, everybody over the age of eighteen puts himself on the car waiting list. Marscha's grandmother did that over ten years ago. Marsha and Anton are now on the waiting list for a telephone line and a *datscha*. But all that is not enough for them.

Anton loves being a chef and feels that he should travel the world to learn about other countries' cuisine. But to him traveling the world and gaining more knowledge doesn't mean going to the Soviet Union and being shown how to make "Soljanka" soup or cook red beet stew, as he himself always sarcastically put it. He wants to go to France, Italy or Spain to broaden his knowledge. He knows it's a pipe dream except when he does what so many do: submits an Exit Application. Anton has an aunt in Cologne. He can declare his wish to be with her. Marscha is not very excited about her husband's plan. She doesn't want to give up what she has for something she doesn't know she may have or have not. Her kids are all for it. In the end she let Anton to

332

do the paperwork.

It comes as a total surprise to them when only after six months they get the news that they can leave East Germany. The only problem is that the family has to cross the border into Giessen: an unexpected twist because they had hoped to go directly to West Berlin. Friends of theirs had already set up an apartment. Now they have to go through Giessen which has a refugee camp with the worst reputation. It is known as a tough and violent place, to be avoided at all costs. But Marsha and Anton don't have a choice, they have to temporarily move into one of the bleak-looking apartment barracks together with refugees from the Soviet Union, Poland, Romania and other East Bloc countries.

Most of those immigrants rightfully claim their German origin but some of them are just notorious criminals and have really no basis to apply for West German citizenship. West Germany's constitution acknowledges all people with German ancestry, no matter where they live, as Germans. Therefore anyone who has German blood can seek German citizenship if they wish to. Eastern Bloc governments don't make easy for those people to leave but in the end money talks. West Germany pays for them directly or indirectly. The people themselves have to give up their properties or any other valuables they may have. It's a dirty trade but like the East German *Nomenklatura* the Russian, Polish, and Romanian Communist elite love a good life. The more they let go the more money comes their way. It's nothing less than money-for-human trade. That the Communist authorities mix in some of their undesirables like Gypsies or outright criminals with those who have German background doesn't matter.

Fights and thefts are part of the daily camp life in Giessen and well documented in news accounts. Anyway, Anton and his family are assigned one room with bunk beds plus a kitchen and bathroom. To watch TV they have to go to the communal room. During the day, when Anton has to deal with the bureaucratic side of becoming a West German citizen, Marscha has to watch her children and protect their personal items. Her new beginning is a far cry from what she had to leave behind. She is not sure how she will make it through the next four weeks, the average time to be processed.

Just about a week into their camp life Marscha develops the first signs of depression. She cannot sleep, cries for hours and is unable to get out their room. Any attempt by Anton to be intimate she rejects. The children start to act out since Marscha doesn't want them to go to public school in Giessen. Anton tries hard to make his family as comfortable as possible. He uses any opportunity to get free clothes or money that several charitable organizations offer to former Easterners. He even picks up some furniture, dishware and linens. With the 100 West Marks Welcome Money he takes his family to downtown Giessen to have lunch. But all that does not minimize Marscha's anxiety. She begins to talk about going back to East Germany. Anton tries harder to expedite their naturalization and he is successful. In a record time of only two weeks he has all the papers together. His aunt, not happy about having her relatives now so close by, is also deeply worried about her niece's mental conditions. She wants to be as helpful as she can and has rented an apartment for them in Cologne, paid for the next six months. Anton, Marscha and the kids take the train to their new hometown.

Their flat is in the outskirts of Cologne city in a low-income apartment complex. Their new neighbors are mostly Turks. Only very few Germans live here. Marscha is as devastated as Anton is disappointed that their aunt had chosen this particular neighborhood for them. The aunt lives in the city with unobstructed views of the Rhine River. The only foreigner she has to deal with is her Polish housekeeper. Her neighbors are fellow German countrymen. No coincidence.

Marsha and Anton have to register with the unemployment agency to receive money until they find work. The school for the kids is close to where they live. Anton finds all kinds of charitable organizations to get more furniture from. He seems happy since things are going in the right direction, or so he thinks. He finds a job as a line cook in a downtown restaurant. It's below his qualifications but he is ambitious. Marscha has a harder time knocking on shop doors to ask for a job as a sales clerk. The children are only two of five German kids in the class of thirty-five students. Marscha cannot afford to stop and remember what she has left behind in East Berlin. The Golden West, of which everybody talked about back home, has no shine for her. She hates it here. She wants to go back. She knows she will go back. Anton is torn. He knows he will make it here if she would let him. But he also has responsibility for his wife and two children. Sure, he endures every day how his boss treats him at work. He mocks him constantly because he is an Easterner. He tells him that he sucks as a cook, doubts that he even is a trained chef. But Anton is sure of himself. The more his boss pushes him around the stronger his will becomes not to give up.

His life at home is a different story. The last time he and Marscha had sex was the night before they left East Berlin. Marscha sleeps in the living room now. If she goes to the bathroom she locks the door and does not comes out for a very long time. They hardly speak to each other anymore. Marscha also has stopped looking for a job. The six months of free rent is almost up. Anton is not sure how they will survive. His earnings are not enough for all their needs. Marscha's only contact with the outside world is her mother. They speak on the phone daily and for hours. Marscha's mother wants her daughter and grandchildren back. Anton realizes that his dream of becoming a world chef will be short-lived.

The Wait Begins

I knew the day will come. I guess our visit to the Permanent Mission has expedited the meeting to review my employment status. I am summoned to the main building of *Der Morgen* at Taubenstrasse, second floor, office of the editor-in-chief, Gerhard Fischer. Another charade with the same players: the representative of the FDGB, the one from the FDJ, the one from the LDPD, my former office supervisor, the editor-in-chief himself.

"It is now several months that you decided to turn against the German Democratic Republic. Since then you have been given numerous opportunities to retract your decision. Again my question is: have you changed your mind?" Fischer's massive body is placed behind his massive desk. His voice deep, certainly intended to be intimidating. He does not look at me. He faces his deputy, as if I am not in the room. Everybody else in the room stares at me.

"I appreciate your concerns about my decision to live closer to my father."

"Come on Herr Schardt, we are not dumb. This is your official version why you want to leave the DDR. The real reason is that you have turned against the people and the government of this country because you are brainwashed by our enemies." Fischer's body is now erect behind his desk. Still he directs his words towards his deputy Fahlenkamp.

"If I just can remind you of something: it was not me who has *turned* as you like to put it. In this very room I told you that I was declined a travel visa to Budapest. It was in this room that I told you after Das Deutsche Theater withdrew its job offer that I felt like an outcast. Both decisions were made without any explanations. I had to accept it. You told me you would get an answer on my behalf. To this day I have not gotten one. So, please don't accuse me of turning. The DDR has turned on me first. I am too young to accept being bullied. And that is the reason why I want to leave the DDR and live closer to my father. I am intelligent enough to make up my own mind. What you call *brainwashing by the enemies* has not happened."

"I gather after that tirade you have not changed your mind."

"Of course not. Does anyone in this room really think I made that decision in the spur of a moment without knowing about the consequences?" I replied.

"That's enough." Fischer slaps down his huge hand on the desk. "Dear colleagues and friends, you have heard it. Herr Schardt has rejected one more time our offer to be re-integrated in our society. I propose to terminate his employment immediately. What is your decision?"

"Herr Schardt has stopped paying his member ship dues. Therefore I cannot represent him," the union guy seconds.

"Herr Schardt is no longer member of the LDPD." The party representative follows.

"Same here. Herr Schardt is behind in his dues for the FDJ. We are in the process terminating his membership." Van Haydn, the FDJ person ends the ridiculous process. This is all rehearsed. No glitches this time.

"Thank you my friends. I think we should vote on the proposed termination of Herr Schardt. For security reasons the vote should be done without him present." Fischer scans the room.

Security reasons? What a stupid thing to say. Are they afraid I will do harm to them? I get up before I am officially dismissed and leave the room. Only seconds after I have closed the door behind me Fahlenkamp shoots out. "Herr Schardt, I will escort you downstairs to the foyer. You have to wait there for our decision." I shrug my shoulders. I open the door to the hallway and keep on walking down the stairs. I hear Fahlenkamp's steps. I am more than angry. I reach the small entrance hall.

"Wait here. We will let you know,"he says.

"I heard you the first time," I snap at him. Fahlenkamp turns around and goes upstairs. I don't see any reason for me to wait. I know I will be terminated. Why give them the satisfaction to tell me in person. "Tell them I have left," I say to the porter and push the door open.

What now? My whole body shivers. Even my teeth click

uncontrollably. I am in deep doo doo. I lost my job. But I need a job. I can't get caught jobless by them and give them a reason to prosecute me. That's how they get a lot of people who have Exit Applications. By taking the jobs away the authorities simply criminalize dissidents and critics. What follows is imprisonment together with the common riffraff. Another clever act to keep the number of political prisoners as low as possible. I know I have to find a job.

First, I have to get myself together. I try to calm myself down with controlled breathing. It seems like my body is separated from my mind. I don't want to shake, but I do. I hold my breath and count to ten. At the same time I concentrate on my surroundings. I start counting how many cars are parked along the street...thirty-six. How many pedestrians pass by me? Four. Slowly I gain my body back. My shirt is wet from my sweat. I feel cold. That's okay. I walk towards Stadtmitte subway station. I will go to the city hall in Pankow to tell the people at the Office for Interior Affairs what just happened to me. Maybe my Exit Application will be put on fast track?

A women clerk lets me in the office after she had checked my ID card. "Earlier today my employment with *Der Morgen* was terminated. I have no job, and very likely no prospect to find a job. Therefore, I think my application should be positively answered as soon as possible."

"I am not assigned to deal with unemployment issues. You have to go to the Office for Labor. You know it's against the law not to work?"

"I know that. Isn't my situation reason enough to get me my papers so I can leave the DDR immediately?"

"I would advise you not to assume that your application to leave the DDR now or in the future even will be processed. What I can tell you is that you have to work. Otherwise you will become a case for the People's Court." She hands me back my ID. I am dismissed.

"I am not stupid. You want to break me by threatening me. I am not a criminal. You know that. I just want to leave this country. A country that made very clear that is not interested in me. "I speak extra loud so I also can be heard in the adjacent offices. I slam the door behind me.

The Office for Labor is one floor down. Again, I face a female clerk. Before she can say anything, I speak. "I lost my job because I have an Exit Application. I guess I have to register with you now." I am agitated.

"What kind of work do you do?"

"I am a reporter."

"Pah," she scoffs, "I don't have any openings for reporters."

"Pah, I have not expected that," I mock her.

"Young man, I have a job as a pipe fitter at Bergmann Borsig factory. Please report there tomorrow morning at 7am."

"Pah, I won't. I am not working in a factory."

"You are not the one that makes that decision," she replies.

"Sure, I am. During my high school years I have been there as part of our curriculum. It's awful there. I will not work there, period."

"You are not in the position to choose."

"Well, we are going in circles. I told you what I won't do. So you can call the *Volkspolizei* right now to arrest me."

She looks like she wants to grab me by the neck. I am close to doing the same with her. A side door opens and a man appears. "No one screams at my colleague. You either calm down, or I will call a *Volkspolizei*."

"I don't think that I was screaming. I just tried to tell your colleague that I won't work in a factory. If this is reason enough to call the *Volkspolizei*, please do so."

"You lost your job today?" he asks.

"Yes."

"What's your plan?"

"I don't have any plan except that I want to leave the DDR as soon as possible."

"Here is a plan. I will give you twenty-four hours to find a job. If you don't have one after that time you either report to Bergmann Borsig factory or we will report you to the authorities." I want to topple the desk in front of me. All I do is turn around and slam the door behind me as hard as I can.

I am very nervous and frantic now. I have twenty-four

hours to find a job. The only chance I have is to try privately owned stores. There are about ten in my immediate neighborhood. There is lamp and a hardware store at Florastrasse. A bakery on the bottom floor of my apartment building, another at Stubnitzstrasse.

I decide to try the Kristall Mueller porcelain store on Berlinerstrasse first. The owner, gray haired and a little bit of a snob (I know him from past visits and purchases) gives me the cold shoulder. "I am not looking for help." He shows me the door.

The reaction at a store for lamps on Alte Schönhauser Strasse is one of utterly disgust towards me. "You are young and healthy looking. Why do you seek work?"

"I was fired because I have an Exit Application."

"We never would hire enemies of the GDR."

The fabric store on Breite Strasse is not looking for a male clerk. The florist on Berlinerstrasse is looking, but only for experienced clerks. The owner of the hardware store on Florastrasse is out and his wife is not sure if they even need help. I run out of options and time.

My next target is Schönhauser Allee, where there is a concentration of privately owned shops. Jeweler Stern is not hiring. Period. Cafe Schönhauser is fully staffed, including the kitchen. That I don't believe. I realize as soon as I explain why I don't have a job no shop owner wants to talk to me any further. I hop on the S-Bahn to get to other neighborhoods. But I have no clue where I should continue. Fear creeps up on me that I won't find anything before the twenty-four-hour countdown is up. Is there any employer who won't care about my Exit Application? Is that even a realistic possibility? Shop owners rely on the good standing with authorities in order to keep their businesses open. An employee with an Exit Application will certainly not put them in the best light. However, I don't think I have exhausted all of my options yet in finding a job as a store clerk. I am determined not to work in a factory.

Stations, backs of apartment complexes, vast rail yards, graffiti-covered bridges and tunnels pass by as I look out of the window of the S-Bahn train. My thoughts are all over the place. But I have to concentrate on my job-finding mission. *I should get off at the next stop and continue my search* I think, but can't make myself move. S-Bahnhof Karlshorst train station is next. I know nothing about this area except that the headquarters of the Red Army is located here as well as the Technical College for Economics, one of the breeding grounds for future foot soldiers of the Party.

I decide to get off here. Down on the street level I decide to turn left. Everything is so unfamiliar. There seem no shops of some sort. I pass by hot dog stands and HO restaurants. No reason to ask for work there. I take the next side street and circle back to the S-Bahn station. After a couple of blocks I see a storefront with two big windows. A huge handwritten sign states: "Grand opening of a Second Hand Store next Wednesday. We sell and buy clothes, furniture, dishes." Below is a little sign: "Help wanted." I look through the window. I can't see anybody. I walk around to the side of the building and find a door. I knock. A tall young man opens the door. Not bad looking.

"Are you looking for help? I am interested."

"What's your name?" he asks. I introduce myself.

"Do you have a job?"

"No, I was fired because I have an Exit Application."

"My wife is out for lunch. Can you come back in an hour?"

"Certainly." I am ecstatic.

I am back in less than an hour. "Hi, I am Elena Nice to meet you." Elena has a beautiful face, short blonde hair. Her body is pressed into tight jeans and a knitted sweater. I can make out a slight accent. "My husband Rolf told me why you are looking for work. Do you have any idea when you will get your permit?"

"No, your guess is as good as mine."

"Mmh, what about the army?" she asks.

"What about it? I never have served. I actually was told I never will be called to service."

"Interesting. However, I have to talk to the Office for Commerce at city hall and ask if I can hire you. I also have to make a call to the recruiting office of the army to find out about your status."

341

Thomas P.W. Schardt

"Sure, but could your first tell me what kind of work I would be doing?"

Elena laughs. "Of course. Sorry about that. You would help out in the store. Besides that, Rolfs needs help transporting furniture. We haul stuff from the sellers. We also offer delivery. We had a lot of calls for the job. But to be honest, we really can't use a woman because of the heavy lifting. On the other hand, men who have inquired decline after they hear what I can pay. It's not much. I can offer you 350 Marks per month for a five-day work week, eight hours a day."

"That's fine with me. I can't be too choosy. At this point I need a job, the pay is secondary." The pay is ridiculously low. After deductions I probably will get less than 300 a month. But I don't have any alternatives at this point.

"How can I reach you after I have talked to city hall?"

"Do you know when you are going there?"

"Later this afternoon. Than I have to call the Military District Commando I should know the answer by tomorrow."

"How about I come back tomorrow afternoon?"

"You want to come all the way from Pankow for that?"

"If I get the job that will be my daily routine. So it's a good exercise for me."

"You really want the job?"

"You are the first one who doesn't seem to care about my Exit Application. And I am pretty certain that the army will give you the answer you want to hear."

"I am from Bratislava. Rolf and I married four years ago, but I never gave up my Czechoslovakian passport. That allows me to travel freely to West Berlin or anywhere in the world. I don't understand why the GDR has such a problem in allowing its citizens to travel freely. So, I fully understand when people want to leave." I like Elena. I cross my fingers. I want to work for her. Tata's saying comes to mind: all bad leads to something good in the end.

I can't wait to tell the lady at the Office for Labor that she can stick the pipe fitter job at Bergmann Borsig factory up her ass. But I have to hold my horses. I have to wait until tomorrow. I don't want to jinx it. On my way back to the station I stop at an ice cream parlor. I reward myself with a scoop of vanilla ice cream. I have accomplished something today.

The letter I find in my mailbox upon my return is from the Karl-Marx University. I know the content before I open it. I am fired as an extern student because my employer *Der Morgen* has withdrawn its sponsorship of me. No other explanation. It doesn't faze me a bit. I hated the farce they call "study of journalism" anyway. I rip the letter into small pieces.

I tell Klaus about my day. He doesn't seem very interested, doesn't ask any questions. His only comment when he hears about the pay is "How will you make it on that?" I am surprised by his question. I thought we were in this together. How disappointing. Another realization that I have to solely depend on myself. For better or worst does not apply to our relationship, I guess. When he says he loves me, what does he really mean by that? Anyway, I don't want get into an argument. I leave his question unanswered. He will not dampen my mood, not today. I turn on the TV and sit next to him on the couch. No touching between us, just two pillows.

My new employers are a fun couple. They certainly know how to circumvent the system. Elena has a lot of friends from West Berlin. They bring desired articles by the bag loads. Even though their store is supposed to be a secondhand shop the new digital watches are a hot item. I overheard that her friends buy them for about ten West Marks per piece. She pays 50 East Marks for each watch. In the store we sell them for 110 East Marks. And that's all off the books. When she goes to West Berlin she buys cheap costume jewelry and sells it for a lot more that she had paid for it. Since she was born in Bratislava and kept her Czechoslovakian passport she has unlimited access to discount retailers like Woolworth any time she needs to restock the store. Because she is a Bratislava native she also has connections to get the desired crystal and hand-blown glassware from her native country. It only takes a couple of hours after we open the door and most of the items are sold.

Store hours are Thursday through Tuesday. On Wednesdays the owners buy for the store. Therefore the busiest day in the store is Thursdays. A long line forms way before our business hours. I am amazed at how much money people are willing to pay especially for the cheap Western ware. One guy, a repeat customer, is only a gardener for the city but he seems to have endless financial resources. He once offered West Marks to buy those cheap digital watches. I think Elena was very tempted but she declined. "He probably works for the Stasi and wants to trick me." I am not so sure about that. She could be right. I certainly question where his money comes from but this guy's shopping habits look legit.

One day during my break I ran into him at the supermarket. "I want to buy my daughter a digital watch. If you get some children's watches, reserve one for me. I'll pay you extra." I mentioned to Elena that we should also sell some girls watches. With the next delivery we got five of them. I put two aside without telling her. The next time the gardener came I was alone in the store. He paid full price for two watches and gave me 20 Marks extra. Nervously I took it. Twenty Marks is a lot of money for me right now considering what I make.

The shop is a limited private business, where the State is part owner. Every month Elena has to go to the commerce department at city hall to show them the books which list every item she has bought and sold. About thirty percent of her sales she has to give to the state. From her seventy percent she has to pay all of her overhead such as rent, merchandise, my salary, etc. This written-in-stone system encourages most the private shopkeepers not only to cook the books but also buy as cheaply as possible and sell as high as possible, so it seems. These semi-privately owned businesses surely fill a void in the otherwise notoriously underperforming state-run economy where almost everything falls short of what the citizen needs and wants. I wasn't aware of the amount of disposable income to be spent on non-essential goods like cheap watches from the West, kitschy glassware and junk jewelry or antiques. But I also learned about the other end of the spectrum. People who sell family heirlooms just to generate additional income, mostly to supplement their low state pensions. A set of dishes once given as wedding present and only used for special occasions ever since, a still life oil painting handed down through a couple of generations or a grandfather clock safely stored away during World War II turn into cash to help to pay for coal to heat the apartment, a son's divorce, or simply to have some savings in the bank.

Sometime it is absolutely heartbreaking when a pensioner brings an antique and has to be told the item has no resale value. It means so much to him but nothing to someone else. One can see it had taken the seller a lot of time and thought to make his way to the store in order to part with an inherited piece to generate some income in order to cover household expenses. We also get customers who just want to pawn a piece of jewelry, a gold watch or fur coat to bridge the time until the next paycheck. We are not allowed to do that because of the type of business license we have. Being a witness to a semi-capitalist business practice I really start to wonder if I am getting a glimpse of my future in the West. The West where free enterprise is a way of life and survival. And only the fittest will make it. Will I fit in? Will I be fortunate enough to belong to the ones who have it and not to ones who don't have it? I see the glow of our customers with wads of money who buy whatever they want. I see the disappointment of the others who leave with a lot less then when they came to strike it rich. Money means so much in our lives. Dealing with it seems so cold and cruel. Joy for one, misery at the same time for someone else.

Klaus Gets His Exit Papers, but What About Me?

I am surprised when Klaus comes into the store. I have another twenty minutes before closing. The owners are out running errands. "I got a letter in the mail from the Department of the Interior. I have to leave in two weeks."

"Wow," is my only reaction. "It's getting serious now."

"I hope you got the same letter. I don't want to go alone. I always thought you would be the first."

"We will see when we get home. Do they tell you what you have to do?"

"They want me to come to office to get further instructions. I told my boss that I won't come in tomorrow. I am really nervous."

"Why? This is what we have been waiting for. Two weeks is a short time to get everything settled! But if that's what they give you then that's what we have to deal with." I can't wait to get out of work and go home.

I don't have a letter in my mailbox. I am disappointed and envious that Klaus' exit is scheduled and mine is not. Fear creeps up that I will be left behind for God knows how long.

"Maybe it's better that we didn't get the papers at the same time. It's less chaotic." I say. I don't believe in my own spin but I want to stay optimistic. "Let's go to your apartment." Most of Klaus' stuff is already at my place. But there is still some furniture that we have to dispose of. "I hope we can find buyers. It would nice to get some money."

"Ralph mentioned he would be interested in my wall unit and the couch. I will call him right away."

We drive over to Klaus' place. He drives through a red light. I offer to drive the rest of the way. Klaus says he will be fine. I'm nervous that we will get into an accident. "I am fine. We are almost there." We take two steps at a time up to his apartment. I am not sure why we rush but somehow it seems like the right thing to do. My eyes canvas the living

346

room. There is really nothing left to keep.

"I would like to take the dining room table and the chairs. Maybe my mother's sewing machine and some of the pictures." I am surprised at that. When we started to make lists of what he would like to take, Klaus added just a few things. Not a piece of furniture at all.

"Well, if that what you want than we should bring them to my apartment tomorrow. We have to get this place cleaned out."

"That sounds good. You are so calm and collected. I feel like my head is exploding."

"Believe me, I am nervous too. And you don't want to know what is going through my head right know. We knew it will be upsetting when the day comes. Think about what lies ahead. We wanted that. Now we have to deal with whatever happens." Klaus puts his arm around me. I feel his tears on my cheek. It's been a long time since we've been physical with each other. I feel nothing as he presses me closer. I've lost any interest in him. I take his arms off of me. I try to be more gentle than I actually am.

I freak out. I have not heard anything about my case: it so ironic that the one who wanted to leave the least gets his papers first. I fear I will never get out. The rumors are rampant. No one knows really what is going on. The news on the Western TV station shows footage of the immigration camps in Giessen and Marienfelde, overcrowded with recently released East Germans. According to Western news organizations, the West German government was caught by total surprise. No one seem to have an explanation why East Germany all the sudden opened the floodgates. The Western Red Cross is in overdrive opening additional locations just to be prepared. The DDR has yet to give any indication how many of its citizens will let go. The West starts to estimate that between twenty and thirty thousand Easterners may arrive. Of course none of that makes the evening broadcasts of the "Aktuelle Kamera." I am glued to the television whenever I can watch. I am excited to see and hear that people's applications to leave the DDR are approved. I only wonder in which order?

Klaus had to take a leave of absence from work to fulfill

Thomas P.W. Schardt

all the requirements precluding his eminent release from
the GDR. No date is set yet but he was told that he has to
complete the to-do list within a week. For instance, he has
to go to every bank to get a release form that he has no
account with them. One bank we have never heard of is on
that list: Die Eisenbahner Bank (Bank of Railroad
Workers). It took several attempts to even locate that bank.
Its office is hidden behind a building along the Spree close
to the Nikolai Quarter. Of course, in order to make it more
difficult and time consuming, some of the personnel at the
bank who have the clearance to issue the required release
are either out of office, in a meeting or busy with other
important work. Klaus says that in most places the people
are very hostile, rude and not polite at all. One bank person
even made the comment to him that she hopes that he will
become a homeless in the West.

The weirdest thing happened at the "KWV" Housing
Authority. They demand that he turn in his coal rationing
card that Klaus, like everybody else, receives prior to the
start of the heating season. This card guarantees a certain
amount coal per household at a low price. Klaus still had
some coupons left when he received the news that his Exit
Application is pending. He didn't think that he would have
to return the remaining coupons so he gave them to his
neighbor. She was very thankful because with those she
could afford to buy more coal. The coal you can buy without
the ration card, if any is available at all, is much more
expensive.

Klaus tells the clerk at the housing authority that he had
given the ration card to his older neighbor. Her response
was "If you don't bring the remaining coupons back we will
not issue a release. And you know what that means do you?"
Klaus had to rush home hoping and praying that his
neighbor had not used the coupons already. She didn't
because she didn't have the money to buy even the cheap
coal. She understood fully Klaus' dilemma and gave the
coupons back. Klaus and I decide that we will buy her coal
for the regular price. Her apartment is badly insolated and
hard to heat.

The least complicated visit for him is to the Department

348

of Culture at city hall. Since he does not plan to take anything like books, paintings, antiques or such he get his release stamp right away. Otherwise, he learns, he would have to compile a list with a detailed description of each object and submit it for approval. If items on the list are older than one hundred years they would have to be inspected by an official reviewer who will determine what is and what is not cultural property of the GDR If an item is declared a national treasure it cannot be taken.

I am glad that Klaus gets all this information. That makes my preparation when, and if, the day comes for me much easier. The other issue for Klaus is his parent's apartment in Dresden. Currently he has subleased it to recover some of the monthly costs such as rent and electricity. Klaus has to make a quick to trip to Dresden to get the tenant out and the needed release stamp from the local housing authorities. He is nervous about that because it is known that Dresden authorities are very devoted Party underlings. They view Berliners as fickle and less ideologically committed to the proletarian cause due to easy access to the Western TV and radio stations. Dresden because of its geographic location is called "The valley of the clueless" because no filthy imperialist airwaves can reach its residents. It's here, where the most loyal foot soldiers, midlevel Party cadres and professional Stasi employees can be found and recruited to advance real socialism. Anyway, Klaus has one day to settle things in Dresden and hopes that the local authorities won't give him any grief.

I try my best to be supportive and focused. But I have to admit that I am jealous of Klaus. I don't know what to do if he gets out and I don't. I contemplate my options. I could wait. But that is not in my nature. I decide to visit the "Department for Interior Affairs" at my city hall again. Klaus, of course, thinks I should wait until hear from them. I don't listen to him. On Wednesday, the day that the store is closed, I make my way to City Hall. As soon I reach the second floor I can sense an atmosphere of activity never seen before. Doors open and close. Clerks carry piles of files. One of the clerks I pass recognizes me from my previous visits.

"Did you get your letter in the mail?"

"No. That's why I am here."

"But you should have gotten one. Come with me." This is the first time that I come here and I don't have to slide my ID card through a closed door slot before somebody will talk to me. Things have clearly changed. I follow the woman into her office. Behind the counter I can see stacks of files piled high. Nondescript, but there is no question in my mind that these are the files of applicants. The woman sifts through index card drawer. She pulls a card out. "Yes, here you are. The letter went out two days ago."

"But, seriously I have not gotten anything in the mail." I try to contain my nervousness.

"I don't know what to tell you, but that is what the note here says."

"So, what should I do?" I feel a pressure in my chest. Be calm, I tell myself. Don't blow this one. "Since I am here, can you give me another set of papers? Maybe my letter got lost?"

"That is very unlikely. And I don't have an extra set of forms." I look at her.

"Please, help me." She looks at me. In the past she was never polite or impolite towards me. She was just very official and impersonal. Never very talkative. Just straight to the point. One or two word sentences as answers. As we lock our eyes for a very short moment I detect a slide flicker in her eyes. Her usual cold stare seem to switch to a warm twitch. She raises her left eyebrow. For a nano-second she loses the harshness in her face. She turns around grabs the very first file on the top of one of the piles and pulls out a handful of papers. "Here, fill these out. You have a week to bring them back. When you get the letter in the mail return the forms so we can use them for somebody else." I try to catch her eye but she is already the official non-committal clerk again. She turns her back to me when I thank her. She won't acknowledge that or my goodbye.

When I reach the massive wooden exit doors of the City Hall I notice my too-tight grip on the form papers. I relax my fingers. Slowly I take the steps down towards the street. No one pays any attention me. Why would they? But I feel so different from when I entered the building less than twenty minutes ago. I look at the pedestrians. I am not one of them anymore. It's little bit over a year when I took the imposing steps in the Ministry of the Interior at Mauerstrasse to submit my Exit Application. And now I am only weeks away from leaving the country I learned to despise so much. I feel happy and euphoric. Energy seems to shoot out of my skin. I wish I could scream. I want to stop every passerby and tell him that I will be gone forever in a short while. I feel taller, confident and good. I want to yell in the faces of those who told me I will never get out. If you want something really bad you will get it. Yes! I proved it again.

Needless to say our days are now really hectic. Klaus has successfully finished his to-do list and has been given his date of exit: February 12th between noon and eight p.m. He seems nervous but does not say so. He has quit his job and is busy selling his stuff. We camp out at my apartment which is filled with his possessions I will officially declare as mine to bring with me. Our friends Marlene and Claudia have volunteered to type the lists for the Department for Culture. I also make good progress with my to-do list. It certainly helps that Klaus had done his. I know when and where to go. The evening news on the Western TV are now reporting non-stop about the massive release of East Germans. They estimate that within a couple of weeks 30,000 will be released.

The East German officials not only want to rid themselves of all the applicants. There are also reports that they will open the prisons to let common criminals go. The West Germans start to question GDR's intentions. Are they getting rid of unworthy elements to quiet down rising dissatisfaction within their borders? Is this a humane act on the East German side to let people go who wish to live in the West? Or is there also the motivation to create if not instability, a massive problem for West Germany who is taken by surprise by this sudden influx of new citizens. The West German constitution sees the East Germans as their own, always a contention for the GDR who never stops to proclaim the existence of two independent countries. By

351

constitutional law West Germany has to integrate tens of thousands of their own. East Germans who cross the borders are automatically West German citizens with the same rights to benefits such as health insurance, workers comp, pensions, etc. Seeing the reports about the long lines and overcrowded refugee camps shows that West Germany seriously struggles to welcome its new citizens. East Germany has the last laugh. I start to worry how will we, Klaus and I, be welcomed in our new country?

It's only a couple of days until Klaus leaves. We start to do things for the last time. Meet friends, enjoy the opera, walk around our neighborhood, have dinner at our favorite restaurants. Klaus gets teary eyed every time. Several times he tries to be physical with me. I want it too, but I have to pretend to like it. At this crucial point in our life I have lost my attraction to him. It's rare that I get hard. He wants me to penetrate him but I never come. At least I make him come. He never asks me why I don't have an orgasm. Maybe he does not want to embarrass me? Or he simply does not care? I don't say a word and pretend everything is normal. But it makes me sad that we have reached that point. Somehow I also try to convince myself that things will get better if and when our lives are in order again.

They don't tell me my date when I deliver my completed to-do-list. Of course I am disappointed but I understand that my list has to be checked and approved by the various officials. I wish I had decided not to take anything that needs approval by the Department of Cultural Affairs. I fear they will deny my Exit Application because of some stupid painting or piece of antique furniture. But it's too late now. I will follow Klaus' advice not to argue when some of the items are taken off.

Klaus and Ferdinand talk on the phone almost every day. Ferdinand was able to secure an apartment for us to sublease for the next three months. I am very thankful that Klaus or I don't have to live in the camp in Marienfelde. The pictures I see every night on the Western evening news are not pretty. People sleep in bunk beds. The communal facilities are in bad shape. There are reports of violence and theft amongst the camp residents. Some West Germans already resent their brothers and sisters from the East and express their opinion in front of the news cameras.

Anyway, we have a place to live without all that negativity. That's good. I am not so sure how we will pay the rent. It seems astronomically high to me: 165 Marks a month plus electricity. For my apartment I pay twenty-seven East Marks plus electricity. Ferdinand says he can lend us the first month's rent. He also says that each of us gets a one-time welcome gift of 100 Marks. Some charitable organizations give out fifty Marks per person. We also would be eligible for unemployment benefits. And he knows a doctor who would attest that we have to be on sick leave for at least a month because of the trauma we have experienced in connection with our relocation. That would make us eligible to receive money from the AOK, the state-run health insurance company. This all sounds very foreign to me, but I trust that we will be able to manage the first couple of months to pay our bills. Who knows how the employment situation will be? So many unknowns. I have to tell myself over and over again to take it one step at a time. I am still here for God's sake and I try to get a handle on things that lie on the other side of the Iron Curtain.

Our friend Ralph offers to build crates for my paintings and some of the furniture. The moving company VEB Kombinat Autotrans made it very clear when I went to their office that they cannot provide any packing material. It was a very unpleasant visit. "What are you doing here?" The clerk snapped at me when I told him that I don't have a date yet for my exit yet. "Come back when you have an exact date."

I tell him that I only wanted some information beforehand so I can be prepared. He shakes his head. His attitude is very clear: "Don't bother me with your questions." But I not that easily dismissed and I want answers. "You have to tell us how many boxes and the number of furniture pieces you are moving. Depending how much it is we will give you a date when we will pick up your stuff. The average cost is about 500 Marks. That only covers the move from your apartment across the border. When you pick your stuff up you have to pay in West Marks depending how long we had to store your stuff in West Berlin."

"As soon as I know my day I will tell you so you can come prior to my departure."

"No. That is not how it works. You don't tell us when to come. We tell you when we come."

"But when I leave I have to give up my apartment. So where would I store my stuff until you can pick it up?"

"That is not my problem, is it. You are the one who want to leave the GDR. So, don't whine to me about it." I feel rage. How dare this person talk to me like that?

Rumor has it that the moving firm Kunzendorf in West Berlin is officially owned by a SEW-Member, the West Berlin arm of the East German SED. That means that this company is owned and run by the Party. Another moneymaking machine to enrich the East German elite. I would like to scream at this person and tell him what kind of a company it is he works for. The only good thing is that Autotrans takes East Marks. Without any more words I leave. Klaus tells Ferdinand about my visit to the moving company and the very uncertain cost we will have when we pick up our stuff in West Berlin. Ferdinand has found out that there would be no additional cost when we pick the stuff up as soon as it arrives at the freight station in West Berlin. It would only cost us when they store it for us and that can be very expensive. He offers us the use of his basement for some of the things and the rest we can bring for the time being to our subleased place. Again, I am so happy that we have Ferdinand as our Western liaison. For a moment I start to wonder how others who are in the same situation as we are but don't have anybody in the West would deal with all that? I can see now how people can go wild in the refugee camps.

Klaus decides to take just one suitcase with his clothes. Even that has to be listed, item for item, and copied three times. Apparently, the border guards will check the list, compares it with each item and keep two copies. Why they have to keep on file how many pairs of underwear, socks and pants someone takes is beyond me. It only can be explained with the sick love of government employees for efficiency without purpose. For some reason I am reminded of the lists the SS compiled of all the personal items prisoners had packed for their last journey to the concentration camps. Those lists were as absurd as the typists were emotionless.

When the day of Klaus' exit comes he asks me not accompany him to Friedrichstrasse station. In a way I am glad. It's not a happy moment for me to be left behind. Since we still have our car I drop him off at the corner of Oranienburger and Friedrichstrasse. He wants to walk the rest of the way. We don't know what to say. What do you say anyway? We hug. It's awkward. In a way I fear that I won't see him again. My throat tightens. "Be good," is all I can manage to say.

"I love you. You will get your exit date soon. I can't wait to pick you up on the other side." I just look at him and tip my head. He gets out of the care and pulls his suitcase out of the trunk. I follow him with my eyes as he melts into the afternoon crowd. He does not turn around. After a couple of minutes I lose sight of him. Once in a while I see his suitcase bumping in and out of wide rows of pedestrians. It is now that I feel lost and alone. My view becomes unclear. I cannot stop my tears. I shift in first gear and drive down towards the Monbijou Park.

Reality sets in. Klaus is out. I am still here. Since I don't have a phone in my apartment there is no way for me to get in touch with him. I expected his departure to be more dramatic, earth shattering on a personal level. But life continues. I pee and poop, eat, do my thing. Sure he is gone. But I don't feel a void. Sure, I miss him but more in a sense of being left behind and dealing with the uncertainty of what and when the things will happen for me? I have to admit, I also feel relieved. Relieved, not to worry and wonder where and with whom Klaus is with when he is not home. For almost eight years I was in that constant state of alert, worry, anger and stress. His constant escapades and drinking binges have numbed my feelings for him. Distance has grown between us. I am sure I won't spend the rest of my life with him. But for now I will stay with him, more out of selfishness than anything else. Ending my life here and beginning it hopefully soon over there...I can't imagine being by myself.

Being solo for the moment I think more than I should about cheating. The thought alone arouses me. Of course, I am not interested in anything serious. Just a fling. Some quick closeness and comfort. Touching bodies, effortless kissing, meaningless compliments, superficial foreplay, lost in climax, walking away without looking back. Being a copycat of Klaus. Slutty. Yes. But, nevertheless desirable. I will not cruise intentionally but I will be open and approachable.

I decide to go back to work at the shop. My bosses need help and, I have time to do so. I like the job. It's easy, noncommittal and not challenging. My bosses are good to me. They also belong to this new growing class of young East Germans who through their private entrepreneurial spirit make serious money. And they spend it as freely and generously. They hang out in restaurants at the Maritime Hotel and Palast Hotel, the Grill Bar at Hotel Berlin or the Espresso Bar under Fernsehturm tower during the day. At night, the Yucca Bar at Eberswalder Strasse or the Penguin bar across from Volksbuehne theater, which are the hotspots for the New-Money-People. On several occasions Elena and Rolf have invited me to join them for their nights out. Now if I want to go alone to these places I am recognized as part of the in-crowd and I'm through the door in a flash. I enjoy that privilege.

The interior at Yucca Bar is so different from the dull looking state owned HO or Konsum Restaurants that you feel as if you're not in East Germany. There is a fake yucca plant of course, a lot light garlands wrapped around pillars, along the ceiling and the bar. The music is a mix of the Puddys, Roland May, Costa Cordales, Abba, Kurt Juergens and Mireau Matteou. The patrons are fashionably dressed in clothes from East German's own high-end Exquisite stores and Intershops. It's a world within a world that makes you forget about the outside. Conversations circle around money, business plans and, yes, who just got the papers to move to the other side of the Iron Curtain. I am sure some of the customers are informants for the Stasi. But no one really gives a damn who could be possibly working for the secret service and who is not! Everybody here, business people or Exit Applicants, know they have already a file in the archives of the Stasi.

That alone makes bars like Yucca a place of perverted freedom. You know you are being watched. Therefore you don't have to limit yourselves to what and to whom you say what. Outside of these confined places, everybody is on edge. Who is the Stasi informant? No one is immune from suspicion: it's a very cleverly implanted fear where husbands could betray wives, children their parents, colleagues their co-workers and so on. Devious but also very efficient.

It is also more virtual than real. Because, if you really sit back and do the math, how many citizens can realistically be Stasi spies? There are sixteen million East Germans. Subtract the underage, very old and the sick; you have eight million potential informants. Even a highly organized and well managed Big-Brother-apparatus can't possibly supervise and organize an eight million-man strong army of Stasi informants. And what about the collected data? Who can shift through it and assess its significance? Therefore, I think the rumors that almost every other citizen is in some way or other working for the Stasi is just that, a rumor. I also believe that those rumors is not fed directly by the Stasi but certainly not discouraged by the apparatus. The real number of informants must be lower.

Finally: I Lose My Citizenship...on My Grandmother's Birthday

"Herr Schardt, the State Organizations of DDR have determined that you have to leave the territory of the DDR on March twenty-second between two and eight p.m. If you decide to leave before or after those set times your papers will be indefinitely revoked. Please hand me your ID." The condescending tone of the voice of the person in front of me is annoying and irritating. Why would I jeopardize what I have waited for for over a year? Who would do that? This threat is just one of their last and pathetic power games. Anyway, I hand him my identity card and in return I get a certificate stating that I am released from GDR citizenship. It did cost me twenty-five Marks. I am now a citizen of the world! For the last time I leave Pankow city hall. For the last time I walk down Breite Strasse. I already feel like a stranger in a foreign country. For a moment I wonder if it is a coincidence that the date of my exit date is the same as my grandmothers eighty-third birthday.

I try to find a functioning public phone to call my mother to tell her the news. I also have to find a way to reach Klaus. I have not heard from him since he left over a month ago. My parents have a phone in their apartment but I wouldn't dare to ask them to call West Berlin. Trying to get a connection at the post office will take hours. Ralph offered that I could use his phone, but he is never home before seven or eight at night. Maybe I can ask a neighbor in my building if I could use their phone. It's asking a lot, I know. All phone calls from East to West Berlin are taped. Lost in my thoughts I almost get hit by a streetcar. I have to pay attention to my surroundings. I continue to hurry home.

"Thomas, Thomas!" I turn in the direction of the call. It's Lisbeth and Arnold Frank. I had hoped I wouldn't run into them ever again. But here they are.

"Good to see you. How are you?" Lisbeth gives me a hug. Arnold and I shake hands. "Everything is good," I respond. "How are you doing?"

"Good. Mother died. You probably know. Now we have the whole apartment to ourselves. Arnold is doing less work for the Party. But we are still involved with the neighborhood association. It's never ending." Lisbeth does the talking as usual. Arnold just nods.

"How is your mother?"

"Good." For a second I think I should tell them that I have my exit date. But I decide not to. "It is so good to see you. But I have to run. I want to order a cake for my grandmother's birthday which is tomorrow."

"Say Happy Birthday to her from us. Please come visit us. You know where we live. Don't be a stranger."

"I won't." I run off without a hug or handshake.

I always liked the Franks. I met them after I became member of the LDPD, and I was asked by my Party group to volunteer in my neighborhood. Arnold Frank was deputy SED Party chairman for Pankow district and a devoted neighborhood activist. He also is Jewish, survived the camp in Theresienstadt and is a steadfast Communist. Lisbeth was never married until she met Arnold 10 years ago. She was in her late fifties and he twenty years her senior. Lisbeth is also member of the LDPD and worked until her wedding at the Buchverlag der Morgen as a secretary. When I met both for the first time we clicked right away. Since both were childless I became their surrogate son. It didn't take long before Arnold suggested that I should be the chair for our neighborhood association. I felt honored. In this position I had to organize block parties for children, clean-up-the-neighborhood events on Saturdays and convince everybody to recycle bottles, newspapers and unwanted textiles. That was the fun part.

The other part was a watchdog function. That meant identifying troublemakers or conduct neighborhood meetings. During my tenure as chair I also had to be involved during Volkskammer parliament election on the local level. I was responsible for reporting who has and who has not hung the GDR flag outside of their window to

Thomas P.W. Schardt

dutifully commemorate the International Workers Day on May 1st, the day of the defeat of the Nazis on May 8th and the birth of the first socialist country on German soil on October 7th. I personally didn't have to walk the street to make the count. I ordered the board members of my neighborhood association to do it.

The same spy mission was asked of us on the day of the election scheme. Officially it was a free and secret ballot procedure. Whoever wanted to could use the enclosed voting booth. All part of the propagandized democratic election process, which was a charade at its core. The voting booth every citizen was welcomed to use was always very inconveniently located. One had to pass the long row of election workers after he or she was properly identified and given the ballot. As soon it was clear that someone was headed for the booth one designated helper recorded the name. No one talked about what would be done with the list of voting booth users, but it was clear that it would go straight to the local Stasi office. I felt sick being part of these charades and spying missions. Fortunately I was neighborhood association chairman for only one year. I resigned the day prior to submitting my Exit Application. Lisbeth and Arnold were shocked and sad when I told them my intentions. I could tell by their expressions. But both were silent, didn't ask any questions or tried to change my mind. They just had lost a surrogate son, and I two friends.

My last day. So far I have not had a chance to talk to Klaus to let him know that I am on my way. It is frustrating. I have no clue when I get through the check point tonight where to go from there. I have Ferdinand 's address but I don't know where that is. There are no maps of West Berlin I could orientate myself with. The only hope I have is Ralph. He had promised to tell his sister so she can tell her Turkish boyfriend who lives in West Berlin and hopefully he can get a hold of Ferdinand. I never planned for a chain of communication with Klaus. How careless and stupid of me.

Ralph will pick me up at around six in the evening. That should leave me with plenty of time to get through border control by eight. Earlier I bought my S-Bahn ticket to Bahnhof Tiergarten. 2.50 Marks. That seemed extraordinarily expensive. An S-Bahn ticket within East Berlin cost 20 Pfennig. I have to get used to a different pricing, I guess. I heard for instance that a movie ticket in West Berlin cost 9 Marks, here it is 1.55. A passport photo is 20 Marks, here 2 Marks. Capitalism versus socialism.

I wanted to get a birthday cake for Tata. The only bakery I could find who would decorate it with "Happy Birthday" is close to the shop where I had worked. I know the owner. He was a repeat customer in the store, and I always would set a couple of newly arrived digital watches aside for him as well. I lost count how many he had bought from the store. But he never blinked at the 110 Marks price point. He was just happy to get them. He told me ones that if I wanted to have a special cake made he would personalize it for me. I had asked the owner of the bakery in my building if she could do a birthday cake for me. It would have saved me the long ride to Karlshorst district to see the watch-loving baker. But she was out of a certain kind of ingredients to make a smooth cream for the engraving. "What's next?" I was thinking. A shortage of flour to bake bread or rolls with? But I didn't say anything. I just felt sorry for her. I took the S-Bahn to Karlshorst. And it was worth it. The cake looks really great. I am very happy. Tata will be surprised.

On my last day in East Germany, her birthday party will be also my last day to celebrate it in her apartment. From now on she has to come to visit me to get her birthday cake. I won't be allowed to visit. I have a one way ticket. The last and final punishment GDR apparatus can impose on its former citizen. A perverted and twisted interpretation of the self-declared greatness and superiority of proletarian dictatorship which seriously considers itself as the ultimate and true grantor of human rights and freedom. If it wouldn't be so disgusting it could be utterly laughable.

It will be a small gathering for Tata. My mother, my aunt and the next-door neighbor of my grandmother. It will be also a somber gathering. No one really knows what will happen from here on. It will be years before I can see my mother and her sister again. They are both far away from retirement age. As soon as someone reaches pensioner status he or she becomes useless in the paradise of the proletariat. From now they only cost money. Therefore they are allowed to travel to the West to seek help from their long lost relatives and friends. And if they decide not to return, so be it. One less body on the state pension rolls.

My mother had begged to come with me to what is known in the vernacular as Traenenpalast or "Palace of Tears" at Friedrichstrasse. But I told her, I don't want any family there. To say goodbye will be bad enough. Why not do it in the comfort of Tata's apartment then do it in public and in full view of the GDR customs service and police. I don't want those bastards to see any tears.

Since yesterday I have had painful stomach cramps. I probably drank too much coffee and did not eat enough. I am also a little bit concerned about the blood in my stool. I don't have time to see a doctor and hope it will pass. Tata thinks I should have some chamomile tea with honey. I have reached the point that I don't want anything, liquids or solid food. But I don't want to spoil her birthday party. It feels like the last supper. We all sit around the table. Everybody admires the two-layered cake but no one really seems too eager to eat a piece of it. Tata is the only one to cheer us up. She pours coffee and offers whipped cream. Her neighbor finally breaks the tension and talks about her son's upcoming soccer game. Some classmate had hit the ball smack into his crotch during practice. She describes the coloring down her son's middle as a rainbow from light purple to black. Everybody offers pity. I feel like I've been hit by a soccer ball too. Not in the crotch but in the stomach.

Six o'clock cannot come soon enough for me. Finally the door bell rings. Ralph. We all jump off our chairs. I start with the neighbor. We shake hands. No words. I hug my aunt. No words. I leave my grandmother's living room, Tata and my mother behind me. "I don't know what to say. But I think everything will be good. I call you as soon as I can."

Tears stream down my mother's face. "You will be always my son. Please, if it does not work out over there for you, you always can come back. Don't forget that. I will help you in any way I can."

"Oh, mother. I know I will be fine. I know I shouldn't say that. But get old quick so you can visit me." I press her face on my shoulder. My shirt gets wet. "Tata, I will see you soon. Sorry, that I had to leave on your birthday. But we will have a happier party as soon as possible." She hugs me. I can see a tear below her left eye. She wipes it off quickly and straightens her blouse. She is in control of her emotions again. I go down the staircase. I look back for the last time. My mother leans against the doorframe. She looks at me with both hands holding on to the wood. It's an image I don't want to remember, ever.

Squeezing Into the West

It's so unreal. I step into the Traenenpalast (Palace of Tears); my two heavy suitcases hit the floor as I maneuver down the stairs. I have been here before to say good-bye to relatives on their way back to West Berlin. But the top of the staircase was as far as GDR citizens were allowed to go. Now I have a permit to walk down. A customs service agent looks at me as I struggle downwards with my bags. I give my name. He checks a list and points towards a table. I lift my suitcases up. He opens the first one and leafs through my stuff.

"Where is your list of contents?" I hand it over. I am nervous as hell. Fearing I might have forgotten an item that's in my suitcase. "You can close that one." The man opens my second suitcase. I want to say something to lessen the tension. But I keep quiet. "Proceed to the check point." I fight with the unraveled stuff in my luggage. It seems like it takes forever until I am able to close the lids. My hands shake. My legs are stiff. Somehow I reach the small aisle I have to go through next. Left is a wall. On the right behind a glass window sits a uniformed man. I am too preoccupied to determine if he is custom or police. The aisle is way too narrow for me and my suitcases. I panic. I don't know what to do. I don't want to do anything wrong. The soldier watches me. I break out in sweat. The only way to go on is to line up the two pieces of luggage and push them with my food forward. It takes all my strength to do that. I fight back tears. I start to panic. Will I ever make it through this narrow aisle?

"I need your papers. What took you so long?" The man behind the glass barks at me. "I am trying." My voice cracks. I finally can push the suitcases far enough to come face to face with the uniformed man. He looks at me, expressionless. I try not to flicker. My knees shake now too. "Go on."

I turn and almost fall over my luggage. I want to go as

fast as I can. Somehow I reach a double door guarded by another soldier. I look at him, not sure what to do. He nods his head. I put one suitcase down and push it far enough against the door so it opens wide enough that I can get through with the rest of the stuff. I am in another hallway. This one is much wider.

I have no clue where I am. Still in the East or already in the West? I have to rest. I am not able to carry my suitcases any longer. Slowly I drag them away from the double door. I don't want that the guard on the other side of the door, now invisible but certainly present, to run after me to pull me back. It seems like I lose control of the rest of my body. My breathing becomes heavy. I sink on one of my suitcases and try to collect myself. It is now that I can look around. There are people standing around. I scan them. No Klaus. I look at my watch. It is 7:10 p.m.

I have to give into the pressure of my body. It is like water pouring out of my body. Without checking it I know it's not water. It's blood. I can't make it stop. I am scared. I lean forward, my elbows on my knees. I feel my life is gushing out.

The next two hours are the worst in my life. Minutes turn into quarter of an hour to a half hour to an hour. Panic sets in. Here I am in a strange place. No idea where to go? Not the right money to make a call. Did my message not get through to Klaus that I would be coming today? Did he maybe decide not to care about me anymore? Is he fucking someone at this minute? Is he even still in West Berlin or even alive? I have not heard from him in over a month. What should I do? I can't stay here in the underbelly of the S-Bahn station forever. Are the fears of my mother and the GDR propaganda about the man-eating society of the West maybe real? I wish I could cry. But no tears can fill my eyes. It would have been a relief. The racing storms of my thoughts seem to become almost material pushing against the inside of my skull. Time and time again the pulsing question: what should I do? More than once I try to count to ten to calm myself. But I can't concentrate enough to beyond five. I sit on my suitcase in an impersonal neon lit hallway. My new life has just started. It's surreal.

Less and less people pass me. I am unable to move out of their way. I have no energy left to push or carry my luggage towards the safety of a wall. It is now that I feel how tight my fingers of my left hand are around the strap of my shoulder bag. My hand hurts. And then I sense the presence of Klaus without seeing him. But I feel he is close. I focus my eyes to the end of the tunnel. Yes, there at the far end. He zigzags towards me. His eyes directed on something imaginary. His face is without emotion. I know that expression all too well. Klaus is drunk. His sight should come as a relief to me but it doesn't. My anguish turns immediately to anger. I now wish he wasn't here. I wish I wasn't here. For a split second I even hope he won't see me and just pass me by. I meet his glassy eyes.

He and I look into blank faces."Do you need help?" Klaus points towards my bags. Without waiting for an answer he bends over to grab one of the suitcases. His hand misses the handle. His right food bangs against the suitcase. He can't hold his balance. He tumbles over, misses the pile of bags and lands sideways on the grounds. As he looses control of his body I gain control of mine. It's like a jolt of energy thunders through me. My strength is back. My brain is free of rage. I want to get out this place. I am focused.

"Let's go." Klaus manages to get up. He reaches out to help me. I brush him off. "I don't need your help with that. Where are we going?" He shrugs his shoulders and turns around.

I follow him through a maze of tunnels, stairs and more tunnels. I don't even try to pay attention. The S-Bahn ride is short. We don't talk. We deliberately avoid eye contact. I am mad as hell. He knows it. I catch myself thinking how to get rid of him and make my start in the West without him. My train of thoughts gets interrupted when we have to get off. I read the station sign, Savignyplatz. For a moment I think I have arrived. I am in West Berlin. The weight of my bags bring me back to reality. I have no feel for time and my surroundings. I just follow Klaus. He stops at a newer-looking apartment building and pushes a button. "Who lives here?" I ask.

"Ferdinand," he replies.

"Welcome to West Berlin." Ferdinand gives me a big hug. I haven't seen him for almost two years. The last time was in East Berlin the night before he made his harrowing trip via Prague and Bucharest to Amsterdam. He has not changed. He pushes me into the living room. The dining table is set with three sets of dishes, candles and plates with cheese, sausage and bread. A bottle of wine sits in a cooler. It looks very nice and very Western. "Come sit down. Let's celebrate." Ferdinand pulls out a chair and presses me down to sit. Out of nowhere I feel sick. Cramps shooting through my belly. I know I have to go to the bathroom. "It's off the hallway." Ferdinand points towards the door.

I don't know how long I hover over the toilet bowl. Every time I want to get up more is coming out of me. I don't know how to stop my body to do this to me. The cramps finally become less frequent. The worse seems be over. My forehead is wet from sweat. Maybe cold water will help? I stand up and hobble over to the sink, my pants around my ankles. I let the water run over my wrists. It feels good. With both hands I collect some water and splash my face. My face is as white as a sheet. Slowly I come back to life again. The pressure in my abdomen is gone. I can't make myself look into the toilet bowl. But I know what I would see. I flush and wonder where all that blood was coming from. Did my intestines rupture? And why? My arrival at my new life should have been different, shouldn't it? I don't know if I had a certain scenario in mind. But something more romantic. Klaus with flowers. Hugs. Words of assurance. Something memorable.

Klaus being late and drunk. Me bleeding uncontrollably. Is that a metaphor of what's in store for me from now on? Is what happened to me in the last couple of hours just a reminder that life is less what we wish it to be than what it really is? But when we have to be careful about our dreams and hopes how can one attempt to change direction and look for a different experience? Why is it that the life's pluses and minuses are always on the same page?

Our subleased apartment has an eerie resemblance to Klaus' flat at Christburger Strasse. It's located on the third floor at the left wing of the building like Klaus'. The smell,

peeling paint and squeaky staircase is like Klaus'. The
apartment is on the left side of the stair landing is like
Klaus'. Klaus unlocks the door. I look into a long hallway.
That's different from his place in East Berlin. Thank God.
The kitchen is to the left. I see a shower stall next to the
kitchen stove. Another similarity. The door next to the
kitchen opens into the bathroom with toilet and sink. At
least we have the toilet in the apartment. I am relieved.
Next to the bathroom is a narrow room set up as a loft. At
the end of the hallway is a large living room. My first home
in West Berlin. This East German style apartment at
Turmstrasse is a thousand times better than the camp
living in Marienfelde I remind myself.

Ferdinand has arranged an appointment for me with a
doctor who can attest to my inability to work, followed by
sick pay. My first action in the West German: working the
system. "Everybody does it. Don't worry," Ferdinand
assures me. Klaus will come with me for the first day to get
the hang of all the bureaucratic steps I have to take.

"You will need a week to get the ball rolling," he says,
"After the visit to the doctor's office we go to Marienfelde to
get you registered. The Caritas will give you 50 Marks as
welcome money. You definitely have to go to the Refugee
Help Organization as well. They may give you money as
well. But more important you have to try to be recognized
as a refugee. That helps with taxes, jobs and unemployment
benefits." I am not sure if I understand anything he tells me.
Taxes. Refugee status. Welcome money. It's certainly a new
life. The first twenty-four hours are a haze. I just will rely
and trust that everything is going to work out.

During my first week everything happens the way Klaus
and Ferdinand have told me. I am officially a West German
residing in West Berlin. I have a temporary ID to show it.
The permanent one is in the mail. I am on disability. At the
refugee organization I was told that I am eligible as a
Refugee with C-notation. The highest status there is,
thanks to my mother who was born in Silesia, now Poland.
The West German refugee law, enacted after World War II,
covers all Germans who were born in the former East
territories of Germany, which were given to Poland and

Czechoslovakia as a result of the Jalta agreement reached by the Western Allies and the Soviet Union. Even if I have never lived in Silesia as a son of a recognized refugee I inherited my mother status. It seems weird to me. But why question the interpretation of a law when the C refugee status means privileges? Why would I miss out on better unemployment benefits, a better position on the waiting list for an subsidized apartment, tax write offs, higher social security and on and on?

Everything else in connection with my immigration process goes very smooth for me as well except I was a little nervous to go into the de·briefing by the representatives of the three Allies stationed in West Berlin. The appointment with the Americans was the longest, but very cordial and friendly. They wanted to know about my apprenticeship in the SED and my work as a journalist. I had nothing to help their very obvious curiosity about the East German army since I never served in it. The meeting with the British and the French was very short and seemed more like a formality. All three representatives wished me luck.

When I had finished my way through the bureaucratic process in Marienfelde I had some cash in my pocket. Between the Red Cross, the Refugee Organization and the Federal Government I netted 300 West Marks. Between Klaus and me we are 500 Marks rich. I also have a one‑month unlimited rider card for using the public transportation system. Pretty soon Klaus will receive his first disability payment. That will help us until I get my first check. I certainly am a little more relaxed knowing that we can pay back Ferdinand, who lent us the first month's rent. We also paid our second month's rent to his friend in advance. Klaus and I had sex for the first time in the West. Things look all right.

First Trip to the Grocery Store
— Too Many Choices

I walk down the aisle. The shelves are filled with jellies and other sweet spreads. I read the labels: Cherry, Blackberry, Raspberry, Kiwi. I have no clue what the latter is. Peanut Butter. Never heard of that before. Nutella. It seems so delicious just looking at it. I take one jar and put it my shopping cart. The next shelf is filled with sweets. I recognize some of the chocolate brand names like Sarotty. Tata always brought them back from her trips to the West, usually the plain milk chocolate. Now I see that there is much more. Dark and white chocolate. With peanuts, almonds, raisins or nougat. I am not sure what white chocolate is so I take one. There are also bags of jelly beans, jelly bears, jelly fish and on and on. Around the corner are the canned goods. Pineapple sliced, diced, crushed. I want them all. In the produce section I feel completely overwhelmed. Piles of bananas next to crates of oranges, peaches and pears. I read a sign that says nectarines. I have never seen those before. They look to me like a cross between peach and plum. I watch customers going through the fruits. Picking one, tossing another one back in the crates. "Look at these bananas. Some are already brown," one woman complains to the one next to her and point at little tiny spots.

Where I come from you would be lucky if you could get a couple bananas at all, I think. If they were mushy or still dark green you would take them without complaint. You never knew when the next delivery would arrive. Fruits from the South, so the official name, were rare as Hungarian salami. A bad substitute and still rare to get were Cuban oranges. Greenish-yellowish with a tight skin. It needed some skills to peel them.

I continue my first visit to a Western grocery store. It is March and I see an abundance of vegetables. Cauliflower. Broccoli. Peppers in all kinds of shades and shapes. There are potatoes from Spain, huge and golden. And so clean. Where I come from potatoes were dark skinned and always covered in dirt. Their shapes sickly irregular. They certainly were not offered in net bags. Carrots. Perfectly shaped bright red and clean as well. Other signs advertised juicy honey melons. I have never seen these. Fresh figs. I don't know how they taste. Strawberries from Israel. Ripe stem tomatoes. I can't decide what I want. I steer my shopping cart towards the cheese counter. I have to look closer to reassure myself that all of the different types of cheese are real and for consumption. I am familiar with Swiss and Edam cheese.

I scan the assortment for the familiar. How can I make a choice by looking at so much different types of cheeses? They are divided by regions. It's like a lesson in geography. I feel relieved to find a piece of Swiss cheese. I go for it. So far I thought butter is butter. Now I realize I can choose between salted, unsalted or sweetened. If that is not enough of a choice, one has to decide if he wants butter from Holland or Niedersachsen. Next question: do I want half a pound or one pound? What should I do? I grab I pack that tells me it's from the Schleswig-Holstein area because I remember Heinz's sister telling me that she went there for a bike tour.

The bread section presents another challenge. Wheat. White. Multigrain. With olives or dried tomatoes. Cinnamon flavor. I feel so stupid not knowing what I should take. Maybe the least expensive. Where I come from a loaf of bread was less than 1 Mark. Here I see prices starting at 2.50 Marks. "Why is bread so expensive?" I ask myself. "I have to cut back on eating it. This is way too much for just a loaf of bread." I go for a small bag of sliced pumpernickel bread for 99 Pfennig. I look down in my shopping cart: Nutella, butter, Swiss cheese and bread. I have a headache. Shopping was so much easier in the East, you would just take what's on the shelf, if you needed it or not. Because you could never be sure the next time you would go to the HO-Kaufhalle they might be out of sugar, onions, marmalade or coffee. You didn't have to make choices, let alone compare prices.

Now it seems that shopping becomes a challenge of

another kind. For instance, I have to calculate if I want eggs in twelve or six pack or buy them individually. After, of course, I decide if I want them from free-range or industrially held chickens, from a nearby farm or Bavaria. The same with milk. Less fat content or more, added calcium or not, from Germany or Holland. The one-salami butcher store in the GDR was so much quicker to navigate than the meat counter here. Salami made from turkey or pork, plain or with pepper corns, rolled in seasoning or smoked with Juniper tree bark and extra-long aged.

The personal hygiene section is similarly overwhelming. Florena was the brand on the other side. The soap variety alone makes my head spin. I recognize the brand 4711 and Lux amongst many others. My mother always cherished a bar of Lux that she got from Western visitors. We never used to wash ourselves with it. She would put the soap bars between our linens and towels in the closet. It made our bed sheets smell so Western. I take a bar of Lux soap.

It's my last pick because I feel I have to get out of this supermarket. My senses and my brain are over stimulated. I am afraid to go on. I could discover other things unknown to me but wanted just for sole fact I can have it. The few items in my cart come to almost 15 Marks. I quickly add it up in my head what that would be in East German currency with the going black market rate of one to ten. I am shocked that I just spent 150 Marks on these few items. Reality holds me back when the cashier counts my change: 5.25 West Marks.

Feeling Unwelcome and Suspect

"Young man. You think you come here and you get your dream job like picking apples from a tree. It's different here than over there." *My first visit to the unemployment office is getting off to a bad start*, I think to myself. "You want to be a journalist here too. So do at least thousand other unemployed citizens who have lived here their whole lives. They are first in line if I have anything. To be honest, I see very little chance for you to work as a reporter. First, I think we have to bring you up to speed and send you to a basic computer class. That's a skill you don't have but you certainly need if you don't want to join the army of the unemployables." The woman pushes a stack of papers in front of me to fill out.

I don't look at them. I am pissed off about the arrogance of the woman whose job is to be helpful and encouraging. What does she mean I have to bring my skills up to speed otherwise I will be unemployable? She is implying that I am second in line to all of the West Germans by birth? What does she know if anything about the labor market "over there," as she calls East Germany? I can feel she resents me. Not me, Thomas Schardt, but me the Easterner. As a Federal office worker she should be more professional and familiar with the constitution of West Germany that guarantees the same rights to all Germans no matter where they are born. She shouldn't classify me as an Easterner. Period.

It's not the first time I am aware that the West Germans like to preach about "our un-free sisters and brothers" in the East. But their compassion is only valid as long "our sister and brothers" stay on the other side of the Wall. Now that some of us crossing into the West fear, jealousy and even anger are prevalent. The boyfriend of the guy we sublet the apartment did not hide his feelings right from our first encounter.

"I can't say I am glad that you got out of the East," he

said, "The fact that all the sudden 30,000 more people are flooding our streets, unemployment offices, apartment rental agencies and health care system puts a big strain on our government. Not to mention that my chances of getting a job once more diminish because of you Easterners." It was kind of an odd welcome greeting. At first I thought he tried to be funny. But I realized quickly he was not.

"I didn't come as freeloader," was all that I could say.

"You Easterners think this is a country of milk and honey, plentiful for everybody. You have to work hard to get ahead. It's an elbow society, except that you Easterners have it made. Citizenship right away, unemployment benefits right away, hand-out money and job placement immediately." This guy did not stop his tirade. I remember looking at Klaus and Ferdinand for some support. But they stayed out of it.

"Don't take him too seriously. He is an unhappy fellow." Ferdinand tried to ease my tension after we left Thomas and his boyfriend. "He is almost forty years old and never had a permanent job except as a waiter. He wants to be an art teacher. For the last fifteen years he's been a student but has never made it to any final exams. When he talks about milking the system he is a perfect example of one who knows how to do it. So, forget about him."

"How can he say all this unflattering things without knowing me? You are from the East as well. Did he attack you the same way he did me?"

"No. I met his boyfriend at restaurant management school. We kind of clicked right away and started to spent time together after class. It took Thomas a while to introduce me to his boyfriend. He didn't like that Thomas was going to school. He wanted him to work and bring the money home so he could be a student. Thomas feels kind of guilty but didn't stop going to school. One day he was crying because he didn't have enough money to pay for groceries. His boyfriend had made it very clear if he comes home without food their relationship was over. I felt bad. Thomas and I went grocery shopping. I paid for it. He invited me for dinner the same day. I told the boyfriend that it was wrong to expect that Thomas should be the one to pay the bills.

That he should take his part as well. But that I would help
them from time to time. I must say I regret that I ever made
that offer, but since then Thomas' boyfriend hits me up
constantly for money. Thomas doesn't know about that. I
want Thomas to finish school. That's why I help out. I don't
have much but enough to help out. Please don't say
anything to them when you see them the next time."

"Of course I won't. But I don't think there will be a next
time with this guy around. The way he acted I don't have
any desire to see him again."

"For Thomas' sake try to be nice to him. He is not that
bad." Ferdinand went on to explain that Thomas' boyfriend
gets his opinion about the Easterners from watching the
news.

A lot is reported about the brawls in the refugee camps
because some of the former GDR citizens spent the welcome
money on alcohol and drugs. There are reports that some of
them destroyed the furniture in the living quarters of the
camp. The evening news anchors and commentators imply
often that the East uses the mass release of its citizens to
send spies undetected into the West. That leads to the
simple-minded perception in the West that most of the
former Easterners are either criminals or Stasi agents. How
can I counter that? Thomas' boyfriend and the woman in the
unemployment office have formed their own opinion,
justified or not. They don't know me, but they fit me in that
grid.

Is their strong opinion about us from the East
changeable? I wonder. And if so how? I don't have a criminal
record. They could say that maybe I was lying. I am not a
spy either. Doesn't every spy say that? I *want* to make it
here. They could brush this off as just a meaningless phrase.
The same way I wanted to convince Thomas' boyfriend that
I didn't come to take anything away from anybody. I am
tempted to tell the woman at the unemployment office that
I left the GDR because of its system of regulated and totally
controlled opportunities. But I have the feeling it would be
wasted time. Action alone will speak louder than words. I
will show her and anybody else who thinks that I came to
take advantage of the system, that I am not who they think

I am.

I start to fill out the papers she gave me. It's the enrollment for unemployment benefits. I have to do it if I want to or not. This is a necessary step before I can and apply for a driver's license and a passport. The AOK, the state-run health insurance agency, also wants proof that I really exist. The same is true for the Housing Authority in order to get my name on the waiting list for an affordable apartment. Weird system. Unemployment as a door opener to enjoy citizenship.

I promise myself that I will only chase unemployment checks for a short time. I have no intention to join the needy minority. I will be part of the majority taking life in big gulps based on my own achievements. I sign the bottom of the papers and give it back to her. "I will let you know when I have an open spot for the computer class. I expect you to check in with me every other week to let me know what you do to find work. One word of advice, don't waste your time and contact any newspaper for job opportunities. There are none." Now she really has me excited. I cannot let that slide again.

"I will not take your advice. I have survived Communist East Germany including frightening interrogations by the Stasi. If they could not intimidate me you won't either. If there is one thing I have learned over there no one ever will tell me to accept my status quo. I can't wait to let you know, hopefully pretty soon, that I have landed a job as a journalist. And please don't throw all Easterners in the same pile. We are not one monolithic mass. I will see you in two weeks if not earlier."

"When did you leave the East?" The career councilor at Freie Universitaet looks me straight in the eyes. He is a balding middle aged man with a belly.

"I came three weeks ago."

"Have you done all of your paper work? Are you an official Westerner now?" He smiles.

"I guess so. Everything went really smooth for me. My partner came before me. He gave me good advice how to speed up the process."

"How long have you two been an item?" That's kind of an odd question, I think. What does this has to do with me trying to get information about studying at the University?

"About eight years. He worked at Deutsche Staatsoper as a locksmith and as a vocational teacher as well."

"I am from the East too. I got out ten years ago. I spent two years in prison prior to that. I was a case for the Human rights Commission of the UN. Long story. I am glad that you got an appointment with me." He extends his hand. "My name is Frank." We shake hands. "Oh, and I am also gay. My partner Knut and I just celebrated our ten-year anniversary." I don't know how to respond. "I think it is a good idea in general for people from the East to update their education. Not all GDR degrees are recognized here in the West. But unlike over there, going to University here costs money. You either have it or you can apply for a fellowship. The latter is not that easy to get. What would you like to study??"

"In the GDR I applied for Ethnography and I was denied. I would like to try again. Maybe in the West I am luckier?"

"We have quotas too. But being from the East you will get preferential treatment. The bigger problem is to find work afterwards. Where would you want to work?"

"I am not sure. The very obvious workplace would be in a museum. I think I could combine the Ethnography with my writing skills, either as a reporter or in a museum setting as a public affairs or outreach officer."

"That's an interesting thought. I will be frank with you, if I may?" I nod my head. "You're twenty-eight years old. You studied journalism and you have worked successfully as a reporter. Try as quickly as possible to land a job at a newspaper or magazine. Get the gist of being a reporter here in the West. It is different from what you are used to. Establish yourself. Find out if you still want to be a journalist. And along the road you will see if you want to specialize in any particular field, even Ethnography. If that's still what you want you can get a degree by being an extern student. This is a very combative society. Dive into it as soon as you can. The biggest mistake former Easterners do is the slow approach, via detour as a full-time student or traveling the world or whatever. Most of them will fail."

As I listen to the counselor I find his arguments compelling. To be honest, by me going back to University is more to satisfy my family and their elite thinking that one is only socially acceptable with a bachelor's degree, better even with a doctorate title than what I think is right for me. A Master's Degree or PhD in front of my name has no meaning for me. It's the journey that has brought me now here. It's not an arrival. I will still travel and probably will forever. I start to warm up to the counselor. He lived where I am from. I like the way he talks and lays out a possible options for me.

"What do you think?" The counselor interrupts my thoughts.

"To be honest I came here determined that I want be a full-time student. Something I always wanted to be but never had a chance to be because of circumstances. However, there are wishes and there is reality. Part of the latter is my age but also my desire to make it here as quickly as possible to enjoy the opportunities I hope to have and came here for. You know, the other day I was at the unemployment office and the women there basically told me I have zero chance to get a job as a journalist. That irked me ever since. Even though that woman means nothing to me I think she represents a majority here who think that we Easterners are good for nothing and just take advantage of the system and have no clue how the West works. I want to show her and all the others that they are wrong. At least about me."

"I know what you are talking about. I have more advice for you. As soon as you stop telling people where you from the better. I know it's not easy. In the beginning I was also so eager to let everybody know because I thought they were interested in my story. For once, the truth is they are not. And they become very suspicious of you and in many cases even hostile towards you. So melt in. Don't have "the Easterner" tattooed on your sleeve."

How true he is, I think. My status as a German is guaranteed by the West German constitution and not questioned by West Germans as long as I stayed on the other side of the Wall. Now I am here I become someone who speaks the same language but otherwise is as foreign as the Turks or the Yugoslavs. The current news whines about long lines at the unemployment offices, the Red Cross and the housing authority amplifying my "unwanted from-the-East-brother" status. I am glad I came here today and met this councilor.

"Thank you for your time. I will refocus my goals thanks to you. You gave me very good advice."

"Don't thank me. That's my job to help. I have the feeling you will make the right choice. If you have any other questions please give me a call. Here is my business card." I grab my bag and get up.

"You know, I really like you. Why don't we have dinner together?" Is this guy hitting on me? I blush.

"That would be nice. I will talk to my partner and give you a call."

"Oh, don't give me the I-will call-you. How about dinner tonight? We have drinks at my place and after we decide where we will eat." I am a little bit put off by his aggressive approach. I also think about the money I don't have to pay for the dinner. He must have read my thoughts. "I know you don't have any money. Dinner is on us. When you have a job and you are settled in I expect a dinner invitation. Here is my address. I see you both at eight tonight."

"Ok. But I have to talk to my boyfriend to see if he wants to do that."

"If you can't come please call."

"I will." I leave his office faster than I should have.

After my head-spinning experience in the grocery store I am a little bit reluctant to venture into the daily life of the West. Sure I am busy establishing my new life and visit all of these offices and agencies. But I also should make an extra effort to explore the new. But something holds me back. Fear. I realize for twenty-eight years I was subjected to propaganda and a world view that was just black and white. I lived in the white, the paradise, the future, the safety zone, the taken-care-of society. The black was behind the protective Iron Curtain where danger, misery, survival of the fittest and inhumanity were the norm. Of course I resisted the brainwash. Life experience also told me that the shades of the world are not just black and white. Now, that I am on the other side I have a hard time getting rid of the propaganda.

With a tight grip I hold on to my bag wherever I go. I watch who walks behind me. I panic when I use an escalator because someone might harm me and then jump onto the opposite escalator to escape. I avoid being outside after dark. I step into protective corners to take money out before I go into a store to buy something. I don't want anybody see how much money I have in my pockets. I stop to let followers pass by. I am angry with myself that I am scared but I can't help it. I want to confront my fears by being normal, unfazed, part of the crowed, blending in. I want to become a normal Westerner.

AIDS

AIDS. I have heard of it once or twice in the East. Something that happens as the result of decadence and ignorance. There is talk about the first AIDS case, a flight attendant. Men dying. But far away. Nothing to do with me. I still really don't know what AIDS is and means other than it's a deadly disease. I more concerned that Klaus will infect me with syphilis again. AIDS is as weird as the name itself is. Now that I am in the West I hear that the city shut down saunas, dark rooms and bathhouses. Since I have not been to those places it doesn't mean anything to me. I read articles about men dying in San Francisco. I live in West Berlin. Dr. Gallo is on the news predicting that he will have a vaccine in less than ten years to treat the disease. I am too busy getting my new life going. AIDS is not part of that.

+

"Thomas' boyfriend is dead." Ferdinand tells me over the phone. The last I knew was that the two went to Thailand on vacation. "Just three days ago Thomas had called me from a hospital in Bangkok to tell me that his boyfriend was diagnosed with pneumonia and he himself has a high fever."

"Wow. I didn't know that you can die that fast from pneumonia."

"I didn't know either."

"Thomas told me about six months ago that they both felt sick. They didn't know what it was. Both would wake up in the middle of the night soaked in sweat. They asked their doctor. He thought it was the flu. Then Thomas' boyfriend started losing weight. The doctor put him on a high-calorie diet. Thomas developed skin discolorations in his face and chest. The doctor thought he must have been allergic to something." As Ferdinand points out their health problems I remembered seeing these almost purple spots on Thomas' forehead.

"And you think all that is the reason he is dead and Thomas now in the hospital?" I say.

381

"I think it is connected. And I think they both have AIDS."

"What? How did they get it?"

"I don't know. Thomas' boyfriend must have gotten it first and infected Thomas."

"Why do you say that?"

"He is, was very promiscuous. Thomas was always faithful."

"Thomas told you?"

"Yes, he is my friend. We tell each other everything. I have seen his boyfriend more than once in these fuck places. He would hump everything with a hole."

"Did Thomas tell you what his prognosis is?"

"He cried the whole time we spoke on the phone. He is overwhelmed because he doesn't know what to do with his boyfriend's body. His family won't help with any arrangements. Of course he is fearful of what will happen to him. He is so scared he will die too."

"Poor guy," is all I can say. "Could you give him any helpful advice?"

"It's hard being here and not knowing how things work in Thailand. But I told him that he has to take care of himself first. His boyfriend is dead. There is nothing that he can do for him. If his boyfriend's family is not able help he should try to get the German embassy involved. Maybe they can pay for the transport of the body or, arrange the cremation in Thailand? An urn is easier and cheaper to transport." Ferdinand the pragmatic one, I think.

"Thomas' voice sounded weak and, he was coughing a lot. To be honest, I think he won't make it either."

"Good God. That would be terrible. I hope you are wrong. I like Thomas."

"I must tell you something because you are my friend," Ferdinand suddenly changes the subject.

"What is it?" I say nervously.

"Thomas' boyfriend fucked Klaus too."

"What? How do you know?" I fall with my back into the wall pulling the phone off the kitchen table. It crashes with a loud bang on the tile floor.

"Are you all right?" Ferdinand shouts through the phone.

"I am so sorry. But you have to know especially now where this guy is dead."

"You think I have AIDS because Klaus gave it to me?"

"I don't know. You know that Klaus sleeps around. They fucked the day Klaus arrived in West Berlin. Thomas couldn't meet us at his apartment. He had asked his boyfriend to be there to give Klaus the key. After I got Klaus to the apartment I left. Thomas' boyfriend stayed. It was very obvious to me why."

"I probably should thank you for telling me but to be honest I wish you wouldn't have. What in the world do I do with this information? Klaus and I don't have much sex anymore. But he fucked me once since I came here. Does that mean I have AIDS? I don't even really know how you get AIDS? They say you get by exchanging body fluids and secretions. Does it mean the AIDS is in his cum I got in my ass?" I am terrified. I have AIDS. I have been in the West one month and I am going to die. That fucking boyfriend of mine. "Ferdinand , what should I do?"

"I am sure you don't have AIDS. Just be careful from now on. Klaus is promiscuous. Don't let him fuck you anymore. Don't fuck him."

"What about kissing? Blow jobs? How can you say I don't have AIDS? How often do you have to have sex before you get it?"

"No one knows for sure. All I can tell you is be careful."

"Okay."

I hang up without saying goodbye. I crouch on the kitchen floor of the apartment of the guy who is most likely dying in Bangkok right now. Klaus is out of town visiting his aunt in Munich. Or is he? He has not called yet. I wonder how he will take the news of the death of his one-night stand. I will tell him when he calls but not that I know that he slept with him. The little love I had left in my heart for Klaus is gone completely. He siphoned it out drop by drop. There is nothing left. Not even pity.

Being better off and stronger by making our life-changing move from East to West together was an illusion. Being with Klaus makes me vulnerable at best. I look out of the window without seeing anything. I am surrounded by silence except for a hissing sound coming out of the radiator. Reality has caught up with me again. A reality that was again created by someone else. Whatever happens from here on it has to be without Klaus. He has done too many firsts to me: rape, cheating, syphilis. Now AIDS. I will not hold his dying hand nor will he hold mine.

Between still running from agency to agency and sending out resumes I try to keep my mind occupied so that I don't too much about AIDS. Klaus' reaction was total silence when I told him that Thomas' lover died probably of AIDS. "How did they get his body back to Germany?" was his only question. Weird response, I thought. Maybe Klaus does not even remember that he had sex with this guy? Or he just is not fazed by it? I did not tell him that I know.

I start to read as much about AIDS as I can get my hands on. There are conflicting reports about the cause and how to get it. Some are upsetting and don't calm my fear at all. I read about the danger of mosquito bites. Some warn not to sit on a public toilet. Hairdressers should be watched that they sterilize there scissors. I start to wonder if sweat on handles of doors or in the subway can make you sick. One morning I woke up drenched in sweat. Didn't Ferdinand tell me that Thomas and his lover had those night sweats? I watch Klaus if he is losing weight. Sometimes I reassure myself that I do not have AIDS since I have gained weight since I arrived in the West. I can't stay away from the chocolate and the abundance of sweets available everywhere. My favorites so far are Mars and Duplo bars. Klaus calls me Duplo monster.

Anyway, I would like to talk to him about AIDS but I don't know how to bring up the subject. We haven't had sex in weeks. I want to keep that way. Klaus, too. I suspect he gets it someplace. I carefully keep our personal stuff separate. In the past we shared our underwear, toothbrushes, towels, razors, wash clothes. Now I have my own boxer shorts and my own tub of face cream. He doesn't to notice. If I see our bath towels touching each other I rearrange them. I catch myself wiping down the toilet seat before I sit down. I even rinse the soap bar under running water before using it on myself. I constantly watch what I touch. At home and in public. I really wish I could find someone to address my AIDS fears to. After I saw a report about what happened to a man when his neighbors found out he has AIDS I am even more scared. The man's landlord told him to vacate the apartment immediately. The owner of the restaurant he works at fired him after guests threatened not to come back until the waiter with the "purple spots on his face" was gone. I don't want to be marked as" one of those." I hate being gay because of AIDS.

Klaus has a job as a locksmith at the ZDF film studios. He finds it difficult to do minute work. He has a "Master" certificate but he is relegated to doing handyman stuff. Fixing plumbing, carrying film set pieces. He is one of the very few Germans in his team. Most everybody else is Turkish. But we both are glad he has a job. Our sub-lease arrangement is coming to end. Not only has a neighbor found out about us and reported us to the landlord, Thomas has also died. His family tries to dispose of his furniture as fast as they can so they can cancel the lease. With Klaus' employment we can now actively look for an apartment. Not an easy task. There is a shortage of apartments, especially at the lower end. Our application with the Housing Authority is still being reviewed. We have to look for something on the open market.

I have not gotten any response on the resumes I did send out. I now start to hit the phones to call HR offices directly. *Der Tagesspiegel* wants more writing experience before they even consider my application. But they wouldn't offer me any freelance stuff either. I should find my own subjects to write about it and submit it. *Die BZ* has no need at this point. I can't bring myself to contact *Bildzeitung*, vilified equally in the East and West for its sensational and borderline-twisting-the-truth reporting. *Zitty* Magazine told me to call them in a week or so. *Berliner Morgenpost* has not responded to my resume. I don't feel discouraged but under a great deal of pressure.

Since he got his first paycheck Klaus starts to make some snotty remarks that I have not found anything yet. "Maybe you should try a little bit harder. What are you doing all day long when I am at work?"

"I am doing the best I can. I spend at least three hours every day on my typewriter to preparing resumes and cover letters."

"Obviously that's not enough. Don't expect that I pay for everything."

"The last time I checked we split our costs evenly. You don't have to pay anything for me."

"Yes, with your unemployment money. Does that make you feel good?"

"Yes, with my unemployment money. What is wrong with that?"

"Pretty soon that will run out and then you are on welfare. After that you will be in line at a soup kitchen."

"First of all, my unemployment payments will be at least for one year. I am not quite a month into it. And why would you think I am on the loser track? You are so unfair. I never ever gave you the impression that I have or want to live off of handouts."

"Remember when you left your job in Leipzig I was the one who supported you until you found a job."

"Remember, that you had suggested that I should come back to Berlin to live with you. Remember that you had offered to take care of me until I would find a new job. And remember, it took me less than a month until I had a job. Why do you bring this up now?"

I feel anger bubbling up inside of me. How dare he to treat me like that? I paid more than my dues in this relationship. Sure he found a job first. But I will soon. "Klaus, I don't like where this conversation is heading? I am not in the mood to argue with you. Sure, I would love it if you encouraged me. Instead you do the opposite. I promise you, you don't have to pay one Pfenning to support me, now or in the future. I came here to make it. And I will." I am get up from the kitchen table, fuming. Klaus' face is without any expression, his eyes look right through me. I slam the bathroom door behind me. I stare in the mirror. I hear our apartment door closing. "I hate you, Klaus," I whisper into my face.

Six Degrees of Separation

Frank, the student counselor and his partner Knut live at Victoria Auguste Platz. A beautiful park is surrounded by stately apartment buildings. Everything here looks very well cared for. It's quiet. Major roads and its traffic noise are blocks away. Even the parked cars here look nice, clean and expensive. What a difference from Turmstrasse where Klaus and I live. As we look for the right street address I feel a little jealous. I want to live here too. The entrance to the building is right next to a restaurant. The awning over the door reads Tomasius. It's a pleasant evening. The doors into the restaurant are pushed to the sides. Tables spill out onto the walkway. The place is crowded. The long bar is near the front. A set of stairs leads to a second level behind the bar. Everything looks very cool.

I ring the intercom. "Hi guys. Come on in. Take the elevator to the fourth floor." I recognize Frank's voice. The door opens into an impressive vestibule with a wide staircase. An iron cast and very ornate elevator shaft goes one flight up. The lift is wood paneled. A huge mirror with a gilded frame is on one side. I feel like I'm in a movie set. I have never been in an elevator this elegant.

Frank greets us at his apartment door. I step back when he tries to hug me. "Hey boy, we hug and kiss here. Welcome to the West," he says and grabs my shoulders and kisses me on the cheeks. I blush.

"This is Klaus," I introduce him to Frank.

"And this is Knut, my partner." I look at a tall, handsome middle-aged man. Eye glasses, slim build. He gives me a hug. He is the more attractive one of the both, I think as we step into their apartment. At the end of a long hallway to the right is the enormous living room. Brown leather couch, coffee table, rolodex desk kitty cornered in front of the windows, TV and bookshelves on the other side. A double door opens into the dining room. The high-gloss table is big enough for ten matching chairs. The cupboard with lead glass windows is part of the set.

"I came here ten years ago, straight from the prison in Bautzen with nothing more than one suitcase. See, ten years later, I have arrived." Frank brags about the one-bedroom apartment next door they own as well, plus a vacation flat on Tenerife Island. Some money in the bank and many long trips per year to different places in the world. "That's the West for you. If you work hard this what you get. Have a seat. Knut, get us some gin and tonic."

I am overwhelmed. Klaus looks impressed too. I sink deeply into the leather sofa. Knut serves the drinks. The ice cubes dance on the surface, pushing against the crystal. The singing sound only created by expensive and heavy glass. Richness on display. It feels damn good to enjoy that. Klaus takes a big gulp. He makes a loud slurping sound. I am embarrassed. Our hosts seem a bit irritated since it should have been them who lift the glasses first for a toast. I detect in Frank's face a slight expression of pity when he looks at me. I redirect my eyes into my glass. I blush again. "You have a wonderful apartment," I compliment Frank and Knut, thinking that their style is not mine. It's puffy and frilly. The polished furniture, the huge chandelier, the bronze figurines, the hand-carved glasses and bowls, the brass floor lamp and velvet draperies are way over the top. But nevertheless it displays calmness and comfort. I like the parquet floors and the oriental carpets.

"I met Knut in a bar. I was not quite here a month. He took me home. I was shocked. The only piece of real furniture was his bed. I had to sit on the floor. An old moving box served as table. I knew right from the beginning that he was the man I wanted to live with. But I also knew that he had no style and sense for a homey home. Am I right, my Knut?" Knut doesn't say a word. He just smiles. I guess Frank is the outgoing one of the two of them. "From my next unemployment check I brought silverware, dishes and a tablecloth. Everything was cheap, of course. I got it at Woolworth's. But it was a hundred times better than what my Knut had."

Frank goes on how he changed the apartment into a home in matter of a few days. When Knut's mother came to visit she couldn't believe what she saw. Frank told her that she really didn't raise Knut the right way. How else could she explain that her son basically lived as squatter before? Frank's waterfall of words only gets interrupted when he lights another cigarette. I feel a little bit uneasy listen to him bragging how he completely changed his lover's life. Looking at Knut shows me that he is used to this kind of talk. He seemed content, smiling inwardly.

Klaus is on his third glass. I know I have to finish our visit very soon. I don't want them to see him drunk. I get the feeling Frank likes me a lot since he looks mostly at me and not at Klaus. I don't mind and hope that I can become friends with him and Knut. Frank and I have a similar background. Both from the East, where we were both journalists, coming to the West because we both were looking for a much better life. We both don't mind to work hard to get there. I am certain I can learn a lot from Frank.

"I think we have to leave. It was very nice of you to invite us over for drinks. Again, you have a beautiful place. To be honest, it inspires me to do anything I can to be there someday where you are today. I hope we can stay in touch."

"What do you mean stay in touch? We want to be in your life, don't we Knut? I liked you right from the minute you stepped into my office. I meet a lot of Easterners through my job. And only very few of them I know right away will make it here. You are one of them. Knut and I will help you if you want to. Let's talk about that over dinner. Knut and I want invite both of you for dinner at Thomasius. It's right next door."

I don't know what to say. My first inkling is not to except the invitation. It's kind of too soon. On the other hand I would like to have dinner with them, but we don't have any money to pay.

"That is very nice. Maybe another time. We really should go. Klaus has to get up very early for work."

"Don't speak for me. If they want to invite us for dinner it would be rude to decline it." That was the first word Klaus has said since we sat down for drinks.

"Your lover is right. It would be rude if you left now." Frank taps me on my back.

"I guess I don't want to be rude. It's just...I have to be honest. I don't have any money to pay. I peeked into the restaurant earlier. It looks very expensive."

"Don't worry. I told you we are paying. End of discussion. Some day you will have enough money to pay. I expect that you invite us for dinner."

"I will. I promise." I get a bit teary eyed. I give Frank and Knut a hug. Both put their arms around me.

Klaus leans against the wall. He seems startled. Frank and Knut didn't hug him. That I don't feel bad about it shows how far away I am from him already. For a split second our eyes meet. It's in that very short moment that we both realize the beginning of the end of us has unmistakably began.

"Who helped you to find this sublet?" We are sitting in Knut's car parked in front of our building at Turmstrasse. After dinner Frank and his lover offered us a ride home.

"Our friend Ferdinand. He escaped a couple years ago and lives here in West Berlin." Frank's head almost snapped as he looks back at me from his front seat.

"What's Ferdinand 's last name?"

"Schlueter," I answer. It is as if the cigarette smoke in the car turned into an explosive cloud.

"Schlueter lives here in West Berlin?" Knut and Frank look at each other. Frank tries to pull out another cigarette. His hands shake. I look at Klaus. I am not quite sure what just happened. Frank takes a long suck on his cigarette. "Ferdinand Schlueter, your friend, was he a waiter in East Berlin?"

"Yes." I feel like I shouldn't answer any more questions regarding Ferdinand. I sense that the direction this conversation is going to take may have not a pleasant ending.

"How exactly did he escape? Who helped him? How do you know him?" The way Frank is gunning the questions towards me I have no way than answer them as well as I can. I wish Klaus would step in. But he doesn't.

"Klaus and Ferdinand were once lovers. After they broke up they stayed friends. I met Ferdinand through the dance company he and Klaus were members of. I joined the troupe as well." The silence in the car was unbearable. We all smoked except for Knut. I want to get out. So does Klaus. He starts tapping his hand on my upper leg. I don't know what to do.

"Why are you asking all of these questions? Do you know him?"

"Pah. Know him? You can say that, right Knut?" Frank lapses into hysterical laughter. Something is terribly wrong. I feel like I have been taken hostage because I don't dare to open the door.

"Ferdinand is one of the worst human beings there is. You are lucky that he didn't do you harm...yet." I feel like protesting Frank's s characterization of my friend. What is he talking about? "Twelve years ago Ferdinand and I were the best of friends. We met at a house party and hit it off. It was never sexual. Just friendship. I trusted him and, he could trust me with his life. Because of that deep trust we confined one day that we wanted to get out of East Germany." Frank's voice starts to crack. Even after all these years he was re-living every second of his botched escape.

I also realize that at some point during Frank's talk I must have grabbed Klaus' hand. I needed the reassurance that I was not part of this terrible event. What added to the surreal situation was the fact that I had heard that story before. From Ferdinand. Except that he did not mention Frank. What is even weirder is the fact that in a way I have become part of an event that happened a long time ago. What is the chance that I would re-connect two people, who saw each other twelve years ago for the last time in the woods between Hungary and Yugoslavia? What are the odds that I make an appointment with a student counselor who knows our friend Ferdinand? Doesn't it make one question if there is really such a thing as coincidence?

"I always wondered what happened to Ferdinand." Frank blows his nose after he is finished.

I feel dizzy. The inside of the car is hot. The cigarette smoke is almost unbearable. "Can I roll the window down?" I dare to ask. Knut pushes the button. I can't inhale the fresh and cool air fast enough.

"When I settled into my life here I started to inquire what

happened to Ferdinand. Through friends of friends I learned that he lived in East Berlin and was working at Ratskeller restaurant. Everybody wondered how he pulled that off. Usually caught escapees go to prison for a long time. After the release they would inevitable get the Berlin ban. When I heard that Ferdinand spent hardly any time in prison and could continue to live in East Berlin I became very suspicious right away. My lawyer got a hold of my pre-trial files. In it were detailed recordings of Ferdinand's interrogations. He blamed me as the mastermind behind our escape plan including finding a schlepper. He also told his interrogator that I was a spy for the West German secret service. I was totally shocked because none of that was true. Ferdinand turned on me to save himself."

My brain is in overdrive. That is not the Ferdinand I know. Frank must have gotten things wrong. Sure, Ferdinand is one of those human beings who know where they want to be in life and then go for it without any detours. Part of me has always wanted to be like him. However, it is quite a different story when someone sells his soul to the devil in order to reach personal goals. I still can't believe Ferdinand would go so far. Sure, I always wondered how he had all these friends from the West visiting him all time. There was this guy who worked as a printer at Springer Verlag publication here in West Berlin. He practically lived with Ferdinand. Then there was the general manager of the theater in Gelsenkirchen who smuggled fake passports into East Berlin in preparation for Ferdinand's successful escape via Prague and Bucharest to Amsterdam.

I asked Ferdinand once how he met all of these people and he was very evasive. Now Frank, his former friend, makes it sound certain that Ferdinand became an informant for the Stasi. How else was he able to return to East Berlin and get re-hired at Ratskeller restaurant? I shake my head. I don't want to fall into that trap again and suspect everybody I know to be a potential Stasi spy. That was part of my daily life in East Germany. That is the past. I am in the West. Ferdinand is my friend.

"Why are you so quiet?" Frank interrupts my thoughts.

"I don't know what to say. This is a terrible experience

you went through. I am so sorry," I answer. "What you just told us about Ferdinand is not the Ferdinand I know and value."

"You don't believe me?" Frank almost shouts at me.

"Of course I do."

"I want you to tell Ferdinand that you have met me. I want to know what his response is. I want that you arrange a meeting so I can confront him." I am stunned at the sharpness in Frank's voice. And I resent his demanding tone. My first loyalty is with my longtime friend and not with Frank. But I also don't want to lose a new potential friend over an occurrence that has nothing to do with me.

"Frank, that is a lot to digest for me. I really have no clue what to think. My head is spinning. It's getting also very late. Can I call you in the next couple of days?"

"I hope that you will call me."

"Thanks for the dinner and the ride home. What an interesting evening it was," I try to ease the tension. The back of the front seat presses into my chest as I attempt to hug Frank. Knut just lifts his hand. Klaus gets out off the car without a word or handshake. I follow him into the badly lit hall way of our apartment building.

Things Fall into Place

All the sudden two things happen at the same time. *Zitty* magazine contacts me to write an article about a citizen initiative to take drive-through traffic out of a neighborhood in Tiergarten and Frank called to say that a former neighbor of his had just died. Her daughter had asked him if he knew anybody who would be interested in the apartment. If so the interested party has to take it in as-is condition, including all of the furniture. The catch is that the potential tenant has to qualify for subsidized housing. Klaus and I do for certain because of our low income but our application for a low-income housing certificate is still being reviewed. I have no idea how much longer it will take to receive it. Anyway, the landlady of the apartment wants to meet us but she has also indicated that she will not wait longer than necessary to rent the apartment. She doesn't have to since there is a long line of potential tenants out there.

Frank knows the landlady because he had rented his first apartment from her. "She loves gay people. She knows they take good care of the apartment," said Frank, "I tell you, when one reads your resume with that street address you've already moved to the front of the line." More news to me. It seems funny that you are judged by where you live. The apartment is on Fasanen Strasse in the Wilmersdorf district.

Klaus works long hours at ZDF Studios. At least that is what he tells me. It really doesn't matter if I believe him or not. The bulk of the daily stress lies on my shoulders anyway. I am overwhelmed but happy. I work best under stress. My first article got published in *Zitty* magazine. They promise to keep me on their freelancer list. I also wrote an essay about my exit from the East and sent it to the editor of chief of the *Berliner Morgenpost*. Frank gave me the idea. Endless hours at the housing authority office paid off. I have our permit to rent a subsidized apartment not bigger than fifty-five square meters. Frank also made the appointment for me with the owner of the apartment at Fasanenstrasse. I have to be at her office at nine o'clock in the morning. Klaus refuses to take time off of work. Therefore I make my way alone to her Dahlem address with a big bouquet of flowers in my hands which was Frank's idea. I am nervous and at her house almost an hour prior to the appointment.

At the given time I ring the bell. A woman in her forties opens the door. I introduce myself and hand her the flowers. Her expression is blank. My heart sinks when I step into her huge office. Another couple is already there. "I apologize that I am late."

"You are not. It's nine o'clock and you are here." The woman tells me in a matter-of-fact manner. Her demeanor is very dismissive and stern. I see my chances dwindle. "What's your monthly income?" she asks.

"My partner makes 2500 Marks."

"I didn't ask you for your partner's income. How much are you making?" I feel like a student in the principal's offices put on notice. I am embarrassed. The couple is listening as well. I thought Frank had told her about our situation.

"I don't have an income yet. I am on unemployment."

"Oh, I didn't know that. You could have saved yourself a trip."

"I am trying very hard to find work. I just got my first article published in *Zitty* magazine. They told me that I am on their freelancer list. I also sent an article to the *Berliner Morgenpost*."

"You are a journalist?" she asks.

"Yes."

"Well, as far as I know it's a very competitive field and very, very difficult to make a decent living as a writer. I don't see how you could afford my rent."

"I promise you we will never be behind our rent. We both came from East Berlin just over two months ago with not a Pfennig in our pocket. We have saved as much as we could. We have about 2000 Marks in our account. I can write you a check in that amount as a security deposit."

She rolls her eyes. "Do you have permit from the housing authority?" Wordlessly I hand it to her. She looks at it and shows no intention in giving it back to me. "I have not made my decision yet who would be my new tenant. I am still interviewing applicants. I will keep your permit for now. If you don't get the apartment I will send it back to you."

That's not right, I think. I need that certificate to apply for other apartments. My chances with her seem close to zero anyway. I spot a copy machine behind her desk. "Can you make a copy of it, please? This is a very important paper for me. As I understand, if I lose it I lose the chance to rent a subsidized apartment. And I have to find a place pretty soon since our sublet runs out shortly."

She looks at me. Her eyes dart over her glasses frame. If looks could kill I would be dead right now. "Don't worry, young man. I won't lose the permit. I think we are done here. You will hear from me." I glance over at the couple. The two ignore me.

I grab my bag. "Thank you for meeting me. I hope we have chance to be your tenant." I extend my hand. She ignores it.

"You will hear from me. Oh, thanks for the flowers. They are very pretty. But you should have saved yourself the trouble and the money." She is one tough lady and very unfriendly, too. I make my way out of her apartment. I failed to be convincing. I wish Klaus was here right now. I dig through my pockets for change to call Frank. He had asked me to call him as soon as the meeting with the landlady is over. "Right away," as he put it.

It takes me about ten minutes to find a public phone.

"Hi, it's me, Thomas."

"Congratulations!"

"What do you mean?"

"Your landlady just called me. She told me that she likes you and, that she will rent the apartment to you. She also told me to tell you not take it too hard the way she talked to you. She is a lesbian, you know?"

I am speechless. "Please, repeat what you just said. I can't believe it."

"You are the new tenant at Fasanenstrasse 3. I knew you could do it." Tears fill my eyes.

"Thank you, Frank. Without your help and connections I

couldn't have made it."

"Oh, don't thank me. I can't wait to come to your housewarming party." I hang up. I can't wait to call my mother. I have rented an apartment at Fasanenstrasse. Even though I have not seen it yet, I know it will be great. It has a balcony, parking spot in the back, central heat, close to the subway. For a second I remember how long I would have waited for a newer flat with fewer amenities over there. Ten to fifteen years at least! I am proud of myself. I deserve a little reward. I see an Eduscho coffee shop. I order a cup of coffee and a piece of cheesecake. I just splurged. I count 1.80 Marks into the hand of the cashier. Klaus will never know about it.

I am in a bind. *Zitty* Magazine wants me to do another survey. But at the same time I have an appointment with the editor-in-chief of the *Berliner Morgenpost*. I feel like I am on a roll and for the first time in my life things are going my way. Now I have to make a decision. Which appointment should I cancel? I will call Frank. He has become such a good and helpful advisor to me in the last couple of weeks. I am so glad we met. The Ferdinand issue has not come up again. I certainly will not bring up that hot topic.

I trust Frank's judgment and knowledge. "Of course you keep the appointment with the *Berliner Morgenpost*. How can you think twice about that? Call *Zitty* magazine and tell them you can do it the next day or so." Frank reinforces my gut feelings. However, I don't have the stomach to call *Zitty* Magazine. I will deal with it after my meeting in the Springer Hochhaus at Koch Strasse. Klaus says I shouldn't go there. He thinks that all things related to Springer publications is so right wing. No serious journalist should work for any of his newspapers. I am totally aware of Springer's right-leaning political views that are demonstrated in his publication on a daily basis. In East Germany Springer was the poster child for distorting reality and brainwashing its readership by scandal-loaded articles. Axel Springer and his company was a favorite topic for the TV show Schwarzer Kanal.

Axel Springer never made any qualm out of the fact that

he hated the GDR. Every article printed in one of his publications that mentioned East Germany had to put DDR in quotation marks. It showed his contempt with a country he believed to be illegitimate. His stern political vision is that someday Germany will be re-united again. To put his money where his mouth is he built the Springer Hochhaus right at the Berlin Wall, very visible from both sides of the Iron Curtain. The East German leaders hated him just for that. I also know that Springer is very controversial in West Germany as well. The left hates him fiercely. Springer became a brand name for the left what's wrong with capitalism.

I honestly don't have a strong opinion one way or the other when it comes to Springer. I always looked at the Springer Hochhaus when I walked down Leipziger Strasse. The golden metal façade looked so cool and impressive in comparison to the uniform and boring high-rise architecture so common in East Germany. The Leipziger Strasse was rebuilt as some kind of a high-end shopping boulevard. Stores, hair salons and restaurants on the first floor of the buildings. Modern apartments above. Whoever was assigned a flat here had special clearance by the State authorities. The rumor was that mostly Stasi employees and mid-level Party cadres were living there. After all, the Wall was very visible no matter which side of the street you were on. Therefore only really steadfast Communists and Party loyalists could be trusted living in the shadow of Springer Hochhaus.

It was also no secret that the Party made Leipziger Strasse into a prestigious avenue in order to stick it to Axel Springer and his "journalistic henchmen." The propaganda apparatus wanted to showcase the achievements of the victorious proletariat right under their windows. However, Leipziger Strasse like others façade projects in East Berlin, is just another Potemkin village. One wonders how stupid the *Nomenklatura* believes their citizens are. You take just one sidestep and you in the gray and depressive reality of the GDR. The Gendarmen Markst is still in ruins, over thirty years after the bombing of Berlin. It takes only a minute by foot from Alexanderplatz and you are in nineteenth-century shabby working-class living quarters. It's the same just outside of the other showcase Karl-Marx Allee where squatters are still a harsh reality that is so perfectly described in the mandatory read *The Moore and the Crows from London*, except that this Karl Marx glorification novel records the horrible living conditions in Liverpool in the late nineteenth century and not the neglected apartment buildings in East Berlin. Just replace any Liverpool street described in the book with Simon-Dach Strasse in Friedichshain district for instance and you get the picture. The time: 1980. The location: Berlin, capital of the socialist German Democratic Republic.

I am nervous and excited. Springer Hochhaus is getting bigger and bigger as I walk down Koch Strasse. I still cannot believe that I will enter the building in a couple of minutes. Past dreams, visions and hopes have really nothing much to do when reality becomes the present. Whatever I imagined back from behind the Berlin Wall about my future did not include a stomach in knots, sweaty palms and flashbacks prior to entering the symbol of capitalist self-esteem. I have to calm my nerves through distractions. I concentrate on what I see. Koch Strasse is a pretty unattractive street. Except for some newer apartment buildings and some restaurants and pubs the street shows that it is on the geographical edge of the city. It runs parallel to Leipziger Strasse. The Wall divides the city.

Springer Hochhaus with all its modernity and its shiny appearance sticks out like it does not belong here. It looks more like downtown and the inner city. The entrance plaza lies a couple of steps below street level. Huge revolving doors push you into an impressive and vast lobby, wood paneled and several stories high. The elegant sitting area complements the confidence of the building and its owner. I show my ID to the doorman behind a big desk to my left. I have to write my name into a logbook. Then he asks me to take a seat. I am way too high on adrenalin that I could relax on a leather couch. I look out of the window without focus. I feel humble and vulnerable. I am in the lobby of a building that is the embodiment of hate and a target for the East German propaganda machine waiting to meet the editor-in-chief of *Berliner Morgenpost*. It feels so good. Didn't I came a long way, a way many close to me thought I chose because I was misguided and it would lead me straight into the abyss of the capitalist mud? What they forgot to tell us over there is the fact that on the other side of the wall are human beings. Not just monsters, rejects and criminals.

"Herr Schardt!" A friendly voice interrupts my daydream. I dry my eyes with my hands quickly before I turn around. An older woman in a black suit looks in my direction.

"Yes, I am Thomas Schardt." I answer and extend my right hand.

"Welcome. I will bring you up to the office Herr Schardt." She leads me to a row of elevators. "It's a beautiful day today, isn't it?" The woman who didn't introduce herself to me pushes an up button.

"Yes, it really is." I am not sure how to get the conversation going. We are alone in the elevator; both of our eyes stare at the display panel. I am glad when the door finally opens. The muffled noise of people's voices, phone ringing and typewriters clacking greet me. I notice the puffs of cigarette smoke that linger over people's heads. "This way." We turn to the right. I am let into a small office with huge windows, which open up to a panoramic view into East Berlin.

"Wow." I whisper to myself. Even though I have been in West Berlin for over three months this surprising outlook on my past life hits me like stone. Yes, I am here, safe and sound, away from what I hated and did not want anymore. I look at the toy-sized traffic of Leipziger Strasse. I see the bridge at S-Bahnhof Friedrich Strasse. I squeeze my eyes to scan the area where my parents live. I detect Brandenburger Tor to the left of me. Yes, and there is the Berliner Dom and the Fernsehturm to my right. I wish I could get closer to the window, but a group of desks block me. I want to scream so that my former co-East Germans would hear me. I fight my emotions.

My past blitzes by. The guy who would bully me in third grade and call me a girl. My Russian teacher at Carl-von-Ossietzky School, who named me a failure after I got a three for a test. The Stasi interrogator who called me a pansy. My stepfather who told me it would have been better if I was never born. My mother who feared I would end up poor and homeless as soon as I crossed the border. And here I am looking at all of that from above, alive, able and proof of how wrong they were. Inside of the Springer Hochhaus. I feel as hopeful and lucky like never before.

The editor-in-chief has stunningly similarities to Fischer, the editor-in-chief at *Der Morgen*. Tall and massive but not fat, a shock of white hair. Otto's big right hand reaches up around my wrist when we greet each other. "So young man, you are from East Berlin?"

I nod my head. "I feel like it's an eternity since I have left the East. But it's only been a of couple months since I got out."

"Well, welcome. I like your little essay. You know how to write. We always look for new blood." His voice is very masculine and self-assured. "Listen, I don't have much time. I wanted to personally meet you. The rest I will leave to the head of our local desk. We would love to have you on our team, young man." With that said he pushes his big frame out of the chair. "Frau Eberhardt, get Marquardt here," he yells through the open door of his office. "I am off to a staff meeting, young man." His firm handshake makes my hand crack. He walks out of the room. He didn't leave me a chance to say anything. As I watch him leave I notice that he has a slight limp. Our meeting did not last more than two minutes. I collect my thoughts only to be interrupted by Frau Eberhardt, the same woman who picked me up in the lobby.

"Herr Schardt, please follow me." She forcefully walks ahead of me towards a corner separated only by removable walls from the huge office room. I see a man sitting at a small desk. His handknit sweater does not match his shirt. What an odd combination, I think as we get closer to him. That must be Marquardt. Something in his appearance makes me think of a mistreated dog.

"Herr Marquardt this is Herr Schardt," Frau Eberhardt introduces me. He almost jumps out of his seat. His eyes are wide open and express surprise and consternation. He really looks like a haunted man, I conclude. I extend my hand. He ignores it.

"Good morning," he mumbles. "I am not sure what Otto wants me to do with you, to be quite honest. I also have very little time right now. We will have to reschedule." Marquardt apparently is one of those human beings who cannot look people straight in the eye, so my attempt is hopeless when I try to meet his. I am disappointed after I the promising encounter I had with the Marquardt's boss.

"Herr Otto said that he would like for me to part of your team," I say.

"Oh he always has these brilliant ideas without consulting me." No love lost between these two, I think. But I won't give up. "The editor-in-chief told me that he liked my essay about my first experiences as a new West Berliner. I have a copy. Can I leave it with you?"

"I don't know when I will have time to read it. But sure, you can leave it. Give Frau Eberhardt your contact information. I really have to go back to work. I am close to a deadline." Again no eye contact. No handshake. I am dismissed.

"I am looking forward to hearing from you. Please give me a chance." I am not sure if he was even listening to me. Marquardt is back in his chair, focusing on whatever lies in front of him.

I make my way back to Otto's s secretary. She is on the phone. On a piece of paper I write my name and phone number and wait until she is done. "What can I do for you, Herr Schardt?" she asks after she hangs up the phone.

"Herr Marquardt said he doesn't have time for me right now. He told me to leave my phone number with you. I know Herr Otto has mine. But I wanted to make sure Herr Marquardt has it as well."

"He told you he has no time right now? I wonder why, because the editor-in-chief told him during the morning conference to meet with you. I will make sure Herr Marquardt gets this." She takes the paper with my contact information. "Sorry about that. Don't be discouraged, Herr Otto wants to try you out."

"I am so glad to hear that. Thank you so much. Do you

Page 411

think I should give Herrn Marquardt a call if I don't hear anything let say in the next two days?"

"Sure. But I am certain you will hear from him before that. I will also mention it to the editor-in-chief."

"Thank you again." I say, and I leave her office in an exuberant mood. I am on auto pilot. Elevator, lobby, Koch Strasse, U-Bahn Station. I can't believe my luck. I have a job, almost. My chest is bursting. I check my pocket. I have 5 Marks. I will go to Wilmersdorfer Strasse, my favorite shopping street. There is an Eduscho coffee shop. Coffee and a piece of cheesecake. Yeah.

I never told Klaus that I had discovered Wilmersdorfer Strasse during one of my visits to the AOK office nearby. I was so mesmerized passing all of these shops and department stores. Not that I could buy anything right now. But the anticipation to do so someday makes me come here any time I can. Towards the end of Wilmersdorfer Strasse is Eduscho. On my first stroll I went in and dared to buy a cup of coffee for 95 Pfennig. Sure I felt guilty spending that kind of money when we needed every Pfennig to buy groceries, get passport photos taken, copies of resumes, you name it. But it also felt so good to enjoy the cup of coffee. Of course I didn't tell Klaus, neither about the coffee nor my window shopping. And I won't tell him about today's splurge. It's my secret. It's my new routine. Eduscho is my reward. No one will take that away from me.

I have been offered a freelance job at *Berliner Morgenpost* as part of the paper's expansion into the different city districts of Berlin that the first regional office will open in Zehlendorf. Besides the bureau chief, all five reporters are new hires on a contract basis. There is Erika, born in Thüringen close to the border to West Germany. Her weekend trips with her family always gravitated near to the forbidden border area. "I never was able to see across. The so-called death strip was way too far away. But I always envisioned myself being on the other side." She got out almost at the same time that I did. In the refugee camp in Marienfelde she met her current boyfriend, an aspiring actor with minor roles at the theater in Stendal. A group reading of Camus *The Plague* in a friend's house got him in trouble. He was fired from the theater. Attempts to find work were unsuccessful. His only way to have an acting future was to leave East Germany.

The other new hire is Frederika who has just had finished a training program as flight attendant but couldn't find any employment. She is now trying a career in journalism. Sonia is a doctor's wife with a lot of connections who wants to be social reporter. Frank just moved from West Germany to West Berlin and has a degree in public policy science and worked previously as a reporter at a paper in Duisburg. Michael the bureau chief has worked for the *Berliner Morgenpost* for the last three years.

I like the diverse group. I am very excited to have the opportunity to be back in reporting. Michael encourages everybody to submit stories of our own findings but he also assigns some to each of us. Nothing time sensitive. He wants stories in reserve. The first Zehlendorf page will be produced in two weeks. After that we have to fill one every day. "There is enough space for everybody to file articles. 90 Pfennig per printed line. If you are good and don't mind long hours you will make a decent living." Michaels is matter-of-fact and seems to draw a line right from the beginning. No personal stuff will muddle our team effort to produce the best local reporting *Berliner Morgenpost* has ever seen. He certainly is driven.

I wonder for a moment if he sets the pace and standard with an impersonal touch because he tries extra hard to cover the fact that he is so obviously gay? Maybe I am just sensitive to the fact that he avoids any direct eye contact with me. This guy has certainly suppressed his issues. I don't care. I have met Michael types before. Fear of being discovered what doesn't need to be discovered anymore. And just because someone is gay doesn't make one automatically sexually desirable to every other gay man. I ignore his attempts to ignore me. Besides, I have no intention of receiving any special treatment because it just so happens that we are both gay. I know I will break the ice, if there is any between us, by being the best reporter he has.

My new boss wants me to write an article about the pros and cons of the installation of speed bumps in residential neighborhoods. I am starting to wonder if that is one of the current main topics in my new hometown since in my first *Zitty* magazine assignment I had to deal with the same issue. Anyway, I am happy to deliver. First I will go to the Zehlendorf town hall to get some insight on which streets are on the agenda to be remodeled to slow traffic down. After that I will interview residents. I feel very confident that I can produce a well-researched article. I also will call *Zitty* magazine and have them take me off the freelancer list. I want to solely concentrate on *Berliner Morgenpost* from now on.

I realize that I have to buy a typewriter. There are two in the office in Zehlendorf, not enough considering the amount of people who need to use them. I could go to a public library and use one of their typewriters. But that would be not very time efficient. If I have my own typewriter at home I am more independent. During the day I can spent my time researching different stories. In the evening I would be able to write at home without any constraints. I already have checked the prices. The least expensive typewriter is around 200 Marks, a staggering price. The funny part is that it's an Olympus made in the GDR.

I am still waiting for the interest-free government loan for ex-GDR citizens which would give me a nice head start. The 5000 Marks are re-payable within in the next ten years. At first I was very hesitant to apply for it. I didn't want any debt. But Ferdinand convinced me after he pointed out that my monthly payment is around 50 Marks. Anyway, the loan is still in the approval stage. I have about 200 Marks in savings. But I am hesitant to spent all my savings. I could ask Frank, who probably would lend me money. But I feel like I shouldn't ask him. There is only Klaus left. He is so weird about money lately. I think he just wants to prove a point to me. You make money, then you can spend it. If you don't then you are out of luck. Our relationship has reached an indefinable stage.

For instance, I really was hesitant to sign a lease with both of our names on it. But in the end I had to be practical. The apartment at Fasanen Strasse is our best bet at this point but I could not have afforded the 450 Marks monthly rent on my own. The apartment came fully furnished. That also saved us a lot of money. I convinced myself I could live with Klaus for another year. After that I hopefully will be able to make it on my own. He has no clue about my plan to end our relationship very soon. I feel bad that I am so calculating. I am not a freeloader. But sharing costs is the best alternative not only for me. All my unemployment checks go into his account. The little I have made so far with my writing went there as well. I only kept all of the money I got during my naturalization process. About 250 Marks in total. My stepfather's sister Hildegard, who I met for dinner without telling Klaus, gave me 200 Marks. I was very surprised and thankful. With that money I opened a savings account at All Bank and, I pledged not to touch it no matter what.

I decide to get off the subway at Hohenzollernplatz and walk the rest of the way home. I need the fresh air after an intense day. My notebook is full of quotes from residents and information I got from the office for public transportation in Zehlendorf town hall. In my head I am writing the beginning of the article. I don't pay much attention to the street or anything else. It's more or less a boring part of the Hohenzollern Damm lined with apartment buildings. There are hardly any shops to get distracted by. There is also a small park in the middle of the street just before the intersection of Fasanen Strasse. I am waiting for the traffic light to switch to green. Without focusing I look around. I do a double take and recognize Klaus, who sits on a bench in the park I was going to cross. That is odd, I think. Why would he sit here just a few steps away from our apartment? Something tells me to watch him undetected. I step back from the curve and hide behind a tree.

After a while Klaus gets up. I follow him with my eyes. All of a sudden I know where he is heading. To the public bathroom. Sure enough he opens the door and goes inside. I don't know what to do. Should I go home and pretend that I don't know where he went? I was certain that Klaus would take up his old habit and cruise for quick sex. But until now I did not known for sure. I feel anger rising up inside of me. It's been about five minutes since he vanished inside the public bathroom. I cross the street straight into the bathroom. It's dimly lit. Its urine smell is not unexpected. I stop for a second to look around. One of the two stall doors is ajar. I follow the muffled noise. With my foot I push the door open and see the exposed back of a guy, his pants down at his ankles. His hands are around the naked hips of another man. I step closer to make sure. Klaus is bent over the toilet, his hands against the wall above to steady himself. The sound of flesh against flesh is getting more intense. Klaus is the first to realize that he was being watched. He turns his head towards me, his eyes flicker with recognition. The guy behind him tries to grab my crotch. I push him away hard enough that both connected bodies lose their balance and fall against the stall wall. I turn around and leave the public bathroom.

For a split second I am inclined to wait outside for Klaus. I am shaking. It is certainly not the first time I have witnessed Klaus with another man. But seeing him bent over in a stinky public bathroom hurts like the first time I saw him getting fucked behind the bushes at a bus stop at Friedrich Strasse. I walk slowly towards our apartment building. But I can't get myself to turn the key in the lock. I keep going. Melting into the evening hustle and bustle of Ku'damm is the only thing that I can stand right now. I don't know why I can't detach myself emotionally from Klaus.

I have developed a daily routine. I leave the house every morning around nine o'clock to be home about twelve hours later, write my articles on my new Olympus typewriter and phone them in afterwards. I could cut down my time being on the road if I had a car. But that is out of the question for the time being. Zehlendorf district is a widespread area, some of which is easily reached by subway and bus. Other parts I can only walk to. My willingness to work a lot of hours and cover any local story they want to write about helps me. Michael gives me a lot of leads. Not so much because he likes me and my writing but because I don't have any problem covering stories late in the day or on weekends. Most of my team members refuse to be available around the clock. I don't. For one there is the money part. My first paycheck was almost 1900 Marks. That means I have sold over 1900 printed lines to *Berliner Morgenpost*. I was able to give back Klaus the 200 Marks he lent me to buy the typewriter. I think he was very surprised when I handed him the money. "How much have you earned so far?" he asked. I told him. "You make that much with the shit you write? Maybe I should be become a reporter, too."

He never appreciated the fact that I wanted to be a journalist. Back in the East he laughed at my articles. So I am not surprised that he still dismisses my line of work. Sure, I would have loved to get some kind of congratulations from him when I brought my first paycheck home. On the other he has inflicted so much pain on me in the past that now he can only touch my feelings on the surface. The more work I take on, the less time I have to spend at home. The distance between us is getter wider.

Klaus is back to his heavy drinking again. In addition, not one week goes by where he doesn't coming home at least one night. Of course I still worry. Not so much about with whom he has sex. I am sure it's a stranger he picks up wherever he happens to be. I still worry that he will get physically harmed. His choices of guys and locations are always indiscriminate. Sometimes I wake up in the middle of the night wondering. More often than not I can't get back to sleep. So I stay awake until I can call his work the next morning to see if he is there. He is always annoyed about my calls. I can tell by his voice. He even told me once that I should not call him at work, ever. By calling him at least once a week he thinks his colleagues will put one and one together. He is so freaking afraid they will find out he lives with a man. Well, that is not really my problem. He is forty-two years old and still has issues with coming out of the closet. In my eyes, that is just ridiculous.

"Please don't call me here anymore. You don't have to worry. I can take care of myself. Always remember, I will always come back to you," he told me the other morning when I called him at work to see if he was okay.

What an asshole you are, I thought and hang up on him. Klaus still seems very secure in our relationship. Why else would he continue his sexual escapades and think at the same time that I will continue to accept it? What he doesn't know is that the countdown is on. For now I have to take it until I am stable enough to be on my own feet. I have to admit that the thought frightens me a bit. I have not lived alone for almost ten years. I don't remember when was the last time was that I hung a picture, wallpapered or replaced a fuse. Klaus takes care of all that and I happily let him. Moving into my own place and taking care of any handyman work, as crazy it may sound, is daunting to me. Also the fact that I will be responsible for a hundred percent of the living expenses instead of only half of it makes me nervous. I know I have to leave him for my own sake. I just still don't know when.

Made in the GDR: My First Typewriter and Camera

"You should take your own pictures. Per published one you will get 55 Marks." Eberhardt , who works at the local desk at Springer Hochhaus, edits my article about a new Kindergarten in the Neukoelln district. He is one of the long-term journalists at *Berliner Morgenpost* whose prime as street reporter has long passed as well as their health. Eberhardt is overweight, a chain smoker and because of his contract, totally safe in his job. He can't wait to retire in about ten years...if he will make it that is. Until then he has to sit at the desk and edit and re-write whatever young and inexperienced reporters deliver. A thankless and tedious job, so it seems to me. Eberhardt, however, appears to have fun being some kind of a father figure to the newcomers. I like him. I appreciate his help and advice and most of all the extra assignments he throws my way. Maybe it has something to with the fact that he also grew up in the East. He somehow saw the Wall coming and took the subway on August 12th, 1961 from Leipziger Strasse to Gesundbrunnen. The next day Berlin was cut into the East and West.

"I don't have a camera. I also don't know if my photos will be in print quality"

"You never know for sure until you try. The next time you get paid buy one. You can get a quality camera for about 250 Marks. Go to Photo Probst at Wilmersdorfer Strasse. They will help you. And I will help you to get assignments where you can also take your pictures to illustrate the articles." Eberhardt is probably right to suggest having my own camera. It would only take five published photos to have paid for the camera. I just shiver at the idea of spending 250 Marks. It's more than half of our rent. Everything in the West seems so expensive. The other day we wanted to go to the movies. We turned around after we learned that one ticket would cost us seven Marks, fourteen Marks for the two of us.

"Thank for your suggestions. I will look into it."

"What do you mean you will look into it? You will buy a camera. If you want to I will lend you the money. You can pay me back in installments."

"Okay. I will go to Photo Probst. Thanks for your offer, but I will try to manage it myself. If I can't I may take you up on your offer." I am humbled by the willingness of him to help me buy a camera to make more money. I have 300 Marks in my pocket, money I wanted to put into my savings account at All Bank. I decide to wait and go first to the camera shop. If I can't find anything decent for less than 300 Marks I will deposit the money.

It's certainly not the first time since I've been in the West that I find out that I have to spend money in order to make some. A totally new concept for me. In the East you earned money to pay for things. Food, furniture, television sets, you name it. But spending money on something to make more money is foreign to me so far. I certainly like the idea of making a ton of money. My 200-Marks investment in a GDR-manufactured typewriter paid off already many times over. Why wouldn't a camera do the same?

But there is also creepy feeling that I am being sucked into the evil of the spending that can easily put me just steps away from poverty and homelessness. I want to shake off my fear. I am still not comfortable and secure enough with my new circumstances. I catch myself more often than not being afraid, assuming danger and feeling sudden panic. At the same time, I am angry because of the indoctrination I was subjected to in the East that still continues to hound me. Pounding into me that everything is white and good is in the East. All the black, bad and evil is behind the Iron Curtain. Now that I am here and see it with my own eyes I feel fouled, betrayed, lied to because I was not told about gray. I am furious that my mental state is still somehow controlled by them. Why can't I get rid of my past faster? They took my citizenship. Why couldn't they also keep my brainwashed cells? I have to learn quickly to take risk and responsibility for my action. From now on I will try not to measure all of my actions here against the fraudulent values injected in me over there. I can think, see and decide for myself. Therefore I will now go to Wilmersdorfer Strasse. I will have a cup of coffee at Eduscho. I will go to Photo Probst. And if I have some money left I will go to Woolworth where I saw a black shirt for six Marks.

Paris

I can't believe it. I am on the top of the Eiffel Tower, Paris below, visible until the horizon touches the sky. We have three full days to explore, to walk, to take photographs. We have already climbed the steps to Sacre Coeur, saw the Louvre and counted all of our change out for a cup of coffee at the famous Cafe de la Paix. But it still feels like we're sleepwalking. More than once I had to stop to tell Klaus "We are in Paris, man." Not even six months ago this city, like the rest of the West, was unreachable, closed off for us, only a dream, not a reality. In the end, just 126 Marks and a twelve-hour Holiday Reisen bus ride was all that was needed to be here.

We crossed the border after showing our passports. No machine guns pointing at us. No dogs sniffing down below the underbelly of the bus to make sure no one tried to stow away. No suspicious eye contact from the customs officer to feel you out and learn of your travel intentions. No, just standard interruptions of a ride from one country to another. No questions asked. No warning to be aware of evil. Just normalcy of travel from one place to another. Accompanied by the euphoria that I can now go places. But there again are the moments of anger when I look at the Chagall murals at the Paris Opera or watch the Can-Can performance at Moulin Rouge. Anger at the Eastern ideologists and their ruthless messing with our brains. "You don't have to see for yourself. We tell you it's bad over there and dangerous. We have done the work for you. Sure you can buy bananas whenever you want if you have the money. But no one is looking out for your safety as the all-knowing Party does."

What is the harm in taking a picture of the Arc de Triomphe? Why would a visit to Notre Dame endanger my life? Why was the *Nomenklatura* so worried for me to buy a ticket to visit Versailles? What is the reasoning for them not to allow me to touch the walls of the Bastille?

413

Klaus works now as a teacher at a city-run vocational school. He is glad that he could quit his little job at ZDF studios. After we read in the paper about a job opening at this trade school I asked Ferdinand if he knew anyone who could get Klaus that job. Of course he knew and, Klaus was in. He would be rather working in a theater environment again but those jobs are hard to find. Anyway, he seems to be content with his teaching job as part of a re-integration program for troubled teenagers. His students are mostly male. I feel a little bit uneasy for obvious reasons when he told me who his students are. Klaus' alcohol consumption is getting out of control. He had it a little bit under control since hard liquor as well as beer cost more than he wants to spend. He, like me, still compares West with East prices. Anyway, wine in cartons at Aldi supermarket is cheap. Somehow he also heard about the so-called wholesale clubs where he can get alcohol for much less than in regular stores. I don't know why I continue to worry so much about his drinking.

Overall, I am very happy with my freelance job at Springer. I get printed almost every day. Eberhardt keeps his word and gives me assignments where I also can take my own pictures. I now make almost a 1000 Marks a month just with my photos. It is ironic that the camera I got, like my typewriter, was also made in the GDR. Both articles are a rare find in the East and quite expensive in comparison to the income levels over there. Here they are the least expensive among comparable items and plentiful. What a difference the Wall makes! We also have discovered IKEA as a reasonable alternative to get household things. Again, this Swedish-owned company gets its stuff made in the GDR.

Lisa and Johanna, Our New Neighbors

Lisa and Johanna met at a food stamp distribution center near the bombed-out Stettiner Bahnhof train station. It was September 1945. Lisa, a war widow with a baby daughter, couldn't feed herself or her child with the one ration card she had been given a week prior. She was here to ask for an additional card. Johanna, strong boned, was eligible for double food stamps because she worked as a construction worker in war-ravaged Berlin. She saw the tears in Lisa's eyes. "I have enough food stamps. You can have some of mine." Johanna took Lisa in her arms to comfort her. It was a meeting by chance that would last a lifetime. Johanna and Lisa are our neighbors at Fasanen Strasse and became our friends the first moment they saw us. "We are so happy to have you live right next to us. We have to stick together." Johanna shakes my hand, manly, to the point it hurt me. Her gray hair is short and groomed straight back. The crisp white blouse was tightly tucked into her gray flannel pants with front zipper and cuffs on the bottom. A man's watch on her wrist, her feet in masculine brown loafers.

"Welcome. Please come in for some tea and cookies. I am Lisa." A petite woman steps from behind Johanna's back. Her hair is gray, the curls are perfect layered. Pearl earrings, a simple gold necklace, a wool sweater loosely touching a straight-cut black skirt, black high heels. Both women appear to be in their seventies. A picture-perfect lesbian couple. No doubt who wears the pants in this relationship. I giggle to myself.

We step into a mirror image of our apartment. Narrow hallway. Kitchen and bathroom to the right. "My bedroom." Lisa points to the door at the end of the corridor. On the left side is the living room. "I sleep on the pull-out couch," Johanna explains. A smaller room next to it "is my daughter's room when she visits us." The apartment is immaculate. The furniture looks expensive, but not

415

ostentatious. Johanna directs us to two cushy armchairs. She sits down on a high back chair and lights a cigarette. "I wish you would stop smoking," says Lisa.

"I know. Sometime soon, darling." Johanna exhales the smoke. *This little exchange has been repeated probably since they met,* I think and smile. After Lisa finishes setting the table with the Meissen porcelain teacups and small plates she takes her place on the sofa. "Tell us your story," Johanna demands. We do.

Both woman listen politely and with noticeable interest. "It's not very often these days that you hear someone has a partner for almost ten years like you. Congratulations." Johanna lights a new cigarette with the end of her previous one. The women exchange a knowing glance. "We've known each other for fourty years. I was quite a womanizer before I met Lisa. With Lisa and her daughter I found the family I always wanted." Lisa looks at her. It seems like there is some sadness surrounding Lisa. "We struggled like everybody else after the war. But I made good money in construction. Lisa didn't need to work. We all had enough to eat."

"I was so happy for my daughter. It was not easy for me after I learned that my husband was killed at the Eastern Front. He had never has seen our child." Lisa takes a sip of tea.

Johanna says, "I did construction for about ten years. Then one day I met this man in the streetcar on my way home. He started talking to me. At first I thought he was coming on to me. 'What a dumb ass,' I thought. Can't you see that I am not interested in men?' But he seemed unfazed and I was very nonchalant during our little chat. He wanted to know what I did for work and so on." Johanna stops for moment to get a new cigarette going. "Well. To make a long story short, he owned a schoolbook publishing house and was looking for a sales representative. He gave me his phone number. At first I didn't think much of it. But I told Lisa about it."

"I encouraged her to look into it. The construction work was really way too much for her. So, one morning I laid out her Sunday suit. Remember?" Lisa looks at Johanna.

"When I saw my suit I thought that woman is getting crazy. I can't go in a suit to work."

"I told her. Today you are not going to work. Today you visit that nice man and ask him if he is still looking for help."

"I did what she told me. I got the job and in the next 25 years I went from school to school selling books. I liked it. My boss treated me very well. Today I get a nice company pension. He always invited both of us to his Christmas party. To him we were Lisa and Johanna. He never asked any questions. He just accepted us. A couple of years after I retired he died. I think one of his sons took over. I don't know. It doesn't matter." Johanna excuses herself to go the bathroom. As soon as she closes the living room door behind her Lisa straightens up.

"You should not get a wrong impression of us. We are not lovers. Johanna never touched me. She knows better. I am straight. Always was. Johanna provided for me and my daughter. There were men who were interested in me. But how could I leave her? She was so good to us. Once I had an affair. I got pregnant. Johanna didn't ask any questions. She drove me to the hospital. She picked me up after the procedure was done. And now it's too late for me to be on my own." Lisa slides back into the cushions of the sofa when she hears Johanna coming out of the bathrooms.

"Boys, again I am so glad you are here. Let us know if you need any help."

"Thank you for inviting us. As soon as we are settled we will have you over." I give Lisa a hug and shake Johanna's hand. I am also glad to have these two women as neighbors. Over the course of the next year we become really good friends, sharing a lot of laughs, tea and cookies together.

One evening Lisa knocked at our door. Only Klaus was home. She asked him to help her to get Johanna off the toilet. At first Klaus thought that was an odd request but followed Lisa into her apartment. When he opened the bathroom door he realized what happened. Johanna had died going to the bathroom. Lisa wanted him to lay her on the couch in the living room. "I will call the coroner tomorrow morning. I want to wash and dress her myself. I need the time, just her and me." The next morning when they picked up Johanna's body Lisa was ungroomed, still in her nightgown. She didn't say a word. She didn't need to. Lisa stared at us neither recognizing Klaus nor me. She was just standing in middle of her hallway. Fragile, disoriented, frightened. Overnight she not only had lost her life partner, she had lost her mind as well. The paramedic helped her on to the stretcher. Tears were running out of the corners of her eyes. I squeezed her hand. She did not react. She just looked at the roof of the ambulance. Lisa died on the way to the hospital.

A Sense of Lost Security

Even though I make a good amount of money every month I am constantly worried about not having enough. The biggest difference between living in the East and here is the fact of lost security. Over there everything is regulated, monitored and secure. (As long as you play by the rules, that is.) Here everything is a challenge. You can take nothing for granted and things can change in an instant. I am now totally responsible for my own existence. No fallbacks, no safety net. Sure you can get unemployment, food stamps, help with the rent, health care. But that is no place I want to be. I went to the unemployment office, stood in line for subsidized housing vouchers and claimed health benefits right after I came here. Plenty of people in need do so, among them a lot recent transplants from the East. However, my experiences were so unpleasant, humiliating and depressing that I will do everything I can to avoid these locations for the unfortunate. I am prepared to pay the price of personal freedom. I had the alternative and hated it.

In the last week alone two journalists at the newspaper were let go. One was in his late fifties and had been on the police beat for two decades. He was told by the receptionists to hand over his press card and desk key. He couldn't even get his personal stuff out his locker. This man was an alcoholic. He never drunk on the job but did so as soon as he left the building. I saw him once going straight to a pub on the corner of Koch Strasse and Friedrichstrasse. At that time I didn't think much of it. He had given his entire professional life to the paper. You could see that he struggled to do his day job. But in the end he delivered at deadline. A new police reporter was hired, young and energetic. After he had learned the ropes the other one was dismissed. Without warning, appreciation or extra pay. Fired straight and went into unemployment without any chance to find another job. His only hope now is to make it somehow until he gets his pension in about ten years from now.

The second dismissal hit closer to home; Erika, the girl from Thüringen. She still lives at the camp in Marienfelde. Erika is certainly what you would call free spirited and air headed as well. She would discuss assignments to death, would refuse to interview any local politician if she or he was a member of the Social Democratic Party and would make no qualms of her hatred of any immigrant from Eastern Europe. But her biggest flaw was that she never stopped talking about her East German past to the point that it was nauseating. The East does not mean anything for the most West Germans. The GDR is another country where people speak just the same language; but so do people in Austria and Switzerland. The talk about a common history, the dream of a united Germany and the felt sorrow for the "poor brothers and sisters" in the GDR is meaningless talk here in the West. Now, when so many from the East were let go, their counterparts in the West are fearful for their own jobs, housing, benefits, and living standards. They are not in the mood to share. East Germans are foreigners like all the others who try to come here.

Erika has no sensitivity for the concerns of her new fellow citizens. She tells her story no matter what. She did so during an interview with a representative of a concerned citizen action group who wants to limit recreational water sports on Lake Wannsee. According to the complaints Erika told him about her denial to access to a higher education in the East just because her father was a Minister. After her monologue she spent about fifteen minutes getting information regarding increased boat traffic on the lake. You would have not known by reading her article that she had spent only a short time getting the background for her story. Anyway, a call to the editor in-chief by the action group resulted in the immediate dismissal of Erika. The tragedy is that she just had signed a lease for an apartment if she could show three months of consistent income as a freelance writer. Her supervisor at the paper had never given her a warning or advice how to conduct herself at assignments. He just fired her.

Erika called me after she got the bad news, crying into

the phone. I could hear her boyfriend, who had so far just daydreamed about buying a boat to sail to South Africa, in the background cursing at her.

"I don't know what to do! I came here because I thought people would care about me and my story. All what I was told about the Golden West is such a lie. Thomas, people here don't care about us. They don't want us. If I could I would go back."

"To do what?" I ask.

"I don't know. But I would be back on familiar territory. Over there I don't have to second guess people. I know who works for the Stasi. So, I will avoid them. I know who I can tell off-the-cuff jokes to. I probably could get a job at the local library, because the director sleeps with my sister. In a way, things are more honest over there then here." Erika was back on her rant.

"I don't think you should give up so easily. Yes, I agree. Things are different here. But isn't that what we wanted. I realize too that some people here really don't want or care about us. Well, we are here. The constitution guarantees us citizen status and rights. We should run with that and leave our past behind. Not forget about it. I don't mean that. But our reality here is what we have to deal with. Don't open yourself up to another alternative."

"But I am sick of living dormitory style. Sharing a kitchen and bathroom with people I don't know and I don't want to know. Every day I have to hide our few valuables at different places. People steal from each other. People fight. It's terrible. I have to get out of this place. I just found an apartment. But at the same time I lost my job."

I am not sure what to say to her. Erika seems to have reached a low point. I just want to get off the phone with her. I catch myself thinking that I really don't care about her. How awful of me. I should feel sympathy for her. But just listening to her makes me realize how much I want to distance myself from my fellow Easterners. This is my new life. I want his new life. I don't want to be dragged down. I am a Westerner, not by birth. But by wish.

"Erika, I can give you a name and phone number of a guy at *Zitty* magazine. I wrote a couple of articles for them before I started at *Berliner Morgenpost.* Call and see if they are looking for people."

"Thanks. I call you later for the information. Right now I am just too upset to think straight." She hangs up without saying goodbye. I feel bad for her. But I am also glad that I don't have her phone number.

Curious Places and Confusing Choices

"Eat your fucking soup you idiot." I am stunned when the bartender hits the man in front of him in the face. I look at Klaus and Ferdinand. Neither they nor any other patron seem to be alarmed about what just happened.

"Why did he hit the guy? Do they know each other?" I ask Klaus.

"Oh, don't play your Mister Innocent again," he dismisses me. Ferdinand giggles without looking at me. "Didn't you read the name of the bar?" I did, but I didn't think anything of it. But now I put one and one together. The name Knast is not just a name, it's also a theme. The bar is framed off with prison-like bars. Whips and handcuffs are visibly displayed. The guy who was just slapped is chained to his bar stool. He gets wacked again because he stopped eating his soup. I look around. It seems that the three of us are the only ones not dressed in leather. I feel threatened for no reason. No one pays any attention to us. But this scene makes me very uncomfortable. I want to leave. I have heard about S&M stuff but it was just talk or some porno clip I have seen. But this here is raw reality. It's not only weird to me. It turns me off.

Today is my first time out onto the gay bar scene of West Berlin. Knast is our second stop this evening. First we went to Oldtimers. It was kind of funny to watch young guys cozying up to the old guys. "You will find a bar for any desire." Ferdinand was the self-appointed gay bar tour guide for the evening. I had looked forward to our time out on the town but expected just different bars, not playgrounds for the weird. Now that I am at Knast I have no wish to see other bars. Needless to say, Klaus was in his element. He had already downed way too many beers. His restless eyes scan the room. "Want to go downstairs?" A tall man asks Klaus. He wears a pair of black leather pants and a harness made out of chains and leather straps.

423

"Let's go." I had guessed that Klaus must have been here before, but now I knew. They both leave our table. I stare at the back of the guy. His ass is totally exposed. "There is a downstairs?" I ask Ferdinand to bridge the awkward situation.

"Yes, it's a dark room." I am not sure what that means but I don't ask. "Want to have a look?"

"No, thanks. I have seen enough for today. To be honest this is not my kind of a place. I will leave pretty soon anyway."

"You have to loosen up. This is not repressed East Berlin. Here you can play out any fantasy you have. No questions asked, no judgments made. Do you mind if I go downstairs as well?"

"No, go ahead." I look at my half-empty glass of beer. A guy passes by me, rubbing his hand. "I just hit a guy down stairs really hard. I think I broke my wrist," he tells a group of men close by. Now I have really had enough. I dart for the exit door. The smokeless air outside feels good and clears my head as I walk towards U-Bahn station Wittenberg Platz. How does one get attracted to hurting others for mutual pleasure? I am glad that I am a normal gay man only fantasizing about a man who I can build a future with.

Sure, I had been to a sauna at Meineke Strasse several times. Excited every time I go in, ashamed when leave. Nothing ever happened there. However I can't deny that I am always hopeful when I pay the entrance fee. But I am not surprised when I leave without a happy ending. East Berlin, West Berlin...nothing has changed when it comes to me being noticed by other men. I am still the invisible guy.

I talk with my mother almost every day. I miss her more now than when I lived in East Berlin. She is one of the few constants in my life. My new life is all about new things. Every day, so it seems, is about making choices. Regardless of the purpose. Shopping is about selection and pricing it out. Taking public transportation is a decision between saving the fare and walking or not. Eating out is a matter of mood, taste palate and cost. What did I know before about Greek, Indian, Chinese, French, Spanish or Turkish cooking? Wednesday is movie night. In the East a ticket was

1.55 regardless what day of the week. Buying a car means you first figure out if you want a German, Swedish, American, Spanish, French or British one, followed by size, power, color and number of doors. After dark, certain parts of the city are off limits for safety reasons. You don't open the door without making sure you know who is on the other side. It's better not to talk about how much money you make because you don't know what one does with that information.

In the past you just grabbed whatever was available and you had the money to buy it. The East is about reaction instead of being proactive. No steaks in the butcher shop, onion shortage at the grocery store, a long waitlist for a vacation spot at the Baltic Sea: no matter what your wants and needs were it was not yours to decide. Here I can choose my dentist based on I don't know what. Here I can buy a washing machine either from Siemens or Miele based upon brand loyalty or price point. Do I want a green, blue or red sweater is based upon my personal taste. When in the past maddening when I couldn't get Rosenthaler Kadarka red wine anywhere it's now stressful to be sure I get the best deal on a vacuum cleaner. By no means do I want to change back to where I came from. I am doing well. And for the first time in my life I feel like things are going in the right directions. No litmus test anymore to prove dedication to any party, leader, the unwavering friendship to one particular country and its heroic citizens. No blind acceptance of one opinion and world view.

It's now about achievement without ideology. It's now about competition without ratting out somebody to authorities. It's now about making a personal and educated decision without final approval by the collective. But I also learn to see the pros and cons of a dictated society versus a democratic society. It's the weakness in some of us that gives the Eastern Bloc its existence. It's the desire for an effortless life by handing over personal competence and ability. The price: every aspect of your life is ruled, manipulated and laid out from crib to casket. It is the strength and self-motivation in others that guarantees the West its existence. The price: some make it and some do not.

425

Attempts to fuse the positives of both worlds as seen so often in the past produce illusion, and most of all failure, in the end. It may be a good exercise for the brain to look for a way into a paradise forever. The goal to better the world is better pursued as an intellectual exchange of like minded individuals than to actually put it to task. The reality is that there is no good without bad, no plus without minus, God without Devil. All the human attempts throughout history to build the land of honey on earth are in the end a journey into the impossible. However, there is nothing wrong with seeking it. I am glad that I can make the journey.

Senior Caravans, Fake Marriages, and Leaving Klaus

Talking to my mother in the evenings is also about comfort and familiarity. I can visualize the chair she sits in when she listens to me on the phone. I tell her about all the positive things that happen to me. My freelance job at *Morgenpost*, furnishing the apartment at Fasanen Strasse, walking through Tiergarten Park, wandering through Karstadt, Wertheim and KDW department stores, my guarded studying of vacation magazines, my new friends Frank and Knut. Of course I have to tell her about my new leather jacket. I paid 350 Marks. The next day, the beginning of the Summer End Sale, the same jacket was down to 99 Marks. I think my mother is relieved that my life on the other side of the Wall is off to a positive start. With every phone call I deflate her fear that I would experience a similar bad beginning like she and her brother had when they arrived in the American Zone after the long and merciless less trek from lost Silesia into the Western part of Germany.

No matter where my exhausted grandparents tried to make a new home along the way they were unwelcomed refugees. Strangers in their own land. Düsseldorf, their final destination in the early Fifties, ended up to be the worst of all stops. The well-to-do relatives here had no space except a dingy basement. Forgotten were the good times they had when they visited my grandparents in their big house with the big dining room table loaded with food. Now, after losing everything, they were reduced to outcast status by their own family as well as by their new neighbors in a shabby apartment house, where my grandmother moved her family because she couldn't take it anymore to live below street level in her cousin's home in the affluent neighborhood of Geressheim.

My mother, being my mother, cautions me at the end of every phone call to be careful and not to take anything for

427

granted. I let her be. Sometimes I wonder if she really addresses me with her warnings or the Stasi agents who without a doubt listen to our conversations. After all, she and her family have to continue to live in the Worker's Paradise.

It's all about routine for me. Settling in and getting familiar with the unfamiliar helps me to feel at home again. Being repetitive day after day makes me feel good and more and more at ease. I am also already able to satisfy my materialistic side. The stores at Wilmersdorfer Strasse have what I want. They also offer all the things my East German relatives would like to have. Nice fabrics my mother can bring to her tailor for dresses, sweaters for my stepfather, jeans for my brother, knickknacks from Eduscho for my parents' household. At Aldi supermarket I shop for chocolate, yogurt, cheese, soap and shower gel. The canvas bag on wheels I got for Tata is easily filled to the top.

My grandmother is now part of a well-organized cottage industry where East German senior citizens function as sherpas to help to ease the notorious shortage of daily consumer goods in the East. Every time I send her off with a full bag at Friedrich Strasse station the crossing point feels like a busy rest stop. It could be almost described as comically entertaining to watch how Westerners get their relatives ready for the border crossing if it wasn't for the fact that almost all of them are elderly, some of them even need walking sticks. Their backs are bent with age. It's a slow continuous caravan that pushes, pulls and drags through the swinging double doors which separate the East from the West, followed by another underground tunnel before the trek ascends to street level. There the human mules are anxiously awaited and unburdened by the Easterners. The mood is always a mix of exhaustion, relief and joy.

Knowingly or not, some of the schleppers break the East German customs rules over and over. I, for instance, never tell Tata that she has more than the allowed amount of coffee and cigarettes in her bag. When I got my mother a small yucca palm tree she wanted so very much for her living room I buried it under boxes of bandages. Plants are on the restricted list. If the border guard would try to check

428

her bag my grandmother could tell him that it's full of needed bandages for her son-in law. This is true. My stepfather had fallen off of the ladder and severely injured his right leg. A misguided treatment left him with an open and seeping wound, constantly needing to be washed and re-bandaged. However, his doctor doesn't have enough bandages and had asked Heinz to get them from the West.

Interestingly enough that doctor is a proud Party member and, never lets a consultation go by without praising the greatness of the health care system in the GDR. He explains the disrupted supply of bandages with the price increase for cotton thanks to the inhuman capitalistic trade practices. "The GDR just cannot afford these inflated prices." What he forgets to mention is that the Soviet Union, one of the major cotton producers, sells its product for hard currency on the world market then trades it with its compatriots in the Eastern Bloc. Another example of the seemingly grotesqueness of a system whose functionality depends so much on the continuous existence of its enemies.

Klaus and I get ready for our ski vacation in the Tatra mountains, our winter destination for many years. Only this time we are going there as West Germans meeting our friends from the East. I am very much looking forward to seeing our friend Monika for the first time since we left East Berlin. However our trip will be not without a tedious detour. The GDR does not allow former citizens to cross over its territory except for three designated roads connecting West Berlin with the West Germany territory. That means we have to go south to cross at the border control in Dannenwald into West Germany. From there we have to ride to the border crossing into Czechoslovakia. After that we turn east paralleling the common border with East Germany to our destination. A ridiculous journey considering that it doubles our travel time. No one is unpunished when leaving the Dictatorship of the Proletariat.

Monika is one of the very few friends who were not afraid to stay in touch with us after Klaus and I submitted our Exit Application. It was amazing and disappointing at the same time to see how many of our good and close friends turned their backs. Not because of socialist conviction but because they were scared of what the GDR authorities would do to them if they continued to be our friends. To what extent some of them would go to avoid us like a deadly disease was baffling, sometimes comically so. One of my former colleagues crossed the street when she saw me coming towards her. Another one hushed by me whispering "I am sorry. Don't think badly about me." Our friend Maria, waiting for the permission to leave East Berlin herself, cut contact with us out of fear that being friends with us would diminish her chance to get her papers. Kirstin, a biologist with a PhD, was on the waiting list to be approved to attend a conference in Austria. Of course she also cut contact with us.

The saddest reason for not visiting us anymore came from Karsten. Shortly before we submitted our application he was informed by the housing authorities that his waiting time for an apartment was now only a couple more months. His waiting time to buy a Trabant was less than three years. He applied to buy a car seven years earlier after his mother had left him some money. "To be honest, the apartment and the car are more important to me than our friendship," he told us when we ran into him at Burgfrieden bar.

Somehow, some of those friends tracked us down after we moved to West Berlin. Kirstin, the biologist, called one evening to tell us that she was in Munich to present a paper and would like to stop by on her way back to East Berlin. "I know it sounds odd contacting you. But you have to understand I could not jeopardize my chance to meet other scientists."

"Don't worry. I think I am the lucky one, not you. You have to go back and duck and conform in hopes of being approved for another trip to the West."

"I wonder if you could help me?" Kirstin was totally ignoring my remarks, "If I stayed with you for a night I could go to the welfare office in your district and declare you as my cousin. That will entitle me to the 25 Marks the West gives to a visiting Easterner."

"Sorry Kirstin but I won't be part of that plot. Remember, *you* gave up our friendship. Now, when it is convenient, you want to reclaim it in order to get 25 Marks. Ask your beloved Party for help." After that I hang up on her. I know I should have been bigger than that. But at that moment I enjoyed my leverage.

A couple of weeks ago Karsten called. I was surprised that he found our phone number. Before I could ask him how he is doing he asks me if I could call him back right away because it was cheaper for me than for him. I felt very tempted not to call him back. But I did.

"You would not believe it, I got an apartment," he started the conversation without any attempt to ask how we were doing. It had been almost six months since we had seen each other for the last time.

"That's great. Where is it?"

"In Marzahn."

"That's pretty far from where you work, isn't it?"

"I know. But the flat is in a brand new building, has a balcony and central heat. There is even a built-in kitchen." As Karsten continues to describe his new apartment I remember witnessing the beginnings of Marzahn. Working as a reporter in the East I had to write about the genius of the GDR apparatus to build a whole new city from the ground up. Marzahn was a creation of the Party as an attempt to ease the shortage of housing in the East. In order to build as many apartments in the least amount of time, GDR architects were ordered to create a fast-system for vast housing complexes. Their answer: modular building systems or Platten-Bauweise. Pre-fabricated concrete walls would be assembled like a puzzle. The result: a beehive for humans. However, the creation of Marzahn was not without controversy and protest from Western Allies. When Berlin was cut up into the four military zones after the War it was also determined that each of these zones could not be altered in any way including adding space to it. East Berlin, the Russian zones, had eight boroughs at the time of the agreement. With the development and incorporation of Marzahn East Berlin grew by one more district. The GDR *Nomenklatura* even called it loudly and proudly the Ninth borough. The Russians and the East Germans authorities didn't care about the post-war Potsdam Agreement or the

Western Allies.

"I finally have my own four walls," Karsten couldn't stop talking about his new place. "The reason I am calling you is I was hoping that you could get me ceramic tiles for my bathroom. A friend's mother, who can travel to West Berlin, could pick them up one box at a time. As you know, it is close to impossible to get nice tiles here. I really would like dark blue ones." Another of our former friends who turned their backs is now asking for help. I cannot help feeling used.

"How many tiles would you need?"

"I measured for about 400 quadrate meter wall space to be covered."

"Wow, that sounds like a lot."

"My friend's mother brought back a brochure, where I read that one tile cost about 65 Pfennig." Is he hinting that we should pay for his tiles? I wonder.

"I really have no clue what tiles cost here. I have to check it and let you know, " I say.

"Maybe there is something I can buy here for you in exchange for paying for the tiles?"

"What do you think I want from the East that I cannot get here?" I laugh at his proposal.

"I know. It was just a suggestion because I didn't want you to think that I want you to pay for my tiles and get nothing in return." Now I am really getting annoyed with him. There is no way that I will pay for his tiles.

"Sorry Karsten, I will not buy you the tiles. If you want to give me the money, sure. Otherwise you have to find somebody else. We just moved here. We are starting from scratch."

"Excuse me that I am asking you for a little help. I see it took only a couple of months and you've turned into a selfish Westerner."

"Karsten, we have to work here for our money too. It does not grow on trees."

"I thought we were friends who would help each other in need."

"Well, you should have thought about it when you cut us off out of fear or whatever." I have had enough and slam the phone down.

What an outrageous expectation: to help just because I could. I didn't leave the East just to be haunted by, it including people who were not able to separate friendships from a sick system that wants everybody to live in fear. If blue tiles are so very important to Karsten than he should leave the country that is not able to produce them. If Kirstin is so eager to have an intellectual exchange of scientific findings across borders than she should demand the opportunity to do so and not give up on friends who decide to leave a system that limits even basic human desires. From now on I will be supportive to friends in the East if they decide to leave as well, but I won't be an enabler who makes their lives over there tolerable so they can continue to be willingly complacent. I left because I couldn't stand what the apparatus did to me. I certainly won't play any part in helping its continuous clinging to life. I am convinced that without the feeding tubes from the West the East would have been dead a long time ago. I am already guilty by supporting my family. I hope that I can cut that life line someday after I have successfully convinced my parents and brother to get out of there as well.

Charlotte, the Stage Manager

Charlotte is one of the stage managers at Metropol Theater. Like many others, working in Berlin is the ultimate career goal for her; at least it was prior to being hired away from Eisenach. Stations before were Rostock, Neubrandenburg, Schwerin and Erfurt. Leaving the "Province" behind didn't only mean saying good-bye to provinciality, tight budgets, meager salaries and deplorable roommate situations. Berlin means Hauptstadt, a sense of worldliness even if that it means also seeing non East Germans walking the streets. Haupstadt comes with perks: fresh potatoes most of the time, Western TV without interference, unobstructed listening to Radio Europe, RIAS and BBC as well as the wellness bath in Friedrichshain district, another prestigious project to showcase socialistic achievement. That this water complex was only possible by cancelling smaller public recreational projects in the rest of the Republic is a scandal in itself, but certainly not a first one. The *Nomenklatura* lives in the Hauptstadt and not in the underbelly of the paradise of the proletariat.

Anyway, Charlotte's wish came true. She had aimed for the Deutsche Staatsoper or even Komische Oper. By landing a job at Metropol Theater was a step in the right direction. She had a foot in the door. Delusion followed in the fast lane. Stage managing lofty operettas like "My Fair Lady" or "Im weissen Roessel" was not a challenge for her. Attempts to be part of the production process were always stopped from above. Christine was not part of any clique. She was outside of the inner circle. She voiced frustration, a sure recipe for being kept at arm's length. She had to make a choice between hanging on to the status quo, going back into the grayness of a second and third rated provincial theater scene or to find a match to her aspirations on the other side of the iron curtain.

A good friend of hers works as a costume designer in West Germany. She could help her land a job there.

Charlotte's friend's boyfriend also had connections. Plans grew into shape, steps were imagined, her escape finalized. Then, luck would have it that Charlotte got a visitation visa for a week in order to attend her aunt's eightieth birthday in Munich. Not for a second did Charlotte contemplate returning to the East after the week of allowed travel to the West. In the middle of the night she would leave her apartment with boxes packed with personal items. She would bring them to trusted friends who would later send the boxes to her. She made copies of her keys, leaving them also with friends. If they had the courage they could come in the middle of the night and take furniture and anything that they were willing to risk taking. It had to be done during the week that she officially was on her Western trip. After Charlotte did not report back, the authorities would realize that she escaped the GDR and her possessions will be taken by the State.

Charlotte felt badly about the left-behind antiques: the Biedermeier desk, her grandfather had used in his family medical practice; the grand piano her mother had played on. Leaving the GDR for good against the will of the dictatorship of the proletariat meant being stripped of your personal past and heirlooms. Everybody knows it. Charlotte knows it. But looking at her apartment for the last time before locking it and making her way to Palace of Tears at Friedrichstrasse station was heart wrenching nevertheless. Shedding what was part of her life felt like dying.

Even though she had bought a railroad ticket to Munich, she got off as soon as the train crossed into West German territory. Her friend and boyfriend picked her up in Paderborn. It felt so good to be out off what lay just a few kilometers behind her. Happy times with good food, wine and an unexpected threesome in a hotel room along the Autobahn on the way to Essen. Charlotte was settled on the sofa in the living room for the time being until she found her own space. Her friend's boyfriend would join her many more times on the sofa. The promised job possibilities at a theater were just that, a promise, and not based in reality. She felt discouraged, nervous at times. After two month as a new Westerner she felt a lump under her left armpit. The biopsy came back in just one day. The follow-up diagnosis was devastating: stage three cancer.

Charlotte felt punished, but she wasn't sure for what. Maybe she should not have challenged her luck and stayed at Metropol Theater and waited for a career advance or retirement. She was forty-five years old and for the first time in her life she had no plan, no path to follow. Worse, no energy to think about a future. She had put all her hopes into whatever would come after the DDR. But she had not mapped out her hopes. She had not prepared for a plan B or C if A fell through. She had not included sickness into her life. It took hold of her unexpectedly and brutally.

She asked her friend if she could stay on the couch. Her friend said yes. She asked her physician for the right amount of morphine. He got her the doses. She reached stage four soon after. The twelve boxes she had carried to friends to be shipped to her later on all arrived and were stacked in the living room of her friend. Charlotte did not open one.

* * *

I am under contract. I am officially a staff reporter at *Berliner Morgenpost.* I am the only one of the freelancer crew who originally started at Zehlendorf office to be given the opportunity. Erika is dismissed. Frederike , rumor has it, will be joining the editor-in-chief's office overseeing the final editing of the paper: a nice jump considering her weak background in newspaper editing. I like her and so does the editor-in chief...in a different way than I do. She is quick and smart, but not pretty in a conventional way. However, a smile and flirting charm opens older men's hearts and pants. When she announced she interviewed with Pan Am to become a flight attendant after she learned she would not be offered a staff contract, the editor-in chief met her for coffee. I am happy for Frederike. I don't think she has what it takes to be a reporter running from appointment to appointment and delivering articles on or before deadline, but she certainly lifts the average age in the editor-in chief's staff office.

After I told Stefan, one of the other freelancers, that I had moved up to staff reporter he asked me bluntly "How did you do that? It must have something to do with the fact that you are from the East." He could not hide his disdain for me and my advancement. Stefan has a degree in French literature and economics and was out of work for years until he landed the freelance job at the Zehlendorf office of *Berliner Morgenpost*. From the first moment he acted like an intimidating and a pompous ass. He would refuse assignments like covering an opening of a new kindergarten or ballpark. He thinks interviewing local politicians sucks.

In his mind they are all corrupt anyway. He never can shut up and infuses his opinion into everything. In other words, Stefan is basically a nightmare for any team leader. His presence makes everybody's eyes roll. Of course, he is totally oblivious of his surroundings. He thinks of himself as the center of the universe. That also includes his physical appearance. Skinny as a rail, always bad breath, greasy hair and stained clothes don't faze him. If he's not talking about his weird world views, he is babbling about women he has laid or is going to lay. Simply put, he is someone I have nothing in common with. On the other hand I am little bit weary of him. He is the type who just can't wait to see somebody else to mess up. I know all eyes will be on me for a while.

I start to believe I was born to be a Westerner. Seriously. Anything I achieved in the East was always coupled with setbacks and struggles to say the least. I was either not smart enough, not fit enough, born into the wrong family, didn't have the right connections, was not pretty to make the cut, not naturally talented to be sponsored, politically not trustworthy, gay and never part of the in crowd. It was a life on a leash. With the voidance of my GDR-citizenship things have changed dramatically. What I was not before I am now: lucky.

I am very thankful. And proud. But I am also torn. Torn not knowing what to do with my personal life. I feel like I should not challenge my good fortune. Maybe I should stay with Klaus to counterbalance my good fortune? Is accepting his indiscretions the price I have to pay to keep the rest in my favor? I know it's up to me to decide to leave the relationship. He will never end it. He needs me. I don't need him. I am convinced that he will endanger me with his reckless lifestyle. I am stressed because I constantly have to defend our home against intruders and people who want to take advantage of us. I feel like, some of our acquaintances think, it is our obligation to help them since we have made it and they haven't. Klaus, in an almost pathological way, will share anything with others just to get his two seconds of satisfaction and attention. People who recently were let go from East Germany and have somehow gotten our address crash on our sofa, invite themselves for dinner, ask to borrow our car, want us to co-sign leases and ask for money. It seems also that the Eastern authorities have become more lenient in giving visitation visa to non-seniors. Some of them also knock on our door. Unlike Klaus, I don't like total strangers staying with us. For Klaus it presents an ample opportunity for hook ups.

He thinks I don't notice. Having lived nine years with a man who fucks himself through life, I have become an expert in knowing when he has had his little side tricks. Scribbled phone numbers on pieces of napkins, cum-smelling underwear, stained bed sheets, whispered phone conversations or just simple slip ups when Klaus tells me about people he knows are sure signs of his indiscretions. I also can tell when Klaus introduces men to me, if they already slept together or they're going to. Their interactions with each other are such a telltale sign and often just hilarious in their attempt to hide their sexual past from me. I don't bother to confront them about their indiscretions.

Even though Klaus makes it easy for anybody to get a piece of his ass, I always wonder about the character of those who know that Klaus and I live together. Value, morals, responsibilities, respect: for them those are just empty words. When I confront Klaus about the fact that our apartment seem to have a revolving door he calls me selfish, unwilling to share. He is right, I am not willing to share what I have with anybody who thinks we should because we can. What is in it for me when I open our door to people who are just selfish, and in many cases losers? I want to align myself with winners who want go places. I can tell Klaus is already very content with what he has. He makes enough money to support his lifestyle. His new job as a teacher at the vocational school is safe and, he never can get fired. That is all the security he wants to continue his he pathological drive for drinking and sex. No other ambition is left.

He laughed at me when I told him I want to put money aside to buy an apartment. He brushes travel magazines off the table when I ask him to look at them so we could make plans to see other countries. Anything to do with the future is an inconvenience to him. He has no plans other than to get his paycheck at the end of each month. Aside from his constant cheating on me, the prospect of stagnation is not attractive to me. Living with Klaus limits me in more than one respect. Why can't I take the next step? What else should happen before I pack up?

I feel like I can't shed my Eastern past. It's like pulling on rubber and never getting beyond a certain point. Our friends Claudia and Marlene have decided that they would like to leave the GDR. I am not surprised about their wish. I am just caught off guard by how they want to get out: they want to marry Klaus and me. It seems so ludicrous to think that the East German authorities wouldn't see how phony that is. It's a well-documented fact that Klaus and I are a couple. Why in the world would the apparatus even accept an application for a marriage license? Claudia and Marlene think that I cut the East Germans too much slack, thinking that they would be able to connect the dots to the result that the marriages would be a charade. I don't agree. I don't understand why they don't just base their request to leave on a family reunion. Both have aunts and uncles in the West. Claudia's reasoning is that she would have to officially disown her parents in order to argue that she now wants to live close to her uncle. Point well taken. I am highly skeptical that Claudia and Marlene will ever get the permission to marry Klaus and me. Not only for obvious reasons.

In order to marry them we would need a permit to go back into East Berlin for the wedding. My many attempts to visit my parents or my grandmother were all denied so far. Not a surprise to me. Of course Klaus and I want to help Marlene and Claudia, but it seems a waste of effort, hope

439

and time. Then my plan to leave Klaus would be stalled. For some reason I think I should stay with him if we want to go through with these fake wedding plans. No one in the East has any indication that I am determined to move out soon. I also have to postpone my plans to meet my parents in Karlsbad because Claudia and Marlene want us to meet in Czechoslovakia as soon as possible to talk about the plan of action in more detail. A meeting there would also show the East Germans that we are determined to be together.

The meeting will be costly since I would to have to pay for the hotel. East Germans only can exchange 25 Marks per day when traveling to Czechoslovakia. Not enough to pay for even a fleabag hotel and food. The least expensive hotel rooms in Prague, Karlsbad or Marienbad run about 30 to 40 East Marks: a sign of a very unbrotherly behavior by two countries in reality restricting their own people from traveling freely because they cannot pay for food and lodging. The ones who try to make it work despite the proletarian hurdles load their cars with as much canned food and bread as they can. That way they don't have to spend any money on groceries. Packing a tent also eliminates the hotel expense. The brave just pretend to travel for two weeks to Czecheslovakia in order to exchange more money, but return after a week. That is very risky because the next time they want to travel to Czechoslovakia they either have to show that they still have money left from their previous trip, shortened by a week, or face the possibility that their entrance into the country will be denied because they deliberately lied about the anticipated length of the previous trip.

As a Westerner I have to exchange a daily determined amount. But since the exchange rate from West Marks into Czechoslovakian Kronen is very, very favorable for me I have way too much money to spend there. There is nothing I want to buy that I couldn't get where I live now. That means I have to book an expensive hotel and eat in expensive restaurants: but expensive in Communist Czechoslovakia does not mean good and high quality. In the end, it does not matter where you come from to visit Czechoslovakia, from the East or the West. The dictatorship takes advantage of their foreign tourists

That all goes through my head as I prepare for a trip to Karlsbad that really doesn't make any sense, and is expensive. Sure, I look forward to seeing Claudia and Marlene. But I would rather got to Italy and not to an unpleasant country like this one.

We are on our way to Karlsbad. The ride is smooth but painstakingly long, because of an annoying detour through parts of southern West Germany in order to cross into Czechoslovakia. Only Claudia will meet us. Marlene has decided not to come. She was too afraid for her safety. I am not sure I understand her fear. What could happen? The East German border control sends her back after they find out that she is going to meet her future husband now living in the West? Or she is arrested because the East German border control finds out that she is going to meet her future husband now living in the West and suspects that this whole marriage plan is a big lie? Either way, I think it only would help her case to get out of the GDR. There must be more behind her decision to cancel her trip on short notice.

Claudia is simply pissed that Marlene did not come with her to meet us. "Marlene has always looked after her own best interests. If we for some reason are never allowed to leave the East she always can play naive and claim that she really never wanted to leave. Not coming to Karlsbad she could show as evidence for her half-hearted intent of getting to the West, arguing she was kind of confused and didn't think everythins through. Marlene thinks only about Marlene."

Our time in Karlsbad is limited. We mostly walk through this once glamorous spa town to talk about our next step. We think that moving around makes it harder to be watched and listened to. Klaus suggests that he and I should get different mailing addresses in West Berlin. When Marlene and Claudia officially apply for the marriage license the East German bureaucrats would be derailed by the fact that Klaus and I live at different residences. I think that's total nonsense. For one thing, they know that Klaus and I are gay. They know that we were a couple when we submitted our Exit Application. And I am sure they know that we are living in the same apartment in West Berlin. Why in the world should we put on a charade that is so easy to figure out? We should do this as straightforward as we can. Let them figure it out.

Claudia agrees with me. Klaus still lives with the illusion that people think he is not really gay. He likes to put up this front whenever he can. That his behavior and appearance makes those attempts just laughable doesn't seem to bother him a bit. Anyway, we decided that Marlene and Klaus will be a couple and Claudia and I will be the other couple. We convinced the receptionist at our hotel to loan us a type writer so that Klaus and I could put on paper our unshakable desire to marry our girlfriends and have them reunited with us as soon as possible in West Berlin. Blah blah blah. These letters will be attached to Claudia's and Marlene's marriage applications.

The weather is nice enough that I could type both letters addressed to the GDR-Secretary of the Interior, Horst Dickel, outside of our hotel. This is another layer of safety we use. We think dictating the letters in the hotel room would have not been a good idea. The room could be bugged. The little park close by seems the perfect spot to bring the typewriter to. What a hoot! Our loud laugh amplified by a bottle of Krim Sekt put smiles on passersby. If they only knew what we were cooking up. What completely slipped my mind was the fact that you cannot find a copy place in all of Karlsbad. Claudia and I split the task of retyping each of the two letters many more times. Tedious but unavoidable so that we all can have at least one copy of each letter.

I am still very skeptical that the East will ever issue a marriage permit. It is so blatantly fake. On the other hand I think by allowing us to getting married the East can fill a statistic that they can show to the world. This statistic could help their tarnished human rights records. Allowing inter-German marriages not only saves face, it can also serve as evidence that the GDR is in compliance with the Helsinki Agreement, an agreement they signed. Marriage permits play very well in their own sick minds; they would rather permit marriage than let people go because of the political reasons. Our marriage adds two more to the list of humanitarian actions by the GDR, which is so eager to be internationally recognized as a sovereign country. The biggest dream of the apparatus is to become a member of the UN. The Party knows how much weight the West puts on human rights.

I have a goal: I want to visit three countries per year. Klaus thinks that's crazy. But I don't care what he thinks. Seeing the world was what made me leave the East. I don't know why; it's just three different countries and not four or six. Three seems just a reasonable number. I have six weeks of vacation and a job that pays well. I am already a travel overachiever. We have been to Paris, London and Vienna. Two weeks in Morocco are booked for the end of the year but I still feel like I am running against the clock. In a way my life started seven months ago when I squeezed through the narrow check point alley below the Palace of the Tears with the burning eyes of the GDR border guard on me. That means I am almost twenty-eight years behind of all of my newly won fellow Western countrymen. How can I catch up or even surpass them? I know I have to relax and be thankful for what I have done and reached so far. But I am so hungry to experience on my own what a system denied me by limiting my mobility and filtering the outside world through a prism that distorts reality. Now I am on a journey where I know the beginning but have no intention to learn about its end.

Wherever I go I collect travel magazines and read them from front to cover. I can get lost standing in front of travel agencies reading their alluring special offers. I could go to any of those places advertised. I have no list with priority countries or regions. China, yes. Fiji, of course. Beach vacation in Kenya, intriguing. Majorca, Tenerife, Malta, sounds good. New York, Rio, Cairo, in a heartbeat. I must admit that I will leave continental Europe for later. Travel means flying for hours, arriving where it is so different. Klaus thinks we should take our car and explore Bavaria, cruise the Rhine, visit Heidelberg and take photos of the Dom in Cologne. I tell him that we can do all these things on a weekend here and there. On my vacations I want to go as far away as possible. Again, it's not so much the destination I have in mind. It's the ride to get there that I long for. I am most excited waiting at the airport terminal full of anticipation and joy and then stepping off the airplane at the destination. I hate, hate coming back.

And now, when the world is at my fingertips, I compromise, give in because of my friends Frank and Knut who tell me I should go to Verona for the Opera Festival. I love opera. I am sure I will enjoy the city and have a picture taken under the famous balcony where Romeo serenaded Julia. But going there for three weeks shortens my overall time off by twenty-eight days this year. I would rather hike through Thailand. But Frank and Knut nagged and nagged until I gave in to join them to go to Gardasee Lake which is very close to Verona. I feel obligated to do so because they have both become very good friends of mine. I run out of reasons why I didn't want to go Italy because there no real reason why I shouldn't go. I have not been to Italy. So what's the problem? It's not a problem at all. But Turkey, for instance, is so much further, so very different, so not Europe. And that is what I really want. Frank and Knut don't understand that, Klaus does not care and I could not stand up for myself.

My parents also want us to meet in Zopot on the Baltic Sea during their summer vacation. My mother's company awarded her a two-week stay there. Poland is a country I can get a visa for without problems but it will be a long journey. Again, I cannot transit directly through the GDR into Poland. I have to use one of the three corridors like the highways from West Berlin to West Germany. Then I have to take a ferry that does not pass through the Baltic Sea waters of East Germany to Poland. The ferry ride alone is twenty-four hours. Since there is only one boat connection per week I will have to stay five days in Zopot. Of course I want to see my parents and my brother...but Poland of all places?

Also, the Baltic Sea is so contaminated that swimming is prohibited. I envision us sitting on the beach looking at an ocean that is basically dead. Then there is the cost factor.

The ferry ride is not cheap and the Poles demand that I exchange my West Marks one for one into Zlotys. A rip off because equalizing a strong and internationally traded Deutsch Mark with a currency that has no weight outside of Poland whatsoever is another sign of the delusional self perception of each the Eastern Bloc countries.

I am not sure what to do with all that Polish money. I will be staying at friends of my parents but they expect me to pay for the room in West Marks. I certainly get their desire to have West Marks, because on the black market it's worth packs of Polish Zlotys. Anyway, I have to accept the rules and regulations of a Communist-run state if I want to see my family. Klaus makes light of it: "You want to see three countries per year. Now you only have to travel to two others next year." If these Communists were normal people I could stay in Berlin and take the subway from my house to my mother's house. But they are not normal people and a twenty-minute subway ride turns into a three-day journey, passing through two countries and one ocean. It's insane.

I rush home. Work is pretty busy these days. *Berliner Morgenost* is opening a new satellite office in the Reinickendorf district to further expand the local reporting. I am one of two staff reporters. Between leasing the right space and getting up to speed, making our rounds to local politicians, business owners, and party offices and interviewing potential freelancers my days at the paper are long and intense. But today I leave earlier than usual. Klaus's aunt is visiting and I want the apartment perfect. Aunt Maria, who I never met, is not really a relative of his. It was his mother's best friend and Maria's son was Klaus' best friend in school back in Dresden. Maria still lives there. Klaus had invited her to come to West Berlin for a couple of days. She is almost eighty years old. Therefore she didn't have a problem getting a travel permit from the East German authorities. Klaus is not home yet. That leaves me time to do the last bit of cleaning, getting her bed ready and setting the table for dinner.

As soon as I open our apartment door I notice that something looks different but at the moment I can't pinpoint what it is. I am too pressed for time. I pull sheets and extra pillows out of the closet in our bedroom. One of the pillows drops onto my desk. It takes a couple of seconds to realize, that the desk is total bare of anything except my typewriter. What happened to the framed pictures I had displayed on the top shelf of the desk? I look at the wall above. Empty as well. I stop what I am doing and look under the desk and behind it. Maybe the pictures fell off the wall? Nothing. That is weird, I think. Did someone break into our apartment? What else is missing?

I reach into the small armoire next to our bed where I keep our valuables and passports. It's all there. I go back to the desk and open the bottom drawer. I have to pull hard because it's stuck. I reach in to the small opening to get whatever is blocking the drawer. I feel items I can't identify, but I am able to press them hard enough so that I can pry the drawer open. I look at the contents in disbelief. I see the picture frames that I had on the desk. I stare at a photo showing Klaus and I under the Eifel Tower. Another shows us embracing during a party at Ferdinand's house. An enlarged photo that was hanging above the desk shows my parents, Klaus and I sitting on a bench in Karlsbad taken during our first trip there to meet my mother and stepfather for a long weekend. I am speechless.

Why would Klaus stuff them in the drawer? It was him in the first place who selected them, framed them and hung them. I go into our hallway. The wall next to the wardrobe that had more of our photos is completely empty. Not even a nail left. Now I realize why I felt that something was out of place when I entered the apartment earlier. But why would Klaus take all of our personal photos and hide them? Things between us are not good, but they're calm. We are now more or less roommates sleeping in the same bed, but not with each other. We spend time with each other whenever we want to.

Agreed, that is not very often. I lose myself increasingly in work, Klaus is involved in his usual pastime; alcohol and the men he picks up. But to our friends we are still a couple. So why would he start redecorating the apartment? Is he sending me a message that we should call it quits? Knowing him he would do it in a more dramatic way like writing me heart-wrenching notes as he did in the past when I was on the verge of leaving. Or throwing all the things I had given him over the years in the middle of the living room. But taking our pictures down does not make any sense. This is really odd and I will confront him as soon as he comes home. Definitely before we go to meet his aunt at the Bahnhof Zoo train station. I pick up where I had stopped getting ready for our visitor. My brain is pounding with more questions about the pictures.

I am on the balcony when I hear the lock turn in our apartment door. Only one glimpse at Klaus and I can see he has been drinking. That certainly does not calm me down.

"Two questions. Why did you take all of our pictures down and, why are you drunk at five o'clock in the afternoon?"I start right into him. His eyes go blank. He retreats behind this imaginary wall I know so well and can't penetrate. Now I am furious. "Klaus answer me. Why did you stuff our pictures in the drawer? I fucking don't care why you are drunk. So, forget my second question." He just stands in the middle of the hallway his eyes and shoulders down. He looks like a little kid that was caught doing something wrong. Despite the fact that my emotions spiral into new negative highs I feel pity for this grown man in front of me. After almost ten years of sharing my life with him I still don't know if he is just a good actor or just a lost soul who can't help being the way he is? I probably will never know the answer. My caring for Klaus has turned into indifference. So, this "poor little me" display does not stop me from confronting him until I have an answer. "Klaus you can't do this. I want to know why you did this."

"I am sorry." His eyes meet mine. Tears run down his face. "I am sorry that I took our pictures down and I am sorry that I am drunk." His voice trembles. "I know it was wrong. But I don't want my aunt to know that we are a couple. My mother killed herself because she found out that I was gay. I don't want her best friend to know about me. Please you have to understand." Klaus sinks to his knees. Now comes the drama part, I think.

"Your mother didn't kill herself because she found out

Thomas P.W. Schardt

you are gay. Stop that guilt thing. She killed herself because she was unbearably lonesome after your stepfather died. If there was a reason for your mother to be upset then maybe it was the fact that she had to find out on her own that you were gay. You should have told her yourself. Running from the truth is not the solution."

I am enraged. It took a lot of energy to keep my voice down. "Don't kid yourself that your aunt won't realize what's going on here. We live in a one-bedroom apartment with one bed. Taking pictures off the wall is a half-assed attempt to cover up what you can't and shouldn't cover up. You tell me all the time how much you need me. That I am your life and you can't live without me. This just a freaking lie."

"I don't know what to tell you. I am really sorry. But what's the big deal to take the pictures down for a couple of days? The fact is that I will not tell my aunt that I am gay or that we are more than roommates." I look at Klaus still kneeling on the floor. Our many years together, our ups and downs have pulled me slowly away from him. What just happened turned him into a total stranger.

"Well, I guess there is nothing much to say. I am hurt. Not so much because you can't tell your aunt that I am the man you spent the past ten years together, I am hurt because I let you hurt me over and over again. Don't worry, your aunt won't know about me because I won't be around." I feel cold shivers running through my body.

I don't know where to go. I only know that I have to find a place for the next few days. I try to collect myself. I need to pack things I would need. I am frantic. Grabbing shirts, pants, socks. Throwing everything on the bed. I have to go to the basement to get suitcases. I am running back and forth. And Klaus is still kneeling on the floor trying to catch my eye. I don't want to look at him. It's over, man. I can't believe it, I am finally doing it. I wish the end would be a little bit more organized and controlled. Right now, all that I can think of is getting out of the apartment. I could scream.

I know what I am doing but I don't know where to go. Maybe I should go to a hotel? I am sure Frank and Knut would let me stay with them. But it does not feel right. The

448

last thing I need is to get advice what to do next and what they would do if they were in my shoes. But I don't need friends right now. I need a place to stay. Ferdinand is out of the question as well. He made it very clear that he never will get involved with others' personal shit. He hates to take sides. I need to make a plan. First I will get my stuff together and put everything in the car. Then we will see. Yes, I will do that. I stop and count to ten. I feel much calmer now. My thoughts stop tumbling. I press my fingertips together. Now, my hands don't shake anymore.

"Please don't go." I jump because Klaus is right behind me, just a few inches from my back. I didn't hear him move. I turn around. His face is red. I can see the dried lines of his tears.

"Don't please me, please. You made me into a problem. The problem will be gone so you can have a splendid time with your aunt. Isn't what you want?" I try to get Klaus out of my personal space. He does not move. He spreads his arms. I feel caught between him and the foot of the bed.

"Klaus let me pass."

"No. You will leave when I tell you to. Not the other way around." I am very familiar with his icy voice. I have heard it so many times in the past. I know what will follow. It has happened so many times before too. The only difference between then and right now is I will not allow him to attack me. I quickly duck under his right arm still spread wide. But he is faster. His hand hit my chest hard. I lose my balance and fall backwards on the bed. He jumps on me and pins my arms to the side. I am totally surprised by his strength. My chest still hurts from his punch. I am spread eagle and unable to move. It all happens so fast. He kneels on my upper arms.

"Klaus stop, please. You are hurting me."

"Thomas please, don't please me." His sarcasm is not lost on me. "I told you, I will tell you when you can leave. Now, I want you to turn on your stomach."

"Oh God, Klaus don't do that, please. Let me go, please."

"Turn."

"I can't. You have to let go of my arms." He lifts one knee of my right arm. I move onto my right side. Quickly he lets my left arm go and presses my body on my stomach. At the same time he swings around and pushes my head with his ass into the bed and positions his knees on my arms again. I start to fight him in order to free my arms and my head. He forces his full body weight on me. I realize I cannot get him off of me.

"You will finally listen to me." I can't see what he is doing next but I feel shooting pains in my arms as he leans forward, his knees still on my arms. Klaus strips my pants downward. He does not make any attempt to unbuckle my belt. I feel the metal part ripping at my skin. "Klaus don't do this. You are hurting me. Stop." My voice is muffled because my face is still pressed into the pillow. I am not sure if he even can hear me. I feel my pants going down my legs. They are now like shackles around me ankles. I know what comes next. I squeeze my butt cheeks together knowing I have no chance to stop his next move.

I lost count how many times he has raped me in the past. However he hasn't made an attempt since we left East Germany. I have put this very dark side of our relationship way back in my mind. We have only had sex a few times since we've been here. But he also never penetrated me. And for the last six or seven months we haven't done anything. How could I have forgotten what he is capable of? And here I am on my stomach waiting for the attack. Over the years I have learned not to fight when the unavoidable is going to happen because it hurts less when I have time to control my breathing. Deep in, holding it for a while, out. I have to start it now.

Klaus swings his body around and kneels between my legs. My ankles can't move. He grabs my hips to lift my ass. Deep in, hold, out. Deep in, hold, out. The pain thunders through my body. I dig my fingers deep into the comforter. I look at the pile of clothes I am going to take with me. Deep in, hold, out. I can't relax. It hurts so much. Klaus is pounding into me like a mad man. When he grabs my shoulders and pulls my back I know it's over. He pulls out and gets up. I feel something warm running down my legs. I turn on my side. "You are getting loose. Look it that. You shit on the bed. You are disgusting. Get the fuck out. I have to change the sheets." I try to get up without making a bigger mess. The burning sensation seems worse than ever. I don't have the strength to step out of my pants. My legs are shaking. I hobble towards the bathroom. Klaus is in the kitchen opening a bottle of beer. For the first time since I've known him I fear for my life.

I am too ashamed to call anybody to find a place to sleep for the night. I also don't want spend money on a hotel room. I need to save every Pfennig. I seriously have to look for my own apartment. I don't know where to go? Should I spend the night in my car? I could drive towards the Wannsee Lake area and find a quiet side street. I could also cruise bars and restaurant until closing. Bahnhof Zoo train station is open all night long. But finding parking around the area won't be easy.

It's now for a second time that I drive down Fasanenstrasse. I don't know how long I can stand to stay seated. I am in so much pain. Klaus made no attempt to stop me from leaving the apartment. He carried my bags just outside of our apartment door. No words. No apology for what he just did. In the past he always said he was sorry. Not this time. It seems true that people's affection for each other go through stages. From unconditional love, to routine love, to oblivious love, to hate love, to finally just hate or simple boredom. I think I am in the stage of hate love and Klaus is where I don't want to be: hate. Will I ever get away from him? I never had the courage to report his rape. To whom, anyway? I look fairly strong. So why would someone force himself on me? I could fight him off, couldn't I? But I never learned how to physically fight.

As a young kid when I was bullied and punched I let it happen. That made me always an easy target. I thought it's better to get hurt that way then hurting myself more by getting into a fight. Whenever it happened to me I always hoped the other kid would stop because I didn't put up any resistance. To be honest I always wished that these punches and slaps would turn into a hug or into a friendly tap at least. Of course it never happened. I was the girly boy anybody could push around. In later years I tried to buy the tough guys affection by offering them cigarettes and alcohol.

Klaus' rapes were always followed by affection, caressing and promises that he would never hurt me again. For so many times I believed him because I wanted to believe, but deep down I knew better. He succeeded to pummel my self-esteem to the point I believed I won't make it on my own. He had caged me. I was too scared to break out. Nine out of our ten years together I struggled with myself to move on without him. I told him that so many times that he stopped taking it seriously. Sometimes me either.

Yes, I am scared being alone: scared of having to take care of my own place. Dreading the idea of looking for someone, the dating spiel, the rejections, the roller coaster of emotions that will follow the hurt and the pain. But this time is different. I can feel it. I will leave Klaus. If I do not get out now, something terrible will happen. The force he used today, the coldness afterwards and his indifference were frightening to watch. I want to live. I am not done yet. I can't be a victim any longer. I know that now than ever. I will be strong. I am a survivor. Disappointment will occur but also so many more opportunities. I came here because I can not only see and hear the world. I can touch it with my own hands, smell it with my own senses, and dance in the middle of it. During my first year in the West I did what I did the previous nine years; tried to keep our relationship together. Tried to fight off all these intruders. Tried to chase after a Fata Morgana called happiness. Hoping someday the constant struggle will be all worth it. Wrong, wrong, wrong. No more wasting time. No more running in circles. No more abuse. I can see a future without Klaus. Yes, all the sudden I know where to go for the night. The satellite office of *Berliner Morgenpost* in Reinickendorf is a converted apartment. One of the rooms is still unfurnished. I can sleep there on the floor. The bathroom has still a functional shower and the kitchen is equipped with a stove. That will do it for one night. Tomorrow is another day with another idea.

Only four people know that I am looking for my own place. Frank and Knut, Tata and my mother. All are very supportive except my mother. She thinks I should work things out with Klaus. "You can't just throw ten years away. You have a past together. I am so worried about you. You hardly know anybody yet. How will you manage?" Again she has doubts. But I know it's for completely different reason. Klaus thinks I am a daily-life idiot. My mother thinks it would be so much easier to stick together a little bit longer until I am really established in my new environment. Well, both are wrong.

Tata, on the other side is very practical. "Make a list of what you own so you know what you will take. I will help you to pack." My eighty-five-year-old grandmother is all business and feistiness. She is not worried I won't make it on my own. She can see with her own eyes that I am doing pretty well so far. A privilege my mother does not have. She can't visit me. We have to meet in strange places in other countries where we not belong.

I didn't take my friends Frank and Knut up on their offer to stay with them until I have found an apartment. However, I can use their home phone to make calls about available apartments. I am very adamant about staying in the Charlottenburg or Wilmersdorf district. I don't want to live in any housing projects. I want as nice an address as I have currently. Since there is still a shortage of apartments it will be a tricky task to find what I want. Anyway, for the last two weeks Frank, Knut and drive to Bahnhof Zoo train station around midnight to fetch Sunday's *Berliner Morgenpost* which has the biggest apartment-for-rent insert. As soon as the paper truck pulls up hundreds of apartment seekers rush to be the first to buy the paper. You would think that I would have at easier since I work at *Berliner Morgenpost*. But the rules are very strict when it comes to the Sunday for-rent issue. I can't get a copy before others. Anyway, armed with the newest edition we drive to the closest restaurant to scan the paper to see what's on the market and what is suitable. Bright and early the next morning I am on Frank's and Knut's doorstep to make my calls.

I moved back to Fasenstrasse after Klaus promised he would leave me alone. I did insist that I would sleep on the sofa in the living room. So far things are as calm as they can be. He has no clue that I am on an apartment hunt. I will not tell him until I have signed a lease. Frank and Knut think I am crazy and that I am playing with fire. Tata offered to move in for the time being but I convinced myself that I can handle whatever lies ahead. I am fearful but act very cordial around the apartment. I deceive with purpose. I feel that if I would move out before I have my own place Klaus would not allow me to come back to get my stuff.

Jackpot! I have a lease for a one-bedroom apartment with a balcony at Traunsteiner Strasse. The rent is frighteningly high at 650 Marks a month. The landlady chooses me right on the spot after Frank told her that I work for Springer Publications. She must have assumed that working there meant that I am a right winger like she obviously is herself. She even threw new wall-to-wall carpeting in. I can't wait to get it painted and furnished. I am so excited. Nervous, of course. But the prospect of finally putting physical distance between Klaus and me is exciting. Putting my signature on the bottom line of the lease felt like signing my divorce papers. What a happy moment. Now, I have to tell him.

"I don't know how to say it any other way. But I am moving out this weekend. I found an apartment." My voice trembles a little bit. I hate myself for that. Klaus, repairing the dishwasher, loses the grip on the screwdriver. It slips to the floor. His head snaps back. His eyes are locked at the ceiling lamp. His body becomes motionless. Everything around him seems to have stopped as well. Only the constant drip from the leaky drain attached to the dishwasher seem to soften the tension-laden air. Seconds turn into minutes. I probably should say something meaningful but I don't know what. There is no proven script to follow for breakups. I lean against the kitchen doorframe and stare at the floor. All of the sudden and seemingly in one move Klaus jumps to his feet. What a scary moment! I step back into the hallway.

"I hope we can stay friends." I feel Klaus' breath on my face as he slips by me.

"That would be nice," is all that I can say, I'm not sure if his asking me for friendship is cynical or serious? I am also surprised by his calm reaction. Maybe he has also realized there is no us anymore. Maybe he is relieved that I took the initiative before it is too late to depart unharmed? Maybe there is a reasonable Klaus under all these layers of superficiality provoked by alcohol abuse, sexcapades, addiction to admirations and violent outbursts? Whatever it is I am too burnt out to continue any longer this quest of analyzing, of finding answers, of making it work and of waiting that hope becomes reality. "Yes, let's be friends," I say.

Klaus and I hardly talk. I am not around too much. I am busy with my new flat anyway. I basically go to Fasenstrasse to sleep. Surprisingly, Klaus is home every night. Something that was not that way when we were officially still a couple. Anyway, I start to pack my stuff whenever I can. The bulky things I will get ready the day I move. Smaller items and boxes I can fit in my car to drive over to my new apartment. Klaus has told me that on the moving day he won't be around. I think that's a good idea. Because of money concerns I will rent a small moving truck for the furniture. Ferdinand and his partner Stefan have promised to help me move. So things seem to go smoothly and calmly. I am glad.

Only a couple more days and a new stage in my life is upon me. It will be the first time in years when I wake up at night and don't have to wonder where and with whom Klaus is at this very moment. I don't have to worry if he is drunk out of his mind, staggering along and getting picked by the wrong people. I remember one night when he brought somebody home to our apartment. We were still living in East Berlin. I was asleep when I woke up because I heard voices from the kitchen. I recognized Klaus' but not the other man's one. I tiptoed closer to the door to listen. Klaus and the unknown person were clearly drunk. Their voices slurring to the point where the conversation did not make any sense. All of the sudden the man started yelling: "What are you, you gay prick. Take your hands off me." That was followed by loud bang. Something was crashing onto the floor. Followed by the unmistakably noise of a hand hitting flesh. I was frightened and did not know what to do.

Then I heard Klaus begging to stop. "I am sorry. Please

don't hurt me. I am sorry. Do you want money? I am sorry."
The other person didn't seem to care for Klaus' plea. The
slapping and kicking appeared to get closer to the kitchen
door. Klaus' screaming was getting unbearable for me. I
knew I needed to do something. But I also was afraid to get
in the middle of the two. I wanted whatever was going on in
the kitchen to end. I got all my courage together and
slammed my shoulder against the kitchen door. It only
moved a little bit. But enough so I could see Klaus' feet. The
rest of his body was pressed against the other side of the
door, shaken by constant pounding and kicking from the
other person I couldn't see yet. With all my strength I
pushed against the door.

"Please let me in. Klaus what is going on? Let me in."

"Who is that? Oh, you bastard. Is there another gay pig
in the apartment? I will kill you both." With that the kitchen
door opened wide enough so I could see inside. Klaus was
crouched in a fetal position on the floor. Crying and
screaming for help. Our two kitchen chairs were tipped over.
The table had been pushed with such a force into the lower
part of one of our cupboards that the wood of the cabinet
doors was splintered open. The kitchen sink was detached
from the wall.

Somehow what was before me did not seem real. And
then the guy. He was clearly agitated. Still shouting
profanities and kicking Klaus at the same time. "Can you
please stop," I begged. The guy launched out at me and
grabbed my arm. It happened so fast that I lost my balance
and fell against his chest.

"You big pig. Get off of me. Is that what you do? One lures
one home and gets him drunk so you can fuck him both? You
got the wrong guy." He pushed me back. My head hit the
edge of the kitchen stove. Now I started to panic.

"Please don't hurt me. I don't know why my friend
brought you to our apartment. But it is not what it looks
like."

"Your lover here wanted to suck my dick. I will teach you
both a lesson, you perverts." The guy grabbed one of the
chairs lifting it high above his head.

"Please, don't," I screamed as loud as I could. But it was

too late. He slammed the chair with all his strength onto the stove. Afraid of what would come next I covered my head with my arms. "Please, please," is all I could whimper. Klaus in the meantime crouched under the sink, not saying a word or trying to help to stop the man from hurting me. Despite all my angst I became so angry at him. What happened here is just because of Klaus. Because he cannot keep his dick in his pants I lie on the floor and fear for my life. My growing anger towards Klaus somehow calmed me down.

Now I was able to look at the stranger in our kitchen. He was tall and slim with a crew cut and small beard just around his chin. Even he seemed very upset he didn't look scary. "You guys are crazy. Why are you cocksuckers always wanting to fuck straight guys? We don't like dicks and hairy asses. You don't get it, do you? I easily could really hurt you. Look at you two. It's just pathetic and disgusting." He lifts his right leg and slams his foot down on Klaus' chest. I still lean against the stove. He smacked my head hard with his left hand. I didn't say a word. I felt the worst was over. All I wanted that this guy leaves our apartment. Before he did he took the almost full bottle of vodka from the kitchen counter. As he went towards the door he kicked the inner panel of the door with so much force that it cracked open. "Assholes," he hissed at us before he yanked the entrance door open. With a loud smashing noise it fell back into the lock. When I heard him going down the staircase I was so glad the nightmare was over.

I didn't know how much time passed before I got up onto my feet. My head and back were hurting. A hot shower felt like the right thing to do. But I just wanted to go back to bed. Klaus was still crouching in a fetal position under the kitchen sink. "How much more can he do to me?" I wondered looking down on him. He almost had me killed. Why would he even try to hook up with a straight guy? That is so crazy.

"Can you help me get up, please? I think one of my ribs is broken." Klaus tried to get up. I was way too angry to help him. I stared at him. "I hope he broke more than one rib. What in the world were you thinking, picking up a normal guy? You are out of your mind." With that said I left the kitchen. I didn't care how he would get off the floor.

457

*

I look straight at the tip of a pair of scissors. It takes me a second to make sure that's really what it is just inches away from my face. My eyes adjust to the darkness slowly. The lights from the streetlamps filter through the window shades and the outline of a figure next to me. It is Klaus. Slowly I drift out of my sleep into fully awareness. My brain still struggles to send the right signals within. Yes, I am awake and it is real what I see. No, I'm not dreaming any longer. In an instant I am fully awake. "What are you doing here?" Quickly I turn onto my side to get my head out of the intended stabbing direction of Klaus' scissors-clutching fist. As fast as I can, I stand up. My thoughts are racing. I have to get Klaus away from me as far as I can. I eyeball the door and try to estimate how long it will take me to run out of the living room and pull the door shut. But what then? Do I have enough time to grab the cordless phone and run out in the hallway? Klaus would outrun me. Why didn't I listen to Frank and Knut who offered me to stay at their place until my new apartment is ready? And why did I not lock the living room door? Klaus is totally motionless. His hand with the scissors doesn't move. His eyes stay on me. Follow my every move. To sprint away would definitely unlock him. I have to talk to him. I have to talk him out of what he had planned.

"Klaus, talk to me. And please, put the scissors away." My voice displays panic. I have to clear my throat. Klaus still has not moved. Maybe he is sleepwalking? But his eyes betray him. They don't let me go. Again, I am fearful of a physical fight. Again, I have flashbacks to my childhood times when I was the perfect target to be hit. Fat and unfit during gym classes. One of the shortest kids in the class. The tough guys always had a field day with me. Pushing me to the ground, slapping me around, ripping the school pack off my back and calling me a "little girl." And I would take it. My only defense: I would not cry. Even my middle school gym teacher would throw his heavy bundle of keys after me when I couldn't get up the rope, jump over the horse or didn't catch the ball during games. I hated him so much that I had nightmares about him. Every time he threw his keys at me he would yell "Catch them, you idiot." Of course, I never would. Sometime they would crash on the floor just short of reaching me. Other times they would hit me on my back or legs. My fellow classmates would laugh at my humiliation. I wanted to sink into the ground. But never ever did I try to defend myself. None of my classmates would ever come to my defense. I was not a popular student. There was nothing to gain by helping me. Only by making fun of me.

And here I am again. An adult. Confident when it comes to making myself heard facing authorities. I look at the tip of the scissor blades. I start to wonder how long Klaus was standing over me watching me sleep. One way or the other I have to change this scary situation. I push myself away from the sofa bed. Forceful enough that Klaus stumbles back a couple of steps. And just that little move seems to get him out of his rigid body stare. His fist opens and the scissors fall to the floor. Klaus let go of his legs and he slams into the armchair.

"I don't know what I was thinking. I wanted to kill you and then me." His voice cracks. He puts his face down in his hands. "Please don't leave me. I know you deserve better. I don't know why I hurt you all the time. Believe me. I really don't want to hurt you." Klaus looks up to me. Tears streaming down his face. "I am sorry. Please don't go. I don't know what I will do without you?" His right hand is reaching out to me. I don't let him touch me. "Please hold me, Thomas, please." I look at Klaus. Small, fragile. He seems to have shrunk in size.

How often have I heard his pleas? How often have I listened to his apologies and promises? How often did I want to believe him? But how often was I not sure which Klaus was the real Klaus? The one who humiliated me, betrayed me, raped me? Or the one who didn't know why he was doing what he was doing? The one who didn't want to humiliate me, rape me, betray me? How many times in the past ten years have I hoped, wanting to believe but was disappointed in the end again and again. But this is the past. This is the final state of our togetherness. I am immune to his cries for forgiveness and his pledges to be better. Moments ago he wanted to kill me. Now he is shaking uncontrollably. I see his tears and I see the scissors on the floor. I don't feel any pity and any sympathy for him. I am done, done, done.

I look at the clock. It's three in the morning. Going back to bed is out of the question. I am not interested in listening to Klaus anymore. I am not taking another chance. I dodged the bullet. Now I have to get out of the house unharmed.

"I am taking a shower," thinking that our bathroom is the only room that I can lock from the inside.

"Thomas, Thomas, please." I turn the key. The shower drowns out Klaus' cries. The warm water feels good. If I get out of this apartment in one piece tonight I will not come back without someone to accompany me.

I still can't believe it. The GDR has approved our application to get married. The ceremony is scheduled for February thirteenth at city hall in the Koepenick district. I will be allowed to enter East Berlin for exact twenty-four hours to get officially hitched to Claudia. What a farce? With the marriage license Claudia will be allowed to leave East Germany unharmed. And I have twenty-four hours to see my parents and my brother. Of course I feel a little bit uneasy going into East Berlin. What if they don't let me leave at the end of the night? I make sure that many people know where I am going on February thirteenth including my colleagues at the newspaper. I also told my editor in-chief. He wanted an article about my journey back to the East, our wedding and short family reunion. I had to talk him out of it. For once, everyone who knows me knows that I am gay and this wedding is not for real. And I am not sure how East Germany would react to an article in *Berliner Morgenpost* about an East-West wedding. It could endanger Claudia's exit. It also could have some repercussions for my and Claudia's family? Klaus and Marlene's wedding is approved as well.

* * *

"Oh, my God I have AIDS." My bedsheets are drenched from my night sweat. I feel like I just came out of the water. Except this wetness sticks to my skin and hair. Don't they say that heavy night sweats are one of the first signs of

460

having AIDS? I want to get out of my bed but I am too scared. What am I going to do? I can't tell anybody about it. Where and how could I have been infected? I try to recall my sex partners since I left Klaus. There is Konstantin. I met him on the Island of Rhodos during my vacation last September. But that was almost five months ago. After I came back from Greece I dated Teo for a couple of weeks. Then there was a one-night stand with some guy. I also jerked off with another one in the steam room on Kurfuersten Strasse.

I push the soaked comforter off me. My sweat makes me shiver. I feel cold. I grab a towel from the closet to dry off. I look at myself in the mirror. I have lost over twenty pounds since I started living alone. I am sure it happened because I started exercising combined with a yoghurt-cucumber diet. But maybe not? They say weight loss is another sign of AIDS. How much time do I have left? Don't they say you can die from it very fast? I step under the shower. Maybe I didn't get it from having sex? Don't they say a mosquito can transfer AIDS? But it is the middle of January. There are no mosquitoes around. I went to the hairdresser just after New Year's Eve. Don't they say AIDS can be transmitted through scissors and hair combs? My last visit to the dentist was in October. Don't they say unsterilized medical tools are carriers of AIDS?

The warm water runs down my body. It feels good. I still can't stop shivering. Oh my God, I totally forgot about the guy in Phuket. It hits me like a boomerang thinking about it. In December Ferdinand, Stefan and I went to Southeast Asia. Our last stop was Thailand. After much sightseeing we went to the beach for a couple of days. One evening I felt that the two wanted some privacy. I went for a stroll on the beach. It was dark. I only could hear the water rolling onto the sand. Not far from me I saw a small light go on, then fade, on, fade. I realized it was somebody smoking a cigarette. And I also felt that that someone wanted to be noticed. I walked towards the cigarette light. "Hi." His voice broke the silence. "Hi," I answered. He rose up and I saw that he was naked. Neither he nor I said another word. The sex was intense and quick. After it was over he left and I searched unsuccessfully for my underwear. Anyway, this was the last time I had sex. Until now I had totally forgotten about it. It happened five weeks ago. Now, I am really scared shitless.

"The test result is negative." The doctor closes the file. "Do you have any questions?" I shake my head, unable to speak. It takes a while for me to let it sink in. I don't have AIDS. Of course I am relieved to hear that, but I have been through the most agonizing two weeks since they took my blood. It seems like an eternity from the time I woke up soaked in sweat until today. I had talked myself into the fact that I have AIDS, for sure. I prepared a will. I have been through so many moments of anger, pityparties and resigned-to-the-fact nights. I lived on coffee more than food. I was tempted to start smoking again. I called the Berliner AIDS-Hilfe not to seek help but to volunteer my time. I wanted to learn how others dealt with the fact that they are infected. I wanted to hear about their pain, struggles and how they cope with the stigma to ease my own roller coaster ride.

More than once I came very close to talking about my night sweats, weight loss and fear of being infected. But I never had the courage to do so. I was afraid of what Frank, Knut and their friends would think about me like "He is sick. You know what I mean," accompanied by a flicker of their eyelids. I wanted to hold on to the clean and healthy me as long as possible. So I kept my raging emotions hidden as well as I could.

Now, sitting in front of the doctor whose name I don't even know I am glad that I didn't alarm anyone, not my friends, colleagues or my family. When they called me from the waiting room I was number sixty-one to protect my anonymity. Now I wish they would call me by my full name. "Thomas Schardt, you don't have AIDS." I am not sick. I am back on the side where healthy people are. Yes, I am happy and smiling again. No, I do not feel guilty about my emotions. Tonight I will answer the phone at the Berliner AIDS-Hilfe and try to help just by listening to men in fear. Fearless.

The editor-in-chief is leaving. It's not unexpected but nevertheless sad for me. The first moment I met him I liked him. He took time to interview me, even if it was for just a freelance job at the time. When I felt I deserved a raise after I was hired as staff reporter and my supervisor saw no need to up my salary I went directly to him and pleaded my case. Again, he gave me his time, listened to me and in the end called our HR department. I think he had no clue what entry-level staff reporters make. I am not sure if I can go so far as to say that he liked me because he seemed very aloof to all of his staff; except when it came to young, attractive and mini-skirted females. Rumors are rampant that he liked to have company after the daily issue of the paper went to print. Cigars, whisky and a pretty intern are supposedly his favorite past times.

Dude Ranch, Stretch Limos, and a Dream

The plane ascends into a clear afternoon sky. The Statue of Liberty is floating above the glistening sea to the left of me. My face is pressed against the way-too-small window. I want to hold on what disappears from my eyesight. The gorgeous skyline of Manhattan flattens slowly as we go higher and higher. Liza Minnelli's "New York, New York" is the fitting soundtrack coming through my earphones. A perfect eleven-day whirlwind through the United States is coming to an end. It still feels like a dream. Horseback riding in Arizona, touring cigarette plants in Virginia, sightseeing in the nation's Mall, enjoying Georgetown's cobblestone streets, taking in Fifth Avenue and the Empire State Building: all part of a getting-to-know-the-U.S. trip courtesy of Philip Morris. Twice a year the company invites journalists from Germany in order to showcase America. I am the first from *Berliner Morgenpost* to partake in that privilege. Not so long ago I was a dismissed reporter in East Germany with an Exit Application and a more than uncertain future. With breathtaking speed I was back in my profession and awarded with a trip I never could have envisioned. The way I am introduced to the United States is equally hard to grasp. Corporate jets, first-class hotels, stretch limos and superb hosts are mind boggling as well. I feel privileged and grateful.

But there were also moments where I felt upset, angry and outraged again. One of those moments: I stand in the middle of Times Square close to midnight after an enjoyable performance of "Forty- second Street" unthreatened, unrobbed and most of all still alive. Wasn't I taught back in East Germany that after darkness New York sinks into an abyss of murder and violence that no one could escape? Didn't they tell us that people in New York don't leave their homes after the sun goes down? Haven't Gus Hall, Pete Seeger and other of the "most favorite Americans of the East

464

German *Nomenklatura*" painted a bleak picture of a swamp called New York City, where people live in cardboard boxes and children get bitten by rats? Liars! Liars! Liars! I look at buzzing traffic, neon-lit billboards and lots of people enjoying what's known as the crossroads of the world. I am unhurt. And I am ready to continue the night at "Second Eye," a nightclub somewhere on 21st Street. I am not scared to do so at all.

Something else has happened to me on this unbelievable trip: Alexander, a fellow journalist and part of our group. At first I was irritated by his attention, then unsure. For almost two years I have not met another guy because I didn't want to. The mere thought of being touched by somebody else revolted me. No desire in sex or masturbation, none of it. But now this tall, dark haired and very handsome guy was obviously flirting with me. I became nervous because I didn't know how to react.

My shyness took hold of me until an itinerary-free afternoon. Alexander suggested taking the Staten Island Ferry. As we stood at the ferry's railing and passed Ellis Island I felt his arm against mine. It was like thunder shooting down to my groin. The close contact just lasted a couple of seconds. We looked at each other. He invited me to meet him later at "Second Eye." He wrote the address down since he is skipping the Broadway show that the rest of our group is going to. Now I am very curious what the club is about. I can't wait to get there. If I still had doubts about Alexander's intentions, as soon as I step into the club they are gone.

We dance, drink and enjoy the ease of the atmosphere. It feels good here and later in my hotel room. The next day we can't wait to spend some time away from our fellow travelers. We rent a rowboat in Central Park. The surface of the lake is flat and unmoving. Only our paddles disrupt its calmness. The tree tops extend seamlessly into Manhattan's skyline. It is magical. I can't remember when I was that happy and wholesome. Our time together is limited. We know without talking about it. The bond between us is instant and deliciously intense. We say things to each other only two lovers full of lust can say. It will be meaningfulness afterwards. The touch of our hands, the scent of our bodies, the roar when we peak: all that will soon be memory. The words, truthful when whispered in each other's ears, will later fade in silliness later when we arrive back in Frankfurt and each goes to his own gate to fetch the next flight home.

But now we are still together, sitting next to each other, blankets over our laps to hide our excitement, listening to Liza Minnelli, accepting the flight attendant's offer of champagne, our heads pushed back in the head rests by gravity. It's a trip of a lifetime, ending in seven hours. What I was allowed to experience will stay. I turn my head toward the window so Alexander can't see my tears. I will come back, hopefully soon! My fingers close around Alexander's hand.

Slow Goodbye

My mother tells me that Tata's mind is slipping. They have to lock her apartment door at night. More than once the police have found my grandmother kilometers away from her home. The last time just dressed in her nightgown, bare feet, shivering. More than once she has not recognized her own daughter, screaming for help when my mother came to visit. No one knows where her jewelry is. Her bank account is empty. The next-door neighbor showed my mother the carpet Tata has given her. Looking for help, East Berlin's elder care officials don't see any reasons to even accept an application to get Tata some kind of supervision since she still has light moments and can tell who she is. When we phone I can detect by my mother's voice that it's an overwhelming situation. I suggest letting Tata come visit me for a couple of days. My mother is relieved by my offer. It will take some planning how to get Tata safe and sound through the border control. We need someone to accompany her. My mother does not want take a chance of Tata getting lost and confused in front of a mean border control officer. My mother at fifty-three years old is not eligible to bring her mother from the East to the West.

The plan is that my stepfather will bring his mother-in law back over the border after the visit. We need somebody Tata would recognize and has the required travel age to come to West Berlin. Finally it is arranged that Claudia's mother, my "official" mother-in-law, will be the East-to-West chaperone.

Like so many times before I wait at Friedrichstrasse station. But it is the first time that I will meet my changed grandmother. I am anguished because I don't know how Tata will react: Will she know who I am? How will I take care of her for the next couple of days? The double door swings open and, there she is. Seemingly the same. We hug. I can't tell if she knows who I am. She introduces me to my mother-in-law as "my new neighbor." What is not true?

Then she looks at me. She doesn't know who I am. But I can see that she tries.

"You really shouldn't have troubled yourself to see me."

"But Tata, I always meet you here when you come visit me."

"That is nice of you." She presses on towards the staircase. I thank Claudia's mother for her help. Physically, Tata is as fit as ever. My eighty-seven-year-old Grandmother tackles the steps going up. No need for help.

I left my car at the Bahnhof Zoo train station. "I have been here before," Tata says as I help her to buckle up.

"Yes, you have been. Nothing really has changed."

"That is true. Only I have." Tata straightens out her blouse and looks out of the car window. "Can I ask you a question? Please don't be upset, but I know you but I have forgotten your name." Her question takes me by surprise. I don't want to show it.

"Tata, I am Thomas, you favorite grandson. Believe me; I forget a lot of things lately as well. We are getting older, aren't we all?"I pet her arm and chuckle. She grabs my hand.

"I thought so. But I was not sure if that was your name?" I detect sadness in her eyes. "Sometimes I think that they have taken my brain out."

"What do you mean? Who do you think took your brain out?"

"I don't know. I am so happy to see you. You are my favorite grandson." I have to drive with only one hand on the wheel. She does not let go of the other. I am glad she doesn't.

My mood can be described as being utterly in shock. I look at Tata with a her long pointed nose, her eyes, one green and brown, her slightly wrinkled face and the raindrop-shaped garnet stone earrings dangling down her neck. Yes, that is still my beloved grandmother, who took me to musicals and operas. Yes, that is still my beloved grandmother, who would sneeze at least ten times before she could stop. Yes, that is still my beloved grandmother, who would fearlessly jump into the ocean without knowing how to swim. Yes, that is my beloved grandmother who

468

accepted the fact that I am gay without addressing it. (Except kind of indirectly when she told me that she had a younger brother who killed himself. I didn't ask her why he took his life. But it seemed there was an understanding between her and me without saying a word.)

But I also look now at a person whose reality is just her own. Strange to others. For instance, after we have a nice normal conversation all the sudden her memory lapses. So as we finish up our afternoon at her favored Cafe Kranzler at Kurfuerstendamm Tata pulls out her money purse obviously attempting to pay our bill. She opens it and puts her fingers inside. I notice her confusion. "What's wrong Tata?"

Absentmindedly she still stares at her money purse. "I can't believe this. Paul must have taken all my money. I had asked him this morning to make sure that I have enough money with me. That is really not nice of him."

"But Tata, Paul is on vacation. He couldn't have taken your money," thinking she is talking about my uncle, her son.

"What are you talking about? I know my son is on vacation. I am talking about your Grandfather." I am stunned. I never met my Grandfather. He died over thirty years ago. His name was Paul. I look at Tata. There is no flicker, no doubt in her expression that her husband is alive and that she suspects him having taken her money. I don't want to correct her.

"Tata, don't worry. I have money. I can pay."

"That is not right. Your grandfather should not have done that. He can't expect that you pay for me. When we get to your place I will call him."

"Okay. We will do that." My grandmother has no phone at her apartment.

For our last evening together we decide to stay home and watch some TV. Tata prepares our supper. Roasted potatoes with ham, tomato and scrambled eggs. She knows it's one of my favorite meals. We sit down on front of the TV set. The evening anchor reads the news. "Do you know this man?" Tata asks.

"No, not really. Why?"

"He is looking at us."

"He is looking at us?"

"Yes. Can't you see?"

"He is reading the news from the teleprompter. Therefore he has to look straight at the studio camera." Why I try to explain that to her, I don't know. I can tell she has no clue what I am talking about.

"I don't like this man. I don't like men looking at me. Let's go into the other room." My grandmother gets up and collects our plates. It is so sad.

The rest of Tata's visit goes by with no major snafus. Only once she wakes me up in the middle of the night, fully dressed and ready to go for a walk. I put my arms around her and lead her to the window. "Look Tata. It's still dark outside. We will go for a walk as soon as the sun is up. I think you should go to bed and sleep a little bit more."

"You are right. It is still dark. What was I thinking? I am sorry, that I woke you." I help her lie down. She closes her eyes. And only seconds later she is asleep again. I pull a chair up next to her. Tata's face is peaceful, her breathing is relaxed. My whole life I was always amazed at how her tiny frame could quell such physical strength and enormous willpower. As I look at her now, I wonder if it is the same toughness that allows her to battle the torment related to her growing dementia. How much does she really know about her memory loss? How many things does she keep to herself, when she goes back and forth between her two realities? Confused at times, knowing at others times she is losing it, sometimes trying to explain her own state of mind. These last couple of days I have not experienced the violence she has shown towards my mother. If there is any noticeable change, she is more gentle. Doesn't mind being hugged or taken by her hands.

I realize how exhausted I am. It's not so much a physical drain I feel. I am emotionally at zero. It is hard to comprehend what might have triggered my grandmother's brain change. What is so difficult to realize is the fact that I can't do anything to bring my grandmother back to the point where I know her again. I can't stop her from going off to a place so utterly strange and crazy. I want to pull her back to me, all of her. Her body and mind. Instead I am made into a bystander helplessly witnessing the disintegration of my grandmother.

* * *

All attempts to stay in touch with Klaus fail me. He clearly is not interested in having any contact with me. Only once we met for an afternoon to drive to Grunewald See for a stroll along the lake. Since he does not have a car I picked him up at his apartment. He did not invite me in; that I found a bit strange. That apartment was my home for almost two years. I was curious how it looked now. I almost said something. In the end I let it slide. It's his home now, not mine anymore, I reasoned with myself. But that afternoon continued to feel awkward. The entire time together felt forced. Our conversation was one question followed by one answer followed by a question and so on. I even caught myself not being very interested in what he was telling me. I started to wonder why we became such strangers in a very short time. Didn't I live with this man for ten years? Didn't I know him as intimately as one only can know another one? Even in our darkest moments I found him physically attractive and exciting. Now I was sitting across from a man seemingly unfamiliar to me. No feelings. Neither good nor bad. Nothing.

From my mother I knew that Klaus calls her almost weekly crying his heart out. Wondering if she could convince me to get back together again. Most of the time during their phone conversation Klaus is drunk, often to the point that he just falls asleep on the phone. Klaus told her recently that he has met somebody from Australia. This guy is somehow involved in the movie industry, the reason why he is currently working in Germany. According to Klaus he stays most of the time with him. There is even talk that Klaus should try to get a permit to live and work in Australia. Of course the Australian guy is not the only man in his life. Igor, an Immigrant from the Soviet Union, is pursuing Klaus as well. So is someone from Lebanon. I feel a little bit uncomfortable when my mother tells me all that. He apparently is doing what he always does: drinking and having as many sexual encounters as possible. What must

471

she think about gay people in general? Hopefully she does not assume that all of us are just man-eating maniacs.

I didn't mention any of the stuff my mother told me during the afternoon with Klaus. I am not the one who's getting cheated on. Let others go through that pain. When I dropped him off at his house he asked me if I got tested for AIDS. I told him that I did. "Good. I did the test, too." Without anything more he got out off the car. *What was that all about?* I thought as I drove off.

London, Turkey, and New York (again)

I am on my way to New York. It's just a little bit over year since I first visited the U.S.A. This time is a working vacation, so to speak. I will be part of Columbia University's summer language program. Alexander was very instrumental in my decision to improve my English. Our intense, short and incredible affair has turned into a friendship I don't want to miss anymore. "If you want to get ahead in life you have to be fluent in at least one more language." One of his many pieces of advice.

Fifteen years younger than me, Alexander seems so much more focused and accomplished than me. Looking at him I am afraid I never can catch up with where he is already. Currently he is working on his PhD in international law. He has a monthly column in one of the leading men's fashion and lifestyle magazines. He is one of the founders of an organization for young journalists; consequently Alexander convinced me to join it. What an incredible opportunity and resource for professional advancement. In less than a year I visited Bonn and London to meet with members of both Parliaments. I am a regular now at power talks with the editor-in-chiefs of leading German newspapers and TV stations.

Another highlight was a fact-finding trip to Turkey. Our group met Kurdish refugees in a camp near Diyarbakir, survivors of a brutal gas attack of Saddam Hussein's henchmen. I watched in amazement at the water-damming project in the North of the country. Near the Armenian border we were allowed into the otherwise off-limits valley of the one hundred churches. And we saw the remains of Noah's Ark, crisscrossed Lake Van and were slapped, soaped and massaged in a Turkish bath. And now, New York here I come again...for five weeks!

I ease into a daily routine of reading *The New York Times* at a coffee shop on Amsterdam Avenue, classes at campus, homework at my little dormitory-style studio apartment on Columbus Avenue and workouts at the Columbia University gym. Most of my fellow classmates are from Japan. When they learned where I was from they started to cling to me in a caring and friendly way. We go out for dinner, listen to the New York Philharmonic in Central Park, and on weekends we go clubbing. I like hanging out with them because the only way to communicate with each other is in English. I deliberately avoid two students from my class: one is from Switzerland, the other one from Austria. I want speak German as little as possible. I have a blast, feel energized and excited. My happiness must be obvious. I get hit on a lot. With some I flirt back, some I ignore and a few I take to my apartment. I live the full life of a student. And it feels good.

Something else has happened. Springer Publications has an in-house foreign news service, the Springer Auslandsdienst (SAD) with offices all over the world including in New York City. Through Alexander I have met Renate, a fellow journalist back in Berlin. She told me that she took a freelance job at the SAD office in New York and suggested that when I am in town I should give her a call. That I did. We met for drinks at the Rainbow Room. After two Long Island Iced Teas each we became the best of friends. I confessed to Renate that I want to live in New York. To do so I would need a job. She offered to make an appointment for me with her boss. Two days later I sat across from Walter Unger. "Tell me about yourself," Unger got right the point. I gave him the rundown of my life so far. He listened without interrupting me. Only once he asks me if I really used my vacation time and money to come to New York to go to Columbia.

"Usually, people ask their superiors for paid time off to do what you do. No one wants to use their precious vacation time other than for leisure and fun. Good for you." Unger seemed impressed with me. "Listen Thomas, I don't have any openings right now. As a matter of fact, we just hired someone. She will start in three weeks. However, I think you would be a good fit for my team. Send me your resume as soon as you are back in Berlin." I can't remember what I said to him, how I got out of his office or back to my apartment. If there was a cloud nine that afternoon I was on it.

After graduation most of my new-found Japanese friends are picked up by cars to spend the rest of the summer in the Hamptons. I only have three more days left before I fly back to Germany. For no pressing reason, other than to get out of the city for a bit, I go to Atlantic City. I am not a gambler. But the Jersey shore seems the most affordable destination for me to get some sun and ocean. I find a rundown hotel only a couple of steps away from the board walk. The weather is pleasant. I take a long walk. The water seems a little bid murky so I skip my plan to take a dip. Instead I soak up the sun. The soothing sound of the waves let my mind drift. Just these four weeks at Columbia University have added so much to my life. Not only do I feel much more comfortable speaking English, but because of my better language skills I can venture further. Germany is no any longer the only place to pursue a career. My limits by yesterday's standards are now less limited. Maybe there are no boundaries as long you are willing to go forward? Directions can change and should. Maybe my new direction leads to New York? An impossible direction not so long ago now looks very likely. I am in a good place.

All of the sudden the warming sun on my face disappears. Must be a cloud. I open my eyes and look straight into a face. "Hi. How are you?" the face talks to me. It belongs to muscular body in blue and white swim trunks.

"Fine." I pull myself up onto my elbows.

"Do you want to go for a walk?"

"I am not sure. Where to?"

"Over there." The guy pointed to a parking lot. "My car is there. It's in a hidden spot." I notice he has a hard-on. Me too. What a weird situation, I think as get my stuff together. He is already a couple of steps ahead of me. Indeed, the guy's car is parked between high shrubs. What follows is quick, steamy, good and releasing sex. It will feel wrong later.

475

Jackpot: Moving to New York

"A Mr. Walter Unger called for you. He wants you to call him back as soon as possible," Sandra, one of my team members, greets me as I step into the office. It's my first day back on the job since I returned from Columbia University. For a split second I don't know who Walter Unger is. I put my bag down trying to recall the name. Then it hits me. Of course. It's the bureau chief for the Springer Foreign News Service in New York. I wonder what he wants from me. Maybe it's just a reminder to send him my resume? But first I should probably deal with another urgent matter.

On my last day in New York I got a call from the HR person of RIAS-TV. She asked me if I was still interested in a job at the TV station. It was a follow up from a job interview I had just prior to taking off for New York. At first I was very excited about the prospect of being part of one of the first morning TV programs in Germany. The editor-in-chief had initiated the contact. He was one of the guest speakers at the monthly power talks conducted in the Interconti Hotel. These so called "Conversations at the Fireplace" connected young journalists with the movers and shakers in the news media. At the end of this particular session, the RIAS-TV-Chief stopped me and asked "Have you ever thought about television? Here is my business card. Give me a call if you think you want to change media." It caught me by surprise, why would he approach me? I only had one very short interaction with him during the question-and-answer part of the lecture. Nevertheless, I was thrilled about his offer to contact him since I'd been thinking for some time about changing jobs. That same evening I wrote him a thank-you note.

Two days later I called his office. After that I didn't hear anything for about three or four months. Literally, one day before I flew to New York I got a call to go in for a job interview at RIAS-TV at Nalepa Strasse. The interview went very well. The big damper came when they told me how much money I would make: it was about 600 Marks less per month what I currently make at *Berliner Morgenpost*. They told me that a decision would be made within the next couple of days. Since I was going to be in New York they wanted me to leave a contact number so they could get in touch with me. The only phone number I could provide was the one of the admissions office for the Summer Language Program at Columbia University. And that was where I got the message that I could have a job as a writer for the morning show. Of course I felt exuberated, but the money part was really a concern. Therefore I didn't call HR right away. I wanted to wait until I was back in Berlin. That would give me enough time to weigh the pros and cons.

I am not sure if I should call New York first or RIAS-TV. I am ninety-nine percent sure that I will accept the RIAS job. It would be a totally new environment for me. It's a challenge I want to face. I am sure that I can manage the salary cut somehow. Hopefully at some point they will realize that I am worth more money. But I am also very curious why the SAD bureau chief had left a message to call him. Without thinking I pick up the phone and dial Unger's number. After only three rings a clearly sleepy voice answers. At the same time I feel like the floor gives away under my feet. I realize that I forgot that there are six hours time difference between Germany and the U.S.A. I just called Unger at three a.m. in the morning. I am so embarrassed and in shock that I am unable to talk. I hang up the phone. I almost ask Sandra for a cigarette, closer to smoking than I have been since I quit three years ago.

The ringing of the phone stops me from falling off the wagon. I answer. "Walter Unger here. Thomas, did you just call me?" I am caught and terrified.

"Yes, I did. I am so, so sorry. It was so stupid of me..."

"Don't be silly. You don't know how often I get calls in the middle of the night from people forgetting about the time difference." I feel relieved to hear that. "Anyway, I am glad you called me right away. From your colleagues I know that's your first day back in the office."

"Yeah, I arrived yesterday afternoon in Berlin."

"Listen, are you still interested in New York?"

"Yes, I am," I'm not sure if fully understand his question.

"The young woman who was going to start this week is not coming. Her boyfriend does not want her to leave. When can you start?"

"Well, in... maybe...I think...," I stutter. I have no clue how to answer his question. I am hyperventilating. I have to give two weeks notice at *Berliner Morgenpost*, three months to get out of my lease. What do I do with my car? My thoughts swirl in a free fall.

"Honestly, I don't know. When do you need me?" I try to sound rational and calm.

"Can you be here by October first?" That is exactly one month from today. I have to bring my breathing under control. This is an opportunity that will come only once. How many of my colleagues at Springer would die for a New York assignment? Tons and tons! I can't let this slip out of my hands. I want this job and I will make it work.

"Right now I don't know how I will manage. But I will be in New York on October first."

"Great. I will help you from this end with whatever I can do. I already contacted Springer Foreign News Service's main office in Hamburg and told them you will be the man for me if you want that job. So, they don't have any choice other than to agree. However, you have to fly there for a formal interview..." Unger rattles down a list of things I have to do. My pen flies over my notebook pages. I am scared miss anything he might tell me.

It's not so much that I can't write that fast, I have a hard time concentrating. I can't fathom what is happening to me right now. If everything goes well I will be reporting for Springer Verlag from New York in a month. It sounds so unreal. Sudden. Out of the blue. Amazing. Frightening. Clearly overwhelming at this moment. "Thomas, I look forward to you joining our team."

"Thanks for saying that. And thanks for offering me this incredible opportunity. It will take a while for it to sink in. I am very excited." I hang up the phone. I am unable to move. I feel like my body is way too small to contain my excitement. My heart races. I can't help it. Tears start pouring down my face.

All of the setbacks and disadvantages, belittling and bullying in the past, the nightmares of my relationship with Klaus, the arguments with my stepfather, the doubts of some of my friends and family members in my decision to move to West Berlin. Was all that the necessary prelude for me to finally receive this gratification? Does one have to pay his dues, as strange as they might be, before his potentials are recognized? Is one allowed to blossom only after enduring pain and disappointments? And at what point does one give up believing in himself? "I am going to New York!" I want to scream and to be heard especially by those who tried to deny my growth. I have reached a peak. I am proud of myself.

It is really interesting how people react when I tell them I have a job in New York. There is Stefan, who has never made a secret out of his hatred for former Easterners. From day one Stefan always has questioned my journalistic abilities and does not hide his disdain for me. He seriously believes that all former Easterners work for the secret service and for the time being are "sleepers" waiting to woken up in the near future when the East decides to spread the World Revolution westwards. Reasonable in his other political beliefs, his opinion about former GDR citizen is unchangeable. Everything that goes wrong in his life he blames on us. The reason that he lost out on apartment is that a former East German got it. Applying for an editorial position at *Tagesspiegel* newspaper went sour because one ex-Easterner was in the running. The increased numbers of beggars on the street is because of losers from "over there." When he heard that I am moving over to Springer Foreign News Service he came running to my desk.

"How did you do it? For years I've been trying to get a job at the SAD bureau in Paris. Here you are, barley established and you are given an assignment within the SAD." He makes no attempt to lower his voice. All my other colleagues stop what they are doing. A deafening silence. But I am way too happy to get intimidated by Stefan .

"First of all, I am not going to Paris. I am going to New York. You ask me how I did it? I saved all of my vacation time to attend Columbia University to improve my English. Oh, I not only used my vacation time. I paid for the course as well. And I made an appointment with the New York bureau chief just to say hi. Anybody could have done the same thing, including you."

"I have no interest in working in New York. I studied French."

"Stefan, listen to you. You are jealous that I am going to work in New York, because you want to work in Paris. You are crazy."

"I am upset because you have not earned that job. You are awarded the job because you are from the East. You got the job by jumping in the front of the line. I know a lot of people who have tried again and again to become part of the SAD team. People, I should add, that are much more seasoned and accomplished than you are. No one should climb the career ladder solely based on the place where he or she was born."

I look at him and around the room. No one comes to my defense. I am a little bit surprised. But I also realize there is no sense continuing that exchange. If most of my colleagues really believe I got the job because I was born in East Berlin than there is nothing that would change their mind. Where Stefan is concerned, he probably has to justify why things don't work out for him. I know that why I was hired for New York has nothing to do with my birthplace. I met the bureau chief at the right time at the right place. And Walter Unger obviously liked my initiative and determination. I certainly will not apologize to anyone for going to New York.

Another weird reaction came from Ferdinand. "I hope you will be happy over there. You know, New York or the U.S. for that matter is not what you have seen in 'Dallas' or the 'Denver Clan.' You should really think it through before you accept the position."

"Ferdinand, do you really think I am that shallow to believe that New York is a perfect place? What makes you think my worldview is based on television shows? You of all people should know better."

"I am just telling you to weigh your options. I am pretty

disillusioned about the West. I thought everything here was about personal freedom and achievement. It's not. It's all about money. Over there, my life was less stressful and challenging. Knowing what I know now, I never would have left." I am honestly shocked about Ferdinand's assessment. He seemed to fit right into the West. He graduated from hotel management school and works now for one of the biggest hotels in Berlin. He travels extensively. He has a nice apartment and a boyfriend.

"What you say really surprises me. You have accomplished so much. I always looked up to you. Anyway, I think it's a wonderful opportunity for me. I am very grateful for that. You say, life over there was so stress free and less challenging. In other words boring and limiting. I thought that was the reason why you and I left?"

"I guess you still see everything through rose-colored glasses. I only hope you won't have a rude awakening. New York is the last place to wake up, so to speak. In any case, I hope you find what you are looking for. Good luck." Do I detect feelings of jealousy in Ferdinand? I remember his letter that discouraged me to leave East Berlin years ago. Now he tries to spoil my excitement over my job in New York. Whatever his motives may be, I am moving to the U.S.A. Frank and Knut's response was "That is great for us. We will have a cheap place to stay when we are in New York."

"Sure you will!" I replied.

Since I've accepted the New York position I had to decline the offer from RIAS TV. "What a great opportunity for you. I totally understand your decision. To be honest, I would have done the same thing. Congratulations!" The reaction from the HR person couldn't have been nicer and more sincere.

I am a little nervous to tell my parents about the job. After years of trying again and again to get them to leave the GDR I finally convinced them to do so. My stepfather has been retired for years, so there is no problem for him to get the permit to leave. My mother on the other hand is still working. She was more reluctant because of the anticipated repercussions she may face at work after she told her boss that she submitted an Exit Application. "Mother, what can they do to you? You are applying to leave the GDR to be with me. East Berlin has accepted family reunions as one of the very few reasons to let people go. Don't wait until you reach retirement age. You are wasting your time. Things will not change for the better."

"You are right. But what about Markus?" My mother is understandably worried about my brother. He has signed up with the National People's Army (NVA) for a minimum of three years. That granted him a place at Extended High School and ultimately a spot at a university.

"I know, mother. Markus made that decision. He is a grown man. Let's see what the future will bring for him. And look at the bright side. When you are in West Berlin Markus has the right to submit an Exit Application because he wants to be reunited with his parents. Don't be afraid. Look at me. I made it here."

Four months ago my parents finally submitted their Exit Application. Since then my stepfather visits West Berlin as much as he can. Together we went to the Federal Labor Administration to submit copies of my parents' work documents to get the registration process with the West German Federal government offices going. The biggest hurdle will be finding an apartment. Berlin still has a housing shortage. My stepfather and I look at apartments, mostly privately owned. A pity about what's available. Through my work I know a member of the city parliament. Not really "kosher" but she opened a door to one of the major housing agencies for me where I could add my parents to a shortlist for apartments. I try to do as much as I can to prepare for my parents' arrival. No one knows when that will be. The latest update is that they can expect to get their papers in November. That would be just one month after I have left for New York. It's unfortunate timing. But I can't wait any longer to break the news about my job in New York.

"I have to tell you something. But before I do I want you to know that you don't have to worry what happens with you," I start.

"What is it? Are you sick?" My mother shifts into mother

482

mode.

"No, I am not sick. I was offered a job..." I pause, "...in New York."

"That is wonderful," my mother says. "Heinz, Heinz come here. Thomas is moving to New York." My mother calls my stepfather closer to the phone.

"What are you saying? Thomas is moving to New York?" I hear Heinz in the background. "Thomas that is wonderful. Is this with the newspaper?"

"Kind of. It's part of Springer's in-house foreign news service. I think I told you that when I was in New York I met with the bureau chief there. He offered me a job. And I have accepted."

"Oh, my Thomas. I am so happy. I can' believe, my son is going to New York." My mother chokes up. I know. She is crying.

"But, Gitti, don't cry." I hear my stepfather's voice.

"I know, I am so silly. But I can't help it. My eldest is going to New York. Who would have ever imagined that? I wish we could be together right now to celebrate that." My mother blows her nose.

"We will, mother," I reassure her.

"So, when will you start?" Heinz is now on the phone. "Well, in three weeks." The silence that follows doesn't sound good. "I know, the timing is off. But they need me there as soon as possible. I probably could have asked for a later starting date. But to be honest, I didn't want to jeopardize my chances."

"Oh, I understand. You did the right thing. This is once-in-a-life time opportunity. You cannot let go of it." My mother tries very hard to sound convincing. But in my heart I know what goes on in her head. How will we manage without Thomas being there? Where will we live when there is no apartment ready for us? On and on.

"Mother, Heinz, I know what you are thinking. Please don't worry. Sure, I would have loved to be here on the day you arrive. I won't. But here is the plan. Whenever you get your papers you will come. I am keeping my apartment. I already talked to my landlady. She is okay with that. So, you will have a place to live. And you don't have to pay rent.

I can handle that."

"Oh that is wonderful. Thank you." My stepfather is on the phone again. I hear my mother still blowing her nose.

"Heinz, there is no reason to worry. Before I leave I will call the housing agency to see where you are on the list for an apartment. My friend Knut works for the Federal Labor Administration. He promised me he would help you with whatever he can. Claudia is also here to help to direct you to all the places you have to go. And I have a phone in New York. You can call me anytime. The first three months I won't get any time off to come to see you. But as soon as I can I will visit you."

"Don't worry. Your parents are old but not helpless. Thank you for all you have done for us." My stepfather sounds confident.

"Can I talk to mother for a second?" He put her on the phone again. "Mother, Heinz can tell you what I just told him. I only want assure you that you don't have to worry. Things will work out. I am only a phone call away."

"Do me a favor. Don't worry about us. Heinz and I will manage. You have your plate full. There must be so much you have to take care of right now. Is there anything we can do for you?"

"Thanks for asking. Maybe later. At some point my company will send the movers to get my stuff to New York. Right now I don't even know where I will live and how big my apartment in New York will be. To be honest, thinking about which furniture to take is way down on my list at this point. When you here maybe you can help to pick what the movers should pack and ship."

"Of course. One last question. Can I tell your brother the good news? Or should we wait until he is on leave?"

"You can tell him."

"I will write Markus right away."

"Do that. Mother, I am sorry. It seems I get further and further away from you. Most children don't venture too far from their families. Not your son. I can't help it."

"I always knew you were different from other kids. But I also knew somehow I didn't have to worry about you. You had to grow up faster than most of your friends. When it was just the both of us you had to take a lot of responsibilities. I always wondered if I overburdened you at too young an age? Maybe I am the one that drives you away from us?"

"I never saw it like that. I don't know why I act the way I act? I still have to figure out if my motive is escape or just curiosity? Right now I am really happy."

"No mother could wish for a better son." I can't hold back my tears any longer. My mother's voice is cracking too. That's enough emotion for me. "I have to run. I call you later in the week."

"Good night."

I have a strange experience at the U.S. Consulate when I apply for a visa. Pages of questions about all kinds of personal stuff, I don't mind except for the required answers regarding my health. I know from friends that they are lying about their AIDS infection on visa applications out of the fear that their entrance into the U.S. will be denied. Some even go as far not as not bringing their medication on the trip in case U.S. customs checks for pills that would give them away. Since I am not infected I can make my marks in the "no" box. But to answer the question if I am gay or not—which is classified as a mental disorder—is so backwards. What would a "yes" answer mean? The denial of my visa? The immediate incarceration into a U.S. mental institution after going through immigration? The land of the free obviously has some limitations. I mark the "no" box and feel bad about lying about who I am.

What really throws me off is the question if I ever been a member of a totalitarian party or organization? Again, I am not sure what will happen when I answer truthfully. After I denied that I am gay I now feel I have lie about another part of my past. I never was a full member of the East Socialist Unit Party. I entered as a candidate to become a full member but started the procedure less than six months into it in order to sever my SED-affiliation. But there is no space in the visa/application/questionnaire to explain all that. It's a yes or no question only. It's a "no" for me again! Of course I wonder how thoroughly they will fact check my application.

Unger has secured an apartment for me. At first I wanted to go with the offer of one of Alexander's friends, who lives in New York and is looking for a roommate. My monthly share would be a $1000, an astronomical number for me. My salary is going to be a little less than $3000, depending on the exchange rate. A third of my income to pay for rent seems like way too much for me. I also have never lived in a roommate situation. The idea of scheduling bathroom times, dealing with piles of dirty dishes in the kitchen sink as well as possible strangers crashing on the couch made me decide to live on my own. The studio apartment on 49th that Unger found will cost $800 a month; utilities included. Hans, a friend of Frank and Knut in New York who I met during my time at Columbia University, was nice enough to check the place out and told me it's okay. I am glad I have a place to live in New York.

News from the East is encouraging since Gorbaschev blasted into the limelight and declared Glasnost and Perestroika as the new policy benchmarks. The most visible sign of change is the amount of visitors from East Berlin. It's not so much the increasing number that is newsworthy but the age of the Easterners who are all of the sudden given "day-passes" to have a glimpse at the "Golden West." Most of them are way below retirement age. Sabine and Volker, former colleagues of mine from *Der Morgen*, are amongst them. Not only are they both in their thirties but they are also married. Unheard of just a couple of months ago that East Germany would let couples travel together. Only one would get the permit, the other one had to stay behind to ensure that the Western-traveling husband or wife would return to the worker's paradise. The loosened travel restriction allows even my single gay friends to come for twenty-four hours. They all share in the excitement of this new period of presumed openness in the East. None of my visitors express any desire to stay in the West. They want to go back to the GDR since they truly believe that things will be different from now on forward. I doubt it.

The fundamentals over there seem to stay in place. The one-leading-party system is still declared as unshakeable. Travel freedom for all without any restriction is still a wish that has to come true. Freedom of the press and assembly is not the law of the land. Sure, there are the Monday Demonstrations all over East Germany, the biggest ones in Leipzig. However, that does not mean the Wandlitz-Clan has given its citizens free hand to do whatever they want to do. I believe more than ever that East Germany, its big brother the Soviet Union, and all of the other satellite countries are not able to reform itself from within. It's the same as expecting a telephone pole can turn into a man. Isn't happening.

I am only half-heartedly interested when my visiting Eastern friends excitingly talk about what is happening right now in their country and that a democratic future can be achieved without throwing the good achievements of the proletarian revolution overboard. What good things? Low rent for mostly substandard housing? Subsidized bread and potatoes but notorious shortages of salami and vegetables? Free education for all but access to universities only for those who pass the litmus test for Party and country? Guaranteed work for life without a career of your choice? I am so over that. I left that behind years ago. I really don't care what comes out of the dictatorship of the world proletariat and its attempt to play dress-up. A wolf in a sheep's clothing is still a predator. A dictatorship with a people's assembly as background is still a tyranny. On my flight to New York I pity my friends and colleagues who willingly go back through the opening in the Iron Curtain.

487

The End

"I know Klaus doesn't want me to tell you , but he is very sick. I don't think he will live much longer." I drive Claudia to the airport in Boston. She just had spent Christmas with my partner Bruce and me in Maine. After the death of her mother it would have been her first holiday alone. I sensed she wanted to get away from it all. I invited her to come to visit. Anyway, giving me the news about Klaus at the end of her visit is totally unexpected. I have seen him once since I moved to the U.S. I still worked for Springer News when he came with a friend to New York. We had dinner at some dive on Christopher Street. I didn't enjoy our time together at all because it seemed like he couldn't stop talking about our past together. If someone unfamiliar with our abusive relationship had listened to Klaus reminisce he would have thought we were once the perfect couple. It was annoying. After that I only heard bits and pieces about him. He apparently tried to move to Australia. But there were a lot of other men in Klaus' life. He was still drinking heavily. The same old, same old. But to hear that he is gravely ill caught me off guard. He was always the epiphany of health and strength.

"What does he have? Its cancer, isn't?"

"No, Klaus has AIDS." I take my eyes of the street and look at Claudia. She sits motionless.

"When did he get infected?" My questions sound stupid. "I mean, I thought these pill cocktails that everybody talks about can keep you alive for a long time, can't they?" I am so removed from the impact and the imminent thread of the AIDS epidemic since I moved to distant Maine I really have not thought much about it at all. I am also in a monogamous relationship with Bruce. AIDS for me is worlds away. Until now. In a way I am not surprised that Klaus has AIDS. I am just surprised by the fact that I am not surprised. If there was ever a poster child for the promiscuous gay lifestyle,

488

Klaus would be it. If I would have stayed with him I probably would have it now, too.

"How bad is he?" I try to bring my thoughts back to the here and now.

"He is in a steady decline. For almost a year he's been on disability. During the last six months he's been in and out of the hospital. The latest is that he can't move his right arm and leg anymore. He is only skin and bones." Claudia pulls a tissue out to dry her eyes. "I wanted to tell you for a long time because I thought you should know. But he made me promise not to tell you."

I try to picture Klaus. I simply can't see him unhealthy skinny, limited in his body movements. "What about medication?"

"You know Klaus. He was never good at establishing some kind of a regularity or routine. He takes his pills whenever he wants to. He still drinks. I guess he doesn't want to mix that with the medication. He is just irresponsible as always." Claudia is now really shaken up. She can hardly speak.

"He always lived on the edge. And he obviously continues so until the end." I feel anger creeping up inside of me. If he is so nonchalant about his medication does he has the same attitude with other men? Does he tell his sex partners? Does he use condoms? I am almost certain I know the answer. "You know, I don't wish anyone any bad disease or something like that. But Klaus always, always danced to his own drummer. He can't help it. He doesn't give a shit if you care about him. I never understood him. "

I try internalizing what I just learned minutes ago. All of the sudden I have these flashbacks to when we were a couple: none of them good. All of them nightmarish but not thought about in years. I feel my chest tighten. Even after so many years my past with him is back in an instant. A good, somber, successful and content life does not make you forget what was once upon a time. I don't want to think about the guy who fucked Klaus in front of me and asked me afterwards why I live "with this slut," wiping off his dick. I can almost feel the pain again remembering the nurse taking a smear test out of my urethra after Klaus almost infected me for the second time with syphilis. Why do these memories thunder back the moment I learn about Klaus' infection?

"Honestly, I am not sure I feel sorry about Klaus. Of course I don't want him in pain or that he dies. But whenever he caught it, it was at a time when there was enough information out how to prevent it. I mean he didn't get it because of a blood transfusion, did he?"

"You are right. Klaus is my friend. I don't want my friend to die." Claudia now sobs uncontrollably. Klaus is not my friend, I catch myself thinking. "Are you angry with me that I told you?"

"Of course not."

"Please don't tell him that I told you. And please, please don't tell your mother. He doesn't want her to know either." I park in front of the Lufthansa terminal at Logan Airport. Sabine and I hug.

"Call me tomorrow, so I know you arrived all right."

"I wish things would be different. I think Klaus is very lonesome and always was. I really believe that he — if he could overcome whatever it is — would want you in his life again. You were the closest friend he ever had. A soul mate. I know he blew it. But that's what I believe. When you left him he unraveled." Claudia and I are still hugging, our heads on the other one's shoulder.

"I really don't want go through all the emotions and turbulence again. It's enough that I can't stop reliving memories since you told me about his illness. All that I said in the past and say here and now again is that I gave it my all when we were together. But at some point I ran dry. I had to leave him. And I am glad that I did." I loosen my arms. "I don't want talk about Klaus anymore. Keep me updated on his status if you want to." A porter takes Claudia's suitcases. "Thanks for spending Christmas in my wilderness called Maine. Please come again." Her face is reddish and puffy from her dried-up tears. One last kiss. No last word. Claudia steps into the opening of the revolving door. I start my car.

The drive back home is mechanical. My right foot moves between the gas and the brake pedal to adjust to the heavy rush hour traffic. My hands move the steering wheel as needed. The windshield wipers are on autopilot to push the falling snow to the side. My mood is sad. Claudia is probably right that I was the closest friend, lover, partner or whatever you call it Klaus ever had. But I don't regret leaving him. Klaus is poison in a relationship. He almost got me. Somehow I feel his disease is his last attempt to recast a spell that he was so successful for having over me in the ten years we were together. It's crazy. Klaus was a master manipulator. He belittled me with his actions and his words. In the soft moments of our relationship he wept for forgiveness and promised forever love.

What were his words when I left him? "You are my life. When you leave me I will die." Now, so many years later it appears his prediction is coming true. Is it his last act to really stick it to me? Does he want to become the ultimate winner by leaving me behind filled with guilt I am responsible for his deadly infection? "No, no," I scream as loud as I can. I have to stop the downward spiral of my ridiculous thoughts. I live 3000 miles away from Klaus. I have not thought about him in many years. I have a new life. I am happy. I want him to get away from me forever.

Epilogue

My dear grandmother died in 1990. To this day I have dreams where I almost catch up with her. Every time that I think I am close enough to give her a hug she disappears behind a closing door.

My uncle Paul died 2001 six months after he was diagnosed with lung cancer.

Klaus died in 2002. Ferdinand was the last visitor to see him alive just hours before most of his vital organs shut down. Ferdinand told me that Klaus was very agitated during his hospital visit but he didn't expect him to be dead just hours later. The heartbreaking tragedy about Klaus' final moments is that he died alone. And that was the one thing Klaus hated the most. During his adult life he would avoid at all costs to have a single moment without somebody around him. I am certain that the almost pathological fear to be alone went back to the very beginning of his childhood. The night his grandparents perished during the merciless bombing of Dresden he was handed over to an orphanage, which would become his home for the next five years. Left there by his mother because all that she was able to do was fend for herself. A break in his abandonment came when his mother married his stepfather and found a home where all three could live together. One day in the mid-fifties his biological father was released from Russian imprisonment and returned to Dresden. He promised Klaus he would be in his life but didn't keep his word. The tragic death of his stepfather during a traffic accident and the suicide of his mother just a month later also meant a turning point in Klaus' life. From now on he would take whatever crossed his path before someone or something else would grab it from him. He numbed his feelings and pain with any pleasure no matter how shallow, short lived and ultimately destructive it will become. He tried to enjoy life the way he thought it should be. But it all was just a physical indulgence, void of

492

time to seek real satisfaction. I am not saying that his life was just misery covered up by men and alcohol. He looked for happiness but had lost trust a long time ago. When my mother heard about Klaus' death she was almost inconsolable. She didn't know until the day he died how sick he was so his death came as a surprise. If it is any consolation for Klaus dying alone it is the fact that he was mourned by my mother as only a mother can mourn a son.

Frank died in 2003 after a long battle with a brain tumor. He never saw Ferdinand again after their fateful night together decades ago in the Hungarian forest.

My first New York acquaintance Hans, who Frank and Knut had introduced me to, gave into his demons in 2004 and jumped off of his apartment building on 55th Street. Hans was a true friend and confidant to me from the minute I had moved to New York City in 1989. He helped me tremendously to adjust to my new life. However, numerous times I had to be a powerless witness to his stifling depression. He told me over and over again that no one could help because no one knows how it feels and what he is going through.

He traced the reasons for his mental illness back to his very beginnings in Germany. When life for Jews became intolerable in the thirties Hans' parents were desperately looking for countries that would allow them to emigrate there. Many governments had closed their eyes and borders by that time. One day his father would hear that Chile is giving out visas. "We didn't even know where Chile was. We had to look it up on the map," Hans remembered. The family made it safe to South America and tried to fit in as well as they could. But Hans' parents didn't really see a future for their son and daughter in Santiago de Chile. Hans was the first one to find a sponsor and moved to New York. There he was hired as an assistant to a jewelry salesman. Their professional relationship became personal as well. Hans was now able to let his sister come to the U.S. His parents were too old and too worn out to make another life-changing move. On the outside Hans and his sister had finally arrived at a good place in their life, except that Hans needed more *and more medication to mentally deal with a world he had not chosen freely: first Chile and then the U.S. At some point he lost his partner, many years his senior. Years later his beloved niece would be killed in broad daylight by her overly jealous husband. No pills, wealth or life's pleasurable distractions could take away his inner demons – until the fateful morning when he took the elevator to the 19th floor.*

Ferdinand died in 2008 after a long battle with the effects of his HIV infection.

My stepfather died in 2010, just two months shy of his 90th birthday.

My Aunt died in May 2014. She was 85 years old.

My friend and dancer Roland returned after only four weeks in West Germany to East Berlin. His boss, chief choreographer Tom Schilling personally went to West Germany to convince him to come back. The promise that he could continue to dance with the ballet of the Komische Opera sealed the deal. Roland stayed on with the troupe until he couldn't deal anymore with the continual suspicions of his fellow dancers that he had signed on as an informant for the Stasi. I can see that Roland's story could have let to that assumption. I never saw or spoke with him after he was back in East Germany. (Not by choice, just by circumstances.) However I followed his career as well as I could. The last I learned about his whereabouts was when I saw his name in playbills of the Friedrich-Stadt-Palast revue theater and later of Das Ei, a smaller venue adjacent to Friedrich–Stadt-Palast a couple of years ago.

It took me many years before I was able to sit down to record this part of my journey. And it took me many more years after that until I wrote the last word of it. I had envisioned a personal account paralleling the circumstances I was surrounded by. Because I was always curious to learn how much weight personal and social structures determined one's existence in the future, and how much experienced societal fabric can tip the scale in one or the other direction. And not least, what power do I have to separate myself from all that to take charge of my own destiny and to what degree? Was my inability to leave my dysfunctional family as well as the abusive relationship with Klaus for a long time rooted in the fact that I lived in a totally controlled and unhealthy governmental structure where individual decisions not only were discouraged but also punished? Or maybe all that doesn't really matter since everybody makes his own bed, so to speak, and it is only his actions alone that decide when to get out of that bed?

I tried wholeheartedly to give an honest account and hope I have not offended or discomforted those I crossed paths with. I lost touch with most of my former friends, colleagues and acquaintances. To ease possible bad feelings I have changed some of their names. But I know some of you will easily recognize yourselves and I welcome the chance to reconnect with those who wish so. I feel so lucky that I have come to the present stage of my life fully aware that I left people and things behind. Not out of disregard. No, all the bad and good in my past helped bring me to my next junction. As I mentioned so many times in this account, I have loved the journey more than anything. But I also have to admit, sometimes I wish I could be more content and less breathless.

About the Author

Thomas Schardt was born in the former East Germany in 1955. He spent the first twenty-nine years of his life in East Berlin and Leipzig, where he worked as a librarian and later as a journalist.

In 1984 he was finally permitted to move to West Berlin where he soon found work as a reporter, and in 1989 he joined a group of foreign correspondents and started reporting from New York for a variety of major German newspapers and magazines.

He strongly believes that our history is the collective result of a larger puzzle that each of us play a role in creating.

Thomas currently lives in Maine.